Water Resources Planning

AWWA MANUAL M50

Second Edition

American Water Works Association

Science and Technology

AWWA unites the entire water community by developing and distributing authoritative scientific and technological knowledge. Through its members, AWWA develops industry standards for products and processes that advance public health and safety. AWWA also provides quality improvement programs for water and wastewater utilities.

MANUAL OF WATER SUPPLY PRACTICES—M50, Second Edition

Water Resources Planning

Disclaimer

The authors, contributors, editors, and publisher do not assume responsibility for the validity of the content or any consequences of their use. In no event will AWWA be liable for direct, indirect, special, incidental, or consequential damages arising out of the use of information presented in this book. In particular, AWWA will not be responsible for any costs, including, but not limited to, those incurred as a result of lost revenue. In no event shall AWWA's liability exceed the amount paid for the purchase of this book.

Project Manager and Technical Editor: Melissa Valentine
Production: Claro Systems
Manuals Coordinator: Beth Behner

Library of Congress Cataloging-in-Publication Data

Water resources planning. --2nd ed.
    p. cm. -- (AWWA manual ; M50)
  Preparation of the manual managed by William O. Maddaus.
  Includes bibliographical references and index.
  ISBN 1-58321-471-2
   1. Water-supply--Planning. 2. Water consumption--Forecasting. 3. Water resources development. 4. Water-supply--United States--Planning--Case studies. I. Maddaus, William O.

TD345.W2685 2007
363.6'1--dc22

2006052622

Printed in the United States of America
American Water Works Association
6666 West Quincy Avenue
Denver, CO 80235

ISBN 978-1-58321-471-8

Printed on recycled paper

Contents

Figures

This page intentionally blank

Tables

Foreword

This publication is the second edition of the American Water Works Association (AWWA) Manual M50, *Water Resources Planning*, originally published in 2001. The manual provides information on how to develop a plan for new water supplies to accommodate projected future water demands.

This second edition significantly enhances the basis of water resource planning provided in the first edition. Additions and improvements include:

Emphasizes the role of successful public involvement in water resource planning with a new chapter on the topic.

Expanded treatment of water losses in the Water Demand Forecasting chapter along with examples.

New section on conjunctive use as a water source option.

Update on drinking water regulations.

New section on Native American Consultation in environmental impact analysis.

Additional case studies on Integrated Resource Planning.

The impetus for M50 stems from the fact that many of the water supplies serving the current population were developed decades ago. During the 1930s through 1960s, the US Bureau of Reclamation, the US Army Corps of Engineers, some state agencies, and water wholesalers actively developed water projects. Environmental regulations were minimal, federal and state money was relatively plentiful, and the public was not greatly involved in water supply decision making. All this changed in the 1970s. Since then, we have seen

- heightened public interest in water resources planning (WRP)

- extensive promulgation of environmental regulations

- greater scrutiny of large public works projects

- an emerging understanding of water conservation, efficiency, and demand management benefits

- a better understanding of how water supply projects affect the environment (and our ability to model the impacts)

As a result of these changes, far fewer water resource projects have been built since the early 1980s.

The traditional mission of AWWA member utilities has been to distribute treated drinking water from sources often developed by predecessors or outside entities. In most cases, the utility's role is now being expanded to include the development of major new water supplies. As noted, limited source of supply development over the past two decades has been influenced by expanded environmental regulations. These regulations have constrained new source development projects, while creating a concentrated focus on capital-intensive treatment process and water quality enhancement upgrades. Increased demand for new sources of supply can be seen in every region of the country. This manual is designed to provide information, previously unavailable through AWWA, to help member utilities meet their customers' needs and the demands of the marketplace in an effective, organized, and responsive fashion.

Water resource planning for potable water supply is a very broad topic. No single manual could cover all possible technical topics needed by resource planners. Issues range from estimating future water demand to evaluating possible new sources of water and dealing with expanding environmental regulations. One method for preparing a water resources plan is integrated resource planning (IRP). Developed in the 1990s, IRP shows promise as a way to tie together all the loose ends through a planning process that usually results in a reason-based, cost-effective, and environmentally sound plan the public can support. But this manual discusses much more than IRP; it provides utilities with substantial detail on how to develop and evaluate the information they need to make informed decisions on the best time and method to expand water supplies.

It should be noted that a standard exists that covers the essential requirements for the effective protection of source waters, AWWA Standard G300, *Source Water Protection*. Successful source water protection programs may vary widely in their details, but it is a premise of this standard that successful programs share six fundamental elements:

1. A source water protection program vision
2. Source water characterization
3. Source water protection goals
4. Source water protection action plan
5. Implementation of the action plan
6. Periodic evaluation and revision of the entire program

Within this generalized framework, individual utilities may establish and maintain source water protection programs that account for their unique local conditions, incorporate the interests of local stakeholders, and reflect sustainable long-term commitments to the process by all parties.

The AWWA Water Resources Planning and Management Committee, which helped prepare this manual, welcomes input on its content and usefulness. Planning is an ever-changing process. Techniques are being refined, and new techniques are being developed and gaining acceptance in the planning and engineering marketplace. Subsequent versions of manual M50 will provide an effective framework for WRP for the beginning of the 21st century.

Acknowledgments

The first and second editions of AWWA Manual M50 were authorized by the Water Resources Planning and Management Committee. Preparation of the manual was managed by William O. Maddaus. The authors were as follows:

Chapter 1, Introduction	*William O. Maddaus*, Maddaus Water Management
Chapter 2, Public Involvement for Water Resources Planning	*Wendy Nero* and *Liz Barksdale*, CH2M-Hill *Terry Cole*, Brown and Caldwell *Michelle K. Robinson*, Tampa Bay Water *Nancy Howard*, Newport News Waterworks
Chapter 3, Water Demand Forecasting	*Jack Weber*, Weber Analytical
Chapter 4, Water Policy	*Kenneth R. Wright*, Wright Water Engineers *Brad B. Castleberry*, Lloyd, Gosselink, Blevins, Rochelle, Baldwin and Townsend, P.C.
Chapter 5, Evaluation of Surface and Groundwater	*David B. Campbell*, Schnabel Engineering Associates *Dr. Najmus Saquib*, WRIME, Inc. *Mark V. Lowry*, Turner Collie & Braden
Chapter 6, Evaluation of Other Sources	*James A. Cathcart*, HDR Engineering, Inc. *David L. Roohk*, HDR Engineering, Inc. *James A. Yost*, West Yost & Associates *Lisa Maddaus*, Brown and Caldwell *Bill Hoffman*, City of Austin
Chapter 7, Water Quality	*Janine B. Witko*, Black & Veatch *Rosemarie Short*, Malcolm Pirnie, Inc.
Chapter 8, Hydrologic Modeling	*Dr. Najmus Saquib*, WRIME, Inc.
Chapter 9, Regulatory Issues	*James A. Cathcart*, HDR Engineering, Inc. *Ronald Sharpin*, Massachusetts Department of Conservation and Recreation
Chapter 10, Environmental Impact Analysis	*Gwen Buchholz*, CH2M Hill *Nancy Howard*, Newport News Waterworks

Chapter 11, Watershed Management and Groundwater Protection	*Ronald Sharpin*, Massachusetts Department of Conservation and Recreation
	Steven R. Roy, GeoSyntec Consultants, Inc.
Chapter 12, Economic Feasibility	*Daniel B. Bishop*, Bishop Consulting
Chapter 13, Integrated Resource Planning	*William O. Maddaus*, Maddaus Water Management
Chapter 14, Case Studies	*Gary S. Fiske*, Gary Fiske and Associates

A special thank you to Fred Bloetcher for his in-depth review of this manual. This manual was developed by the AWWA Water Resources Planning and Management Committee. The membership at the time it approved this manual was as follows:

Alison Adams, Tampa Bay Water, Clearwater, Fla.
Aziz Ahmed, Malcolm Pirnie Inc., Phoenix, Ariz.
John Andrew, California Bay-Delta Authority, Department of Water Resources, Sacramento, Calif.
D.B. Campbell, Schnabel Engineering Associates, West Chester, Pa.
Max Castaneda, Corpus Christi, Texas
Brad Castleberry, Lloyd Gosselink et al., Austin, Texas
J.A. Cathcart, HDR Engineering Inc., Lake Forest, Calif.
O.L. Chen, Olivia Chen Consultants Inc., San Francisco, Calif.
W.Y. Davis, Chair, CDM, Carbondale, Ill.
K.E. Dennett, University of Nevada, Department of Civil Engineering/MS 258, Reno, Nev.
Nass Diallo, Las Vegas Valley Water District, Las Vegas, Nev.
M.A. Dickinson, California Urban Water Conservation Council, Sacramento, Calif.
D.D. Dunn, HDR Engineering Inc., Austin, Texas
D.F. Edson, Prism Environmental Inc., Westborough, Mass.
Scott Forbes, Paller-Roberts, Westchester, Calif.
T.L. Frederick, Rivanna Water & Sewer Authority, Charlottesville, Va.
E.A. Harrington, American Water Works Association, Denver, Colo.
Uli Kappus, Parsons, Denver, Colo.
Paula Kehoe, SF Public Utilities Commission, San Francisco, Calif.
J.C. Kiefer, CDM Inc., Carbondale, Ill.
M.V. Lowry, Turner Collie & Braden Inc., Austin, Texas
W.O. Maddaus, Maddaus Water Management, Alamo, Calif.
Saquib Najmus, WRIME Inc., Sacramento, Calif.
P.E. Peterson, Malcolm Pirnie Inc., Newport News, Va.
Perri Standish-Lee, Black & Veatch, Sacramento, Calif.
Lorna Stickel, Portland Water Bureau, Portland, Ore.
Alyson Watson, RMC, San Francisco, Calif.
J.A. Whitford, HNTB Corporation, Indianapolis, Ind.
Ray Yep, Santa Clara Valley Water District, San Jose, Calif.
T.T. Yurovsky, SRT Consultants, San Francisco, Calif.

Chapter 1

Introduction to Water Resources Planning

According to a recent report by Johns Hopkins University, nearly half a billion people around the world face water shortages today. By 2025 the number will increase fivefold to 2.8 billion people—35 percent of the world's projected total of 8 billion people.

Although 70 percent of the Earth's surface is water (mostly in oceans), only about 3 percent of all water on Earth is fresh water. Because much of this fresh water is locked up in ice caps and glaciers, only about 1 percent of all fresh water is reasonably accessible for use. Only about 0.001 percent of the world's total supply of water is considered easily accessible for human use.

The world's population, now at nearly 6 billion, is increasing by about 80 million per year. As of 1995, 31 countries, with a combined population of 458 million, faced either water stress or water scarcity. Although the United States does not currently face critical shortages, there are problem areas:

- Overall, groundwater is being used 25 percent faster than it is being replenished. In particular, the Ogallala aquifer, which underlies parts of six states and irrigates 6 million hectares (14,826,300 acres), has been overexploited and, in some areas, half its available water has been withdrawn.

- The Colorado River, which flows through several southwestern states, has fed agriculture and enabled rapid growth of desert cities such as Las Vegas, Phoenix, and San Diego. Demands have so drained the river that it no longer consistently reaches its mouth in Mexico's Gulf of California. The river's overuse has been a source of contention between the United States and Mexico.

These are merely two examples of a growing water resource crisis. Water wars are being fought in the humid southeastern United States. Restrictive withdrawal policies are being applied to groundwater and surface water sources in nearly every region. Growing demand for water is being met with growing recognition of the impacts that unconstrained diversions have on water resources. In the United States, relatively few water projects are being planned or built to accommodate population growth, certainly not enough to keep pace with the increasing water demand. In the past, many water utilities could often rely on federal agencies, such as the US Army Corps of Engineers or US Bureau of Reclamation, or a state agency, to build water supply projects. Today, that is less often the case. Water utilities, individually or with others, are more and more often planning and building water projects.

The mission of the American Water Works Association (AWWA) has traditionally focused on treating water, because utility members meet the requirements of the federal Safe Drinking Water Act (SDWA) and respond to customer-based issues. The 21st century will see an expanded focus for AWWA's member water utilities. Virtually every water utility will plan to meet growing water demands by balancing demand reduction programs and new supply development. With this manual, AWWA offers its member utilities a focused guidance document in the area of water resources planning (WRP). Analyzing and evaluating water supply projects is complicated and includes technical issues about yield of potential new sources as well as regulations and permits that require extensive environmental analysis. Surface water, groundwater, desalination, reuse, and other source options all have their own special issues and concerns. Utilities must answer many questions on the impacts of proposed projects before regulatory agencies can approve projects and grant permits.

WRP for potable water supply is a very broad topic. No one manual can incorporate all the methods or procedures that may be required. This manual attempts to introduce the utility planner to many techniques and methods that may be needed to prepare a proper plan. Integrated resource planning (IRP) is an underlying theme for tying all the loose ends together, but this manual also provides significant additional technical guidance and supporting information. It provides enough information to inform a utility manager or to help a planner get started, but managers and planners should use the reference lists provided with the chapters to pursue technical issues in greater detail. The manual is a guide and covers most, if not all, of the needed topics.

THE WATER RESOURCES PLANNING PROCESS

This manual was prepared by the Water Resources Planning and Management Committee and associated volunteer authors to help water resource planners meet the challenge of accommodating a growing demand for water, while complying with the myriad regulations that govern the development and use of new water supplies. No two water resource plans are alike. The manual is presented in a logical order and format; however, planners are expected to use the parts of the manual that apply to their situations. The issues discussed in this manual should allow the planner to develop and implement a comprehensive work plan that responds to technical questions that must be addressed before deciding how to develop new water supplies.

Planning Issues and Components Included in This Manual

Figure 1-1 shows the overall water resources planning process advocated in this manual. The fundamental basis of WRP for water utilities is water demand forecasting, which establishes how much water the planning area will need in the future. Normally, a forecast is prepared and the planning process begins following a triggering event, such as the release of new demographic forecasts that show a relatively high growth rate, a recent water shortage that indicates current supplies are inadequate, or other problems that develop with current supply sources.

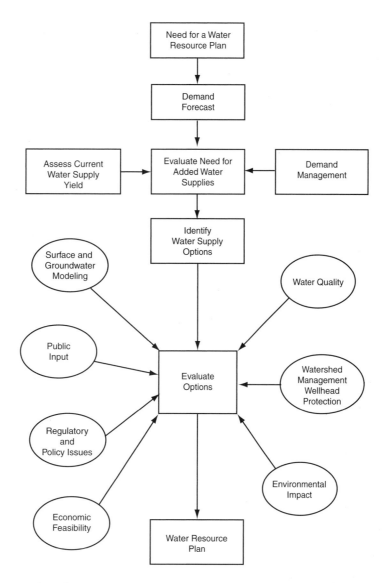

Figure 1-1   Water resources planning process

Once demand forecasts are developed, the need for added supplies should be assessed. This requires estimating the yields available from current supply sources. In some cases, yields will decrease over time as a result of a number of factors, including

- sedimentation of reservoirs (storage loss, clogging of intakes)
- increased upstream diversions
- falling groundwater levels
- contamination of sources
- reallocation of water resources to other entities
- increased minimum in-stream flow or groundwater level requirements

Demand-side management may reduce future water needs, allowing supplies to last longer. Demand reduction can be treated as an additional source of water. It has a cost, a yield, and environmental considerations, as do other sources of supply. An early assessment of demand reduction is appropriate, because this source may obviate the need to develop new supplies or defer the need for a new source for a number of years. Demand management efforts should be documented because they can provide convincing evidence of the need for additional supplies when sources need to be expanded.

The next step is to identify feasible new sources that, individually or combined, make up the identified supply deficit for an estimated future time period. These can include

- new or expanded surface supplies
- new or expanded groundwater supplies
- desalinated water
- reclaimed water
- conserved water
- transferred water from other water purveyors
- purchased water from other suppliers

A rigorous evaluation process should be designed, reflecting the nature of the alternative new sources identified. All relevant issues should be addressed, including

- water quality of new sources
- protection of current and new sources
- regulations
- water rights and policies
- yield of new sources and impacts on other sources (assessed through modeling)
- environmental impact assessments
- economic feasibility and financing considerations
- long-term viability (design life)

These evaluations are intended to identify a preferred plan that balances conflicting factors. Criteria will generally include

- cost-effectiveness
- financial feasibility
- public acceptability
- environmental issues

As previously mentioned, IRP is the WRP process advocated in this manual. IRP is a way of tying all the issues together in a comprehensive process. A hallmark of IRP is its open and participatory process. All interest groups, including water agency staff, regulators, environmental groups, public interest groups, the public, and elected officials, participate in and contribute to the decision process.

Selecting the Project Team

One of the most important issues a water resource planner must face is who to involve in the planning process. Those involved are called stakeholders because they have a vested interest in how the process turns out and which alternative is selected. No longer are plans prepared in a vacuum, released for approval after all the technical work is completed and the alternatives evaluated. Planners have found that this closed-door approach necessitates starting over when opposition to the proposed project surfaces, possibly more than once. An open approach requires a slower, more painstaking process. Although involving all stakeholders may slow down the technical work, the final decision and project approval are invariably reached sooner and more amicably.

One way to involve the stakeholders is to develop and implement a public participation plan. Stakeholders are identified and may be invited to serve on an advisory committee. The committee reviews key-issue papers and technical memoranda, identifies additional issues that need to be addressed, and helps select the recommended plan. Supplemental techniques include newsletters, media coverage, public meetings, and hearings. The committee's objectives are to be proactive and to solicit input at a time when it can be helpful, not after decisions are made. Every alternative will have its detractors. Therefore, a significant amount of listening, learning, negotiating, and balancing of conflicts is required.

Developing the Project Framework

Every planning process should begin with a carefully thought-out work plan. This plan should address issues identified in an initial scoping paper. Tasks should be laid out with detailed descriptions of activities, products, budget, schedules, and assigned responsibilities.

Defining the need for action.   The impetus for preparing a water resource plan may come from many events or preliminary assessments. Nearly every plan is a significant undertaking and requires approval from appointed or elected officials. A preliminary assessment is often needed just to receive authorization to identify issues, validate the need for the plan or a new supply, and prepare a work plan. The Need for Action statement is generally triggered by some event, such as a recent water shortage, a current or potential problem with supplies, or a projected high growth rate, expected to outstrip the yield of current sources.

Identifying the issues.   Often a white paper or scoping paper is needed to define the issues surrounding planning for a new source. The white paper can be developed by water agency staff but should involve input from key stakeholders. Its purpose is to gather sufficient background information to prepare a work plan that will identify and address all issues including the need for consultation with Native American tribes, characterize relevant potential new sources, and provide a sufficiently rigorous overview evaluation. The decision-making process should be thought through so decision makers have timely information to guide the process along the way and the information for selecting the best plan.

Developing a work plan.   The purpose of the work plan is to organize the efforts to complete the water resource plan. Completing the plan will involve staff, possibly consultants, and stakeholders. These people deserve a carefully thought-out work plan so time and money are not wasted. A task-flow diagram should be prepared to identify the flow of information and analysis, leading to a decision on a recommended plan. Once tasks are identified, they should be described in sufficient detail so that the cost of completing the work, and the time required, can be reasonably estimated. The next decision is who will do the work. This can be staff, consultants, or both. If consultants are used, the scope of their work should be defined, with budgets, deliverables, and schedules established. The final step in the work planning process, or one of the first tasks in the work plan, is to create a public involvement plan that will involve the stakeholders previously identified.

Working With Regulators

Water resource projects are subject to varying degrees of regulatory approval. Developing new sources or expanding withdrawals may require permits. Such permits could include a state water allocation or a federal Section 404 permit, often requiring a long and involved approval process. Planners should address permit requirements in the water resource plan, although detailed aspects of the permit approval, such as detailed environmental impact analyses, will occur after the plan is approved. Regulatory officials need to be consulted, and applicable guidelines and permit requirements addressed, in the plan.

Understanding permit requirements. Chapters 9 and 10 can help the planner understand the types of permits that may be required. State regulatory officials should be consulted as the work plan is prepared so that likely permits are identified, and the considerations required or implied are included in the alternatives analyses.

Assessing environmental impact. Each state has its own framework for assessing the environmental impacts of water resource projects. The state's water allocation agency can identify the lead permitting agency and help identify the types of environmental work that will likely need to be performed. Detailed environmental assessments or impact statements are not usually undertaken until after the preferred alternative source is identified. However, the planning process leading to that selection should include preliminary consideration of all issues likely to require detailed assessment. Preliminary environmental screening needs to be integrated with the alternative assessment process. This will help justify the alternative selection and reduce the time required to complete environmental assessments or environmental impact analysis for the recommended project and needed permits.

The manual follows the IRP process. Each chapter covers a part of the process.

Chapter 1—Introduction to Water Resources Planning

WRP involves many technical and nontechnical issues. The organization and order of the chapters in the manual generally follow the flow diagram, Figure 1-1. WRP begins with establishing the need for a water resource plan, including a comparison of forecasted water demands with available supplies. Techniques to evaluate identified resource options are included in the manual. The underlying theme for developing the plan is called *integrated resource planning*, which is described in detail in chapter 13.

Chapter 2—Public Involvement for Water Resources Planning

Chapter 2 provides an understanding of public participation techniques and the important role it can play in water resources planning. It covers the process of setting goals and developing work plans to involve the public in the water resources planning process. It also describes the key elements of plan implementation that include chartering the project team, monitoring and managing change. A variety of techniques are illustrated in the four case studies. Finally, an appendix provides suggestions for addressing historic/cultural resources and environmental issues.

Chapter 3—Water Demand Forecasting

Chapter 3 begins by summarizing common forecasting methods ranging from simple per capita models to more complex statistical forecasting methods. It then describes types of data normally used for forecasting, including water billing data, weather data, demographic and economic data, and other explanatory variables, and provides examples of forecasting with per capita coefficients, land use water factors, and regression analysis of disaggregated demand data.

Examples also are provided to illustrate the effects of seasonality, weather, and price responsiveness. The use of dummy variables to account for factors of limited duration is explained. Identification of indoor and outdoor water use is described.

This chapter demonstrates how planned water conservation programs are integrated and identifies water use reductions that have occurred in the past. Sensitivity analysis is used to evaluate the variation in projections caused by errors in the explanatory variables. Sensitivity analysis can be used to develop a confidence interval around the projected water demand.

Chapter 4—Water Rights and Policy

Chapter 4 describes the role of water rights in water resource management. Two distinct systems of water rights are defined and described: riparian rights, used primarily in the eastern United States; and appropriation doctrine, used in the western United States. Water rights systems for groundwater include absolute ownership, reasonable use, correlative rights, and appropriation permit systems. Federal rights also are described, including federal reserved rights, water rights for water not reserved, rights of navigable water, and federal contract rights. Chapter 4 presents the guiding principles of AWWA water policy. Also, impacts to water rights are covered including instream uses and environmental flows and impacts of the Clean Water Act and Endangered Species Act.

Chapter 5—Evaluation of Surface Water and Groundwater Sources

Chapter 5 describes new conventional water sources. Included are descriptions and parameters for

- surface water, including source identification, screening, and site selection for direct river withdrawals, on-stream reservoirs, and pumped-storage reservoirs

- groundwater, including confined and unconfined aquifers

- conjunctive use of surface water and groundwater

Chapter 6—Evaluation of Other Sources

Chapter 6 describes other sources including

- conserved water

- reclaimed water

- desalination

- water marketing and transfers

Also, chapter 6 discusses how to identify the timing and magnitude of new source development. This includes a comparison of current yield and demand forecasts, use of surplus/deficit projections, factors affecting project development, and project step size considerations.

Chapter 7—Water Quality

Chapter 7 explains water quality interactions and the hydrologic cycle, including physical, chemical, and biological components. This chapter defines various measures of water quality and describes the relationships between water uses and water quality. In addition, impacts of natural influences, point sources, and nonpoint sources on water quality are defined, as are the major factors affecting quality of various types of surface water. Similarly, the major factors affecting groundwater quality include common contaminants and transport considerations.

Chapter 8—Hydrologic Modeling

Chapter 8 explains when to use models, when they are cost-effective, and how much modeling is enough. The dominant processes of the hydrologic cycle are described, including

- precipitation
- interception
- evaporation and evapotranspiration
- infiltration
- groundwater
- runoff and streamflow

Uses of models, including data needs, calibration, sensitivity analysis, and error analysis, are described. Guidance for project managers includes how to conduct a modeling study, various types of models, organizations that distribute models, and commercially available models. Steps for developing successful models are laid out for the practitioner.

Chapter 9—Regulatory Issues

The major federal laws affecting water resource development are the SDWA, as amended, and the Clean Water Act (CWA). The 1986 amendments to the SDWA include

- Volatile Organic Chemical Rule
- Surface Water Treatment Rule
- Total Coliform Rule
- Lead and Copper Rule
- Disinfectants/Disinfection By-products Rule
- Others

The 1996 amendments to the SDWA added important other rules as well as federal funding, including

- Microbial/Disinfection By-products Rules
- Arsenic Rule
- Sulfate Rule

- Radon Rule

- Groundwater Rule

From a water supply development viewpoint, an important part of the CWA is Section 404. Other important aspects are regulation of wastewater and agricultural discharge upstream of withdrawal points. Section 404 regulates the discharge of dredged or fill materials into all surface waters of the US. The US Army Corps of Engineers issues permits for reservoirs or projects that involve changes to surface waters; the US Environmental Protection Agency (USEPA) holds veto power over the process. For surface water source of supply projects, this process usually dominates the framework of the overall process.

Chapter 10—Environmental Impact Analysis

Chapter 10 stresses that environmental impact analysis should be an integral part of the WRP process. It describes how to initiate the environmental impact documentation process and explains the types of environmental documentation and the critical issues in preparing the documents. These issues include the study area, study period, baseline conditions, and level of detail. The information in environmental documents includes biological, human, and physical resources. Chapter 10 also describes permits and approvals in the environmental process, including those required by relevant federal acts such as

- National Environmental Policy Act

- Endangered Species Act

- Clean Water Act

- Clean Air Act

- Archaeological Resources Protection Act

- Wild and Scenic Rivers Act

How these acts apply to potential projects governs the scope of the environmental documentation process.

Chapter 11—Watershed Management and Groundwater Protection

Watershed management is equivalent to source protection. Chapter 11 describes the process to prepare a viable watershed protection plan. The following steps are explained:

1. Delineate/characterize the watershed.

2. Identify relevant stakeholders and form a planning team.

3. Identify regulatory and desirable community goals.

4. Classify and rank goals.

5. Develop an outreach education program.

6. Compile criteria to measure achievement goals.

7. Identify activities posing a threat to achieving goals.

8. Quantify activities and impacts on goals.

9. Rank threats.

10. Identify control methods to reduce or eliminate threats.

11. Quantify efficiency and effectiveness of control measures.

12. Identify administrators of control measures.

13. Rank control measures.

14. Develop a watershed/reservoir protection plan.

15. Implement plan.

Chapter 11 also describes the state and federal regulatory efforts in groundwater protection. SDWA established the wellhead protection program, and thereafter most states have developed wellhead protection programs approved by USEPA. The chapter describes the seven elements of a wellhead protection program.

In 1992, USEPA published guidance for a Comprehensive State Ground Water Protection Program. This program is designed to build a comprehensive approach to groundwater protection that includes all stakeholders. States were requested to coordinate their groundwater protection actions through six strategic activities:

1. Establish a groundwater protection goal.

2. Establish priorities to guide program efforts.

3. Define authorities, roles, responsibilities, resources, and coordinating mechanisms.

4. Implement efforts to accomplish the state's groundwater protection goal.

5. Coordinate information collection and management.

6. Improve public education and participation in all aspects of groundwater protection.

Chapter 12—Economic Feasibility

Chapter 12 describes economic feasibility as one of several factors that must be decided in WRP. Perspectives on how to portray costs and benefits are explained. Types of costs include internal costs such as capital and operations and maintenance. External costs include imposed costs to deal with project impacts and environmental costs. Defined benefits include the value of additional water sales associated with the project and avoided costs and external benefits, such as recreation, flood control, and environmental benefits.

Methods of comparing alternatives are described. Common parameters include the value of time and the discount rate. Methods illustrated with formulas and examples include

*   annualized costs

*   present value

*   benefit–cost ratio

*   internal rate of return

Chapter 13—Integrated Resource Planning

IRP is described as a method that ties all the elements of water resource planning together. AWWA's definition of IRP is given, and the differences between IRP and traditional water supply planning are used to help explain IRP. The chapter includes an outline for an IRP report. The IRP process, illustrated in a diagram, includes

- forming resource combinations, including traditional and nontraditional sources such as demand management and wastewater reclamation

- evaluating resource combinations by considering costs, reliability, environmental impact, public acceptability, and ranking methods

- plan selection and implementation considerations, including cost-effectiveness, environmental permitting, and financing

Chapter 14—Case Studies

The final chapter presents several examples of WRP that have occurred recently in the US. These examples illustrate the vast differences in WRP processes. No judgments are made as to whether the processes were successes or failures, as such a determination is subjective. Case studies include

- King William Reservoir, Virginia

- Regional Water Planning in Texas

- Portland Regional Water Supply Plan, Oregon

- City of Colorado Springs, Colorado Integrated Resource Plan

- Denver Metropolitan Area, Colorado

- Kentucky–American Water Company's Integrated Resource Plan

- Wichita Integrated Resource Plan, Kansas

- Ware Creek Reservoir, Virginia

- Southern Nevada Water Authority

- Eugene Water & Electric Board, Oregon

Each case study describes the planning process and plan outcomes.

REFERENCES

Engleman, R. and P. Leroy. 1995. *Sustaining Water: An Update*. Washington, D.C.: Population Action International.

Henrichsen, D., B. Robey, and U.D. Upadlhyay. 1997. *Solutions for a Water-Short World*, Population Reports, Series M, No. 14. Baltimore, Md.: Johns Hopkins School of Public Health, Population Information Program.

Pimentel, D. and M. Pimentel. 1992. *Land, Energy, and Water: The Constraints Governing Ideal U.S. Population Size*. In Grant, L. ed. *Elephants in the Volkswagen: Facing the Tough Questions About Our Overcrowded Country*. New York, N.Y.: W.H. Freeman and Company.

Postel, S. 1996. Sharing the Rivers. People and the Planet. *Jour AWWA* 5(3):6–9.

UNESCO. 1997. *Groundwater: Managing the "Invisible" Resource*. Environment and Development Briefs, No. 2, p. 4. New York, N.Y.: United Nations Educational Scientific and Cultural Organization.

This page intentionally blank

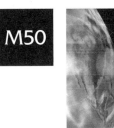

Chapter **2**

Public Involvement for Water Resources Planning

INTRODUCTION

Overview of Relationship between Water Resources Planning and Public Involvement

Water Resources Planning evaluates supply and demand issues while taking utility, community, and environmental concerns into consideration and then proposes strategies to address future needs based on that input. The planning and decision-making process should be open with affected stakeholders invited to participate. This chapter will assist in developing an understanding of public participation and the important part it can play in water resources planning. The public involvement planning process described herein is based on the process described in the American Water Works Association Research Foundation's (AwwaRF) "Public Involvement Strategies: A Manager's Handbook" and "Public Involvement Phase II: Making it Work."

Public Involvement as a Critical Project Component

As a result of changing public attitudes and regulatory requirements, public involvement in the planning and implementation of a project has become a more critical component. It has evolved from a courtesy during a project to an analytical process that identifies affected populations and integrates public input into decision-making.

In some cases, public involvement becomes consultation as a regulatory requirement. The National Environmental Policy Act (NEPA) and the National Historic Preservation Act (NHPA) require consultation when there is potential to impact historic or cultural resources. The groups that value historic or cultural resources can be a community, a neighborhood, an institution, a Native American tribe, or even the nation as a whole.

If the group involved is a federally recognized Native American tribe, consultation is taken to another level. Federally recognized tribes, numbering nearly 600 throughout the country, are recognized under law as sovereign nations. NEPA and NHPA require that consultation and collaboration with impacted tribes be conducted in a formal government-to-government manner.

Also under NEPA, the issue of Environmental Justice (EJ) can invoke the need for consultation, not only with Native American tribes, but also with other socio/economic groups. The goal of EJ consultation is to assure that lower income and/or minority communities, including Native American tribes, do not bear a disproportionate share of environmental impacts from federal actions, and this includes projects requiring a federal permit.

The NEPA and NHPA consultations aspect of public involvement is described in some detail in Appendix at the end of Chapter 2.

Benefits of Effective Public Involvement in Resource Planning

Today's water suppliers must balance multiple, often competing organizational and political demands while also providing safe, high-quality, and affordable drinking water to their customers. The water resources planning process seeks to frame resource decision-making in terms of community values as well as technical and cost criteria. Therefore, the planning process should be designed to not only solicit community input, but to use that input in a meaningful way during decision-making. Benefits of meaningful public involvement include:

- Demonstrating the utility's commitment to efficient investments while competing for public dollars.

- Listening and learning from the public.

- Increasing public access to accurate information about current water quality and quantity, and other affected water resources thereby increasing trust in the utility and providing a counter balance to misinformation that may be communicated through other avenues.

- Increasing the public's baseline understanding of water quality regulations that have dramatically increased the need for more costly, advanced treatment technologies.

- Increasing public support for balancing development of limited water resources and increasing emphasis on water use efficiency.

- Providing more and better information that is otherwise unavailable.

- Increasing elected officials' comfort level with complex decisions about long-term investments in a community's future by building a public mandate for sustainable, high quality water.

- Reducing the potential for protracted win/lose battles with project opponents, lawsuits, and the odds that needed permits may be denied.

Linking water resources planning and public participation can add credibility to a project. Public involvement can help utilities garner the support necessary to move a project forward. Further, public involvement can help projects succeed by reducing the risk of failure, ensuring compliance with regulatory agencies, and gaining acceptance with the public and elected officials.

PLANNING FOR PUBLIC INVOLVEMENT

Ideally, initial planning for public involvement begins in the conceptual planning phase of a water resources planning project. The decision to include the public requires that an honest assessment of water supply alternatives and benefits will be the basis for the planning effort, and that the public's input will have a bearing on the final decision-making process. Assuming that the planning process will be collaborative, the development of an effective public involvement program should begin with careful, thoughtful planning. Essential elements to successful planning include

- Defining the project and assessing potential risks to successful completion of the project.

- Assessing the "owner's" (utility or decision-making entity) readiness for public involvement.

- Consideration of the budget and staffing needed.

- Understanding stakeholder concerns and expectations for involvement.

- Identifying techniques for involving stakeholders.

- Developing the public involvement work plan.

When projects have potential impact to federally recognized Native American tribes (sovereign governments) or to other special socio/economic groups, there are additional issues to consider. With Native American tribes, it is recommended that consultation begin with them prior to involvement of other stakeholders because some of their issues may involve sensitive information, such as locations of sacred sites or burial places. For details on how to consult with Native American tribes, or to satisfy EJ requirements, refer to the section in Appendix A entitled: Public Consultation on Historic/Cultural Resource and Environmental Justice Issues.

Defining Goals and Expectations of Effective Public Involvement

The term *public involvement* is often used interchangeably with public information, community relations, and, in some cases, marketing. Clearly defining the role the public will play in water resources planning is more than semantics, and it will help to manage both the public's and the decision-makers' expectations.

Marketing is a communication strategy designed to *sell* the public on a decision that has already been made. Community relations and public information are strategies to distribute information throughout a community, with opportunities for feedback but no real influence over decision making. Projects, such as water resource planning, that attempt to identify and prioritize resource development issues from both a technical feasibility and a public acceptance perspective indicate that a collaborative decision-making process is appropriate. Truly *involving* the public in identifying, prioritizing, and assessing the value of resources, therefore, will require a process for reaching interested members of the public, educating them on the issues, and providing a meaningful way for them to express their opinions and influence the decision making, enabling them to be effective partners in the decisions that are made.

A necessary step to help manage expectations of the public involvement (or other communications strategy) process is *framing* the project. Determining the specific problems that will be solved and identifying the boundaries of those problems helps to frame the project in terms that both internal and external interests can understand. Facts that establish the need and the scope of the process are clearly defined and assumptions used in the process are identified. Once these boundaries are understood, it will be easier to establish achievable goals and expectations.

Distinguishing facts from assumptions is critical when defining water supply alternatives. Facts are limited to what is known about an option; they can be readily agreed upon. Project facts may focus, for example, on water supply capacity or permitting constraints. Assumptions often form the basis for disagreement, so it is important to uncover differing opinions about data sources, uncertainties, regulatory projections, and planning horizons—first within the sponsoring organization and then among key members of the public. During this planning phase, list facts and assumptions separately as distinct line items to ensure all potential obstacles are anticipated.

Developing a clearly defined water supply *need statement* is an important component of the planning process. The need statement consists of a few sentences describing why the utility must resolve particular problems. The need statement should be shared with staff, the media, elected officials, and the public. Doing so will foster internal alignment, gain the attention of the public, and lay the groundwork for consensus-based solutions. Sometimes needs can be defined jointly between the utility and the stakeholders.

Resist the temptation to develop solutions to problems too early in the process. It is natural to want to present solutions when describing a problem to the public rather than just communicating about the problem. Instead of bolstering credibility, this position can alienate the public, forcing one to try to sell the project, while pushing the public into positions of support or opposition. At this stage, it is essential that a public forum be established for discussing problems. In this way, managers can resolve public concerns rather than brokering positions on a project. In the field of mediation, this approach is referred to as *interest-based* negotiation rather than *position-based* negotiation.

Determine the Process and Opportunities for Public Involvement

Planning for public involvement should be accomplished at the same time as the overall water resources planning process. For public involvement to be meaningful to both the participants and the decision makers, the public's input should feed into the process at logical points. Once the opportunities for public involvement are identified, planning can take place for appropriate activities or venues.

To gain public confidence, look for opportunities to demonstrate that the owner listens and is capable of acting on public input. Start by reviewing, with interested members of the public, the full range of decisions that must be made during the water resource planning process. The following questions may be helpful in identifying when the public should be involved:

- Do opportunities exist for informing the public about the problem?

- Do project alternatives exist? If so, how can the public be involved in developing or ranking alternatives?

- Does an opportunity exist for the public to participate in some aspect of water supply development, particularly location of facilities, site configuration, aesthetics, or timing?

- Are there opportunities to create other community benefits such as parks or environmental centers related to this project?

Assess Risks and Priority for Each Resource Being Evaluated

Project *risk* is the potential impact of the failure of the project or program on the organization. Types of risk to water resource projects may not be inherently clear. Not developing a plan at all or in time to begin development of resources to meet future demands can be risks. There can be potential risks to individual water supplies under consideration. The investment in public involvement should be proportional to the risk posed to the organization, although with a low-risk project, some minimal level of public involvement is always needed. Public involvement should not be viewed as an *insurance policy* against project failure. However, projects that include high risks or significant controversy should include robust public involvement programs.

When assessing a project's risk, these variables should be considered:

- Consequences of not developing a feasible water resources plan

- Risks that eliminate water supply options

- Impact that lack of public involvement may have on internal and external plan approval

After assessing risk, focus can be shifted to resources and projects that are more controversial than others, that require public support, and whose success is key to the water resource plan as a whole.

Determine Public Involvement Priorities and Develop Budget

Public involvement is typically linked with project implementation, however budgeting for public involvement activities should be aligned with each phase of water resources planning activities. This will ensure that resources and staff are available during the planning process when needed. Implementation of a public involvement plan is typically *front-end loaded* with a bulk of the planning and public involvement activities taking place early in the water resources planning process.

Begin by focusing on the overall plan. Then, consider each project. Any special needs of the individual water supply options should be taken into consideration at this time. The risk associated with each of these projects will be assessed by simultaneously considering project issues (or risk factors) and the priority of the project. Project issues raised in the past by customers, activists, elected officials, other communities, or the media should be factored in.

Securing the resources necessary to implement meaningful public involvement programs is a fundamental challenge. Because staff and financial resources are limited, the focus should target future projects with the greatest risk of opposition, delay, or failure. Examining future projects in this manner will prompt a series of questions about the nature of the challenges a project might face and will assist in developing a strategy on how to allocate resources to each water resources project.

Assign Responsibilities

To ensure a credible and sustainable public involvement plan, it is important to assign responsibility for individual public involvement activities. Determine who has lead responsibility and what support will be needed to provide the appropriate technical input, logistical support, and production assistance for public involvement materials.

A well-planned public involvement initiative will include both labor and expense budgets for each task. The number of professional hours for each person and all expenses should be budgeted for each task. Then, evaluate workload and determine whether outside consultants will be needed. They can help balance workload without the time or expense of hiring full-time staff, and they offer expertise that may not be available in-house.

A strategic planning process will ensure that at-risk alternatives have the appropriate level of public involvement, can help the owner garner internal and external support for public involvement, and will guide the development of a strategic, implementable public involvement work plan.

PREPARE PUBLIC INVOLVEMENT WORK PLAN

After determining the elements of the planning process that will need to interface with public involvement activities, a work plan should be prepared. The work plan will outline specific tasks to be performed in concert with the water resources planning process. These activities include:

- Identifying stakeholders

- Identifying public involvement techniques

- Matching public involvement activities with water resources planning elements

Identify Stakeholders

The public is not one group, but many groups or individuals—each with different viewpoints about the utility or agency, the problems, and the potential solutions. These interested groups or individuals are called *stakeholders* because they have a stake in the outcome of the decision. It is important to remember that stakeholders are not limited to groups or individuals in favor of the water resources planning process or friendly with the agency. Stakeholders often include opposition groups and vocal detractors. While not always pleasant, including all stakeholders is key to a successful public involvement program. The following questions will help identify key stakeholders:

- Who has information?

- Who is likely to be concerned about the problem?

- Who will be impacted by potential solutions?

- Whose support is needed to implement the plan?

Project managers often think they know and understand stakeholder concerns, but these perceptions are sometimes wrong or have changed over time. To ensure that stakeholder views are clearly understood, schedule one-on-one interviews with the people who are likely to shape opinions about the project. Interviews with these *opinion leaders* often correct assumptions that you might have about public opinion. These interviews are an opportunity to measure the credibility of the organization, further expand the network of project stakeholders, and plan for information dissemination. To conduct a successful interview, come prepared with a list of questions designed to achieve the following objectives:

- Understand a group or individual's specific concerns about a particular problem or set of solutions.

- Determine which interests will be satisfied with receiving timely, appropriate information and which interests will seek to influence the decision-making process.

- Identify other stakeholders to interview.

- Determine if any of the stakeholder values are contradictory.

- Identify where and how interested groups or individuals are likely to find their information.

Stakeholders will have varying levels of interest and expectations on any given project. Typically they will fall into one of three groups:

Group A – expects to be informed but not involved

Group B – expects to be able to exchange ideas with the project team

Group C – expects to be able to influence the outcome of the project

Understanding the stakeholders and their level of expectations will help in determining which techniques will work best and how to link public involvement activities to project tasks. The following worksheet is an example of how to organize information gained from stakeholder interviews.

Stakeholder	Issues and Concerns	Expectations for Involvement (A, B, or C)
Resident	Cost and impact on property value	A + B
Local politician	Impact on constituents, tax revenue	B + C
Environmental	Compliance with regulations, environmental impacts	B + C

Identify Techniques

When selecting public involvement techniques, project needs must be linked with stakeholder expectations, the owner organization's culture, and the time and money available to devote to public involvement. Some techniques are suitable for providing information to the public, others are better suited for two-way communication, while others enable stakeholders to participate in some aspect of project decision making. Water resources projects most likely will use some techniques from all three categories. Efforts should focus on the most critical tasks associated with the water supply alternatives. A few common techniques are listed in the following worksheet.

Getting information to the public	Getting information from the public	Exchanging information with the public
Newspaper advertisements	Questionnaires or surveys	Information line telephone number
Bill stuffers	Legal notices	Web site
Door hangers	Public comment period	Storefront, trailer, street kiosk
News releases	Focus groups	Talk shows
Fact sheets	Informational workshops	Speakers bureau
Newsletters	Interviews	Door-to-door canvassing
Displays	Dedicated Web sites	Advisory groups
Briefing books		Public meetings/open houses/ workshops
Information repositories		
Articles in existing publications		
TV/radio		
Cable TV		
Videos		

Match Public Involvement Needs and Opportunities with Each Planning Process Element

Identifying opportunities for incorporating public involvement includes combining what is known—about stakeholder interests and expectations for involvement—with what can be done to include the stakeholders in the decision-making process. One way to identify strategies for linking stakeholders to a project is to evaluate the project's task schedule.

A task schedule is a common project management tool often developed as a Gantt Chart using Primavera© or some other type of project planning software. Its purpose is to illustrate the relationship of one task element to another over time. This is the project manager's *road map* and the key to understanding how to incorporate public interests into the decision-making process.

To enhance support for and implementation of a public involvement work plan, all public involvement activities should be displayed graphically on the project schedule. The goal is to link public involvement tactics with the other project tasks so that public involvement becomes an integral part of the project delivery process.

Understanding the relationship of the project tasks with the concerns of stakeholders is critical to the success of a public involvement program. An effective public involvement program can be crafted once the stakeholder concerns are linked to specific project decisions. The information gathered from stakeholder contact will help link the project tasks with public concerns.

IMPLEMENT THE PUBLIC INVOLVEMENT PLAN

Public involvement, like any other project component, requires focused, strategic implementation of the work plan. The implementation phase may consist of three major steps:

- Chartering the public involvement project team (who may be internal or external to the utility)

- Monitoring the project

- Managing change

If the organization already has established project management processes, use them. While it may be necessary to modify the processes to address both the needs of the public involvement program and technical aspects of the project, existing tools are a good starting point.

Charter the Team

The first step in implementing the public involvement work plan is to identify team members and their roles. Team members might include the program manager, other task managers (e.g., planning, permitting, funding, and design), project champions, consultants, and outside stakeholders. Note that senior members of the water resources planning project team are included on the public involvement team. In addition, the public involvement task leader should be considered a key member of the project management team.

When chartering the project team, it is helpful to identify an internal project *champion*. The champion is the designated senior-level manager who is visible in the community, has access to political decision-makers, and has a passion for the project to succeed.

Champions have a big-picture view and are able to accommodate temporary setbacks; they consistently communicate both internally and externally about the progress being made; and they are able to maintain project momentum during controversy. External champions are also essential project team members. They are typically allies in the community who act as a conduit about public sentiments. They often serve as contacts and symbols for elected officials, especially during controversial projects, because they demonstrate knowledge of community values, understand project priorities, and illustrate sensitivity to local politics. They can be important local opinion leaders who speak on your behalf.

A chartering session at project start-up provides the forum to establish team responsibilities and define schedule, deliverables, budgets, and communication processes. The chartering session is also ideal for developing and endorsing the project need statement, differentiating project facts and assumptions, beginning stakeholder profiles, and identifying conflict resolution strategies. Ideally, the chartering session for the entire water resources planning project includes chartering for individual tasks, including public involvement.

Monitor the Project

Predicting and managing project changes involves monitoring the status of a public involvement work plan almost daily. Regular communication with project team members and advisory bodies facilitates this process. During the monitoring phase of plan implementation, the manager must be aware of the interrelationships between the project's public involvement activities and schedule of technical tasks to ensure a consistent workflow. Understanding the sequencing of tasks is also important because the plan must build on successful completion of a preceding task before the next one can be implemented.

The schedule should be actively managed and the team members kept apprised of upcoming tasks. Active monitoring of the project will indicate where the public involvement program is working and where it needs improvement. Even the most thoughtfully created plan should be assessed periodically to determine how effectively the individual tactics are meeting the intended goals. Assessment should focus on those tactics geared toward addressing the most critical issues or stakeholder groups, because these could presumably stop or significantly delay the planning process. The means of making these assessments include

- Asking key stakeholders their opinions,

- Conducting public surveys to measure change in attitude or position,

- Tracking media coverage,

- Monitoring attendance at public meetings, and

- Detecting Web site hits.

When developing assessment tools, choose the methods that best meet the needs of the project. Their *scientific defensibility* may not be as important as their ability to gauge how targeted stakeholders feel. Use the feedback received to correct previous assumptions about opinions on proposed projects.

Manage Change

Change on any project is inevitable. Public involvement programs must address public concerns and perceptions, which are often in flux and can be hard to predict. Even the most subtle change in public sentiment can cause a shift in the public involvement strategy, timing of program elements, and program goals. Public involvement programs must be flexible to respond to events such as election results, pending rules, evolving community issues, and changing stakeholder needs as awareness grows.

Because some changes in public opinion can be anticipated, it may be valuable to assign monitoring responsibility to the most probable risk-related changes. For example, the team member assigned to address political issues should also monitor local elections, candidates, and platforms. Ideally, the public involvement team should develop a change management plan that identifies potential changes in project parameters and public opinion, and methods for addressing them. Creating a flowchart that maps out hypothetical scenarios will help to display the plan. Sometimes public information committees have been used to guide needed mid-course corrections so that the goals of the public involvement plan are met.

CASE STUDIES

This section provides a brief overview of four public involvement projects that used a decision support system approach similar to the one previously discussed. Although the case studies are drawn from different resource management projects (water, wastewater, and storm water management), they provide good examples of how to successfully integrate the public into the process on any type of utility project.

Case Study 1

In this case study, Tampa Bay Water, a regional water supply wholesaler in Tampa Bay, Florida, was charged with developing a variety of new water supplies to meet growing demand and offset pumping cutbacks at long-producing well fields. One project concept proposed to withdraw groundwater from a linear well field adjacent to Tampa Bypass Canal. The Bypass Canal is a flood control channel designed and excavated by the Army Corp of Engineers to divert high flows from the Hillsborough

River around the City of Tampa. During construction of the Bypass Canal in the 1970s, the top of the Floridian Aquifer was breached, creating a constant flow of groundwater into the surface water canal.

- **Goals and expectations:**
  - To site and permit a linear well field along the Tampa Bypass Canal, capable of producing at least 10 million gallons per day of new water supply for the region; to develop and implement a public involvement program to facilitate public participation in the project's decision-making process. (A separate public involvement program was implemented during the final design and construction phases.)

- **Project risks:**
  - Delayed or impeded project development could prevent the agency from meeting its contractual requirements to reduce groundwater pumping from 11 long-producing well fields.
  - Without the project, the region could potentially face a water shortage, resulting in more stringent water restrictions.
  - Without the project, environmental stress would continue to occur in the vicinity of 11 long-producing well fields.
  - Negative public perceptions of groundwater withdrawals, underscored by the agency's commitment to reduce withdrawals at 11 regional well fields.
  - A permit challenge could affect the project's timing, implementation, or yield.
  - Public disagreement about the need for new water supplies.
  - Public perceptions about who would receive the new water.
  - The agency lacked a public involvement track record.

- **Budget:**
  - The public involvement budget was approximately $78,000 of a total budget of $400,000.

- **Stakeholder identification:**
  - Stakeholders were identified by developing a list of potential concerns or issues and by determining which persons or groups might have an interest in the issues identified. This effort also included identifying whose support was needed to implement the project. Stakeholders identified included nearby residents, environmental groups, the local government officials and staff from the city in which the project was located, and local and regional regulatory agencies.

- **Techniques used:**
  - **Project articulation and key message development:** An integrated project team consisting of engineers, hydrologists, environmental and public involvement consultants first worked together to identify and clearly define the need for the project. The team then developed key messages to communicate the need for the project and project attributes

to establish a starting point of communications between the project team and key stakeholders.

— **Focus groups:** Two focus group sessions were held to determine the public's perceptions about the need for new water supplies, groundwater pumping, alternative supplies and conservation.

— **Early contact with individual stakeholders:** Initial conversations were held with individuals in the community to discuss the project and obtain feedback. That information, combined with the focus group results, was used to develop a public involvement program for the project.

— **Speakers/media training:** Annual speakers/media training sessions helped project managers sharpen their speaking skills and practice handling difficult questions from angry citizens.

— **Public meetings:** A series of public meetings were planned to introduce the project to the community, explain the decision-making process, answer questions, and obtain input. The first meeting was noticed and held as an open house, with display boards and team members positioned around a room. This format, although successful for many other Tampa Bay Water projects, was met with some opposition by local citizens for the Tampa Bypass Canal project. As a result, the project team and a board member met with a group of community leaders to fully explore their concerns and their preferences for communicating with the agency. This input was used to modify the public participation program.

The format of the next two public meetings was modified to start with an open house, followed by a traditional presentation, and concluded with a question and answer session by the community. The purpose of the meetings was to a) convey project information, b) explain how community input had shaped the project to date, c) answer any questions, and d) obtain additional citizen input.

— **Fact sheets:** Fact sheets were updated regularly to keep stakeholders informed about the project.

— **Newsletters:** Newsletters were mailed directly to project stakeholders to keep citizens apprised of project milestones, project modifications, and to give feedback on how citizen input was used.

— **Q&As:** Detailed question and answer packages were developed and updated regularly to answer questions frequently asked by citizens.

— **Public notices:** All community meetings were public noticed through display ads placed in local daily and weekly newspapers.

— **Direct mail:** Stakeholders on the project mailing list were notified of public meetings and updated on the project through direct mail.

— **Group presentations:** The project team kept local civic, environmental, and community groups apprised of the project through periodic briefings and presentations. These briefings provided additional community input to the project team.

— **One-on-one briefings with elected officials:** Tampa Bay Water's Board of Directors is comprised of two elected officials from each of the three counties it serves and one elected official from each of the three cities it serves. Briefings were scheduled with individual city or county elected officials to provide project information and obtain feedback. Additionally, copies of all direct mail and fact sheets were sent to local elected officials in the event they received calls or letters from their constituents.

— **Web page:** Tampa Bay Water's Web site featured a Master Water Plan link that directed citizens to information on each potential new water supply project.

— **Media relations:** Local reporters were briefed and provided news releases prior to each public meeting. Additionally, editorial board briefings were conducted to provide updates on all Master Water Plan activities, including the Tampa Bypass Canal project.

- **How the public involvement plan matched project tasks and milestones:**

  — A detailed project schedule was created using Primavera software. From this schedule, the project team identified key milestones where public input was needed as well as milestones where the team needed to provide information to the public. Additionally, the team determined all the points in the project where public input could be used.

- **Assessment of public involvement program success:**

  — During the public participation process, citizens voiced a strong preference for surface water withdrawals, instead of the linear well field proposed by the agency. After detailed technical evaluations and coordination with another project, the Tampa Bypass Canal project became a surface water withdrawal project. Through a proactive public involvement process, the project was successfully designed and permitted. Currently, the facility produces an average of 25.5 million gallons per day—far more than the 10 million gallon per day yield the agency initially sought. In addition, the public participation process improved the agency's relationship with the community as it continued feedback on how the public's recommendations were used.

Case Study 2

Coordinating officials from 15 jurisdictions and four counties can be a daunting task. When the effort is intended to produce successful implementation strategies to protect a multijurisdictional river across a diverse watershed, the challenge can seem enormous.

However, when the right approach is employed, as that used in the Alcovy Watershed Protection Project in north Georgia, a successful outcome is possible. By using a process with credibility for stakeholders, the Northeast Georgia Regional Development Center overcame a variety of obstacles, including logistics (how do you ensure the attendance at a strategy planning meeting of busy key stakeholders from locations many miles away? The NE Georgia Regional Development Center chose to invite everyone to a working breakfast meeting, which met this challenge), naturally antagonistic relationships (can the upstream polluter and the downstream *victim* share the same space?), and different needs (will recommendations for a heavily developed community be right for its rural neighbor?).

- **Area growth prompts action:**

  — The Alcovy Watershed Protection Project was devised by a few farsighted elected officials in the counties and cities in the Alcovy River watershed, a rapidly changing area east of metropolitan Atlanta. The river provides high-quality drinking water to thousands of residents and businesses, recreational opportunities, and a unique ecosystem.

    The Northeast Georgia Regional Development Center, a state-funded resource center for local governments, facilitated the watershed-wide effort and managed the day-to-day activities of the project. A consultant was hired to study existing water quality and model future outcomes based on a collection of implementation options tailored to each community. The goal of the Alcovy Watershed Protection Project was to formulate a plan to protect water resources in the watershed. Existing policies for managing growth and protecting natural resources were insufficient for water quality given the projected area growth rate. Various land management options were tested, and the result was a set of policy recommendations for local governments using the watershed. Each government could adopt its own combination of these recommendations.

    As a show of support, the Georgia Environmental Protection Division contributed a portion of project funding. The remaining funding was supplied from the four counties involved, which based contributions on their populations.

    To define the project and give it an identity, it was named *Team Alcovy: Neighbors for Clean Water*. The name reflected the nature of the project, which was the cooperative spirit among neighboring jurisdictions and agencies, the recognition that everyone in the area has an impact on river quality and everyone can be part of preserving it, and the protection strategies uniquely suited to each community to help all communities protect a precious shared resource.

- **Organizing major players:**

  — Given the expanse of effort and multitude of interests involved, the project team first established a formal mechanism for jurisdictions to have ongoing involvement in the project—a representative. The chosen representative's input and guidance was seen as critical to developing a watershed protection plan. Bringing elected officials and policy planners into the process after recommendations were formulated would risk the rejection of resulting ordinances and policies.

    It also was determined essential that the representatives sit together at a table during discussions to establish or enhance relationships between jurisdictions and to help neighboring communities become familiar with each other's concerns. In many cases, these representatives had never previously met nor discussed the problems that one jurisdiction was imposing on another.

    The project team developed a two-tiered approach including representatives in the process. To accommodate elected officials, who would be the most difficult to involve given their busy schedules, the Policy Committee was formed. The committee consisted of elected and appointed officials from each jurisdiction and met periodically during the 2-year project. Major components of committee discussions were regulatory requirements, the need for watershed protection measures, and implementation options that would be realistic and acceptable for their communities.

A second group known as the Technical Advisory Committee (TAC) consisted of two representatives selected by each county — typically a planning director, water or wastewater utility official, or other department-level official. This committee met monthly with the Northeast Georgia Regional Development Center and the consultant to oversee the technical details of the project. This group tended to be well-informed on regulatory requirements.

Implementation was a key focus of the discussions from the beginning, and committee input proved invaluable by moving forward with the right amount of information at the right stage of the project.

- **Stakeholder involvement:**

— The next step was developing a public involvement plan, which would serve as a bridge between project needs and stakeholder concerns. The initial step in developing the plan was a brainstorming session attended by center staff and the TAC to identify several goals, which ultimately included the following:

 ♦ Employ an easy-to-understand format to foster informed public opinion about the importance of water quality for the Alcovy.

 ♦ Seek to understand the values and attitudes of stakeholders.

 ♦ Provide opportunities for meaningful input and feedback on recommended solutions.

 ♦ Create a foundation for ongoing programs supporting citizen involvement in Alcovy water protection.

 ♦ Design and employ a basin-wide approach with flexibility for individual jurisdictions.

 ♦ Incorporate public input into the approved management plan and encourage broad-based support for plan implementation.

Taking the pulse of key opinion leaders and the media was also seen as crucial. With an understanding of current issues and the history of the area, audiences could be identified, messages tailored toward them, and information disseminated to reach as many of them as possible.

Research for the Alcovy project consisted of four steps. At the beginning of the process, center staff and TAC members were interviewed for a broad overview of issues and opinions. In addition, this informal, one-on-one dialogue allowed TAC members to share possible opportunities and challenges associated with public involvement.

Next, during the early phases of the project, TAC members received a brief written survey asking them for additional information, including key opinion leaders in their communities, the main drivers behind the Alcovy project, and their vision for public input to the final plan.

Contact then was made with local media in participating communities. This was done because the press was seen as critical in providing information to key opinion leaders, identifying controversial subjects, and providing a history of local issues.

Finally, historical news articles were gathered to complement the information gathered informally from local media representatives. With these four steps, stakeholders were identified, topics of interest were placed in perspective, and an ongoing picture of each community emerged.

- **How stakeholders were identified:**

  — To develop a watershed protection plan that would be implemented and not merely shelved, the public must be involved from the inception, including developers, farmers, homeowners, neighborhood organizations, conservationists, and industrial and commercial representatives. To be efficient and target information to those most interested in the project, the project team spent considerable time researching key stakeholders.

  From the list of prospective stakeholders, TAC members selected 15 for informal interviews on how best to engage the public, what issues were of particular interest to citizens, and what challenges might be anticipated. After interviews were completed, a summary report was submitted to center staff and TAC. Stakeholder information was maintained on a master database, and updates and materials were sent to stakeholders throughout the project. These stakeholders also were targeted for presentations and one-on-one discussions about the project. They were presented with the various policy options and provided feedback—ranging from the establishment of a storm water utility, adoption of a transferable development rights program for waterfront property protection, or establishment of a conservation subdivision ordinance or land trust program providing incentives for open space.

- **Techniques used:**

  — **Reaching the public:** Members of each community also were recognized as vital to successful implementation. Public meetings were an effective forum for direct input, and the project team conducted three such meetings during the project. One meeting was held at the beginning of the project to chart a course and to introduce concepts to the public. A second meeting was scheduled midway through the project to discuss implementation options for watershed protection. The final meeting was conducted after a draft plan was created to allow further public comment.

  These meetings featured an open-house session, which allowed attendees to visit information stations manned by members of the project team, who answered questions and gathered comments. The open house was followed by a group sit-down session to address any remaining questions. This format was selected because of the nature of the project—many residents traveled more than 50 miles to attend meetings, and an open house and Q&A session made it less critical for attendees to arrive and depart on time. Meetings were announced in paid advertisements in major newspapers. In addition, notices were mailed to the 15 stakeholders and posted on the project Web site. The public meetings complemented the next component of public involvement: *community presentations.*

  Presentations to community groups also were seen as an effective method for reaching the public because they can accommodate busy schedules and take place at already scheduled meetings. Making a presentation at these meetings informs a community that already has many time demands. It also focuses discussion and reinforces specific messages. For example, speaking to a group of cattlemen at their monthly meeting informs them on how they can be involved with watershed protection while ensuring that their concerns are heard.

The project team conducted more than 20 presentations and reached more than 500 people. Concepts presented in the final protection plan were introduced at these meetings based on guidance from TAC and the Policy Committee. Presentations were 15 minutes long, followed by a Q&A period. In some cases, a written survey was distributed asking attendees about the challenges of and opportunities for protecting the Alcovy. The goal of the presentations was to gather information to tailor implementation strategies for each jurisdiction. The center and TAC received a summary of all meetings, including public comments.

Because of the rural nature of much of the watershed, the Internet was an important tool. The project team developed a Web site (http://www.negrdc.org) with up-to-date and detailed project information. The site proved valuable in providing timely information to the public and broadcasting information about upcoming community presentations, public meetings, and other news. The site also included an extensive sampling data section as well as easy-to-understand explanations of the findings. This section allowed residents to click on a location near their homes and see actual sampling results with information relating it to water quality. By providing this level of detail, the project team assisted the public in making informed decisions about solutions for water quality in the Alcovy.

— **Tapping stakeholder energy:** The project team anticipated that as residents became informed about water protection efforts, they would seek ways to help. To help participating governments harness this dynamic resource, the team looked for ongoing water quality programs, such as adopt-a-stream groups, Girl Scout and Boy Scout merit badge programs, and neighborhood stream clean-up programs that would also offer cost-efficient and image-building avenues for citizen involvement. The project team researched and established a dialogue with state, federal, private sector, and nonprofit organizations already active in the watershed to present the participating governments with options for worthwhile partnerships.

— **Keeping the press informed:** Media relations were seen as important in spreading the word about the project and in keeping local stakeholders and opinion leaders informed. The project team developed a master database of media contacts within the 15 jurisdictions and wrote periodic press releases at key milestones of the project. Newspapers in particular responded to these releases and provided sufficient coverage.

By developing a strategic approach to bringing elected officials and planning staff together across multiple jurisdictions, combined with a one-on-one campaign targeting key stakeholders, and a broader effort to reach the public at large, the Alcovy Watershed Protection Project team coordinated stakeholders for a successful effort. In the end, a watershed protection plan was formulated and tailored to the unique needs of each community and that could be successfully adopted and implemented across the broad watershed.

Case Study 3

In Case Study 3, a Monroe County, Florida, utility developed a wastewater master plan in an environmentally sensitive area. The majority of existing residents had on-site treatment systems such as septic tanks. As with water resources planning projects, the team was faced with developing solutions that would be accepted and implementable. The team explored multiple options and combinations to determine the best possible solutions to the wastewater issues the community faced. The same steps can be followed for water resource planning projects.

- **Goals and expectations:**
  - To develop a wastewater master plan that offered sound economic and efficient wastewater treatment alternatives and that would be supported by residents, business, and environmental groups.

- **Project risks:**
  - The unique challenges for the project included
    - Disagreement on the true quality of the current treatment systems, i.e., some felt that the current systems were adequate and no changes were needed.
    - General fear that the cost to replace the current systems would be greater than the residents could bear.
    - A lack of trust in the local government to make equitable decisions.
    - A community that expected to be involved in the decision process.

- **Budget:**
  - The public involvement budget for this project was approximately $250,000 out of a total project budget of $2,200,000.

- **How stakeholders were identified:**
  - The public involvement team developed a master interest list at the start of the project that was updated continuously until project completion. The Master Interest List started with local media contacts, civic, business, and environmental groups as well as utility customers.

- **Techniques used:**
  - **Public forums:** Three initial public forums were held to share information about the project and provide an opportunity for meaningful public input regarding the development of the wastewater master plan. Promotion methods for the forums included announcements at related meetings, press releases to the media, and mailings to stakeholders. A total of 38 members of the public and 6 members of the media attended the public forums.

    Three additional public forums were held near the end of the project during the public comment period. The purpose of these public forums was to share information about the master plan solutions and provide an opportunity for questions and meaningful public comment.

— **Stakeholder meetings:** Initial stakeholder meetings were scheduled to discuss and obtain feedback. A number of civic, business, and environmental groups were identified at the start of the project and were contacted for these meetings. Meetings were scheduled over a series of four one-week periods. In addition, each interviewee was asked if there were others that they believed should be contacted. Some of the meetings were held with those individuals or organizations whose name was frequently mentioned. A total of 32 meetings with various civic, business, and environmental groups were held. A total of 44 stakeholders participated. Neighborhood workshops were very successful.

Additional stakeholder meetings to discuss proposed master plan solutions and answer questions were ongoing during the project. Final presentations were made to various groups at the end of the project.

— **Rack cards/information booklets:** Three one-page fact sheets were initially produced and distributed. More detailed brochures (rack cards) were prepared to convey key project milestones and other information to the public at large. These rack cards consisted of 4 color pages and included photos and graphics. The three rack cards were completed and distributed through mailings and hand delivery. Extra copies were made available to the public in libraries, utility offices, government agencies, chambers of commerce, and other places where residents would have access to them.

— **Media activities:** Media training of staff and project team members was conducted to develop and finalize key messages and prepare them for potential reporter inquiries. A media library of local newspaper articles concerning the master plan was created and was maintained throughout the project. In addition, newsletters from various organizations were collected. A master interest list of stakeholders and a media list was developed for comprehensive mailing of press releases, articles, and rack cards.

Press releases were distributed to the media containing detailed project information as well as announcements about the public forums, commission meetings, and technical advisory committee (TAC) meetings. Several meetings were held with reporters which resulted in positive articles.

Radio talk shows were initially identified and prioritized for use during the project. Appearances were made on a local radio morning show. Project team members also appeared on local television programs and answered caller questions during live tapings.

Template articles were written to provide more timely information on project milestones and were distributed to homeowners associations and special interest groups for publication in their newsletters. Press releases were used to alert the public of upcoming events. Opinion editorials were distributed to local papers.

— **Project videos:** A short project video was completed and distributed to the utility, TAC members, and to local television stations for regular airing. The short project video was aired weekdays for a period of 1 year.

A half-hour television program was filmed and aired on local television stations for 6 weeks.

— **Internet connection:** A Web site for the wastewater master plan was developed at the beginning of the project. Regular updates were made up until project completion. These updates included quarterly progress reports, press releases, presentations made to commissioners, a posted meeting schedule, and other project information. There was also a contact form page that allowed the public to send the project team comments and mailing information.

— **Other activities:** A project library of materials was established and contained all materials produced for the wastewater master plan as well as reference items that were pertinent to the project. These materials were cataloged and available for public viewing. In addition to these activities, staff participated in a school based outreach program for middle school students. Meetings with several teachers from local schools were also held throughout the project.

— **Decision solutions:** Citizen and key stakeholders directly influenced the development of the decision model and evaluation process, identified key issues to be addressed, and defined the elements of an acceptable master plan.

- **How the public involvement plan matched project tasks and milestones:**

  — The project team created a Gantt chart outlining the tasks involved in the master plan project. Specific activities were aligned at key points during the project. The timeline for collective public involvement activities covered the entire project schedule.

- **Assessment of public involvement program success:**

  — The public involvement program for the wastewater master plan enabled the project team to gain an understanding of community concerns, develop a plan to meet the public needs, and ultimately gain the support of the commissioners. Interacting with and involving the public was an important element in developing a plan that could ultimately be implemented. Interaction with the public throughout the project helped shape the contents of the wastewater master plan.

Case Study 4

In Case Study 4, permitting requirements forced a utility in Alexander City, Alabama, to change the current Advanced Wastewater Treatment Plant (AWWTP) discharge location for the industrial wastewater it was producing.

- **Goals and expectations:**

  — Stricter permit requirements, the need to prepare for future economic growth, and the need to protect the environment forced the utility to consider other treatment and discharge alternatives. Engineering evaluations revealed that relocating the discharge to one of the state's most pristine lakes, was the utility's most effective alternative. The utility was aware that local public acceptance and regulatory permitting would be difficult and chose to implement a comprehensive public involvement program prior to the submittal of the permit application to gain public consensus and increase the chances of the getting the permit.

- **Project risks:**
  - The industry creating the wastewater employed approximately 45 percent of the community's population. With increasing concerns about the trend for industries to relocate to other areas, efforts to expand the community's economic base were becoming increasingly important. The economic future of the utility and the community depended on the ability to discharge the treated wastewater in accordance with permit requirements.

- **Budget:**
  - The public involvement budget for this project was approximately $50,000 out of a total project budget of $780,000.

- **How stakeholders were identified:**
  - The potential stakeholders were identified by developing a comprehensive list of issues and determining what persons or groups might have a vested interest in the issues identified. The issues on the list were prioritized by identifying the issues that must be resolved and the stakeholders who would be too powerful to ignore. The public involvement efforts focused on these stakeholders while addressing the broader concerns of the general public. The preliminary stakeholders identified included: a local environmental organization, property owners, fishermen, community leaders, economic development organizations, regulatory agencies, and the media.

- **Techniques used:**
  - **Stakeholder interviews:** Initial stakeholder meetings were held as person-to-person interviews with representatives from each of the interest groups identified. During these meetings, stakeholders received information about the proposed outfall relocation, expressed their concerns, and asked questions related to the project. These interviews allowed the utility to assess the levels of concern among stakeholders, the level of misunderstanding related to the AWWTP, along with levels of opposition and support. Approximately 20 stakeholders were interviewed, and the information provided helped the utility to determine the essential topics that would need to be addressed as the public involvement efforts progressed.
  - **Citizen advisory committee:** Once stakeholder interviews were complete, a 13-member Citizen Advisory Committee (CAC) was formed. The CAC members were selected from the community and were representative of a broad cross-section of interests. Members of the CAC were asked to participate in four meetings and a tour of project-related facilities. The overall mission of the CAC was to provide informed public input to the utility regarding the proposed relocation of the AWWTP outfall. The work product of the CAC was a summary report detailing the committee's findings and recommendations. The information in this summary report was provided to policy makers for use in making

decisions related to the project. CAC members also were asked to help build community awareness about the facts related to the project by sharing information with their peers and participating in other community educational activities. The input obtained from CAC members was considered by policy makers when decisions were made about the project.

— **Workshops:** Because the CAC process only targeted a small segment of local residents, the utility chose to hold a public community workshop for those interested in learning more about the project and providing their own feedback. The workshop was set up to allow citizens to walk through a series of displays. Most of the outside experts who presented information during CAC meetings were available to answer questions from each individual. These experts were locally recognized, respected experts in their fields. Forms for comments related to the project were placed at each table and at the entrance and exit. Those who attended were given 2 weeks to return the forms and had the option of whether to include their name. More than 100 citizens attended the event and many completed comment forms. One hundred percent of the forms returned to the utility showed support for the project.

— **Other activities:** The utility made the commitment to continue to openly exchange information with the public as the project moved forward. Because many of the homes in the area were seasonal residences, an article describing the project and the CAC findings was placed in a local coffee table magazine that was popular among residents. After the pipe for the project was delivered, a news release was sent to the local media. Information packets were readily available and mailed to seasonal and weekend residents whose property was near the pipeline route or new discharge site. Facility tours were offered to the public as well. When the draft NPDES Permit public comment period began, a news article ran in the local paper encouraging residents to forward their comments to the regulatory agencies. In addition, a letter-writing campaign was initiated to demonstrate public support for the project. Instead of only receiving comments opposing the permit, regulatory agencies received comments supporting the permit.

- **How the public involvement plan matched project tasks and milestones:**

  — The project team created a Gantt chart outlining the tasks involved in the master plan project. Specific activities were aligned at key points during the project. The timeline for collective public involvement activities covered the entire project schedule.

- **Assessment of public involvement program success:**

  — Because of the public involvement program, the utility was able to build strong public support for a project that would have otherwise faced strong opposition. The CAC's findings and recommendations proved to be valuable to the utility in negotiations with the state regulatory agency and USEPA. The open exchange of information led the state regulatory agency to become a strong advocate for the utility in its decision to implement the project. In addition, the distribution of meeting summaries and project-related materials provided beneficial documentation for the utility's use in the permitting process with state regulators and USEPA.

Supplement to Chapter 2

PUBLIC CONSULTATION ADDRESSING HISTORIC/CULTURAL RESOURCE AND ENVIRONMENTAL JUSTICE ISSUES

As Chapter 2 has emphasized, public involvement is a critical aspect of scoping a water resources project. Under the National Environmental Policy Act (NEPA) and the National Historic Preservation Act (NHPA), timely public participation is required for many situations. These include the presence of historic or cultural resources where a federally permitted project is being considered. Where environmental justice issues must be considered, public involvement is also required.

If federally recognized Native American tribes are impacted, there is a requirement for *consultation and collaboration* with them as separate and sovereign nations. Under the NHPA, agencies must also make a *reasonable and good faith effort* to identify Native American tribes who may attach religious and cultural significance to a site but who live in another location. This can require considerable research, because of the forced relocation of many tribes during the 1800s far from their indigenous roots.

PUBLIC INVOLVEMENT AND CONSULTATION REGARDING HISTORIC AND CULTURAL RESOURCES

Historic resources or properties are defined as physical places included in or eligible for the National Register of Historic Places, which is maintained by the National Park Service. Cultural resources can be defined as those parts of the physical environment—natural and built—that have cultural value of some kind to some sociocultural group such as a community, a neighborhood, or a tribe as well as to archeologists, architectural historians, folklorists, or cultural anthropologists.[*]

Consultation typically involves the lead federal agency, the Advisory Council on Historic Preservation (ACHP), a federal executive board that reports to the president and has general oversight of national historic preservation site work, and the state historic preservation office. If a federally recognized Native American tribe is involved, they may have a tribal historic preservation officer as part of the consultation, in addition to tribal council.

Section 106 of the NHPA requires two things:

1. that federal agencies take into account the effects of their actions on historic properties, and

2. afford the ACHP a reasonable opportunity to comment on their actions.

Consultation with stakeholders is needed to take into account the effects of actions. Its purpose is to stimulate analysis of proposed effects and ways to avoid,

---

[*]King, Thomas F. 1998. *Cultural Resources Laws and Practice: An Introductory Guide*. New York: Altamira Press, p. 9.

minimize, or mitigate adverse effects.[*] Consultation leads to an agreement, termination, or project abandonment. If there is agreement, it should result in a *memorandum of agreement* between parties that includes the ACHP, among others.

For water supply projects, consultation is the process for scoping how and where to get the water. It facilitates the gathering of information and viewpoints from interested parties, looks at how people used the landscape, wetlands, and rivers in the past and how they are using them today. It deals with changes in how people relate to land and water resources, and seeks balance in respecting needs while providing for growth. The challenge and goal of consultation is to use it as a tool to find a win/win situation for groups that may have divergent interests. A good source for detailed guidance on consultation under Section 106 is the ACHP Web site: http://www.achp.gov/.

PUBLIC INVOLVEMENT AND CONSULTATION REGARDING ENVIRONMENTAL JUSTICE

Environmental justice (EJ) can also invoke the need for consultation. EJ is the result of a 1994 Presidential Executive Order (#12898). Basically, EJ is the pursuit of equal justice and equal protection for all people when addressing environmental regulations. The goal of EJ is to assure that lower income and/or minority communities, as well as Native American Tribes, do not bear a disproportional share of environmental impacts from federal actions. Environmental justice is coordinated through the Office of Environmental Justice under the US Environmental Protection Agency (USEPA).

There are several environmental regulatory authorities, including NEPA, NHPA, and the Endangered Species Act, that provide a planning context for consideration of EJ issues by calling for

- analysis of environmental effects, including effects on minorities, low-income communities, and Native American tribes;

- mitigation measures of effects through an environmental assessment (EA), an environmental impact statement (EIS), or a record of decision (ROD) and addressing of significant and/or adverse environmental impacts to these populations;

- opportunities for effective community participation in the NEPA process, including consultation with impacted communities; and

- review of NEPA compliance to assure these issues have been addressed.

Guidance about EJ from the Council on Environmental Quality (established by Congress within the Executive Office of the President as part of NEPA) includes

- consideration of the human composition of the affected area;

- consideration of direct, indirect, or cumulative impacts;

- recognition that certain characteristics of a minority community—cultural, social, occupational, historical, or economic—may amplify an impact of an action.

- implementation of effective public participation strategies that address linguistic, cultural, institutional, geographical, and other barriers to meaningful participation;

---

*Ibid p. 6.

- early and meaningful community representation in the NEPA analysis process and review; and

- interactions with Native American tribes that are consistent with government-to-government relationships between the US and tribal governments, acknowledging any treaty rights that may be involved.[*]

CONSULTATION/COLLABORATION WITH FEDERALLY RECOGNIZED NATIVE AMERICAN TRIBES

Within the United States, there are about 570 federally recognized Native American tribes or governments. Unlike other groups or communities, federally recognized Native American tribes have a unique status that requires a *government-to-government* relationship with such tribes when one consults with them regarding federally permitted projects. What do *sovereignty* and *government-to-government* relationships mean?

Each federally recognized Native American tribe is considered a sovereign government, *an individual nation*, that has the status, dominion, role, or power of a sovereign. Tribes have the power (sometimes limited by Congress) to make and enforce laws for their tribe and reservation, and to establish courts and other forums for resolution of disputes.

In many ways, tribal governments operate parallel to state government with many of the same powers and regulations. (There are a few state-recognized tribes, and in these cases, they function under State law.) Implicit in this relationship is the recognition of tribal sovereignty as individual nations within the US and the US government's obligation to protect tribal lands.[†]

Effective Consultation/Collaboration

To consult and collaborate with impacted Native American tribes is to recognize them as stakeholders in the process. In its guidelines for federal agency historic preservation programs, the National Park Service provides the following definition of consultation:

> . . . the process of seeking, discussing, and considering the views of others, and, where feasible, seeking agreement with them on how historic properties should be identified, considered and any impacts managed or mitigated. Consultation is built upon the exchange of ideas, not simply providing information.[‡]

According to the ACHP, effective consultation occurs when the involved parties do the following:

- keep an open mind;

- state interests clearly;

---

*US General Services Administration Web site on Environmental Justice. From Fact Sheet. http://www.gsa.gov/Portal/gsa/ep/contentView.do?contentType=GSA_DOCUMENT& contentId=19393&noc=T

†Office of Environmental Justice (USEPA). 2000. *Guide on Consultation and Collaboration with Indian Tribal Governments and the Public Participation of Indigenous Groups and Tribal Members in Environmental Decision Making*. Washington D.C. Addendum A, p. 30–31.

‡Ibid. p. 28.

- acknowledge that others have legitimate interests, and seek to understand and accommodate them;

- consider a wide range of options; and

- identify shared goals and seek options that allow mutual gain.[*]

Consulting during project scoping with Native American tribes who may be impacted by a project is especially important before any sort of public discussion takes place. There are several reasons for this.

- The tribe(s) may have concerns about potential impacts to cultural or spiritual situations, details of which they do not want disclosed to the public.

- Involving impacted tribes from the beginning communicates that their concerns are being heard and addressed. People are more willing to consult and negotiate when they are part of the process and part of the solution.

- Obtaining information from the tribes during scoping (under NEPA) means that an agency will be better informed from the beginning of a project, helping an agency to make better decisions.[†]

A good source of guidance on meaningful consultation and collaboration is a document published through USEPA: "Guide on Consultation and Collaboration with Indian Tribal Governments and the Public Participation of Indigenous Groups and Tribal Members in Environmental Decision Making." It can be downloaded from USEPA's Web site at: http://www.epa.gov/compliance/resources/publications/ej/ips_consultation_guide.pdf.

Creating an Environment for Effective Consultation

The attitude surrounding the consultation process with Native American tribes is critical, particularly when crossing cultural boundaries.

1. **Openness.** Being open to learning and appreciating new cultures and values is essential when working with Native American tribes. Indigenous people have close ties with nature that some in the dominant cultures may not understand. A project that will bring change to the natural environment may be perceived as an attempt to destroy the link between Native people and the natural environment.

2. **Respect and validation.** Many in the dominant culture have limited knowledge of Native culture, their ties to the land and water, and their spirituality. Respect for values not shared or understood is critical when trying to build a positive, consultative relationship with another culture that leads to desirable results for all concerned. Lack of familiarity with a culture or lack of understanding does not lessen its validity.

   Native American tribes represent well-developed subcultures that are gaining power and influence. This is a result of many factors: an enhanced self-knowledge and respect of their own culture, increased education, and enhanced economic clout as a result of the gaming industry and other industrial pursuits now taking place on many reservations.

   Finally, native cultures share a past that deserves respect and validation. Research into the history of the arrival of white settlers in the

---

*ACHP Web site on consultation. http://www.achp.gov/citizensguide.html.
†Office of Environmental Justice, op cit., Addendum C, p. 46.

United States and the repercussions that resulted against indigenous people is an effective way to gain empathy toward and respect for Native Americans, for their ability to survive into the twenty-first century with so many of their indigenous values and practices intact, and yet still be part of the overall culture.

3. **Protocol.** Because federally recognized Native American tribes have a government-to-government relationship with the federal government, it is important to approach tribes with respect due any government. Appropriate protocol dictates that interaction through officials be at comparable governmental stature and authority. Tribal leaders are of the highest levels of tribal government and should be treated accordingly.

   A USEPA publication titled *Working Effectively with Tribal Governments* provides insight on the history and values of Native Americans. It can also be downloaded through the Internet at http://www.epa.gov/indian/resource/intro.htm.

Consultation Tips

To achieve successful consultation, application of the following can be beneficial:

1. **Priority.** Make historic/cultural issues a top priority. It is a serious error to think there is not enough time to invest in the research, patience, and attention to timely consultation and protocol for a culturally sensitive project. Failure to invest this time may result in a continuing onslaught of resistance to the project, negative publicity, and lawsuits.

2. **Training.** A critical path to understanding and respecting Native culture is to obtain training from experts about the Native culture, their history, and their values. Training of this nature can be obtained through government agencies, tribal organizations, universities, and consultants. For example, the National Preservation Institute (www.npi.org) offers short courses in Native American consultation and various aspects of cultural resource management.

3. **Continuous development of relationship.** Working with tribes involves the same skills used to create and maintain both professional and personal relationships. It requires understanding, mutual respect, and continuous attention to the relationship. With time, relationships with tribal governments can develop that will enhance the effectiveness of a utility, and enhance the tribal government's ability to best serve its people.

To summarize, effective consultation can be time-consuming and requires research and considerable communication skills. It may also require the patience to learn about another culture and its norms, and to be able to find common ground between the groups. The investment of time in effective consultation, however, can provide project planners with information needed to help make good decisions regarding the project and also help to avoid future public outcries that can delay or derail a project.

This page intentionally blank

Chapter **3**

Water Demand Forecasting

Sound water demand forecasts are critical in water resources planning. In particular, the adequacy of supply, optimum facility location and size, and sound transmission and distribution system design depend on the accuracy of demand forecasts. No single method of forecasting will satisfy the varied needs of all water utilities. The forecasting method used and the data needed to correctly apply the method depend on the situation. For example, when a forecast of average annual demand is the primary requirement, a simple per capita approach might be sufficient. When major new capacity must be added in different locations within the utility's total service area, a multivariate analysis of disaggregated demand by area and customer class will more accurately specify the size and character of facilities required. These two examples illustrate the interactive and building block nature of the forecasting process. An initial forecast might identify capacity constraints, which in turn prompt more detailed area and seasonal (peaking) demand forecasts.

Criticality of forecasting accuracy depends on the project objective and the inherent costs and risks related to forecast errors. Detailed and accurate forecasts are especially important when determining supply alternatives, modeling water use in the distribution system, and sizing facilities. Accuracy is generally not as critical when addressing environmental impacts, determining some aspects of water quality, making water policy decisions, and dealing with regularity issues. However, all factors that may affect the need for accuracy must be considered when selecting forecasting methods with emphasis placed on the potential costs and risks of forecast errors.

The data required to develop an accurate demand forecast will come from a variety of information sources. Most of the data required to develop good demand forecasts, such as consumption data, should be maintained in the utility's engineering, hydrology, operations, and financial departments. Some demographic and housing data must also be collected from the planning departments of cities served by the utility. How the data are treated, analyzed, and presented for decision making

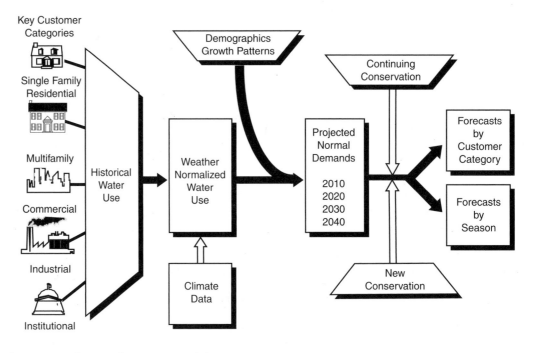

Figure 3–1   Information flow in forecast model

is more demanding. The data categories required in a detailed demand forecast and the general steps used in the forecasting process are illustrated in Figure 3-1. The approach taken in this chapter is to identify and discuss essential data requirements and the typical analytical methods applied to define historical patterns of demand, as well as to dynamically project these patterns into future years.

The overall demand forecasting process incrementally assesses the need for additional information and analysis. The rule of thumb is if a simple process suffices, use it. If more details are needed, collect and analyze the essential data. A continuum of complexity should be used, from a single projection of per capita demand to identifying water use factors and growth rates for numerous customer types by a three- or four-digit Standard Industrial Code. The incremental application of effort and cost usually achieves smaller increments of results; there is a diminishing marginal return. Usually, prior forecasts and a good sense for capacity limitations will suggest a particular level of analysis. The cutoff for analyses occurs when forecasters are comfortable that all the major factors that can be addressed have been addressed.

The forecasting method selected will depend largely on the data available, the complexity of the utility's service area, and the degree of forecast reliability required. When data are limited, a simple model should be used. In fact, a relatively simple model may be satisfactory even though extensive data are available. For example, if a new treatment plant that will meet demand requirements for the next 20 years needs to be built, fine-tuning a demand forecast that will not affect supply reliability until the end of this period is unnecessary. In these cases, excess capacity is common for many years after the construction. The clear objective must be to match accurate reliable supply with accurate demand forecasts for the period that additional capacity is needed. Temporary or continuing shortages of supply that emerge over time will then prompt efforts to curtail water use until a temporary supply crisis is over or until additional supplies are provided. For the very long term (30 to 50 years or more), highly accurate forecasts are usually not critical, especially if a realistic range of demand is developed. Several stepped increments of supply may occur during the lengthy period that allows adjustments to changing projections. For facilities designed to serve for 5 to 10 years, however, poor accuracy in forecasting demand can result in costly replacement of undersized mains or facilities, if demand is seriously understated; or wasted capital costs (debt service on bonds) from building excess capacity, if demand is overstated.

In summary, the steps in the forecasting process are as follows:

- Collect the data that will be needed for the analysis and projections.

- Select the method of analysis and identify historical water use patterns.

- Identify the potential for conservation by analyzing the key measures in place or available programs that might be considered.

- Estimate unbilled water use and system water losses and assess the water loss savings that are feasible over the forecast period.

- Integrate all these elements into a demand forecast, usually over an extended period of 20 to 40 years.

The forecast should include an assessment of forecast sensitivity for key components. The scope of effort for each of these measures is discussed in the following sections.

FORECASTING METHODS

The underlying method of analysis in most forecasting is some form of regression analysis, although it is sometimes not recognized as such. Regression analysis is a statistical technique that mathematically defines the relationship of one dependent variable with one or more independent variables that statistically explain the dependent variable, in terms of either a fixed or a causal relationship. This process can be applied simply with per capita and extrapolation methods, and more rigorously using multiple regression models. The multiple regression models are often used to define or describe relationships between water sales and causal influences rather than to actually make the projections.

Several methods of demand forecasting are often combined, even within a single utility. Several commonly used methods are discussed in this section, although there is usually significant overlap in their use. Specific examples of these methods are provided in the section Identifying Water Use Patterns appearing later in this chapter. The amount of data economically available will usually determine the degree of sophistication in the method of forecasting applied.

Per Capita Models

As its name suggests, the per capita model simply calculates the total production or consumption per capita for a historical period and applies the current year per capita consumption (sometimes with a trend) to the population projections for future periods. This is the simplest forecasting method and requires only historical production or consumption data, historical population, and a forecast of population through the demand forecasting horizon. The per capita models produce satisfactory results as long as the population forecast is accurate, and the customer mix does not change substantially. The more critical element in forecast accuracy, using this method, is usually the population projection, not the per capita water use factor. The obvious exception is when a very heavy-water-using firm enters or leaves the utility's service area.

Extrapolation Models

Extrapolation models plot, in a scatter diagram, annual or monthly consumption related to time or to population and draw a line manually (or with a spreadsheet statistical package) to capture the *slope* or relationship between the variables. The relationship is then extrapolated into future periods. This process can be applied to total water use or to components of the total, such as residential and nonresidential use. Again, the data requirements are simple: historical production or consumption data, historical population, and projected population. The relationships to time and population are forms of single explanatory variable (bivariate) regression analysis without detailed structural analysis. The linear form of this model is

$$D = a + bx + e \qquad \text{(Eq 3-1)}$$

Where:

D = water demand

a = the vertical axis intercept term (a constant)

b = the derived regression coefficient (slope) of the independent variable

x = the independent variable (time or population in the example)

e = an error or residual term

The b term is also referred to as the slope of the relationship between the dependent and independent variables (i.e., the change in demand [dependent variable] associated with a change in time or population in this illustration [independent variables]).[*]

Disaggregate Water Use Models

The billing systems in most large water utilities permit at least some disaggregation of total billings, usually by residential, commercial, industrial, and municipal or public facilities. Further breakdowns are often available for single family and multifamily residential, institutional, and irrigator accounts. Many utilities can also provide billing data by land-use patterns, region, district, pressure zone, microclimate area, and topography areas. Forecast accuracy is generally improved by disaggregation as long as the water use or trend patterns are different among the segments. If two or more segments (e.g., Area A and Area B) are experiencing the same water use and growth rate, separate forecasts are unlikely to improve the accuracy, and additional forecasts are unnecessary. Nevertheless, separate forecasts for residential and commercial accounts are usually made even if their mix is not different or changing.

The basic approach applied to disaggregated segments of total water consumption is usually to isolate gallons per day per unit (m^3 per day per unit) for each segment, which is then applied to projections of the base units into future years. The base unit used could be utility accounts, employment, floor space or acreage, population, or any other unit of measure that makes sense for a particular segment.

---

* Extrapolation models can also take on nonlinear shapes, drawn freehand or using polynomial curves (such as $D = a + bx - cx^2$) or logarithmic functions (such as $D = a + b * \log[x]$) or a power curve (such as $D = a * x^b$).

The method of deriving the m^3 per day per unit can be as simple as taking an average of recent consumption divided by the unit (e.g., accounts) to arrive at gallons per day per account (gpd/a; m^3 per day per account [m^3 pd/a]); or it could be as complex as performing a regression analysis that normalizes for weather and accounts for seasonal variations, price, household income, family size, growth, lot size, and conservation effects. The more detailed analysis is generally not done using cross-sectional regression analysis that measures the impact of each explanatory variable for a point in time or pooled time-series and cross-sectional regression analysis that tracks the cross-sectional pattern over time; rather, the process is to isolate unique patterns of water use by area within the total service area and forecast each of these segments separately if their growth patterns are different. The different segments are often captured via meter reading routes. For example, neighborhood routes are usually read on one day; one route may have small houses and lots (in the central city area) with lower water use compared to a suburban route that has larger houses and lots with high water use. These differences would cause a variation in the per account per day consumption that cannot be explained by seasonal or weather variations. Greater accuracy can be achieved by forecasting the unique segments separately if their growth patterns are substantially different. Forecasting by unique segments (different microclimates) or areas (urban versus suburban) is a virtual requirement to account for the change in mix or composition of total demand as between urban and rural customer water use or different micro climate areas when applicable. Consequently, disaggregate water use models probably are the most commonly used to isolate and forecast the shifting patterns of component elements within the total demand structure.

Multiple Regression (Multivariate) Models

Multiple regression models simultaneously evaluate a combination of independent variables that can include population, households or dwelling units, household income, lot sizes, land use, employment, and various weather variables. Dummy variables are frequently included to measure the effects of dichotomous (on–off) conditions. A dummy variable is assigned a value of *1* when the condition is "on" and a *0* in all other periods. For example, the impact of water use restrictions during a 3-month drought period in 1998 could be captured in a regression coefficient by setting up a variable (call it restriction) with a value of *1* during the 3-month period and a value of *0* in all other months. Some forecasters refer to multiple regression models as econometric models when the structure of the model primarily addresses economic variables such as household income, marginal and average water prices, and employment.

When the regression model includes only variables that vary over time for a single stratum of the utility service area, the model is designated as a *time-series model*. For example, monthly consumption for a city as a function of population and temperature would be a time-series regression model. When the regression model slices through a point in time and addresses independent variables that cause the dependent variable (water consumption) to be different for different strata in the service area, the model is designated as a *cross-sectional model*. For example, consumption in ten communities within a service area for a given period (e.g., summer 1998) as a function of household income, home value, family size, lot size, and marginal prices would be a cross-sectional regression model. When the regression model allows for the differences in behavior stemming from the cross-sectional attributes and the changes over time, the model is referred to as a *pooled time-series, cross-sectional model*. The simple form of the multiple regression models is an extension of the single variable model

$$D = a + b_1 x_1 + b_2 x_2 + \ldots + b_n x_n + e \qquad \text{(Eq 3-2)}$$

in which the *b* values are the coefficients (slopes) of the additional *x* independent variables.

Land Use Models

Land use models concentrate on current and projected uses of residential, commercial, industrial, and public lands within the ultimate boundaries of the water utility. Residential land use is frequently divided into two or more density classifications, and the nonresidential categories are also segmented if there are different patterns of consumption. Growth rates are established (in concert with city planning departments) for each land use segment, usually by census tract, allowing for public land, infill development, and growth into undeveloped areas. Water use factors are developed for each land use segment and applied to the projections of population, households, employment, and other variables used to forecast the segments. Although a land use model is often viewed as a specific forecasting method, all demand forecasts include an evaluation of land use to some degree. For example, the per account models recognize the varying demands of different account groups, and the varying growth patterns for urban and suburban residential accounts. Each category with a different water use or growth pattern should be forecasted separately.

Univariate Forecasting Models

Univariate models have limited applicability to water demand forecasting. In univariate or single variable forecasting methods, only the dependent variable is needed: water production or consumption. Two univariate methods are sometimes applied to short-term water forecasting. These methods are the Box–Jenkins or AutoRegressive Integrated Moving Average (ARIMA) method and the method of exponential smoothing. The univariate methods generally are inappropriate for long-run forecasting, but components of these methods (identification of autoregressive patterns, seasonal patterns, and trends) can be of considerable value in developing other forecasting methods. Univariate methods can be used for water demand forecasting, but in virtually all long-term and most short-term situations, a combination of time-series and regression analysis produces superior results.

The Integrated Model

The integrated model is not so much a separate method of forecasting as it is a repository for the results of all the other methods. Planners will find that using computer spreadsheets makes it easier to construct a model that structures all the relevant variables in demand forecasts. For the simple per capita model, the spreadsheet must include, at a minimum, population history and projections and water use history in gallons per capita per day (gpcd) or (m^3 per capita per day [m^{3}pcd]) with a measure of trend if applicable. For the disaggregate model by customer class (and possibly by land use or area), the model is likely to include 10 years of monthly consumption history for 10 or more customer areas, or density segments, with weather normalization, a moving average that tracks cycle and trend, linked sheets or files with projected outcomes of conservation measures, a price response factor for projections, and any number of other factors that are relevant to a given utility. The integrated model will also contain tabular and graphic output displays. The advantage of developing this fully integrated model in the utility is that it allows planners to judge the relevance and potential forecast accuracy during the building process. The disadvantage, especially in a highly complex utility, is that developing a fully integrated model can require a high level of statistical skill and much effort. Many utilities engage consultants to conduct part or all of the forecasting process.

DATA REQUIREMENTS

The data required for analyzing consumption patterns depend on the methods used in the forecasting process. If a simple per capita approach to forecasting is selected, the data requirements could be as easy as securing historical annual water production or sales for 5 to 10 years and total historical and projected population in the service area. The forecast could then be prepared by multiplying the latest year's per capita rate (possibly including a trend factor) times the projected population. This approach might be appropriate for a very small, mostly residential community but, with increasingly tight water supplies in many parts of the country, even relatively small communities must often analyze the components of demand to conserve water. Utilities can employ some of the more complicated methods of analysis even with relatively sparse data. Therefore, the utility should collect all readily available relevant data in case they are needed and assess the need to compile additional data on a benefit–cost basis. Often more data are collected than are useful in the analyses, but it is difficult to determine what is useful until the process is under way. If the utility takes an incremental analysis approach, the saturation point becomes apparent as additional variables are added to the analysis. The data needed for effective forecasting fall into eight broad categories:

1. Periodic (monthly preferred) consumption (or billings) and number of accounts by customer class

2. Daily and monthly production

3. Weather data

4. Demographic data

5. Conservation history and objectives

6. Rate structure and pricing data

7. Economic data

8. An assessment of current and projected water losses in the system

Each category is discussed in the following sections.

Consumption Data

Ideally, the utility should forecast using monthly consumption from a period of at least 10 years and the related number of accounts for every relevant customer group and location. The difficulty with this prescription is that, in the first-time situation, the forecaster does not know which customer groups and areas should be forecasted until the data are analyzed to determine whether there are differences in water use or growth rates that should be treated separately. When forecasts are updated in subsequent years, the forecaster should know which data are needed. The initial rule should be to collect readily available data and test customer class/area segments to see which current or additional segments are warranted.

Data from a 20-year period are most beneficial if the overall period includes one or more drought crises that must be analyzed to measure their temporary and permanent effects on consumption. The ideal data permit the forecaster to develop a statistically sound seasonal pattern, measure the response to significant price changes, identify indoor and outdoor consumption segments, and track historical consumption long enough to identify conservation results, cyclical patterns, and trends that might be present. Customer groups could include single family residential, multifamily residential, commercial, industrial, institutional, municipal, irrigation, agricultural, and system losses. The areas analyzed depend on differences in consumption and growth patterns and on the level of demand detail needed for specific facilities planning. When combined, relevant customer classes and areas can result in 10 to 20 forecasting series. When the number of forecasting series exceeds 10, the utility should implement stringent justification rules to prevent a proliferation of data. Only if data are justified by being significantly different in water use and growth should they be added as a separate series. A series can be considered significant if adding it changes the forecasting fit over the historical period (backcast) by a specified degree of accuracy, such as 1 or 2 percent. The actual accuracy trigger point for inclusion will differ with each agency based on the total variance in the dependent variable (total consumption).

It is usually more efficient and accurate to analyze consumption patterns on a m^3pd/a basis by customer class than to work with total consumption for each customer class with the number of accounts as a separate independent variable. This approach neutralizes the uneven effects of growth in the water consumption data related to variations in account growth. Of course, the number of accounts must be forecasted independently to be combined with the gpd/a or m^3pd/a to generate the demand forecasts. For account classes other than single family residential, it is sometimes preferable to work with consumption per employee, per square foot (meter) of floor space, or per equivalent account where the equivalent could be typical single family customer use or average use for the customer class being analyzed. The need for using some form of equivalent customer is usually apparent when a small number of very large accounts dominates the consumption in a category. Very large new accounts are not usually added each year; so the average gpd/a or m^3pd/a before a large new account is added is not a good basis for typical new account usage. Using equivalent residential accounts (or some other equivalent such as meter size) solves this projection dilemma as long as the size of new accounts can be predicted. Agencies that have connection, development, or capacity fees for new accounts can often accurately estimate the expected water use for major new accounts.

Production Data

Production data are needed for two reasons: to identify system losses and to identify peaking characteristics (peak hour, peak day, and peak month) within the system. Many utilities routinely perform a water audit analysis. If such an analysis is not done, total system water losses can be derived as the difference between monthly production and monthly retail water sales (billings), combined with metered but unbilled use, allowing for the time lag in reporting billings. However, this approach is crude and does not provide adequate information as to the source of the water losses. The amount or percentage of unbilled water (including water losses) must be added to the retail sales forecasts to derive total system demand. The peaking data, which are needed in the capacity planning for new facilities, are usually recorded daily and archived for use by facility planners.

Weather Data by Location

Monthly weather data for the same periods as the consumption data are needed to identify seasonal patterns and weather impacts on consumption. These data also provide the base for weather normalization of the consumption when projecting future demand. The forecaster should collect and test all readily available weather variables (via regression analysis) to isolate those that display the best causal relationship with changes in consumption. A highly efficient approach to using weather variables in regression analysis is to express them as departures from normal weather (long-run average weather). For example, in July 2003, the actual mean high temperature in a city might have been 90°F (32°C) compared to a 30-year average of 85°F (29°C). The statistical test is to determine (for all months analyzed) how the departures of actual temperature from normal affect consumption. Consequently, the forecaster must derive an average month for each variable over a lengthy period to measure the departures from average. A minimum of 10 years will suffice to derive the average, but a 20- or 30-year average is desirable. Local weather stations and the National Oceanic and Atmospheric Administration (NOAA) usually keep such data, which are available on the Internet. Relevant weather variables available from NOAA include

- Temperature variables usually include the high for each day and the average high for the month, mean daily temperature for the month, number of cooling degree days in the month, and days per month greater than a high temperature such as 90°F (32°C).

- Precipitation variables usually include daily precipitation and the total for the month, and the number of rain days in each month.

- Some locations might also have data on evaporation or evapotranspiration, which often closely correlate with changes in water consumption.

Mean high monthly temperature, total monthly precipitation, and evaporation or evapotranspiration are frequently the most significant variables in the regression analyses. The next level of significance is usually degree days and rain days. Additional weather variables, such as sunny days, snowfall, and wind speed, are seldom significant in analyzing water use.

Demographic Data

Demographic data are needed for two purposes: (1) to provide independent variables, such as population, households, household income, and number of occupants, for the regression analyses; and (2) to derive the basis for projecting the historical patterns into future periods. The amount of data that should be routinely collected in a database depends on the availability and reliability of data.

City planning departments are often the best sources for population, housing values and density, land use by area, and projections of expected growth in city and county plans. It is extremely helpful, if not mandatory for political reasons, that the city or county planning department's population or household growth forecasts reasonably coincide with the water forecasting practitioner's forecasts. This may require a compromise. If an irreconcilable difference remains (usually related to a specific issue such as unpredictable industrial growth, ultimate land use allocations, or similar difficult issues), the planning department's projections are generally used, and the forecaster simply states the potential sensitivity of the issue on the water demand projections in the forecasting report.

City planning departments are usually repositories for demographic data from many sources, including the US Census Bureau, the local Chamber of Commerce, area university studies, and local businesses that do their own economic projections. If data are unavailable from the cities, census data can be obtained directly from the Census Bureau for all but the smallest locations; however, it is available only once every 10 years. Sometimes the census data are updated every year or two by universities in the area or by local commercial or industrial firms. Even if the census data are of questionable value, key elements of the data should be collected if only to corroborate data from other sources. Key data from the Census Bureau should include

- population: composition by city, town (age, births, deaths, and migration optional);

- family formation: number of households, single family, multifamily; and

- number of firms and employment by sector: commercial, industrial, municipal.

Conservation Data

Conservation measures in place by customer class and locality (if applicable) are important factors, as are any potential new conservation measures. This information can sometimes be analyzed statistically to identify the specific impacts conservation measures have had on water use; however, more frequently, the impacts of measures that are undertaken concurrently cannot be isolated statistically. It is nevertheless reassuring to observe that downturns in water use likely result from an intense combination of conservation measures during the same period. The impact of specific conservation measures applied to individual customers can be measured with accuracy if before-and-after-intervention water use is available for each customer and all the customers in a group have been exposed to the same measures.[*] The key tests that will identify conservation savings are comparisons of before and after mean water use and matched pairs analyses of before and after periods.

Currently implemented measures. A description of specific measures, including the design, goals, cost, and implementation period, is highly desirable. This includes any water restriction periods, utility leak detection and repair programs, drought pricing periods, indoor or outdoor fixture giveaways or rebate programs, or aggressive public awareness programs. It is very helpful to know the percentages of single family and multifamily housing that have conservation measures in place.

Potential conservation measures. More than 100 specific conservation measures can be identified for a service area that includes single family and multifamily residential, commercial, industrial, municipal, and irrigation accounts. To complete a long-run demand forecast, the agency management's (and city council's or board of directors') intent and commitment must be clearly identified so the potential results can be included in the forecasts. Most of the data required to assess conservation potential are available in the consumption and demographic data requirements already identified. For example, indoor and outdoor consumption can be derived by customer class and area from consumption or billing data and used to identify opportunities for effective new conservation measures. Similarly, household size (occupants) data and number of bathrooms and fixtures form a basis for a program to replace old residential fixtures with modern, low water-using fixtures. If

[*]Weber, Jack A., Tracking & Measuring Water Conservation Performance, a workshop identifying and demonstrating methods and results, AWWA Water Sources Conference, Las Vegas, January 27, 2002.

the conservation effort is also directed at nonresidential customer classes, the forecaster needs to obtain a list of the largest water users in each customer class. Depending on the size of the utility, this could represent the top 25, 50, or 100 accounts in each class.

Rate Structure and Price Data

If water prices have historically increased in line with the local consumer price index, they are unlikely to have had any statistically measurable effect on water consumption. On the other hand, if a harsh conservation or drought rate structure has been used temporarily or continuously, a response to these rates will have occurred. If a form of multiple regression or econometric analysis is used in the forecasting process, it is quite feasible to incorporate water price data in the analysis and measure price responsiveness (elasticity). However, the forecasting practitioner should be extremely cautious about accepting the results of any price analyses undertaken concurrently with severe nonprice measures during a drought or other crisis period. In such situations, any derived measure of price elasticity would be suspect because it is virtually impossible to statistically isolate nonprice factors, such as restrictions, fixture replacements, education and awareness programs, and the sympathetic restraint of customers during a period of crisis. In normal times, if real dollar price increases are large (at least 10 percent), price elasticity analyses can be a necessity in planning both revenues and water demand. To conduct these analyses, it is necessary to have the water utility's monthly price history, which is usually available from the finance department. If a multiblock rate structure is employed and consumption varies within the utility's service area (because of microclimate, household income, and topography), elasticities will have to be developed that allow for the different average and marginal prices paid in the different areas. Price elasticity results can also be used to project future demand, but not without great care because historical elasticities are generally not applicable to future periods and are not directly transferable between utilities or areas within a single utility.

Economic Data

Economic factors, such as price indexes, housing starts, occupancy rates, employment rates, home values, lot size, and household income, can be precious pieces of information in certain circumstances. For example, water consumption per account decreased sharply in some communities in central Arizona from 1990 through 1993, recovering to the pre-1990 level in 1994 and 1995. These communities typically experienced a high seasonal population (as high as 50 percent) that did not visit Arizona during these difficult recession years. The decline in water use was highly correlated with the occupancy rates in this area and with the number and value of new construction starts. Another important use of economic data is in cross-sectional analyses, where it can be shown that water use is higher in homes with larger lot sizes, higher incomes, and larger family sizes.

Building a Database

All the data identified (possibly excluding items that prove to be not significant in the analytical process) should be combined in a structured database. From an analytical standpoint, a simple spreadsheet file (or linked sheets within a file) with time in the first column and each variable in additional columns works fine because this format is most useful for regression analysis. If a number of area demand forecasts need to be compiled using a number of communities and possibly different microclimates, the process of building files grows more complex. Frequently, the database can be maintained in a separate file or on separate sheets within a single file and then linked to the forecasting model, which makes updating data relatively easy. Also, for large utilities with many cities within their service areas, the most economic approach might be a relational database such as those generated in Oracle®, Focus®, Microsoft Access®, or similar application programs. As an alternative, the utility can regularly maintain readily available data in the database, with the balance of requirements generated only when the demand forecasts are updated (every 5 to 10 years).

IDENTIFYING WATER USE PATTERNS

Data needs now have been specified for various circumstances, and various methods have been identified of using the data to forecast, at least in skeletal form. It would be tedious and somewhat unproductive to review each forecasting method with various levels of data availability. Instead, two examples will be provided that encompass these methods to some extent. The first will conduct a relatively simple combination of the per capita, extrapolation, disaggregate water use, and land use model concepts. The second will combine the disaggregate water use, land use, and multiple regression models with related analyses of seasonality, indoor/outdoor use, weather normalization, price elasticity, and conservation integration to put together the integrated model results.

To illustrate the methods, actual examples will be used from various water agencies. The agencies are identified only by general area because, in some cases, the use of incomplete data prompts further questions, and it is not feasible in this text to discuss all the details required to fully explain each situation.

Example 1: Per Capita/Land Use Model

In this simple model, the agency, located in the San Francisco Bay area, serves raw water to six municipal customers (169,990 people served) and treated water directly to approximately 60,000 connections (200,000 people served). Using annual data, the per capita total water demands for cities served with raw water are specified. Demands in the treated water area are addressed by areas of housing density and by customer groups in each density area. The results of these analyses are provided in Table 3-1 for the raw water customers and in Table 3-2 for treated water customers.

Table 3–1   Example of water demands for raw water customers with per capita use—San Francisco Bay area agency

Area	1996 Demand (gpcd)	1996 Population	1996 Demand, mgd	2020 Population	2020 Demand, mgd	2040 Population	2040 Demand, mgd
City 1	160	65,000	10.4	92,500	14.8	136,250	21.8
City 2	164	12,800	2.1	43,900	7.2	64,630	10.6
City 3	177	29,380	5.2	30,510	5.4	31,640	5.6
City 4	218	14,220	3.1	43,300	8.4	70,690	12.3
City 5	172	42,440	7.3	59,880	10.3	87,790	15.1
City 6	179	6,150	1.1	29,450	5.2	43,530	7.6
Total		169,990	29.2	299,540	51.3	434,530	73.0

Table 3–2   Example of baseline demand for treated water customers, disaggregated by customer type and land use

Land Use Classification	Density, *du/acre*	Use Factor, *af/ac/yr*	1996 Acres in Use	1996 Demand, *acre-ft*	2020 Acres in Use	2020 Demand, *acre-ft*
Single Family Residential						
Low density	1–3	1.0	3,718	3,788	4,776	4,776
Medium density	3–6	2.0	1,135	2,269	1,431	2,861
High density	6–9	3.0	176	529	222	667
Multifamily Units						
Low density	6–12	3.60	1,090	3,923	1,373	4,941
Medium density	12–20	4.50	299	1,346	377	1,697
High density	20+	6.00	242	1,449	305	1,827
Commercial						
General		2.5	280	701	353	884
Office		1.5	1,917	2,875	2,417	3,625
Industrial						
Light		1.5	135	203	171	256
Heavy		1.5	59	88	74	111
Rural county area		2.0	10	19	15	29
Public and Institutional						
Parks and public recreation		3.0	307	621	361	783
Schools		2.5	97	242	122	305
Misc. public		3.2	54	172	68	217
Total this segment			9,519	18,225	12,065	22,979

The projection of raw water demand shown in Table 3-1 appears to be straightforward in this table; however, the 1996 gpcd was normalized to reflect typical weather, using methods that are described later in this chapter. The effects of trends were detected by scatter graphs in city 4 and city 6. These basically rural areas showed decreasing demands in gpcd of 1.0 and 0.1 per year (respectively), which were factored into the projections. The gpcd in 1996 for all other locations was simply projected to the populations in 2020 and 2040. The actual model included 5-year projections and a dozen or so industrial customers that are tracked and billed separately from the cities in which they are located.

The application of customer classes to land use categories requires considerable effort to segment the total service area by densities and calculate the normalized water use for each category. This analysis included a projection of baseline demands by 5-year segments by area, capacity constraints, and demand at buildout for each area. A broad conservation program has been undertaken that will reduce consumption differently in each density and customer class category. These conditions are not reflected in the forecast, which shows only the baseline conditions for the base year and 2020. The forecasts in Table 3-2 also exclude system water losses, open space, highways, and rivers, and the demands for specific large accounts that are derived individually (because they do not fit the norms for any category), and included in the total summary of demand.

Example 2: Disaggregate Demand/Regression Analysis Model

The analysis in this section differs from the simple per capita models in that monthly data are used, introducing factors of seasonality, indoor/outdoor use, price responses, and weather data. In addition, multivariate analysis is used to determine the simultaneous effects of variables on water use. The analysis must be performed for each customer class, area, density, or combination of these segments for which separate projections are required. The utility may decide to analyze five customer classes separately without any special justification, but it is often unclear at the outset that different areas or densities of single family residential accounts should be analyzed, or that apartments should be analyzed separately from other multifamily dwellings. When analyzing demand, the key is to be flexible in adding (and deleting) complexity; some measure of economic analysis should be performed before gathering additional data and adding complexity. Sometimes the time and expense of gathering data appear warranted, but the results of the analysis are not useful. However, the time spent is usually justified. A spreadsheet model is then developed for additional data that are generated. The spreadsheet workbook will become the integrated model for all relevant data at the final stages. At present, the spreadsheet model contains columns for time by month, total consumption (billings), number of accounts, calculated gpd/a, m^3pd/a, and weather variables.

Seasonality. A distinction should be made between the influence of season and the influence of weather on water use. The winter seasonal influence on water use, for example, is determined by the 20 in. (50 cm) of snow on the ground in the Upper Peninsula of Michigan during the winter, not the fact that the temperature is 10°F (–12°C). Summer water use is characterized by extensive irrigation, whether the temperatures in July average 80°F (26°C) or 85°F (29°C). During the summer, however, the variation of weather can affect water use considerably. The difference between 80°F (26°C) and 85°F (29°C), without precipitation, can cause residential water use on a given day to increase by 3 to 6 gpd/a (0.02 m^3pd/a) per degree of temperature above normal. For a month, the overall weather effect is reduced by the interspersion of cool days so that the impact is only 1 to 3 gpd/a (0.004–0.011 m^3pd/a) per degree of temperature above normal. The annual impacts of weather deviations from normal are even smaller, about 0.5 to 1.5 gpd/a (0.002–0.06 m^3pd/a) per degree of temperature different from normal, because of the offsetting warm and cool, wet and dry periods during the year.

The effects of season and weather can be identified directly with multivariate analysis by assigning a variable to each month.[*] This approach adds the complexity of dealing with at least 11 more variables both in identifying and in applying the weather impacts. An efficient way to allow for seasonality without the structural clutter is to define a monthly seasonal index that captures the "normal" seasonal pattern, including the transitional spring and fall seasons that frequently do not appear significant in regression analysis applied separately to each month. Most statistical computer programs compute a centered and weighted 13- or 15-month moving average of the time series data that is centered on the middle (seventh or eighth) month. Then each month is expressed as a ratio to the moving average, and the average ratio for each month becomes the index for that month. For 10 years of data, for example, there would be 10 ratios for July, which might range from 1.30 to 1.50, with an average of 1.40. Similarly, the index range for February might range

---

[*] In actuality, only 11 months are treated as separate dummy variables. The twelfth month is identified by the intercept variable.

from 0.60 to 0.80, with an average of 0.70. The variation in the monthly ratios over the years usually reflects abnormal weather. If a statistical program is unavailable, it is relatively simple to develop the seasonal index in a spreadsheet using the 13-month weighted moving average method.

A typical seasonal index for single family residential consumption in the Mesa, Ariz., area is identified in Figure 3-2. Because the seasonal index is based on an average over at least 7 years (10 years or more is much better), the index represents the average or "normal" monthly consumption pattern, absent irregular weather effects. Consequently, in regression analysis, the seasonal index, coupled with weather variables expressed as departures from the normal, will explain departures of consumption from its normal pattern. In regression analysis, the seasonal index alone will usually explain 85 to 95 percent of all variation in monthly consumption.

Weather impacts and normalization.   When weather is differentiated from seasonality, as described previously, the weather variables have an increasingly moderate impact on water consumption as the period of time summarized is increased. When analyzing daily water use, abnormally cool or hot temperatures combined with little or no precipitation can cause decreases or increases in water use from normal of –15 to +30 percent. However, when analyzing monthly data, the range is typically –5 to +10 percent; with annual data, the range is typically –1.5 to +3.0 percent. The lower impacts with monthly and annual data result from averaging weather that includes the offsetting positive and negative effects.

The impact on consumption of monthly weather deviations from normal is shown in Figure 3-3 for Mesa, Ariz. The weather variable on the bottom axis is a combination of mean high temperature departures from normal temperature (Fahrenheit) and monthly precipitation departures from normal precipitation (inches), expressed in an index form. The vertical scale shows the departure of single family residential consumption from normal in gpd/a (m^3pd/a) resulting from the weather departures from normal. For example, if the temperature/precipitation index were four points above or below normal, the typical result would be consumption of

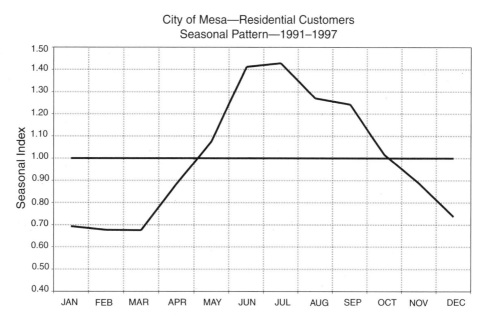

Figure 3–2   Single family residential—typical seasonal index, Mesa, Ariz., area

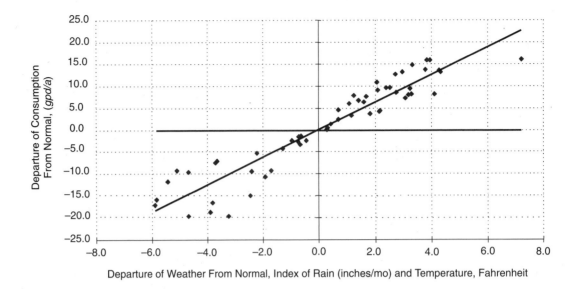

Figure 3–3   Effect of weather on consumption, typical to Mesa, Ariz., area

14 gpd/a (0.05 m³pd/a) above or below normal. The actual weather coefficients in this case were 2.0 for temperature and 8.0 for precipitation; so a combination of 3°F (1.7°C) above normal and 1 in. (2.54 m) of precipitation below normal would cause a 14-gpd/a (0.5-m³pd/a) effect on consumption.* In many regression analyses, only temperature or only precipitation is statistically significant; in these cases, the horizontal axis would reflect only the significant variable.

With extreme weather in either direction, the impact on consumption is about ±20 gpd/a (±0.08 m³pd/a), which is about 5 percent of average summer consumption.

Because the coefficients for each significant weather variable are known, the impacts of weather can be removed by simply subtracting its effect as it was derived in the previous paragraph. This is referred to as weather normalizing or removing the weather effect. For example, the month that had the combination of 3°F (1.7°C) above normal and 1 in. (2.54 cm) of precipitation below normal would have actual consumption reduced by 14 gpd/a (0.05 m³pd/a) to estimate normal consumption for that month. The consumption for all other months would be adjusted similarly, up or down.

Dummy variables.   Dummy variables, also called dichotomous variables, 0/1 variables and on–off variables are very useful tools to capture conditions that are present or not present or that can take on qualitative values at times during an evaluation. The dummy variables are simply columns (as in a spreadsheet or statistical program) that have a 0, a 1, or other numeric values in applicable months. Several types will be discussed to show the broad range of use:

- On–off conditions. By coding a 1 in periods that apply, such as when restrictions are in force for time-series analysis or a swimming pool or automatic sprinkling system is present in cross-sectional analysis, and a 0 in all other situations, the regression program calculates a value for the

---

* Temperature above normal increases consumption, and rainfall below normal increases consumption. Some forecasters derive the departure values as follows: Actual – Normal for temperature and Normal – Actual for rainfall so the positive and negative coefficients calculated in the regression analysis have the same positive and negative effects on consumption.

situations with the 1 in them. Because the 1 is a single discrete value, the coefficient is a constant, just as the vertical intercept is a constant. The coefficient is algebraically added to the intercept to get the predicted value when the dummy variable is active.

- Qualitative categories. Dummy variables are often used to distinguish among different degrees of a condition, such as low, medium, and high income, or low, moderate, or high degree of irrigable lawn space, and so forth. Each condition is a separate variable and for any variable where the condition applies, the variable is coded 1; for all other conditions, a 0 is coded. In the income example, three dummy variables would be used and a separate coefficient is derived for each to identify the unique impact that low, medium, or high income has on water use for the sample tested.

- Quantitative values that apply some of the time. An example that frequently applies is where temperatures apply only during summer months because winters are cold and wet and very little outdoor water use occurs. The winter months are then coded with 0 and the summer months with the departures of temperature from normal. When this variable form is compared with a form that derives its coefficient from the temperatures of all months, the summer-only variable frequently is more statistically significant because the winter weather has no bearing on irrigation, because there is no irrigation in winter (in cold climate areas). Another example is to include a monthly trend for a part of a long period of analysis (say, 2 years of recovery from a drought with values of 1 to 24). All the other months are coded 0. The coefficient in this case will provide for changing values for each month as it is applied to the increasing consumption following the drought.

Weighted moving average and trend. As the statistical data become available, the spreadsheet model must now be expanded to include the seasonal index and weather-normalized consumption. At this point, it is useful to have the spreadsheet calculate the centered 13-month weighted moving average (WMA), which provides a good tracking device for cyclical and trend movements in the time series. In Figure 3-4 for the Tualatin Valley Water District (TVWD) in Beaverton, Ore., the WMA reflects the effects of two distinct events:

1. The TVWD area experienced a severe shortage of water (drought) in 1992–93. The water use increased above normal in May through July 1992, and dropped drastically (20 percent during the June to September 1993 period, 12 percent for the year) as voluntary drought restrictions were imposed. When the restrictions were lifted during the winter of 1993–94, water use increased but not to the predrought level.

2. During the drought, this utility introduced various conservation measures that kept annual water use since 1994 well below the predrought level. There was some upward drift in the 1998-2000 period, but revitalized conservation efforts in 2001 and after have kept consumption since 2001 at 16.6 percent below the predrought level. Note that the conservation results from specific methods employed since 1993–1994 have yielded results (12.3 percent) through 2000 in the same magnitude as achieved from drastic (but voluntary) measures during the crisis of 1992–1993. Specific conservation measures through 2003 have now exceeded the voluntary effort of 1992–1993.

The WMA is calculated for the weather-normalized consumption. For utilities that have had no crises or pronounced price changes during the period of historical analysis, the WMA is often virtually a flat line (1985 through 1989 in Figure 3-4 is quite stable), which can be extrapolated into future months for forecasts. A weather-normalized forecast can be obtained for future months by multiplying the seasonal index times the WMA. If no external forces dictate change, the forecast of gpd/a is identical for all future years, and the forecast of total demand is the product of the m^{3}pd/a times the number of projected accounts. As forecasts are undertaken more often than not in or after periods of crisis, a good deal of judgment must be exercised in extrapolating water use patterns. In Figure 3-4, for example, the forecaster must determine most of the cause for the increased downturn in water use from 2001 through 2005 to be confident that this level of use will continue. In many post-crisis situations, such as in 1994 for TVWD, water use recovered substantially toward the pre-crisis level because there was no concerted effort to continue the drastic (but voluntary) measures temporarily imposed.

Indoor and outdoor water use. Identifying indoor and outdoor consumption is critical in evaluating price and conservation impacts on water use. Indoor and outdoor water use can be estimated with acceptable accuracy in the spreadsheet model for all the historical months and for the forecasted periods. The recommended method for this task is the following:

1. Select the month with the lowest seasonal index as a proxy for indoor water use. The month is usually February with an index of about 0.60, meaning that 60 percent of average monthly consumption is the estimate for indoor use. This estimate is fairly reliable for areas that have a cold winter climate with no irrigation. For warm weather areas that have irrigation during winter months, this approach must be refined. One alternative is to estimate water use for the number of occupants in single family and multifamily residential housing.

2. Multiply the index for the designated indoor month (or adjusted ratio) times the WMA for each month. The result is the estimated indoor consumption for each month. If annual indoor water use is to be estimated, the index would be multiplied by the average month WMA for the year times 12 months.

3. Subtract the calculated indoor water use from total water use to estimate outdoor water use by month. Using this method, indoor and outdoor and total water use can be derived for each month and for the year. Using this method, the indoor savings for TVWD are 21.7 percent in the 2002–2005 period, and 6.7 percent for the peak summer month. It is easy to see the indoor savings on Figure 3-4 where the winter water use is down to 160.7 gpd/equivalent residential unit (eru) compared to 205.2 gpd/eru during the pre-drought period. The peak summer savings are also visible but not as clear in the graph due to peak use variations.

Price responsiveness. Water use does not usually decrease when water prices are increased reasonably in line with inflation, that is, when there is no significant increase in the real cost of water. However, large increases implemented either to provide funds for major operating or capital projects or to induce lower consumption levels are likely to have statistically measurable impacts. Numerous studies of price responsiveness (elasticity) are available in water industry literature that should be reviewed for methods and unique situations. Discussion in this chapter will be limited to a basic description of the process of analysis with

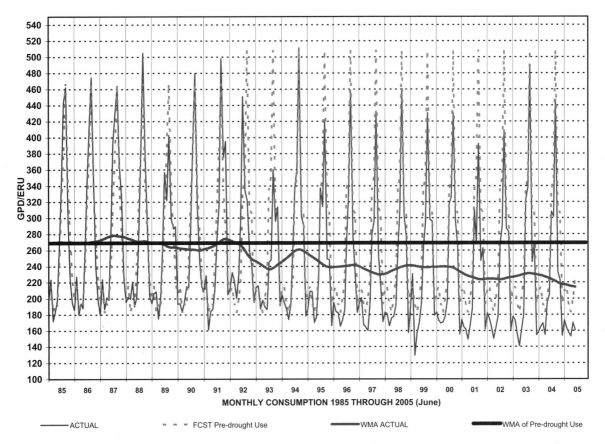

Figure 3–4 Illustration of single family residence water use model components, water utility in Tualatin Valley Water District, Beaverton, Ore. (Units for TVWD are designated eru*)

discussion of some pitfalls. Price elasticity is defined as the percentage change in consumption divided by the percentage change in price and can be expressed in various formula formats. One of the most practical expressions is

$$E = (dq/dp)*p_i/q_i \qquad \text{(Eq 3-3)}$$

Where:

E	=	elasticity
dq	=	the change in quantity consumed
dp	=	the change in price
dq / dp	=	the regression coefficient of price (the slope of the relationship)
p_i	=	the price at some point on the demand curve (average price is most frequently used)
q_i	=	the quantity consumed at the same point on the demand curve that was used for p_i.

(Note: Price elasticity, or other elasticity measures, depend on the functional form of the demand model. For instance, in the case of a double log functional form, the coefficient of the price variable is the price elasticity.)

---

*Residential customers using meters larger than 5/8 in. are restated in terms of 5/8 in. equivalents based on capacity.

The uses of water, particularly for residential customers, are quite different in winter and summer. Winter use is primarily for hygiene, cooking, and sanitation, which allows relatively little discretionary use. Summer consumption, on the other hand, typically includes a high percentage of discretionary use, particularly for irrigation. Measured elasticity is always less in winter months than in summer months for residential accounts. Consequently, indoor and outdoor or winter and summer consumption should always be identified and analyzed separately for measuring price responses.

The purpose of elasticity analysis is often to identify the magnitude of change that has occurred in the past or might occur in the future under various conditions. For example, elasticity analysis allows forecasters to estimate the impact that a large rate increase has had in recovering the capital cost of new treatment facilities, or to measure the impact of drought rates on water use during a period of supply crisis. It can also help forecasters estimate the effects of implementing conservation rates to tone down water use over an extended period. All these potential uses of elasticity analysis could be entirely new to a utility, making it difficult to assess the impacts of major rate changes for specific applications. Selecting an example used in another utility and applying the steps require caution because the conditions under which the elasticity was derived in one utility are rarely the same as those found in another utility. In fact, elasticities derived in a given utility for a given situation are rarely transportable to the same or similar future situations in the same utility. It is usually better to apply elasticity factors in an order-of-magnitude context rather than as a precise response. The response will usually be affected by the history of rate increases. If rates have been repeatedly increased, the demand could be hardening (more inelastic) because the discretionary water uses have already been eliminated. Often a utility has measured the response to its price changes in various situations that can be used for an order-of-magnitude estimate of customer sensitivity. In any case, predicting the response to price changes in specific situations is not an exact science; it is highly recommended that a utility create a revenue stability fund before taking price action and maintain this fund throughout the response learning period to absorb any shortfall in revenues that might occur. This approach is especially important when implementing drought pricing.

COMPILING A DEMOGRAPHIC DATABASE

Compiling a demographic database includes assimilating the data described in the Data Collection section and projecting key elements each month for 1 to 5 years and annually for 20 to 50 years. The key units that should be projected are those that match the water consumption variables. For example, if the water consumption is expressed in gallons (m^3) per account for residential accounts and in gallons (m^3) per employee for industrial accounts, demographic projections must meet these needs directly or indirectly. Industrial employment might be a direct variable, but the number of residential accounts must often be derived from single family and multifamily dwelling information and the number of occupants per dwelling in each locality. Technically, there is no need for the monthly forecasts; however, historical monthly data must be analyzed to normalize consumption for weather factors and to identify indoor and outdoor water uses. From this base, forecasting monthly water use is a simple task, and the monthly forecasts can be used very efficiently to monitor revenue projections and conservation program results.

A demographic database could also include price indexes, and various other economic indicators used for historical analyses but not forecast into future periods. The demographic data that must be combined with water use factors (gpd/a [m^3pd/a], for example) can be included in each model in designated columns or put into separate sheets (pages) to be linked with the water use factors.

This manual does not provide a detailed presentation of the methods for projecting demographic data. The references at the end of this chapter include sources that will be very useful to the forecaster. Some of the basic sources and methods are identified below.

- City and county general plans

- Regional government forecasts of population and employment

- Local and regional trend analysis: linear and nonlinear

- Cohort analysis: births, deaths, migration, and age distributions

- Housing formation and density patterns

NATURALLY OCCURRING AND PROGRAMMED CONSERVATION

Natural water conservation occurs as commercial and industrial facilities and residential homes age and less water-efficient processes and fixtures are replaced with more water-saving practices and devices. The level of naturally occurring conservation depends in large part on the age of the buildings within the utility's service area. This information is gathered from the US Census Bureau data and customer surveys that are linked to housing attributes in the utility and replacement rates. The life expectancy of fixtures or processes determines the specific replacement rate. For example, a residential clothes washer may be replaced after 15 years with a more water-saving model. The overall age of the houses and buildings in a community and the remodeling rate will determine the cumulative effect of conservation caused by replacement needs.

Naturally occurring conservation also includes the effects of previous conservation programs, such as commercial landscape ordinances that remain in effect for new construction. As community development occurs, the water use for each sector may gradually shift to less water consumption. The cumulative effect over 20 to 40 years can be significant, and water use reductions of 4 to 8 percent can be expected.

Each programmed or *active* conservation effort should have a specific purpose, such as reducing demand during a temporary supply crisis, or delaying or averting specific capital expenditures for new supply or treatment facilities. If the utility's goal is to moderate peak consumption, its choice of conservation measures will differ from one whose goal is to address average consumption (see chapter 6).

The targeted demand reduction from active conservation efforts used in a forecast model should be based on a conservation program assessment, which is discussed in chapter 6. Summer and winter (outdoor and indoor) targets should be separately identified and then combined to derive the annual target. The summer target might be 10 percent of total use (as much as 25 percent of irrigation use); the winter target might be 5 percent of indoor use, and the annual target would be 7 to 10 percent. The target must be established based on specific programs and must allow for the reality of expected responses to these specific conservation programs. Utilities often must take sequential steps to attain target reductions. An initial annual goal might be to reduce consumption by 10 percent, but the first cut of affordable and economically justifiable measures might produce only 7 percent. Second- and third-tier measures can then be implemented. Sometimes measures that cannot be economically justified are implemented to attain a required target. These are usually political decisions. Naturally occurring and programmed conservation water savings should be incorporated into the demand forecast model.

Conservation Pricing

Two rate structures are being used more frequently to encourage conservation in areas that have chronic water shortages or limited capacities. The first approach is to use seasonal rates that are implemented for water consumed during a utility's peak-use season, either as a means of recovering the incremental cost of providing water during this period or as an inducement to conserve water because of inadequate or constrained supply. The second approach is to implement inclining-block or tiered-block rates that use two or more rate blocks with increasing unit rates as consumption increases from one block to the next. Tiered-block rates also are sometimes used seasonally when the primary goal is to reduce peak consumption during a crisis. When long-term conservation is the goal, the tiered blocks often remain in use all year. The winter effect of tiered rates is often negligible.

Tiered-block rates are commonly applied separately to residential and nonresidential customers because of the large differences in water use. The rate-blocks for customer classes other than Single Family Residential (SFR) are generally based on percentages of average winter or average monthly water use for each customer to allow for the large variations in water use. Separate rate schedules for each customer class allow utilities to apply an appropriate rate to encourage large volume customers in each class to reduce usage. The blocks in each class can be set to reflect the usage characteristics of each class or of each customer within each class.

Crisis rates should not form the basis for a conservation rate structure. Conservation rates should be part of a broader conservation program in which the rates are a constant reminder that water is a precious commodity that should not be wasted. Significant and enduring conservation results can be achieved when water rates are combined with indoor and outdoor conservation programs such as irrigation efficiency audits, residential home audits, and toilet replacement measures. Nearly 50 percent of the potential annual conservation from single family accounts can be derived from indoor conservation, which is only indirectly affected by summer conservation rates.

Intensified conservation efforts, including higher water rates, reduce water sales that must be anticipated when developing the rate structure and the rates. Utilities should recognize that response to higher water rates cannot be identified with a high degree of accuracy. The difficulty in defining specific price responses is that customers' attitudes play such an important role. A rate increase of 10 percent might not generate any reduction in water use by itself, but if the rate increase is part of a broad conservation program that ratepayers believe is important to the community and to themselves, in a crisis situation, the total response from price and community support could be substantial as evidenced by the 20 percent reduction in water use in TVWD (Figure 3-4), prompted solely by an appeal for community support.

When utilities develop rates, they must anticipate the reduced consumption from conservation programs. The cost of conservation programs and some nominal savings in operating costs (pumping, chemicals) must also be included in the net revenue requirement analysis. The seasonal or tiered rates must include a forecast of water sales that is as accurate as possible and should include a safety factor for a margin of forecast error in the responses to rates and other conservation efforts.

IDENTIFY SYSTEM LOSSES

Forecasting water demand must include measuring and predicting water losses and the application of sound practices to remedy wasteful water use. Increasing population growth and the related increases in domestic, commercial, and industrial demand for water, given a limited supply of water in the long run, if not in the short run has created a forceful thrust among water agencies to change their practices related to water use. It seems that the major emphasis over the last decade or two in seeking efficient use of water has been focused on conservation that relates to the end uses of water. However, in a larger context of the totality of water supply, water utilities are users of water as well as purveyors, and they also should engage in whatever practices are economically justifiable to not waste water.

New momentum to address systems losses more vigorously emerged with the privatization of the water industry in the UK in 1989. Striking inefficiencies in water system and management practices came to the surface in terms of leakage losses, prompting the formation of various industry initiatives and organizations that established what is now generally considered to be the most advanced system of water loss control in the world. The International Water Association (IWA), in concert with participants form other countries around the world, including AWWA representing North America, organized task forces in the late 1990s to develop the IWA Manual of Best Practice: *Performance Indicators of Water Supply Services.*[*] AWWA has adopted the practices developed in the UK system, and these methods are expected to become the standard methods utilized in the US and Canada to establish reliable processes for water accounting and loss control of drinking water supplies.

This chapter on forecasting can address only the integration of the IWA Best Practices provided in Appendix A to this chapter. For practitioners who must deal directly with issues of water supply and efficient use, the manuals produced by IWA and AWWA identified in the references to this chapter are essential reading.[†‡]

COMPLETE THE INTEGRATED FORECAST MODEL

The development of the integrated model has already been discussed in terms of some of its elements, such as the seasonal index, a weighted moving average, weather-normalized consumption, indoor and outdoor consumption, pricing, and conservation programs.

Baseline Forecast Model

A separate spreadsheet baseline model is needed to track historical use and project future use for each data series. The data series could include each customer class, broken down by density, locality, weather zone, or a unique combination of these attributes. Each data series model will include historical data, a model fit that is often derived from regression analysis, and projections. Forecasts by month for 1 to 5 years allow utilities to track consumption against conservation expectations and revenues against plans. Long-run projections are usually made by 1- or 5-year increments for 20 to 50 years. If the impact of weather on consumption is evaluated, the model will include weather-normalized data from past years as well as forecasts. Such information provides an improved basis for identifying the historical and

---

*Alegre, H., Hirner, W., Baptista, J. and Parena, R. *Performance Indicators for Water Supply Services.* IWA Publishing 'Manual of Best Practice' Series, 2000.

†Thornton, Julian, et. al. *Water Loss Control Manual,* McGraw-Hill, 2002.

‡Manual of Water Supply Practices. American Water Works Association M36, *Water Audits and Leak Detection.* 1999.

projected impacts of tariff and conservation measures. The models for different data series are usually kept on separate spreadsheet workbooks because four to six sheets or pages of each model are needed for supporting subanalyses, including graphics. All the models can be identical in structure, so it is quite simple to aggregate any combination (say, five residential area models) or all of the customer class models to derive total utility data. Selected variables, such as weather and demographic projections, can be included in each model or on separate pages or worksheets that are linked to the appropriate model worksheets.

The spreadsheet model should also include interactive graphs that reflect actual water consumption, the moving average of consumption, fitted consumption and deviations of actual from fitted consumption, a monthly forecast of normalized consumption per account, and a total forecast (in gallons, m^3, 100 ft^3, or acre-feet) for the forecast horizon. Figure 3-5 displays this type of data for the same single family residential customer class that was portrayed in Figure 3-4 for the utility in the TVWD. Figure 3-5 includes monthly forecasts of predrought and current level of use for the balance of 2005 and identifies the reduction in water use associated with naturally occurring conservation (the dashed line below the WMA normal line). The difference between the actual WMA and the naturally occurring conservation reflects the conservation or reduction in water use that results from specific conservation programs or that cannot be assigned specific causes. Analysis of the impact of specific conservation measures has not been completed; so the substantial savings must be attributed to the combination of conservation measures that include free showerheads

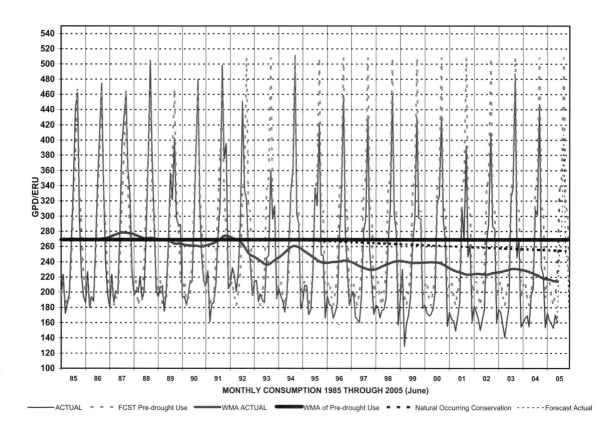

Figure 3–5   Illustration of monthly forecasting with conservation; water utility in Tualatin Valley Water District, Beaverton, Ore.

and toilet inserts, toilet rebates, residential audits, education programs, public relations, media pressure, or simply positive customer participation in the plight of the utility during a time of crisis. Over time, the results of key specific measures will be derived to assist in assigning more of these unexplained savings to specific causes.

Figure 3-6 displays the sum of the forecasts for all customer classes for approximately a 20-year period by 2-year increments, and for buildout. This forecast is for a utility in the Phoenix, Ariz., area that also includes estimated system water losses. The forecast shows the projections with and without the estimated naturally occurring and programmed conservation measures. The annual savings from conservation in 2020 represents 7.7 percent of the baseline demand, 9.0 percent at buildout. These significant savings percentages support the need for accurate projections of conservation in the process of long-run demand forecasting. (The time scale to buildout on the horizontal axis is not linear with the time scale to 2020.)

Figure 3-7 displays the indoor and outdoor total consumption (excluding system water losses) for the same Phoenix, Ariz., area water utility. Indoor use declined from 60.9 percent of total in 1997 to 57.7 percent in 2020 as the indoor conservation effects were larger than the outdoor.

This modeling process will generate various statistical measures related to the accuracy and appropriateness of the statistical methods, including R^2, standard error of the estimate, a mean absolute percentage error (MAPE), regression coefficients and their standard errors and t-values, Durban–Watson values, and other tests of significance. The typical results of these models is an R^2 of 0.85 to 0.97, a standard error of about 5 percent of mean consumption, a MAPE of about 5 percent, a Durban–Watson value significantly close to 2.0, with all t-values for variables used at 2.0 or higher reflecting a 95 percent confidence interval. These measures could also be stored in the spreadsheet model or simply provided as supporting documents to the forecasting process.

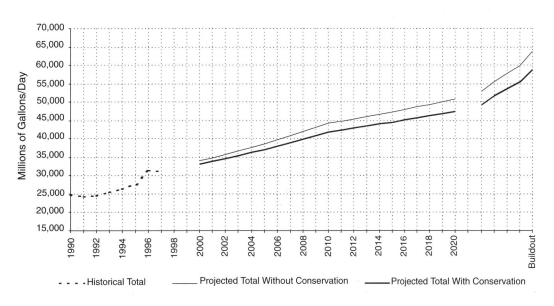

Figure 3–6   Total historical forecasts with and without conservation for rapidly growing utility in the Phoenix, Ariz., area (includes system water losses)

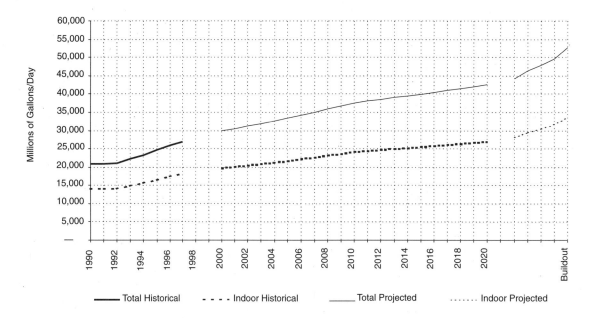

Figure 3–7   Total and indoor water history and projection, excluding water losses, including natural and programmed conservation, for rapidly growing utility in Phoenix, Ariz., area

Integrating Conservation Performance

When integrating conservation program performances into long-run demand forecasts, the permanent and temporary elements of conservation in the historical performance pattern should be recognized. Conservation efforts that respond to drought conditions are usually accompanied by a temporary drought rate structure and by large customer education programs that produce large conservation results. Some of these results, such as fixture changes and Xeriscaping programs, are relatively permanent. Many commercial and industrial process changes will also produce permanent conservation. The customer restraint impacts (rate induced) and the community support impacts, however, will diminish, quickly at first when the crisis is ended, and then gradually until consumption approaches the new level that includes the permanent conservation response. In Figure 3-5 the effect of conservation programs is projected to remain the same in during the balance of the forecasted year, 2005.

Long-run demand forecasts do not account for occasional droughts that are accompanied by restrictions and short-run pricing programs. These short-run restraint measures, however, could have long-term residual effects on water use that were not anticipated in the comprehensive conservation program built into the demand forecast. Furthermore, the demand hardening that occurs as the discretionary use of water diminishes will lessen the impact of future short-run measures during periods of crisis. A utility should anticipate these effects as part of its drought management program.

Measure Conservation Performance

A simple and effective way to measure the continuing response to summer and winter conservation programs is to track the ongoing consumption pattern against the preconservation pattern and measure the volume and percentage reductions.

Consumption during the lowest winter month (usually February or the average of January and February in areas with winter weather) will provide a good base for indoor water use that can be used to measure performance, which is reflected in the difference between the use before and after conservation measures were implemented. Most of the conservation stemming from fixture changes will continue; the conservation from gray water use and customer restraint will dissipate as the crisis situation fades from the public's memory. Outdoor consumption can be similarly analyzed by removing indoor uses (February average) from both the preconservation and the conservation periods being analyzed, and measuring the change in current use from the preconservation base period. This type of analysis will not identify the specific causes of the reduced water use, but it will identify the continuing pattern of overall reduction that can be integrated into long-run demand projections.

This approach can also accommodate the use of time-line conservation target performances. For example, a target of 15 percent annual conservation might be established to be achieved by 2010 from a comprehensive group of conservation programs. A linear or nonlinear achievement line can be included in the demand projection and monitored with individual program adjustments that keep the overall program on track.

SENSITIVITY ANALYSIS

All forecasts will include some unavoidable margin of error. If the total demand forecast is carefully constructed, the volatile elements can be isolated and tested for their simple and joint sensitivity in the total forecast picture. The elements of permanent variation compared to temporary variation must be isolated. For example, a sensitivity analysis of demand for single family residential accounts would include variation for key variables such as the projected number of households, the base gpd/a, (m^3pd/a) and the expectations from naturally occurring and programmed conservation measures. These components will have an effect on demand. Sensitivity of demand in any given year (or month) can also be undertaken for variations in the deviations of weather from normal. Weather sensitivity analysis deals with temporary aberrations which are important for peaking weather considerations but not for long-term average demand planning which assumes normal weather.

Variables that are most sensitive to error in the long-term demand forecasting process must be identified. Usually long-term forecasts of population and employment are more sensitive than extrapolations of gpd/a (m^3pd/a), per dwelling unit, per employment, or per population. Projecting industrial account growth by standard industrial code is more sensitive than projecting single family residential growth, and so on.

Several methods can be employed to define the variation related to the use of selected variables.

Standard Error of the Estimate

The least squares method of deriving regression coefficients identifies a regression line through a two-dimensional or larger array that minimizes the squared deviations of actual values of the dependent variable from the fitted values. If the model is properly specified and unbiased, the residuals (forecast errors) will be normally distributed around the regression line. The measure of dispersion that results from the regression analysis is called the *standard error of the estimate*, which is similar to the standard deviation that can be calculated for any single variable. The usefulness of the standard error is that probability theory can then be employed to define confidence intervals around the regression line for the period of fitted data and for a forecast period. The standard error reflects a type of joint or conditional probability in the sense that the probability distribution is around an estimate of the dependent variable that was derived from the input of any number of significant independent variables in the regression equation.

This type of regression analysis is particularly useful in developing understanding of the relationships among the causal variables in explaining the dependent variable; however, the multiple variable model is rarely used for projecting long-term water demand for several reasons:

1. The difficulty in projecting the independent variables such as weather, price, lot sizes, and so forth.

2. The lack of transportability of some variables; for example, the coefficient related to price increases would not be directly applicable to future periods.

3. Customer mix changes and other parameters are difficult to integrate into a single regression model.

4. The greater the departure of the estimated values of the independent variables from their mean, the greater will be the *standard error of the estimate*, so that forecasts of 20 years or more will have such a wide confidence interval as to be meaningless.

In a small utility where minimal information is available, the regression equation of water use per capita related to population is likely to be the only practical basis for forecasting. In a large utility with many forecast segments related to customer classes and mix within classes, micro weather patterns, different topography, different growth areas, and other segment attributes, separate forecasting models for each unique segment are necessary to optimize accuracy in the combined forecast. Each of these segments is assumed to be an independent series. A simple way to undertake this task for each segment includes three steps:

1. Calculate historical water use per unit (account, household, ERU, population, square feet of floor space, employment) including the removal of abnormal weather effects. Also include a measure of dispersion around the mean values.

2. Forecast for the required period the unit values (population, households, ERU, etc.) for all the units that will be used, including a measure of dispersion around their means.

3. Multiply the mean water use per unit times the mean forecasted units to derive mean forecasts for the desired future periods.

4. Calculate the joint probability distribution (if desired) of the combination of unit water sales and the forecasted unit (accounts, population, etc.) used in each projection.

Standard Errors of Coefficients

Each independent variable in the regression equation has a calculated coefficient, significantly different from zero, that expresses its effect on the dependent variable for the addition of each unit of that independent variable; and a standard deviation can be calculated and applied to each variable coefficient to define a probability range around the coefficient value. Some variables that are highly significant in predicting water demand will have a narrow probability distribution around their coefficient; others that are not as strongly identified in predicting water demand will have a much wider probability distribution around their coefficients. The magnitude of the coefficients multiplied by the variable values, combined with their dispersion, defines the importance and volatility of the variable in demand forecasting.

Joint Probability Analysis

It has been stated a number of times in this text that limited data for small utilities often necessitates making forecasts with only historical water use per capita related to population projections. Similarly, in large utilities with many forecast segments related to customer classes and mix within classes, micro weather patterns, different topography, different growth areas and other segment attributes, separate forecasting models for each unique segment are necessary to optimize accuracy in the combined forecast. After normalizing for aberrant weather effects, the key forecasting variables for each segment are usually some form of per unit consumption related to a forecast of the unit. For example, forecasting single family residential water use by density area could be the product of the gpd/a and the account forecast in each area. The two elements used in making these projections are assumed to be independent series, which is not unreasonable. Of course, all base forecasts of this type must be adjusted for natural or programmed conservation and for unbilled water and water losses to get total demand requirements.

To test demand sensitivity, it is often useful to combine the dispersion (probability distribution) of the per unit factor (e.g., gpd/a) with the dispersion of the unit forecast (account growth). The seasoned forecaster will know that there is no best way to define the probability distribution around the key variables. To be sure, whatever quantitative data that can be applied should be applied, but the parameters of the distributions often must be established by good judgment. A practical method is for the seasoned analyst (or a forecasting team) to estimate the high and low value of each variable that would not be exceeded more than 10 percent of the time if numerous occurrences were possible. To derive the standard deviation for a series, divide the difference between the high 10 percent value and the mean value of the variable by the probability factor (from normal probability table) for 10 percent in one tail of the distribution, which is 1.28. For example, if mean water use is 400 gpd/a and the high value not exceeded more than 10 percent of the time is 650 gpd/a, the estimated standard deviation would be: (650 - 400)/1.28=195. Applying similar logic to households with a mean estimate of 70,000 and a high 10 percent estimate of 80,700, an estimated standard deviation would be: (80,700 - 70,000)1.28=8,360.

The primary value of calculating the joint probability distribution is that it will reflect less variation than a distribution that is derived from the extreme values of the two independent variables. The inference is that, in facility planning, one should not plan for the "worst-worst" case, which would be made up of the extreme adverse impact of each variable occurring at the same time. The joint probability distribution allows for offsetting (high and low) occurrences among the set of variable combinations.

This concept is illustrated in Figure 3-8 for single family residential demand using just two variables: projected number of households and consumption per household in gpd. Average water demand (28 mgd [0.12 m^3/d]) is the product of 400 gpd (1.51 m^3/d) of water use per household times the 70,000 forecasted households, but the upper level of demand (50 mgd [0.19 m^3/d]) is well below the product of the extremes of gpd (m^3/d) water use (1,000 gpd [3.8 m^3/d]) and the number of households (95,000), which would indicate water demand of 95 mgd (0.36 m^3/d). The joint probably allows for the fact that the extreme conditions are not likely to occur at the same time. For two variables, the following "propagation of errors" formula will

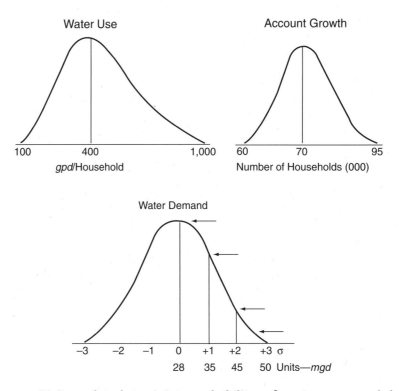

Figure 3–8 Forecasting sensitivity related to joint probability of water use and household projections

give the standard deviation of the joint probability distribution that is virtually identical to the Monte Carlo result.

$$\text{joint standard deviation} = S_j = [S_u^2 \times S_h^2 \times M_u^2 \times S_h^2 \times M_h^2 \times S_u^2]^{1/2} \qquad \text{(Eq 3-4)}$$

Where:

S_j = Joint standard deviation of the water use (u) and number of households (h)
S_u = Standard deviation of water use
S_h = Standard deviation of the number of households
M_u = Average or mean of water use
M_h = Average or mean of the number of households

In this example the calculated joint standard error is 8.6 mgd and the 97.5 percent upper confidence limit is 45.2 mgd (mean of 28.0 mgd + 2.0 std errors for 97.5 level of confidence times the joint std error of 8.6 = 45.2). This result is virtually identical to the one calculated using the Monte Carlo method.[*]

Scenario Analysis

In scenario analysis, the most important method should most likely include the probability elements previously described. Too often in practice, purely judgmental high and low scenarios are included with the average or *most probable* forecasts that

_____

[*]Using @Risk, statistical software by Palisade Corporation, Newfield, New York.

result from regression analysis. The extremes are selected more on a *what-if* basis than a probability basis. Using the joint probability approach by itself is not the answer either, because it does not allow for external forces not in the regression equation that could profoundly affect demand. A more reliable approach blends the defined variability of water use and conservation variables with the long-term demographic and economic sensitivity associated with the area for which demand is being forecast. For example, there has been very rapid growth in the Sun Belt states in the last two decades for many reasons, including migration of retirees and the relocation of industries to more economical cities and labor markets. Forecasters should be careful to combine whatever resources can be gathered when defining the boundary scenario, in particular, because it may determine the ultimate sizing of key facilities built to meet long-range demand.

SUMMARY

Water demand forecasting can be a very technical and intensive process in certain situations. The first rule should be to evaluate the degree of disaggregation and complexity necessary to provide the required accuracy and usefulness to the forecasts. If the forecaster cannot easily access the database for disaggregated account groups and areas, or if the accuracy of the data is suspect, the forecaster should try an 80 percent solution. One hundred percent accuracy is impossible, no matter how much effort is expended. Even 95 percent accuracy is unlikely for all elements of a long-run forecast no matter how much effort and money is expended; it makes sense to initially apply the 80 percent rule (Pareto's Law) with 20 percent of the total potential effort and get 80 percent (or more) of the potential results. If the results come up a little short, the forecaster can extend efforts based on expected incremental yield. Most of the time, relatively simple methods will produce good to excellent results.

The forecasting process used will differ depending on each agency's needs and analytical abilities. More complex agencies should follow some variation of the steps provided below.

1. Collect and edit 5 to 20 years of production, consumption and accounts, weather, demographic, and economic data as available or as needed.

2. Build spreadsheet models for each customer class/area (sector) that will be forecasted.

3. Define seasonality with seasonal indexes for each sector.

4. Define weather impacts on water use with regression analysis and normalize consumption.

5. Develop water use factors gpd/a or m^{3}pd/a for each sector and weighted moving averages of historical water consumption and trends.

6. Identify indoor and outdoor consumption for each data series in gpd/a (m^{3}pd/a).

7. Project water use per unit (account, employment, and household) for all sectors through the forecast period before conservation effects are integrated.

8. Analyze historical and proposed conservation measures and define the current and projected effects on water use. Measure historical conservation performance.

9. Analyze and project demographic data through the forecast horizon.

10. Project indoor and outdoor demands through the forecast period in a baseline demand forecast in million gal, m^3, 100 ft^3, or acre-ft.

11. Modify the baseline forecast to include the impacts of naturally occurring, and planned programmed conservation measures that will be implemented.

12. Summarize all sector forecasts into a total agency forecast.

13. Include projected unbilled water and system water losses that include improvement results.

14. Conduct sensitivity analysis on key variables and scenarios to identify the upper and lower bounds of the forecast under various conditions.

15. Include monthly forecasts for one to five years and monitor for revenue and conservation performance tracking.

To some degree, all forecasts are inherently flawed. The key to efficient forecasting is to identify the important variables for the type of forecast prepared. Household formation is of paramount importance for long-run forecasts; variations resulting from extreme weather conditions are not (except to normalize historical demand). Rarely do water demand forecasts include more than four or five significant variables. Those usually found include seasonal pattern, account growth, employment, population, lot size, weather, conservation measures, and, sometimes, price. Once a forecasting model has been properly specified, it is far more efficient to recognize the inherent error level and work with it to identify upper and lower bounds of potential water demand than to try to fine-tune a model to achieve the last possible percentage of efficiency from a limited database.

SUGGESTED ADDITIONAL READINGS

Forecasting Methods and Models

Agthe, D.E. and R.B. Billings. 1980. Dynamic models of residential water demand. *Water Resources Research*, 16(3).

Agthe, D.E., R.B. Billings, and J.M. Dworkin. 1988. Effects of rate structure knowledge on household water use. *Water Resources Bulletin*, 24(3).

Agthe, D.E., R.B. Billings, et al. 1986. A simultaneous equation demand model for block rates. *Water Resources Research*, 22(1).

American Water Works Association. 1999. AWWA Manual M34, *Water Rate Structures and Pricing*. Denver, Colo.: American Water Works Association.

American Water Works Association. 1992. *Drought Management Planning*. Denver, Colo.: American Water Works Association.

American Water Works Association. 1992. AWWA Manual M34, *Alternative Rates*. Denver, Colo.: American Water Works Association.

American Water Works Association. 1999. AWWA Manual M36, *Water Audits and Leak Detection*. Denver, Colo.: American Water Works Association.

Billings, R.B. 1982. Specification of block rate price variables in demand models. *Land Economics*, (Aug.).

Billings, R.B. 1983. Revenue effects from changes in a declining block pricing structure: Comment. *Land Economics*, 59(3) (Aug.).

Baumann, D.B., J. Boland, et al. 1988. IWR-MAIN Water Use Forecasting System—Version 5.1. Ft. Belvoir, Va.: Institute for Water Resources, US Army Corps of Engineers.

Billings, R.B. and D.E. Agthe. 1980. Price elasticities for water: A case of increasing block rates. *Land Economics*, 56(Feb.):73–84.

Billings, R.B. and D.E. Agthe. 1981. Price elasticities for water: A case of increasing block rates: Reply. *Land Economics*, 57(May):276–78.

Billings, R.B. and C.V. Jones. 1996. *Forecasting Urban Water Demand*. Denver, Colo.: American Water Works Association.

Bishop, D.B. and J.A. Weber. 1996. *Impacts of Demand Reduction on Water Utilities*. Denver, Colo.: AWWA Research Foundation and American Water Works Association.

Boland, J.J., B. Dziegielewski, et al. 1984. Influence of Price and Rate Structures on Municipal and Industrial Water Use. US Army Corps of Engineers, Engineer Institute for Water Resources, Contract Report 84-C-2.

Box, G.E.P. and G.M. Jenkins. 1970. *Time Series Analysis: Forecasting and Control*. San Francisco, Calif.: Holden-Day.

Brown, R.G. 1959. *Statistical Forecasting for Inventory Control*. San Francisco, Calif.: Holden-Day.

California Urban Water Agencies. Feb. 1992. *An Evaluation of Urban Water Conservation Programs: A Procedures Manual*. Planning and Management Consultants, Carbondale, Ill.; Brown and Caldwell Consultants, Walnut Creek, Calif.; and Montgomery Watson, Walnut Creek, Calif.

California Urban Water Agencies. June 1994. *Long-Term Water Conservation and Shortage Management Practices: Planning that Includes Demand Hardening*. Davis, Calif.: Tahors, Caramanis & Associates.

Carver, P.H. and J.J. Boland. 1980. Short- and long-run effects of price on municipal water use. *Water Resources Research*, 16(4) (Aug.):609–616.

Chicoine, D.L., S.C. Deller, and G. Ramamurthy. 1986. Water demand estimation under block rate pricing: A simultaneous equation approach. *Water Resources Research*, 22(6).

Chicoine, D.L. and G. Ramamurthy. 1986. Evidence on the specification of price in the study of domestic water demand. *Land Economics*, 62(1):28–32.

Croxton, F.E. and D.J. Cowden. *Applied General Statistics*. 2nd ed. Englewood Cliffs, N.J.: Prentice Hall, Inc.

DeKay, C.F. 1985. The evolution of water demand forecasting, *Jour. AWWA*. Vol. (Issue):54–61.

Frank, R.E. 1966. Use of transformations. *Jour. Marketing Research*, III (Aug.): 247–253.

Griffin, A.H. and W.E. Martin. 1981. Price elasticities for water: A case of increasing block rates: Comment. *Land Economics*, (May).

Hertz, D.B. 1964. Risk analysis in capital investment. *Harvard Business Review* (Jan.–Feb.).

Hogarty, T.F. and R.J. Mackay. 1975. The impact of large temporary rate changes on residential water use. *Water Resources Research*, 11(6) (Dec.).

Houston, D.A. 1983. Revenue effects from changes in a declining block pricing structure: Reply. *Land Economics*, 59(3) (Aug.).

Jordan, J.L. 1994. The effectiveness of pricing as a stand-alone water conservation program. *Water Resources Bulletin*, 30(5) (Oct.).

Judge, G.G. et al. 1985a. *Introduction to the Theory and Practice of Econometrics*. 2nd ed. New York, N.Y.: John Wiley & Sons.

Judge, G.G. et al. 1985b. *The Theory and Practice of Econometrics*. 2nd ed. New York, N.Y.: John Wiley & Sons.

Maddaus, W.O., J.A. Weber, et al. 1998. *Water Resources Planning*. Denver, Colo.: American Water Works Association.

Martin, W.E. and J.F. Thomas. 1986. Policy relevance in studies of urban residential water demand. *Water Resources Research*, 22(13) (Dec.):1735–1741.

Miaou, S.-P. 1990. A class of time series urban water demand models with nonlinear climatic effects. *Water Resources Research*, 26(2) (Feb.).

Miller, J.W. and M.D. Ludlum. 1985. *Water Demand Forecasting and Risk Management*. Proceedings from 1985 AWWA Annual Conference.

Murdock, S.H., D.E. Albrecht, et al. 1991. Role of sociodemographic characteristics in projections of water use. *Jour. Water Resources Planning and Management*, 117(2) (March/April).

Nieswiadomy, M.L. and D.J. Molina. 1989. Comparing residential water demand estimates under decreasing and increasing block rates using household data. *Land Economics*, 65(3) (Aug.).

Olson, C.L. and Picconi, M.J. 1983. *Statistics for Business Decision Making*. Glenview, Ill.: Scott Foresman and Company.

Pindyck, R.S. and D.L. Rubinfeld. 1991. *Econometric Models and Economic Forecasts*. 3rd ed. New York, N.Y.: McGraw-Hill.

Prasifka, D.W. 1994. *Water Supply Planning*. Malabar, Fla.: Krieger Publishing Company.

@RISK statistical software by Palisade Corporation, Newfield, New York.

Rodrigo, D. 1994. *Integrating Water Conservation Into Long-Term Water Supply Planning*. New York, N.Y.: Proceedings from 1994 AWWA Annual Conference.

Saleba, G.S. 1985. *Water Demand Forecasting*. Proceedings from 1985 AWWA Annual Conference.

Schefter, J.E. and E.L. David. 1985. Estimating residential water demand under multi-part tariffs using aggregate data. *Land Economics*, 61(3) (Aug.).

Schefter, J.E. 1987. Increasing block rate tariffs as faulty transmitters of marginal willingness to pay. *Land Economics*, 63(1) (Feb.).

Schneider, M.L. and E.E. Whitlatch. 1991. User-specific water demand elasticities. *Jour. Water Resources Planning and Management*, 117(1) (Jan./Feb.).

Thomas, J.F. and G.J. Syme. 1988. Estimating residential price elasticity of demand for water: A contingent valuation approach. *Water Resources Research*, 24(11) (Nov.):1847–1857.

Weber, J.A. 1989. Forecasting demand and measuring price elasticity. *Jour. AWWA*, 81(5):57–65.

Weber, J.A. 1993a. *Statistical Analysis of Inverted Block Rates*. Proceedings from 1993 AWWA Annual Conference.

Weber, J.A. 1993b. Integrating Conservation Targets Into Water Demand Projections. *Jour. AWWA*, 85(8):63–70.

Weber, J.A. 1996. *Measuring Overall Conservation Performance*. Proceedings from AWWA-sponsored CONSERV96, Orlando, Fla.

Weber, J.A. and W.J. Bishop. Sept. 1995. *Impacts of Metering: A Case Study at Denver Water, Denver, Colorado*. International Water Supply Association Biennial Conference, Durban, South Africa.

Wilson, L., and R. Luke. 1990. A Critique of "Forecasting Urban Water Use: The IWR-MAIN Model," by B. Dziegielewski and J.J. Boland. *Water Resources Bulletin*, 26(3).

Winters, P.R. 1960. Forecasting sales by exponentially weighted moving averages. *Management Science*, VI(3) (April):324–342.

Conservation/Drought Modeling

Alegre, H., Hirener, W., Baptista, J. and Parena, R. *Performance Indicators for Water Supply Services*. IWA Publishing "Manual of Best Practice" Series, 2000. ISBN 1 900222 272.

Beecher, J.A., P.C. Mann, et al. 1994. *Revenue Effects of Water Conservation and Conservation Pricing: Issues and Practices*. Washington, D.C.: National Regulatory Research Institute.

Behling, P.J. and N.J. Bartilucci. 1992. Potential impact of water-efficient plumbing fixtures on office water consumption. *Jour. AWWA*, 84(10):74–78.

Billings, R.B. and W.M. Day. 1989. Demand management factors in residential water use: The southern Arizona experience. *Jour. AWWA*, 81(3):58–64.

Cameron, T.A. and M.B. Wright. 1990. Determinants of household water conservation retrofit activity: A discrete choice model using survey data. *Water Resources Research*, 26(2) (Feb.):179–198.

Chesnutt, T.W., C. McSpadden, and A. Bamezai. 1994. *Ultra Low Flush Toilet Programs: Evaluation of Program Outcomes and Water Savings*. Los Angeles, Calif.: Metropolitan Water District of Southern California.

Chesnutt, T.W., C. McSpadden, and J. Christianson. 1996. Revenue instability induced by conservation rates. *Jour. AWWA*, 88(1):52–63.

Chesnutt, T.W., C. McSpadden, and J. Christianson. 1997. Workshop: Cost-Effectiveness Analysis of BMPs for Urban Water Conservation. Sacramento, Calif.: California Urban Water Conservation Council.

Clark, D.M. and P.C. Mann. 1994. *Conservation Surcharges: An Application of Marginal Cost Pricing*. Proceedings from 1994 AWWA Annual Conference.

Cuthbert, R.W. 1989. Effectiveness of conservation-oriented water rates in Tucson. *Jour. AWWA*, 81(3):65–73.

Cuthbert, R.W. and P.R. Lemoine. 1995. *A Review of the Effectiveness of Conservation-Oriented Water Rate Structures*. Proceedings from 1995 AWWA Annual Conference.

Cuthbert, R.W. and P.R. Lemoine. 1996. Conservation-oriented water rates. *Jour. AWWA*, 88(11):68–78.

Dziegielewski B. 1994. *Reliability of the Estimates of Water Conservation Savings*. Proceedings from 1994 AWWA Annual Conference.

Gregg, T., J. Curry, and C. Grigsby. 1994. *Xeriscaping: Promises and Pitfalls*. Austin, Texas: City of Austin, Texas, and Texas Water Development Board.

Kiefer, J.C., E.M. Opitz, and R. Brown. 1990. *Estimated Water Savings From a Plumbing Retrofit Program*. Los Angeles, Calif.: Metropolitan Water District of Southern California.

Little, K.W. and D.H. Moreau. 1991. Estimating the effects of conservation on demand during droughts. *Jour. AWWA*, 83(10):48–54.

Macy, P.P. 1991. Integrating conservation and water master planning. *Jour. AWWA*, 83(10):44–47.

Macy, P.P. and W.O. Maddaus. 1989. Cost–benefit analysis of conservation programs. *Jour. AWWA*, 81(3):43.

Maddaus, W.O. 1987a. The effectiveness of residential water conservation measures. *Jour. AWWA*, 79(3):52–58.

Maddaus, W.O. 1987b. *Water Conservation Handbook*. Denver, Colo.: American Water Works Association.

Maddaus, W.O., G. Gleason, and J. Darmody. 1996. Integrating conservation into water supply planning. *Jour. AWWA*, 88(11): 57–67.

Maddaus, W.O., E.H. Thornhill, and E.M. Opitz. 1994. *Water Savings From Water Conservation Best Management Practices in Southern California*. Proceedings from 1994 AWWA Annual Conference.

Mann, P.C. and D.M. Clark. 1993. Marginal-cost pricing: Its role in conservation. *Jour. AWWA*, 85(8):71-78.

Nelson, J.O. 1994. *Water Saved by Single Family Xeriscapes*. Proceedings from 1994 AWWA Annual Conference.

Rothstein, Eric. 1992. Water demand monitoring in Austin, Texas. *Jour. AWWA*, 84(10):52–58.

Thornton, Julian, et. al. *Water Loss Control Manual*, McGraw-Hill, 2002.

Weber, J. A., Forecasting Demand and Measuring Price Elasticity. *Jour. AWWA*. May 1989.

Weber, J. A., *Tracking and Measuring Water Conservation Performance*, Seminar presented at AWWA Conservation Workshop, Las Vegas, Nev., January 2002.

Weber, J.A. 1996. *Measuring Overall Conservation Performance*. AWWA Proceedings of Presentations at CONSERV96: Responsible Water Stewardship, Orlando, Fla.

Weber, J.A., J.B. Gilbert, and W.J. Bishop. 1990. Reducing water demand during drought years. *Jour. AWWA*, 82(5):34–39.

Whitcomb, J.B. 1993. *Water Reduction From Retrofitting Indoor Water Fixtures*. Proceedings from 1993 AWWA Annual Conference,

Supplement to Chapter 3: Summary of IWA Best Practices for Water Loss Control

FEATURES OF INTERNATIONAL WATER AUDIT METHODOLOGY

Through research with hundreds of utilities, five essential features of best practice have been identified:

- Using rational, standard terms and definitions that accurately isolate all key components of the water system, and are used in Figure 3S-1.

- All water is accounted for as a consumption or a loss as shown in Figure 3S-1.

- All components of consumption or loss are accounted for in units of volume for the period of reference.

- All components of water consumption or loss are assigned an appropriate cost that reflects its impact to the water utility based on the prevailing economics. Reduction in losses should include the savings that accrue to deferral or avoidance of major capital costs for capacity.

- Robust performance indicators are used that go beyond simplistic output/input indicators.

A careful examination of Figure 3S-1 will reveal that all water is accounted for.

Own Sources	System Input	Water Exported	Authorized Consumption	Billed Authorized Consumption	Revenue Water	Billed Water Exported
						Billed Metered Consumption
		Water Supplied				Billed Unmetered Consumption
				Unbilled Authorized Consumption	Nonrevenue Water	Unbilled Metered Consumption
	(Allow for known errors)					Unbilled Unmetered Consumption
Water Imported			Water Losses	Apparent Losses		Unauthorized Consumption
						Customer Metering Inaccuracies
				Real Losses		Leakage on Mains
						Leakage and Overflows at Storages
						Leakage on Service Connections up to Point of Customer Metering

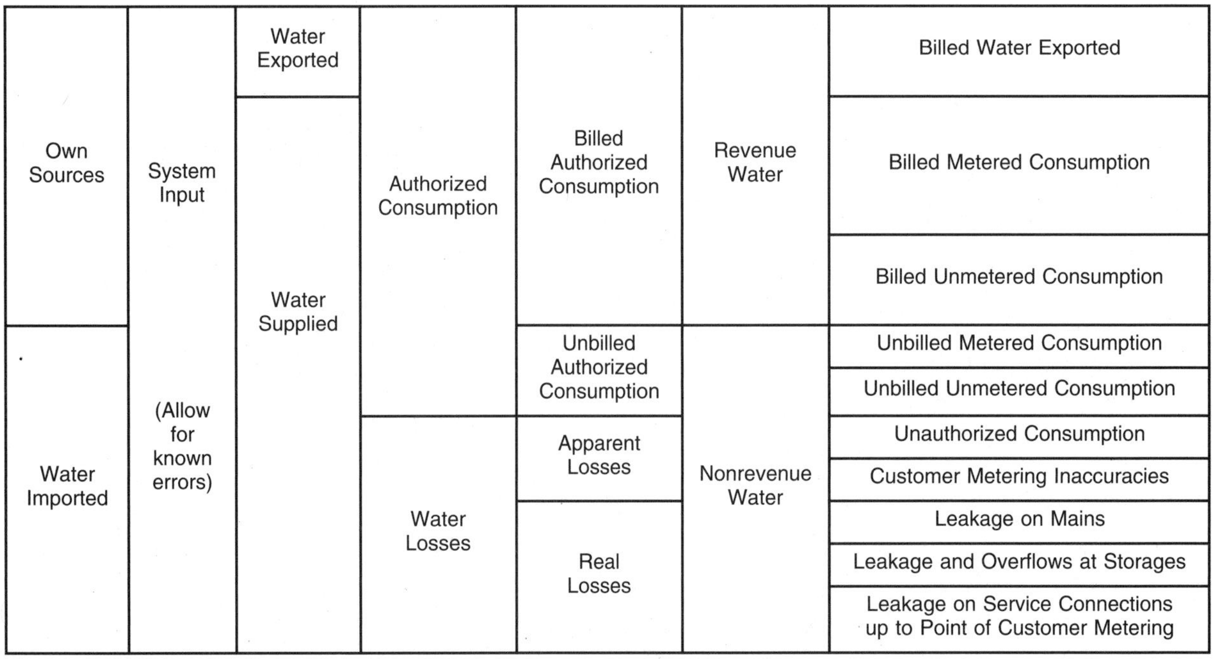

Figure 3S–1   The International Standard Water Audit Format

Some of the water is billed but not metered, and some is metered but not billed. Efficiencies can be developed and applied in many of the audit categories, but the key areas for improvement are in the Apparent Losses and Real Losses categories.

- Real losses are the physical losses of water from the distribution system and include leakage and overflows. Real losses are generally valued at the short-term marginal production or purchase cost.

- Apparent losses include customer meter inaccuracies, billing system errors, and unauthorized use. Apparent losses are valued to include the revenue impact to the utility.

MAGNITUDE OF SAVINGS POTENTIAL

Two examples of water savings related to the above methodology are provided to demonstrate the enormous potential that can exist in many utilities, even those that might think that they are currently doing an exemplary job with total water systems control.

- England and Wales—The privatized utilities in the United Kingdom began applying the methods they had developed in the early 1990s. During the severe drought in 1995–1996, the government regulator, the Office of Water Services (OfWat) drew upon the findings of the utility efforts and imposed new conditions on the utility companies. It has been estimated that up to 85 percent of the recoverable leakage initially measured was eliminated in England and Wales since this structure was put in place.[*]

- City of Philadelphia—In Fiscal Year 1991, the application of IWA Performance Indicators identified the partial results related to water losses as shown in Table 3S-1.

Table 3S–1   City of Philadelphia 1991 Water Audit; Summary Performance Results

Performance Category	Results
Water resources performance indicator	25.8% – Real losses/system input
Operational performance indicators	
Water losses total	83.4 mgd = 62.5 tgal/connection/year
Apparent losses	14.5 mgd = 10.9 tgal/connection/year
Real losses	68.9 mgd = 61.7 tgal/conn/yr; 142 gpd
Infrastructure leakage index (ILI)	Real losses/UARL[*] = 12.7 times
Financial performance indicators	
Nonrevenue water	85.8 mgd or 32.1% of system input
Nonrevenue water costs $ annual:	
Unbilled metered	$27,041
Unbilled unmetered	$107,476
Apparent losses	$11,601,515
Real losses	$2,399,146

*UARL = Unavoidable Average Real Losses

---

*Lambert, A., International Water Data Comparison, Ltd. personal conversation with G. Kunkel, January 2001 re: Interpretation of United Kingdom Office of Water Services (OFWAT) reported leakage results.

MAJOR COMPONENTS OF EFFECTIVE LOSS CONTROL_____

The major methods of leakage control in the International Water Association methodology for the Water Audit and Performance Indicators are outlined below. For details of implementation, refer to the IWA manuals.

Controlling Real Losses

1. Pressure management changes impact all variables in the system

   a. Pressure modeling via innovative methods such as the fixed and variable area discharge paths model

   b. Controlling pressure close to, but not greater than, the minimum standard of service

   c. Limiting maximal pressure levels or surges in pressure

   d. Nighttime pressure reduction where feasible to reduce losses from small leaks

2. Pipeline materials management

   a. Select materials appropriate for site conditions

   b. Ensure proper installation

   c. Establish maintenance routine

   d. Rehab when required

   e. Replace when required

3. Speed and quality of repairs

4. Active leakage control

   a. Regular inspection and sounding of all water main fittings and connection, leakage surveys

   b. Leakage modeling via innovative methods such as the bursts and background estimates

   c. Metering of individual pressure zones

   d. District metered area metering: measuring total inflow per day, week, or month

   e. Continuous or intermittent night flow measurements

   f. Short-period measurements at any time of day

   g. Temporary placing of leak noise detectors and loggers

Controlling Apparent Losses

1. Customer meter management: Reliable selection, installation, testing, and rotation of customer meters

2. Data handling controls: Procedures and auditing to minimize error in data transfer and analysis functions

3. Policy and enforcement: Police unauthorized usage and impose penalties

4. Water accounting controls to ensure that all users are monitored and billed, and water usage data integrity is safeguarded

The reader should refer to the water audit references for the mechanics of conducting the water audit.

This page intentionally blank

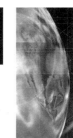

Chapter **4**

Water Rights and Policy

Water laws spring from water policy and represent the institutionalization of water policy. Water laws and water policy change as societal needs change. Water policy is dynamic, both in the East and West.

The laws defining water rights and the institutions involved in allocating water resources represent the framework for managing America's water resources. Water rights law and water allocation arrangements reflect differing traditions and conditions across the country. This chapter focuses on three distinct sources of water policy: general water rights, federal water rights, the Public Trust Doctrine and American Water Works Association (AWWA) water policy. The appropriation doctrine in the western US and the riparian system in the eastern US illustrate how water policy adapts itself to differing environments. Both federal and AWWA water policy demonstrate the priorities and ideals affecting modern water management.

Despite the broad-ranging influences, water rights and water allocation programs have largely been the provinces of the states. At this time, there is no national water rights system. Depending on the jurisdiction, some state water laws rely on common law doctrines and court decisions to resolve private disputes; other states have established sophisticated statutory and administrative arrangements to define water rights and allocate available resources.

In most instances, groundwater and surface waters are not distinct systems, but interrelated resources. Although water laws traditionally considered groundwater withdrawals and surface water withdrawals separately, such laws cannot resolve conflicts resulting from the interdependency of groundwater and surface water.

Resolving the issues involved in developing and managing water resources does not lend itself to the regulatory approach seen in typical environmental programs. In the area of water resources, the challenge for government is not one of regulation, but of fair and even-handed allocation. When demand exceeds supply, more sophisticated water allocation arrangements are required than when supply is plentiful.

Water rights and water allocation arrangements should be designed to avoid and resolve conflicts between competing uses. To do so, water rights need to be defined clearly, logically, and predictably, so water utilities and other users can rely on them for future planning. To be predictable, water rights need to be quantified and

81

defined. Water allocation systems built on undefined rights, such as the right to make *reasonable use*, may be outdated and ill-suited to current societal demands.

Critical to managing water resources is the degree to which water is consumed and not returned to the hydrologic system. Water allocation arrangements need to pay special attention to the effect of consumptive uses, including evaporative losses and interbasin transfers. The goal in managing consumptive uses is to ensure optimum availability and efficient reuse of available water resources.

Under the prior appropriation and the riparian doctrines, the concepts of *beneficial use* and reasonable use of water recognize the fundamental tenet that water should be used efficiently. In practice, however, some water rights systems encourage inefficient use of water resources. Systems that provide credits for water conservation efforts and allow those credits to be sold or banked for future needs avoid penalizing those who conserve.

Although no water rights plan can ensure sufficient quantities of water, water allocation arrangements should provide predictability and security of tenure (granting rights for a sufficient period of time and protecting against interference from others). Such security is essential to water utilities.

To encourage involvement in developing water resources and conservation projects, the water rights system needs to establish rights for previously developed and conserved water and protect those rights against claims by others. Some common law doctrines, particularly in riparian states, do not provide adequate protection for rights in developed waters. To ensure water for environmental uses and human needs, integrated resources planning processes and water allocation decisions should consider the entire system.

Many states need to take a more active role to balance competing demands on water resources. States that develop water rights arrangements that recognize the challenge of integrated water resource management are in the best position to make wise decisions. States should be encouraged in this process.

GENERAL WATER RIGHTS

The law of water rights in the US has included two distinct systems: *riparian rights* in the East and the *appropriation doctrine* in the West. A more accurate picture presents three systems: (1) *riparian rights*; (2) *regulated riparianism* (which lays a system of government permits and regulation by state agencies on top of the traditional court-made riparian doctrine); and (3) the *appropriation doctrine*. Groundwater policy is often some blend of these options. A state-by-state array of water systems is presented in Table 4-1.

Riparian Rights

Riparian rights are the basic rules to allocate water in the eastern US—considered to be roughly east of Kansas City. These policies evolved almost naturally in an environment where water was generally plentiful and excessive government involvement was unwanted. The riparian doctrine, sometimes called the *rule of reasonable sharing*, is patterned after water policy in England where water resources are similar to those in the eastern US.

Under the riparian doctrine, the right to use water from a stream (or lake) belongs to whoever owns the land on the bank. (*Ripa* means riverbank in Latin.) Such a landowner is a *riparian owner*. Every riparian owner is entitled to use water from the stream. This right is defined as the right to enjoy the advantage of a reasonable use of the stream as it flows through the landowner's property. This right, however, is subject to an equivalent right belonging to other riparian owners.

Table 4–1   Summary of water rights of the 50 states

State	Surface Water				State	Surface Water			
	Appropriation	Riparian	Regulated Riparian	Groundwater Permit Required?		Appropriation	Riparian	Regulated Riparian	Groundwater Permit Required
Alabama			X		Montana	X			X
Alaska	X			X	Nebraska	X			
Arizona	X			X	Nevada	X			X
Arkansas			X		New Hampshire		X		
California		Other*			New Jersey			X	X
Colorado	X			X	New Mexico	X			X
Connecticut			X	X	New York			X	X
Delaware			X	X	North Carolina			X	X
Florida			X	X	North Dakota	X			X
Georgia			X	X	Ohio		X		X
Hawaii		Other*		X	Oklahoma	X			X
Idaho	X			X	Oregon	X			X
Illinois		X			Pennsylvania		X		
Indiana			X		Rhode Island		X		
Iowa			X	X	South Carolina		X		X
Kansas	X			X	South Dakota	X			X
Kentucky			X	X	Tennessee		X		
Louisiana		X			Texas	X			
Maine		X			Utah	X			X
Maryland			X	X	Vermont		X		
Massachusetts			X	X	Virginia			X	X
Michigan		X			Washington	X			X
Minnesota			X	X	West Virginia		X		
Mississippi			X	X	Wisconsin			X	X
Missouri		X			Wyoming	X			X

*This state's water rights system contains aspects of all three systems.

Two rules govern how much water a riparian owner may use. The older rule held that the landowner must leave the *natural flow* of the river unchanged. Each riparian owner downstream was entitled to have the water in its natural condition, without others' altering the rate of flow or the quantity (or quality) of the water. The more modern rule of reasonable use is that each riparian owner may use the water, regardless of the natural flow, as long as their use does not cause an *unreasonable injury* to any other riparian user.

Regulated Riparian

With time, increasing population and development in the East have increased the problems of water distribution. The proliferation of problems and an increased faith in government regulation have caused most states to overlay the traditional riparian system with new administrative schemes, such as permit systems, for regulating water use. This has been described as *regulated riparianism*.

The most important feature of regulated riparianism statutes is that direct users of water must have a permit from a state administrative agency to use water. Although the standard for granting the permits is typically similar to reasonable use, reasonable use may be applied differently from the common law riparian doctrine.

Appropriation System

The environment of the western US is less conducive to the use of the riparian system than that of the East. As trappers, miners, and settlers migrated west, they encountered a hostile environment. Early explorers referred to the Great Plains as the *Great American Desert*, and not all believed that it could be settled. It was obvious that most of the land would require irrigation. Limiting use of streams to only adjoining landowners was not practical; such an action would drastically curtail the settlement and development of the new lands, because nonriparian lands would be practically useless.

The early miners are credited with finding a solution to the problem. By custom, they all accepted the fact that the first miner who used water from a stream to work his placer claim was protected against latecomers. Soon this custom expanded to include the use of water for all purposes, not just for mining. Finally, as the land was organized into territories and then into states, the custom became law through express recognition by court decisions, constitutional provisions, and state statutes.

What emerged was a flexible and useful concept, designed for western conditions and created from experience. It became known as the doctrine of prior appropriation. The federal government promoted development of this concept by enacting legislation that encouraged settlement of the West in conformity with each state's water rights laws.

The result was that no western state completely adopted the riparian doctrine. About half, bowing to logic and precedent, retained and modified some of its features, but the others repudiated it altogether. Those states that originally retained some riparian features have found that, by and large, its vestiges prohibit the full development of limited water resources; therefore, they continue to modify their water law and erode its riparian principles. All 17 contiguous western states and Alaska embrace the main principles of the appropriation doctrine. Hence, the appropriation doctrine is firmly established as the principal rule relating to water resources in the West.

The appropriation doctrine envelops several interrelated concepts. The two major concepts are

1. A water right is a right to the use of water; the right is acquired by appropriation.

2. An appropriation is the act of diverting water from its source and applying it to a beneficial use.

The priority of an appropriative water right is the superiority of the right over all rights of other appropriators of later priority when the available water supply is not enough for all. In other words, the oldest rights prevail.

Under the appropriation system, the right is a *right of use*, a usufructuary right. The actual title to the flowing stream is always considered as belonging to the people, or public, or to the state for the use of the people.

A fundamental philosophy expressed in western law is that public waters must be used for a useful or beneficial purpose. Thus, if an appropriator has no immediate use for the full appropriation, the law requires that only the amount presently needed be diverted, allowing the excess water to remain in the stream. Further, once the water has served the beneficial use of the appropriator, any waste or return flow water resulting from this use must likewise be allowed to return to the stream. This requirement protects not only the public, but other appropriators as well.

A water right is acquired by taking waters and applying them to a beneficial use. In some states, no permission of any kind is required. However, in most states, water may not be taken or used until the user has obtained a permit from a water administration official, usually the state engineer.

A basic concept of the appropriation doctrine is that the earliest water users have priority over later appropriators during times of water shortage. Obviously, each appropriation on a stream is related to all others on the same stream. Consequently, all states have developed some system for determining relative rights and priorities through an administrative agency, whose actions are subject to court scrutiny, or through special court proceedings that result in a court decree listing and determining the relative rights and priorities of all water users from the same supply.

Table 4-2 contains a side-by-side comparison of riparian and appropriation water system components.

Groundwater

Water rights systems for groundwater include absolute ownership, reasonable use, correlative rights, and appropriation-permit systems. The rule of absolute ownership is the oldest of the doctrines applied to groundwater, stemming from the principle that land ownership encompasses everything beneath the land to the center of the Earth. Of course, the migratory nature of groundwater distinguishes it from most substances found beneath the Earth and makes it impossible to apply the concept of ownership in a literal sense. Practically, the rule of absolute ownership is a rule of capture; a landowner may use all groundwater that can be captured from beneath that owner's land. Thus, when conflict develops, the person with the deepest well and the biggest pump prevails.

As with the rule of absolute ownership, the rule of reasonable use holds that groundwater rights are an incident of land ownership. A landowner may generally withdraw and use groundwater. However, if his use interferes with groundwater used by neighboring landowners, he is privileged to continue only if his use is reasonable. Conversely, a person is liable for harm caused to others by unreasonable use of groundwater. Thus, a landowner has only a qualified right, rather than an absolute right, to use groundwater.

The rule of correlative rights holds that the right to make an overlying use of water is not absolute but is relative to the rights of other overlying users. The rule is used primarily when the groundwater supply is insufficient to satisfy the needs of all overlying users and sharing is required. In some cases, sharing is accomplished by prorating the supply on the basis of overlying acreage, although the recent trend suggests a more flexible approach.

The appropriation-permit system is sometimes called an *appropriation system* but might be more accurately called a *permit system*. The concept most strongly associated with the appropriation doctrine is the rule of priority. To the extent that priority is applied in groundwater, its principal use is to limit the number of permits issued to prevent overdevelopment of the aquifer. The distinguishing feature of the permit system is administrative regulation and management of groundwater. This contrasts greatly with the relatively unregulated nature of groundwater use under the doctrines previously discussed.

Table 4–2   Comparison of riparian and appropriation water rights systems

	Riparian	Appropriation
How are rights acquired?	Riparian rights are acquired by acquiring riparian land, which is defined as property touching the water of a lake or stream. A riparian right is for the use, not the ownership, of the water.	An appropriation right is independent of land ownership. The right to a certain quantity of water may be acquired by appropriating and applying the water to a beneficial use. The basic principle is that when the supply cannot fulfill the needs of all the perfected appropriations, the last or junior rights are the first to be shut off— first in time is first in right.
What uses may be made?	Water may be used for any reasonable purpose.	Water may be used for any beneficial use as defined by the states' codes. Common beneficial uses may include irrigation, mining, stock watering, manufacturing, municipal uses, domestic uses, and recreational uses.
May water be impounded?	Generally it is unclear whether riparians have the right to impound water at high flow for later use or release. Some riparian states have initiated a permit system for storage for mill or hydroelectric operations.	Impoundment for later use is common.
Where can water be used?	Often in riparian states, water use is limited to riparian lands, but many states permit use on nonriparian lands if other users are not harmed. Additionally, water use may be limited to the watershed of origin.	Water may be used anywhere, and if there is no injury to vested rights, water may be used outside the watershed.
When may water be used?	Whenever it is available.	Often an appropriation right may be limited to a specific time, i.e., day or night, summer or fall.
What is the nature of the right?	Except for domestic uses, riparian lands on a watercourse are co-sharers and have an equal right to make a reasonable use of the water. No riparian land is ever ensured a definite quantity, unless a prescriptive right is obtained.	Appropriation rights are never equal because first in time appropriators are guaranteed an ascertainable amount of water. If an appropriator's needs can be met by use of less water, that appropriator is entitled only to the lesser quantity.
What happens if the water right is not used?	The right does not depend on use. Therefore, it is not lost by nonuse and is not subject to abandonment.	The right is held only as long as proper beneficial use is continued. Appropriation rights are subject to abandonment.

FEDERAL WATER RIGHTS

Federal water rights consist of federal reserved rights, water rights for water not reserved, rights of navigable water, and federal contract rights.

Reserved Rights

The federal reserved water rights doctrine, frequently referred to as the *Winters doctrine* after *Winters v. United States*, states that when the US sets aside or reserves a part of its lands for particular uses or purposes, it reserves by implication the right to enough of the unappropriated waters on or adjacent to the lands to meet its uses and purposes. This implied reservation usually takes priority at the time the lands are reserved.

Although the rights reserved by the US are junior to the rights of prior appropriators, they differ from appropriated rights in several ways: (1) the waters need not be put to use promptly or within any particular period of time; (2) although the rights are ultimately subject to measurement by the water requirements of the purposes for which the lands were reserved, they need not be quantified at the time the reservation is established or within any particular period of time; (3) they are not subject to loss by nonuse or abandonment; and (4) the water may be used for purposes other than those for which the land was reserved, as long as the alternative uses do not increase consumption.

Although beneficial use, in relation to the purposes for which the reservation was created, ultimately determines the measure of such rights, it is not limited to such purposes. Rather, regardless of the purposes by which the rights are measured or quantified, the water may be put to other beneficial uses as long as they do not increase consumption. In short, particular beneficial use is the measure, but not the limit, of the rights.

Water Rights for Federal Lands Not Reserved

Not all federal lands are reservations. The Bureau of Land Management administers millions of acres of unreserved public lands under congressionally authorized programs. These programs may require water.

Does the government have water rights under federal law to serve congressionally authorized uses of unreserved lands? The question has raised a great deal of debate. Central to the debate is the issue of state control over appropriations. Some commentators contend that the federal government must comply with state law in acquiring water rights for use on unreserved lands; others contend the federal government can establish the rights based on congressional mandate. Between 1979 and 1981, three attorneys offered three opinions on the scope, and, indeed, the existence, of these rights. The US Supreme Court, in a decision that predated the attorneys' opinions, directed the federal government to comply with state law but only as far as the state law is consistent with Congress' objectives. At least one earlier court case supports the government's right to use water on its unreserved lands.

Federal Rights on Navigable Waters

Under the commerce clause, the US retains control over all navigable waters in the interest of navigation. In this connection, the US has a dominant servitude over such waters and the beds and banks of lakes and streams that contain them. All proprietary rights of others related to such water and the land beneath it are subject to this dominant servitude or easement for navigation and may be impaired or extinguished by the US without compensation.

Contractual Water Rights

Federal contract rights usually relate to the US Bureau of Reclamation (USBR) and the US Army Corps of Engineers (Corps). Under the Reclamation Act of 1902, the Secretary of the Interior, acting through the USBR, is authorized to construct, operate, and maintain water storage and distribution facilities in the 17 western states. The USBR is also authorized to make water from such projects available to users for irrigation and other purposes. Section 8 of the act directs the Secretary of the Interior to act "in conformity with [state] laws relating to the control, appropriation, use, or distribution of water used in irrigation." The act also states that "the right to the use of water acquired under the provisions of this act shall be appurtenant to the land irrigated, and beneficial use shall be the basis, the measure, and the limit of the right."

To acquire water rights, the USBR usually files an application to appropriate a specific amount of unappropriated water in a river and/or acquires vested water rights by purchase or condemnation. After constructing the dam and storage reservoir and, if necessary, the distribution works to deliver project water to individual users, the USBR executes after-delivery contracts with irrigation districts or other similar entities according to terms of the Reclamation Project Act of 1939.

The USBR may also enter into contracts to provide water for municipal and industrial uses. These contracts make project water available in return for the users agreeing to repay a portion of the construction, operation, and maintenance costs over a specified period.

The Corps' historic mission to maintain and improve navigability on US harbors and navigable rivers was gradually broadened during the early 1900s to encompass flood control. Beginning in the 1930s, the Corps was authorized to construct dams to control floods and regulate streamflows to maintain navigability. The Secretary of the Army has no authority to provide storage and delivery of water for irrigation, but Congress has authorized the provision of irrigation water in a number of Corps projects under the supervision of the Secretary of the Interior pursuant to the reclamation laws.

THE PUBLIC TRUST DOCTRINE

The Public Trust Doctrine is a legal framework for resource planning and management that has been used to clarify water rights. Its origins are historical, and the doctrine is a currently evolving concept relating to the ownership, protection, and use of essential natural and cultural resources. It is receiving increased attention in the US because of the growing awareness of the duty of care owed the environment.

The Public Trust Doctrine is a common law doctrine. The essence of the doctrine is the legal right of the public to use certain lands and waters. The right may be concurrent with private ownership. The legal interest of the public is not absolute; it is determined by a balancing of interests.

History

The Public Trust Doctrine has its roots in the *Institutes of Justinian*, the body of Roman civil law that was put together by the Roman Emperor Justinian's top legal scholars in 530 A.D. One of these laws stated that running water, the sea, and consequently, the shores of the sea were common to all mankind. Therefore, no one was forbidden from approaching the seashores. England, in adopting much of the Roman law, recognized waters and shores as public in nature. As commerce became more important, so did the public's interest in the shores. Eventually, the shores came to be recognized as property owned by the king in trust for the public.

In America, as the colonies began to acquire charters from the kings of England, the law of public shore lands came to America. The waterways were so vital for commerce and sustenance that the original thirteen states kept the shore lands under their control when they granted the Northwest Territory to the federal government. As the rest of the states joined the Union, they did so on equal footing with the original thirteen and kept the shores under their control. This land was deemed to be owned by the states in trust for the public, hence the name Public Trust Doctrine.

Application to Water Rights

Title to these water resources or the common is held by the state, as sovereign, in trust for the people. The purpose of the trust is to preserve resources in a manner that makes them available to the public for certain public uses.

Until recent decades the predominant commons recognized as subject to the Public Trust Doctrine was tidal and navigable waters. American cases have held that title to lands underlying tidal and/or navigable waters is held by the state in its sovereign capacity as trustee for the benefit of the citizens of the state who have the right to use the waters and adjacent land for navigation and to "fish, hunt, or bath. . . ." In other words, tidewaters to their farthest reach, tidelands, navigable waters, and permanently submerged lands, including those extending lakeward or seaward to the limit of state ownership, are subject to the Public Trust Doctrine.

In the US, the National Environmental Protection Act (the environmental impact statement law) declares that, "[I]t is the responsibility of the Federal Government to use all practicable means . . . to . . . fulfill the responsibilities of each generation as trustee of the environment for succeeding generations. . . ."

State Regulation

The Public Trust Doctrine originated as an instrument of federal common law used to ensure protection of the public's interest in navigation, fishing, and recreation (except in Maine and Massachusetts where use is limited to fishing, fowling, and navigation). Also, many state constitutions incorporate the Doctrine, like the Hawaiian Constitution, which declares that, "All public natural resources are held in trust by the State for the benefit of the People." This allows the legislatures to regulate and control submerged lands underlying tidal and navigable waters through the enactment of statutes and ordinances. These laws then enable the states to more easily resolve disputes within their own courts.

This doctrine has been advanced in the area of water rights in some states, particularly in California. In the 1983 California Supreme Court case *National Audubon Society v. Superior Court of Alpine County*, the waters of Mono Lake were at issue. In this case, the California Supreme Court determined that the state had an affirmative duty to consider the public trust value in both permitting initial allocations of water as well as reviewing past allocations. The Court then required examination of the diversions of tributary flows to Mono Lake by the City of Los Angeles and the state ultimately reduced the amount of diversion allowed under California water rights to allow Mono Lake levels to be increased. Although other western states have dealt with public trust issues, some states such as Idaho have acted to limit the scope of this doctrine. The Public Trust Doctrine has been used most often by instream flow interests to attempt restoration of over appropriated rivers and streams. Because of the uncertainty of the Public Trust Doctrine and because its application is dependent on specific state constitutions and laws, other techniques to restore stream flows have been attempted with mixed success. The retroactive application of the public interest test has been used successfully in some circumstances to accomplish similar goals to the Public Trust Doctrine.

AWWA WATER POLICY

The AWWA policy on water rights and water allocation is presented in the following 14 guiding principles.

1. Water allocation and water rights arrangements should be compatible with hydrological science. Water allocation laws should recognize the relationship between groundwater and surface water and avoid artificial distinctions between them. Water allocation systems should recognize that water resources need to be managed in the context of hydrologic units, which do not necessarily follow political boundaries. Resources within a water basin are shared, regardless of political subdivisions.

2. Water allocation and water rights systems should be based on sound, comprehensive water resource planning and integrated resource management by all users.

3. Water allocation and water rights arrangements should be based on government serving in a harmonizing role.

4. Water allocation and water rights systems should be tailored according to consideration of the relative availability or scarcity of the resource.

5. Except in unusual conditions, water allocation and water rights systems should be directed toward managing water as a replenishable resource.

6. To deal with increasing competition among users for finite resources, water allocation and water rights systems should define allowable uses clearly, logically, and predictably.

7. Water allocation and water rights systems should be able to consider and differentiate between management of consumptive water uses (those that do not return withdrawn water to the system) and nonconsumptive uses.

8. Water allocation and water rights systems should promote conservation and the efficient use of water.

9. Water allocation and water rights systems should promote economic efficiency.

10. Water allocation and water rights systems need to provide sufficient security of water rights to encourage investments in infrastructure and enterprises reliant on the availability of water.

11. Water allocation and water rights systems need to provide adequate flexibility to facilitate changes over time in light of changing hydrologic, economic, and environmental conditions.

12. Water allocation and water rights systems need to provide protection for those who undertake development and conservation projects (such as reservoirs and artificial recharge projects) to ensure they obtain a fair return on their investments.

13. Water allocation and water rights systems need to recognize environmental values and be able to balance and provide for the legitimate water needs of in-stream water uses, such as fish, wildlife, and wetlands preservation.

14. Water rights and water allocation arrangements need to provide a forum that reconciles competing uses and needs. States should be encouraged to incorporate in their water rights systems forums that encompass the state perspective and broad national priorities (interstate water pacts, endangered species, wetlands, and other issues). At the same time, the federal government should refrain from adopting single-purpose statutes and programs that override and derail state water allocation efforts to achieve the balance for wise water management.

WATER QUALITY IMPACTS TO WATER RIGHTS

Traditionally, water rights and water quality regulations have been viewed as separate and distinct creatures of law. Water rights are founded on the principles of preventing waste and requiring beneficial use of the resource. Regulations affecting water quality are based on the principles of limiting impacts, trying to eliminate them, and protecting existing beneficial uses of the resource. They also address remediation of contamination so that beneficial uses can eventually be attained (e.g. total maximum daily load [TMDL] requirements.) Although their paths have different origins, water rights and water quality regulations can, and often do, converge.

Early on, stream quality was not impacted by the use of water. Initial demands for water were simply not that great. As the population has continued to grow, however, and more demands have been placed on existing resources, quality impacts on the use of water must be considered. This is no more evident than in the debate over environmental flows. Over the last two decades, many western states have grappled with the issue of granting water rights for consumptive needs, while still protecting environmental flows. The delicate balance between human and aquatic needs is something that many states are still struggling to achieve. While the use of water is something thought of more akin to diversion and consumption, some consideration must be given to leaving a portion of water in its natural flowing state.

Select pieces of federal legislation seek to balance water use and water quality regulations. The Clean Water Act (CWA) and the Endangered Species Act (ESA) have both played a factor in the use of water resources. The CWA has impacted water rights in the environmental flows arena, whereas the ESA may curtail the use of water to protect endangered species. Both the CWA and the ESA have sought to balance environmental needs with human needs, but there have been prolonged legal battles to define the exact meaning of these laws.

Instream Uses and Environmental Flows

Water suppliers across the arid West are well aware of the term *environmental flows*. Generally considered the amount of baseflow needed to protect riverine and estuary health, environmental flows are essential to tourism, fishing and ecology industries across the country. The debate over environmental flows has not so much focused on whether some amount of flow is necessary to protect aquatic health, but more about who is authorized to hold rights for environmental flows, and how much flow is truly necessary for each stream segment or estuary.

Of the western states that follow the appropriation doctrine, the majority address environmental flows in a manner consistent with reserving such water from appropriation. Although some states allow one agency to assign an amount of water to another state agency, this action is still consistent with reservation. The intent of reservation is for the state to withhold some amount of water, which would otherwise be available for appropriation, and to reserve that water in the public trust for the benefit of the environment. There are some states that allow individuals, including nonprofit organizations, to apply for and receive appropriative rights for environmental flows, but there is great debate over whether such action truly constitutes an appropriation for more physical storage or diversion of water for beneficial use.

Clean Water Act

The CWA impacts water rights through its requirement to establish and maintain water quality standards for all water bodies to protect a specific detail list of beneficial use. A water quality standard defines the water quality goal of a water body by designating the uses of water, and by setting the criteria necessary to maintain that use. The CWA has established that whenever attainable, water quality standards should provide for the protection and propagation of fish and wildlife, and for recreation. Water quality standards are the foundation for the CWA's controls of pollution. For example, the level of treatment technology required for water reclamation centers is not the same across the nation because different stream segments have different water quality standards. The TMDL is one way used to tailor standards to specific stream segments.

Water quality standards may impact the diversion and use of water resources. For instance, stream segments with low dissolved oxygen or elevated temperatures may need to maintain higher baseflows to maintain aquatic health. One tool that can be used to maintain baseflow is to limit diversions during low flow events. Many western states employ some form of stream flow restrictions, or special conditions, when granting appropriative rights in order to maintain water quality standards.

In addition to water quality standards, the CWA also has a permitting regime for the addition of pollutants into water bodies. The National Pollutant Discharge Elimination System (NPDES) requires authorization before discharging from a point source. Many water supply projects contemplate moving water from one source to another. Depending on the situation, such action may require authorization under the NPDES permitting regime.

Endangered Species Act

Congress enacted the ESA in 1973 to counter the population decline and potential extinction of numerous animal and plant species. Over the last two decades, the ESA has generated conflict over the use of private property inhabited by endangered species. The ESA reaches private control of land and resources through its general prohibition against the *taking* of endangered species. Under the ESA, "the term 'take' means to harass, harm, pursue, hunt, shoot, wound, kill, trap, capture, or collect, or to attempt to engage in any such conduct." *Harm* is the broadest and least precise term in this definition.

In the water rights context, the ESA has impacted the use of both surface and groundwater. In Texas, the ESA has been used to impose pumping limits in the Edwards Aquifer to protect the fountain darter. In New Mexico, the ESA has been used to limit diversions of surface water to protect the silvery minnow in the Middle Rio Grande. As part of the habitat for endangered species, the ESA recognizes the flow of water, either underground or surface water, as being imperative to the survival of aquatic species. Recognizing that certain water supply projects may reduce the flow of water, the ESA has become an effective tool for restricting or limiting the diversion and use of water resources. It also requires Section 7 consultation for any project that needs to obtain a federal wetlands permit within the CWA.

SUGGESTED ADDITIONAL READINGS

Blumm, M. and Schwartz, T. 1995. Mono Lake and the Evolving Public Trust in Western Water. *Arizona Law Review*, 37(3).

Checchio, E. and B.G. Colby. 1983. *Indian Water Rights: Negotiating the Future.* University of Arizona Water Resources Research Center.

Checchio, E. and B.G. Colby. 1993. *Indian Water Rights: Negotiating the Future.* University of Arizona Water Resources Research Center.

Covell, C.F. 1997. A Survey of State Instream Flow Programs in the Western United States. *University of Denver Water Law Review*, 1(2).

Davidson, J. 1999/2000. Indian Water Rights, the Missouri River, and the Administrative Process: What Are the Questions? *American Indian Law Review*, 24.

Dellapenna, J.W. 1990. Riparian Rights in the West. *Oklahoma Law Review*, 43(1).

Dellapenna, J.W. 1997. Population and Water in the Challenge and Opportunity for Law. *International Journal of Environment and Pollution*, 7(1).

Dellapenna, J. 2002. The Law of Water Allocation in the Southeastern States at the Opening of the Twenty-First Century. *University of Arkansas at Little Rock Law Review*, 25(3).

Dellapenna, J. 2000. The Importance of Getting Names Right: The Myth of Markets for Water. *William and Mary Environmental Law and Policy Review*, 25(4).

Gallagher, L.M. 2003. *Clean Water Act Handbook.* 3rd ed.

Getches, D. 1997. *Water Law in a Nutshell.* 3rd ed.

Getches, D., Tarlock, A.D., and Corbridge, J.N. 2002. *Water Resource Management, A Casebook in Law and Public Policy.* 5th ed.

Gillilan, D.M. and Brown, T.G. 1997. *Instream Flow Protection: Seeking a Balance in Western Water Use*, Island Press.

Gleick, P.H. 2000. *The World's Water 2000-2001: The Biennial Report on Freshwater Resources.*

Gould, G.A. 1986. Water Rights Transfers and Third-Party Effects. *Land and Water Law Review*, 23.

Gould, G.A. 1989. Transfer of water rights. *Natural Resources Journal*, 29(2).

Gray, B. 2002. The Property Right in Water. *Hastings West-Northwest Journal of Environmental Law and Policy*, 9(3).

Kaiser, R. 2001. Deep Trouble: Options for Managing the Hidden Threat of Aquifer Depletion in Texas. *Texas Tech Law Review*, 32.

Kaiser, R. 1996. Texas Water Marketing in the Next Millennium: A Conceptual and Legal Analysis. *Texas Tech Law Review*, 27.

Kauffman, B. 2003. What Remains of the Endangered Species Act and Western Water Rights After Tulare Lake Basin Water Storage District v. United States? *Colorado Law Review*, 74(1).

McMahon, M. and R. Collins. 1983. *Federal Water Rights.* Washington D.C.: National Center for Continuing Legal Education.

Moore, M.R. 1996. Water Allocation in the Arid West: Endangered Fish Versus Irrigated Agriculture. *Natural Resources Journal*, 36.

Neuman, J. 1996. Run, River, Run: Mediation of a Water-Rights Dispute Keeps Fish and Farmers Happy for a Time. *University of Colorado Law Review*, 67(1).

O'Connor, S. 2002. The Rio Grande Silvery Minnow and the Endangered Species Act. *Colorado Law Review*, 73(1).

Reisner, M. 1987. *Cadillac Desert: The American West and Its Disappearing Water.*

Sax, J. 2003. We Don't Do Groundwater: A Morsel of California Legal History. *Denver Water Law Review*, 6(1).

Tarlock, A.D. 2000. Putting Rivers Back in the Landscape: The Revival of Watershed Management in the United States. *Hastings West-Northwest Journal of Environmental Law and Policy*, 6(4).

Tarlock, A.D. and Van de Wetering, S. 1999. Growth Management and Western Water Law: From Urban Oases to Archipelagos. *Hastings West-Northwest Journal of Environmental Law and Policy*, 5(4).

Thompson, S. 1998. *Water Use Management and Planning in the U.S.*

Votteler, T.H. 1998. The Little Fish that Roared: The Endangered Species Act, State Groundwater Law, and Private Property Rights Collide Over the Texas Edwards Aquifer. *Environmental Law Journal*, 28(4).

Wood, M. 1998. Reclaiming the Natural Rivers: The Endangered Species Act as Applied to Endangered River Ecosystems. *Arizona Law Review*, 40(1).

Wright, K.R. ed. 1990. *Water Rights of the Fifty States and Territories*. Denver Colo.: American Water Works Association.

Wright K.R., ed. 1998. *Water Rights of the Eastern United States*. Denver Colo.: American Water Works Association.

Chapter **5**

Evaluation of Surface Water and Groundwater Sources

One of the most important steps in planning a new water supply is identifying and evaluating all possible sources. This chapter characterizes the following common sources:

- surface water
- groundwater
- conjunctive use of surface water and groundwater

This chapter provides guidance on evaluating sources, including yield, costs, and issues specific to the source type. An appendix provides an overview of the conceptual layout and preliminary costs for dam projects.

SURFACE WATER

In most regions, surface water sources are viable candidates for meeting water supply needs. Generally, the three alternative surface water sources are the following:[*]

Direct River Withdrawals

This option requires either (1) a locally available source with sufficient base flow to allow dependable direct diversion throughout a wide variety of flow conditions

---

[*]Surface-influenced groundwater withdrawal, which has some characteristics of a surface water diversion and some characteristics of a groundwater withdrawal, has been considered as a groundwater source.

(without significant diversion storage for release during low-flow periods), or (2) the availability of water from alternative sources that can independently be relied on to meet water supply requirements during periods when the river diversion source may be unavailable (e.g., conjunctive use of groundwater as discussed in chapter 8).

On-Stream Reservoirs

On-stream reservoirs rely on usable reservoir storage capacity and natural basin runoff for meeting water supply needs. During periods of low flow, water supply diversion requirements are met or supplemented through reservoir drawdown. During periods of plentiful runoff, water supply needs can be met by streamflow with storage recharge provided by excess runoff. These facilities offer the benefit of low operating cost, because reservoir recharge is derived from natural runoff.

When located in upland areas, pumped transmission to treatment facilities can sometimes be minimized or eliminated; with delivery by gravity pipe flow or by stream channel releases with downstream diversion at or near the water plant site. Main stem (on-stream) reservoirs many times will have a greater level of overall environmental impact than reservoirs on smaller tributary streams, because of typically increased wetland and habitat disturbance, impediments to fisheries resources, disruption to free-flowing streams, and other factors discussed in chapter 10, Environmental Impact Analysis.

Pumped-Storage Reservoirs

If significant pumped diversions are provided to a reservoir as a reserve for meeting demands during droughts or other periodic service interruptions, the project alternative is considered a pumped-storage reservoir project. These facilities are also known in some regions as *skimmer* or *side-stream* reservoirs. For this project type, storage recharge is provided by diversions from outside the reservoir's natural watershed, which are to some degree supplemented with natural basin runoff. The pumped-storage reservoir option can many times best balance environmental concerns with water supply development needs.

To better protect aquatic life and accommodate downstream consumptive uses, minimum in-stream flow requirements are becoming more strict. These restrictions can significantly reduce both the viability of direct river withdrawals and the available yield of on-stream reservoirs. They are somewhat more capital intensive because of the need for pumped diversion facilities (intake, pumps, and additional pipeline construction), but pumped-storage projects can be more responsive to overall environmental concerns for a variety of project settings. Additionally, many streams of sufficient size for water supply purposes lack the appropriate topography and geology for developing a cost-effective dam and reservoir site. They may also require a large and expensive spillway, or the valley areas may have infrastructure development that would be affected by a reservoir. If better settings for a dam and reservoir are found on small tributary basins, the source of supply and storage facility can be separately considered to minimize overall development impacts.

Source Identification and Preliminary Screening

Alternative supply sources are usually evaluated in phases. An initial, primarily qualitative characterization of site benefits, costs, and impacts is used to develop a list of viable candidates for further assessment. These sites are then scrutinized to identify a preferred development option, as discussed later in this chapter. Many of the screening variables used to assess the relative merits of alternative development options (e.g., yield, environmental impacts, water quality, regulatory concerns, and cost) are discussed in detail in other chapters and appendixes. Additional factors may also need to be included in a surface water alternatives assessment to reflect local issues of concern, utility preferences, project staging and expendability, political considerations, or other specific influences that may be important within the framework of a proposed water supply development.

Demand deficit projections[*] should be available before the alternatives identification and analysis phase is initiated, to allow the yield of alternative source facilities and their responsiveness in meeting identified needs to be characterized. The background understanding of a water supply system's additional yield requirements should include consideration of staging source development. This option allows the utility to defer a portion of the capital cost burden and provide for a larger future revenue base to better accommodate project expansion costs. As an example, a recently completed source of supply study for a county in the Atlanta metropolitan area provided recommendations for developing a reservoir site for initial operation as an on-stream facility with a yield of 12 mgd. With further growth in demand, pumped diversion facilities would be added to increase the project's yield to about 35 mgd. This yield expansion would meet long-term county needs and significantly contribute to water supply demand growth in adjacent counties.

United States Geological Survey (USGS) quadrangle maps provide a natural starting point for initial surface water alternative site identification and assessment. Where large demand growth and a large geographic search area are anticipated, USGS 15-minute series maps help with preliminary site identification. USGS 7.5-minute series maps should be used for initial identification where more moderate demand growth is anticipated, or to provide a greater level of detail in reviewing sites initially identified on 15-minute series maps. Initial review of these maps should focus on site settings conducive to each type of viable surface water alternative.

Direct river withdrawals. Where large rivers are located within a reasonable distance of the service area, direct withdrawals for water supply may be practical. Primary issues to be considered in investigating river withdrawals are diversion allocations, river water quality, contamination potential (highway crossings, barge traffic, industrial discharge potential, etc.), watershed protection measures, the need for a backup or independent short-term supply, and proximity to the service area (in terms of transmission costs). However, minimum in-stream flow requirements will significantly reduce or eliminate the sole, direct uses of a direct river diversion, because mandated minimum in-stream flow values may approximate or exceed periodic low-flow availability. For example, the Rappahannock River near Fredericksburg, Va., has a drainage area of about 1,500 mi^2, but the safe yield of an isolated, direct river withdrawal is zero due to a lack of dependable flow and minimum in-stream flow requirements.[†] Therefore, direct river withdrawal from this basin is viable only if interruptions in supply can be accommodated by use of other sources that can reliably deliver water during periods of low river flow. Other independent source facilities or pumped-storage in conjunction with river diversion are viable options.

When investigating direct river withdrawals from large rivers, consideration should be given to hydropower and lock facilities. Reservoirs can generally accommodate use of more simplified withdrawal facilities than direct river diversions that lack an impoundment. Additionally, these impoundments many times provide

---

[*]Based on findings from population projections, service area growth estimates, demand forecasts, and available yield (see chapter 3).

[†]The state safe yield criterion for a direct river diversion is the 1-day, 30-year low flow. Seasonal minimum in-stream flows and allowances for downstream users must also be maintained.

significant storage. Initial inquiries and possible followup discussions should be held with the owners of these facilities to assess opportunities and impediments related to adding water supply diversions to their current system demands. A hydropower site with 100 ft of head will generate less than $30 in gross revenue per million gallons released (at 10¢ per kilowatt-hour). Even if a final negotiated cost for allocation of water supply diversions is several times the lost revenues to the power company (to accommodate power replacement with more costly peaking sources), this option can be very cost-effective when compared to most other water supply development alternatives.

Reservoir sites.   Sites that appear conducive to reservoir development should be initially identified from inspection of USGS quadrangle maps and supplemented with information from soil and geology maps. Preliminary examination of potential sites by topographic map study can be effective for developing a general site characterization and identifying many key features, such as those identified below.

Dam site. Dam size, inferences regarding likely dam type, foundation conditions, spillway requirements, etc. (e.g.[*], *broad valley bottom with moderately sloped abutments; considerable depth of residual soils to bedrock likely in valley bottom; probable earth dam site with abutment emergency spillway; a large dam, approximately 100 ft high and 1,500 ft long, can be accommodated*).

Reservoir area. Surface area, storage capacity, geometry, likely extent of wetlands and other valued habitat, affected utilities, roads, buildings, etc. (e.g., *long, narrow, deeply incised reservoir [approximately 500 acres]; reservoir splits into two main branches, can provide approximately 5 billion gallons of usable storage; possible wetland areas appear limited to upper reaches of pool and several small tributary stream areas, one county road and three local roads affected; no major utilities identified fewer than five structures affected*).

Basin runoff characteristics. Basin development and land uses, steepness of basin slopes and channels, screening of point and nonpoint source discharges, major roadways over tributary streams (especially those in close proximity to the proposed reservoir), etc. (e.g., *City of Collier is located along the main stem of reservoir, about 7 miles upstream of dam site; significant basin relief, especially in upper basin [flash flood flows]; spillway design flood roughly estimated at 30,000 cfs; two wastewater treatment plants discharge into basin streams and a large coal strip mine is located in the headwaters area; need to assess spill potential from US Highway 43 [four lane], which crosses the main stem and two tributaries just south of Collier*).

Proximity to service area and general notes. Distance from treatment plant and distribution system, likely levels and types of treatment required, topographic, geologic, and land use interferences for transmission facilities, etc. (e.g., *reservoir site 30 miles from service area; two major divides will need to be crossed [pumping and pressure control will be significant issues]; will likely provide water of high quality [limited basin development]; significant pipeline rock excavation may be required, transmission route will need to avoid the Benton Springs Wildlife Preserve*).

Potential fatal flaws. Map reviews of potential sites, as discussed, should highlight the presence of potential fatal flaws, such as

- *extensive wetlands or critical habitat areas*

- *protected lands (wildlife management areas, scenic rivers, etc.)*

- *natural gas pipelines or high-voltage electric transmission lines*

---

[*]Italicized text is included to illustrate features and conditions noted from inspection of topographic, soil, and geology maps for a potential reservoir site.

- *historically or archaeologically significant sites*

- *extensive development within the reservoir*

- *significant pollution sources in the basin*

Some of these characteristics may be sufficient cause for eliminating a site from further consideration, but in most circumstances the characteristics should be documented and examined in more detail during a followup field reconnaissance visit. The latter three assessment categories (basin runoff characteristics, proximity to service area, and potential fatal flaws) are also helpful in characterizing direct river withdrawal sites.

Reservoirs should also be identified and screened for expansion potential. Primary benefits of reservoir expansion can include reduced cost and reduced environmental impacts compared to a new facility. Many of the wetlands and habitat impacts associated with a new dam project are generally related to the floodplain and bottom land areas of a reservoir. Where a reservoir is in place, the environmental impacts of incrementally raising the pool can be much less than for a new reservoir. When the contributing watershed is large enough, expansion can directly increase the yield of on-stream sources. For smaller watersheds, reservoir expansion can be integrated with diversions to convert the project into a pumped-storage facility. Dams should be assessed to identify whether reservoir expansion would impinge on upstream development and whether the site characteristics are conducive to expansion.

Yield estimates.   To initially assess the yield of on-stream sources of supply, the generic reservoir yield correlations for the region should be determined first. Yield values at this stage need to provide approximate diversion rates available from alternative sites. Therefore, a simple but effective approach is to develop preliminary spreadsheet yield analyses. Local USGS streamflow data, representative of the study region,[*] can be used and converted to flow per square mile of contributing drainage area. Preliminary yield analyses should be undertaken for a range of usable reservoir storage volumes, and for a reasonable range of basin sizes. A literature search of available hydrologic publications is advisable because a government or university investigator may have already performed this task.

In nonmountainous areas, rainfall and runoff for nearby drainage areas can be considered to be similar. In these cases, stream base flows will generally vary approximately as the ratio of the drainage area. Where this assumption is reasonable, a range of basin sizes can be approximated by applying drainage area ratios to the streamflow data. Rough estimates of reliable yield potential for a range of usable reservoir storage volumes and drainage areas can then be quickly developed and presented graphically as illustrated in Figure 5-1. For preliminary assessment, the approximate yield can be interpolated from the curves for combinations of storage and basin area.

Similarly, generic yield curves can be developed for assessing potential pumped-storage sites. The drought of record flow data (or synthetically derived data) for the major streams or rivers available for pumped diversions must be obtained. Also, the actual or estimated total minimum in-stream flows and prior diversion allocations for downstream users must be obtained. Because water rights and water allocations can vary significantly from state to state (and in some cases, for a given river basin), the investigator needs to identify the rules that will apply to the area in question. Unless diversion to a pumped-storage reservoir is from another reservoir, daily flow data will generally need to be used in the yield assessment.

---

*See Chapter 7 for an expanded discussion of reservoir yield analyses.

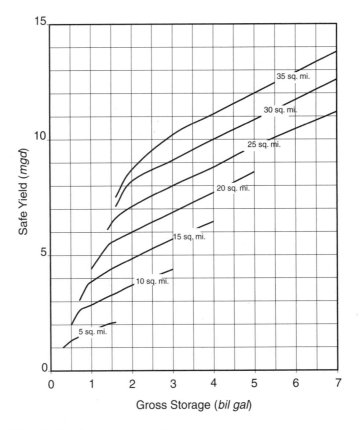

Figure 5–1   Safe yield of on-stream sites

When the tributary basin for a pumped-storage site is small, local inflow can generally be omitted from the preliminary spreadsheet analysis or considered to offset reservoir evaporation and seepage losses. For pumped-storage project assessment, usable reservoir storage and diversion pumping capacity are varied to generate a family of approximate yield curves, as illustrated in Figure 5-2. For preliminary assessment, an approximate yield line can be developed near the maximum rate of slope change for each characteristic curve to estimate the point of significant diminishing returns.

Available flows for diversion are limited by minimum in-stream flow considerations and the size and operating constraints of the diversion facilities. Lacking other detailed information, it is generally reasonable to assume that total pumping capacity will be provided by two pumps, with the larger pump sized at twice that of the smaller. The operating range would then be determined from the minimum operating discharge of the smaller pump to the total installed capacity.

Short-Listing Matrix Rating, and Site Selection

Based on the initial site characterization and yield estimates, a list of viable sites was developed for further scrutiny. Sites defensibly judged to be either of marginal merit or highly flawed should be eliminated.

Short-Listing. Depending on the size, complexity, and number of alternative sites identified as viable candidates for meeting increased yield requirements, a one or two-phase short-listing process can be used to narrow the choices. Generally,

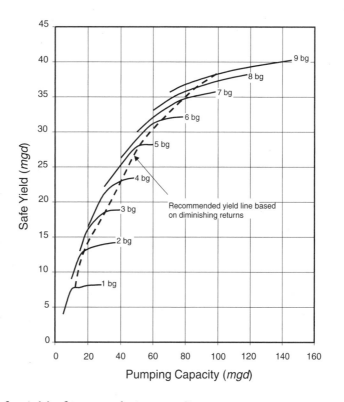

Figure 5–2   Safe yield of pumped-storage sites

where 10 or more candidate sites are identified, a two-phase evaluation approach is merited. Where two evaluation stages are used, an initial matrix rating can be developed based on the general project characterization from map studies (discussed earlier), a review of aerial photography and higher resolution topographic maps (if available), and an initial reconnaissance of each site under consideration.

The reconnaissance should focus on verifying the initial map-based characterizations, identifying recent land development in or near the reservoir area, and enhancing the project team's overall understanding of site conditions. Helicopter flyovers can be useful where a large number of sites need to be assessed, or where access to critical areas is difficult. Flyovers, documented with videotaping of dam sites, reservoir areas, and key watershed features, have proved to be very effective site reconnaissance tools.

A matrix rating table was developed using the acquired information to characterize key variables for each alternative development option (discussed later). The top ranked sites (generally four to six) should then be included in a final short-list for more detailed scrutiny and preferred alternative selection.

For a single short-list, or a second phase evaluation, the project alternatives are evaluated in greater detail than discussed earlier. The level of additional detail will depend on the anticipated level of regulatory scrutiny, complexity of the project setting and needs, number of closely ranked alternatives, available budget, and local factors. Single phase short-list evaluations should incorporate site reconnaissance and other activities, as discussed earlier.

Typically, sites on a single or second phase short-list are further assessed through the following activities:

- Preparing site-specific safe yield analyses

- Conducting archival and publication searches and discussions with local specialists for ecological and cultural resources information relating to the proposed sites or site vicinities

- Using an ecological field reconnaissance of the reservoir and downstream channel areas to develop enhanced qualitative or quantitative assessments of wetlands, wildlife habitat, and other project impacts, and to characterize likely mitigation needs and sites

- Developing conceptual sketches or plans of the proposed project facilities and potential impact areas

- Preparing enhanced project development cost opinions, including project facilities capital and life-cycle costs; land acquisition; environmental mitigation; infrastructure relocations and improvements; and legal, permitting, and engineering fees

Rating parameters and rating values. Matrix rating parameters for surface water source alternatives should be selected to include all substantial issues related to source development. These will generally include ratings of the following:

- *Technical viability.* This factor assesses the likelihood of complications in the technical development of the project site, its location with respect to the water system infrastructure, water quality characterization and variability, potential for contamination, proximity of upstream wastewater treatment plants and industrial discharges, expendability or regional use potential, infrastructure impacts, and operation and maintenance concerns.

- *Environmental considerations.* These factors measure the likelihood of project impacts on wetlands; wildlife habitat; rare, threatened, and endangered species; natural resources; cultural and historic resources; minimum in-stream flows; protected lands; and other important ecological issues.

- *Project cost.* This factor encompasses project development costs, including all significant facilities, land acquisitions, mitigation, negotiated rights, and other site-specific factors important in determining costs when comparing the relative merits of alternative sites. The project cost is usually a cost per mgd of yield that provides reasonable assessment of sites of varying yield. Refer to the Preliminary Cost Guide for Water Supply Dams (Appendix A) for additional guidance on impounding structure costs.

- *Political acceptability.* This factor includes a preliminary assessment of anticipated public and political response to a given alternative. Relevant issues include overall citizen support for or opposition to the project, enhancement of local or regional quality of life or recreational value, regional or statewide support, financial stability, tax and water rate implications, and general environmental soundness.

- *Permitting issues.* These factors provide an overall assessment of permitting requirements, permitting and resource agency support or opposition, and the viability and acceptability of likely mitigation measures from a regulatory agency viewpoint.

Other rating factors can be accommodated (where of significant local or regional importance), or some of the listed factors can be eliminated or incorporated into other factors, to craft the matrix to circumstances relevant for the specific project area. Most important is developing an analysis tool that responsibly represents the relevant concerns that will affect acceptability and performance. This is best accomplished using integrated resource planning techniques discussed in chapter 13.

Rating values are based on a scale developed by the investigators. Typically, a 1–5 scale provides a sufficient basis for rankings, given the complex issues to be assessed and the limited level of understanding of the project alternatives at this stage. Some parameters, such as yield and cost, can readily be quantified; others will necessarily be judged on a mixed or qualitative basis. One end of the scale is reserved for factors of exceptional value; the other end is for those having a substantial adverse impact. Each project alternative is rated in each category and the ratings summed. Separate category weighting factors are generally not recommended. However, some issues, such as environmental concerns affecting project cost, are reflected in more than one category.

Site selection.   The overall rating values are the first guide to site selection. Sometimes, the numbers will speak clearly and show one alternative of exceptional merit that conforms to the investigator's intuitive judgment. However, many times the rating process will result in two or more similarly ranked alternatives, or a ranking that is counterintuitive. In these cases, additional scrutiny and discussion should be conducted to verify the merits of the preferred project alternative and the fairness of the applied factors.

These analyses will be scrutinized by citizens' groups and regulatory staff who will not likely accept a biased presentation. An initial fair, balanced, and reasonably comprehensive presentation will pay tremendous dividends down the road. Remember that the project will need to move from initial site identification and planning through what can generally be characterized as a rigorous, time consuming, and costly public input and permitting process.

When sources other than surface water are being considered, similar analyses and rankings are performed for comparison. Based on further analyses required for permitting, an initially selected site may be found to be flawed (e.g., an endangered species was found in the reservoir area). Therefore, several top ranked sites should be considered for possible development until further studies of sufficient detail for regulatory review and approvals are completed.

GROUNDWATER

Groundwater, or waters found beneath the surface of the Earth, is a very important source of supply. In terms of storage, the total freshwater reserve in the groundwater basins is about 10.5 million km^3, which represents about 96 percent of the total unfrozen fresh water in the world. The other major sources of unfrozen fresh water, rivers and lakes, store only about 91,000 km^3. The total freshwater reserve in the world is approximately 35 million km^3, of which about 69 percent (24 million km^3) is frozen in glaciers and permanent ice covers in the Antarctic and Arctic regions.

In terms of water use, groundwater supplies about 25 percent of total water needs (domestic, agricultural, and industrial) in the United States. Comparable numbers for the United Kingdom and Canada are 20 percent and 2 percent respectively. In some countries, such as Austria, groundwater supplies more than 50 percent of water needs. In the United States, more than half the population depends on groundwater as the primary source of drinking water. From state to state, this ranges from a low of 20 percent in Connecticut to a high of more than 90 percent in Hawaii, Idaho, Mississippi, Nebraska, and New Mexico.

Groundwater Development

The development of groundwater is more complicated than that of surface water. Groundwater is a resource that (1) is hidden from view; (2) is not amenable to delineation of basin boundaries from a topographic map; (3) is usually in a state of dynamic equilibrium; (4) does not necessarily follow surface watershed divides; (5) may comprise several aquifers in different geologic layers that have different areal extents, different flow directions, and different recharge or discharge areas; (6) may have significantly different water quality in different vertical aquifers in the same topographic location; (7) may have different hydraulic potential in different aquifers (such as confined and unconfined) in the same location; and (8) is affected by the quality of sediment and rock materials through which it passes. As a result, groundwater source identification, development, and continued management require consideration of numerous environmental factors.

The primary options for groundwater sources of supply include

- Groundwater wells for direct withdrawal. Groundwater extraction wells are holes drilled into the ground to a formation that will permit water to be extracted from it. These water-bearing formations are called aquifers. In most aquifers, extraction of water can only be accomplished through the use of pumps because the groundwater surface is below the ground level. Artesian aquifers are aquifers that are under pressure. Artesian aquifers will flow to the surface, which may limit the amount of pumping needed.

- A collector well or subsurface drain (or horizontal well) that intercepts interflow in permeable materials or infiltrating surface water and discharges into a sump whose bottom is below the invert of the gallery screen and casing.

- Infiltration galleries, which are often exposed to the surface, but intercept groundwater.

Groundwater development often begins when an individual digs a hole in the ground, pumps the water out of the ground, and uses it for domestic purposes or for irrigating the crop fields. As the population grows and additional holes are dug, the need for organized groundwater development arises in the face of reduced yield at the wells and poorer water quality. A discussion of the water well development is provided here, followed by a methodology for planned development of groundwater.

Development of Groundwater Wells

A groundwater well is a hydraulic structure that allows water to be cost-effectively withdrawn from water bearing formations (aquifers). The utility of a well is not limited to water supply; wells are also used to monitor water levels and water quality, drain agricultural lands, prevent saltwater intrusions, recharge aquifers, discharge wastes, and relieve pressures under dams and levees.

Primary considerations for developing a groundwater well are

1. Location of potential groundwater aquifer that will yield a sufficient amount of water.

2. Purpose of the proposed well and desired yield.

3. Distance between the location of the well and where water is needed.

4. Groundwater development regulations, permitting requirements, and local design standards.

5. Environmental regulations governing well construction, operation and maintenance, and well abandonment.

6. Economics of well exploration, construction, maintenance, and compliance with regulations.

7. Cost-effectiveness of the well in regard to purported use and alternative sources of water.

8. Thickness and nature of the unsaturated materials (vadose zone) above the water table.

9. Thickness and sedimentary nature of the aquifer materials in the saturated zone.

10. Transmissivity, hydraulic conductivity, and storage coefficients of the aquifer.

11. Historic water level conditions, trends, and recharge sources.

12. Design and construction features of previously constructed wells in the vicinity.

13. Performance history of wells in the vicinity.

14. Location of potential contamination sources.

In a real-world situation, all this information is seldom available to a planner. Often what is available at best, in addition to the regulatory and administrative standards, are desired yield, location of use, and approximate location of a well. This available information is supplemented by hydrogeologic reports and maps of the area, geohydrologic reasoning based on current information, inferences through correlation with known information about hydrologically similar neighboring basins, and drilling a pilot hole in the ground if a sizable (yields greater than 100 gallons [0.38 m^3] per minute) well is planned. A pilot hole is a cost-effective way to obtain additional necessary information, such as location of static water level, type and nature of the aquifer materials, characteristic properties of various subsurface strata (lithologic log), drilling time log, and water quality samples. If the well site is found to be unsatisfactory for any reason, the pilot hole can be abandoned in accordance with the regulations and thus save the significant costs related to drilling a production well and then having to abandon it. If the site is suitable for development, final design specifications can be developed and the test hole can be converted into a production well. This pilot hole approach is essential in developing large-size wells to minimize uncertainties and risks during construction, operation, and maintenance. For smaller wells, the cost of a pilot hole may be almost the same as the cost of the production well. As a result, smaller wells are drilled with a preliminary design developed on the basis of readily available information; and necessary adjustments and refinements in design are made during drilling and construction, as appropriate to maximize the well yield.

Well construction and development consists of several steps:

1. Drilling of the well (there are a number of methods for drilling).

2. Installing a surface casing to seal the earth from the well except where water is to be withdrawn.

3. Installing the casing to the production zone pump chamber casing.

4. Placement of the well screen and gravel or filter pack (as needed).

5. Installing a drive shoe to reinforce the bottom of the casing (if needed).

6. Placement of grout for sealing to prevent surface water or poor-quality groundwater from entering the well.

7. Installation of pump and column pipe—submersible pumps are commonly used as they reduce surface equipment and limit air intake in the raw water lines.

8. Construction of elevated well seal or foundations (these can be used for vertical turbine pumps that are surface-mounted).

9. Development of the well to minimize sand, silt and colloidal production during operation to limit the wear on the pump.

Detailed procedures for well design and construction can be found in text or reference books on groundwater, such as the AWWA M21 *Groundwater*, or the *Groundwater Manual* published by the US Department of Interior. The following design principles, if used, will likely result in a good well design, reduced construction and Operations and Maintenance (O&M) costs, and enhanced well performance:

- Target highest yield, consistent with the current demand and demand growth, with minimum drawdown.

- Provide sand-free operation at maximum specific capacity.

- Provide good-quality water with proper protection from contamination.

- Use materials that will provide a long service life (approximately 25 years).

- Use drilling methods and construction techniques that befit the hydrogeologic conditions of the aquifer.

- Strike a balance between short- and long-term costs (that is, do not oversize a well for probable growth and do not use poor material to cut initial costs).

- Minimize head losses and drawdown by choosing proper screen opening, screen length, and distribution of screen openings.

- Mitigate the damage to natural hydraulic environment caused by drilling operation.

- Alter the hydraulic characteristics of the aquifer near the well to increase the rate of free flow of water to the well.

Infiltration Galleries

Infiltration galleries are constructed when subsurface conditions do not permit groundwater development using vertical production wells. Such conditions occur in thin aquifers or where a thin freshwater layer is underlain by saline water. A typical example is a river valley where thin alluvial deposits lie above bedrock where the water is plentiful, and the hydraulic conductivities are high, but the aquifer transmissivities are inadequate for well development because of the thinness of the aquifer. In such cases, a subsurface drain or horizontal well is placed in permeable alluvial material and water is collected in a sump connected to a pump. Significant amounts of water can often be extracted through infiltration galleries because of high hydraulic conductivity of alluvial material and their proximity to a recharge source, such as a stream.

Infiltration galleries can either be constructed under the streambed or adjacent to the stream or surface water body. The yield from infiltration galleries beneath a water body is normally twice the yield from galleries adjacent to the water body. However, constructing infiltration galleries is usually more difficult under a water body. Infiltration galleries below a water body tend to have higher turbidity and higher bacteria count because of less extensive filtration. Where such withdrawals are considered to directly affect the quantity or quality of surface flows, many of the considerations presented for direct surface water withdrawals will need to be followed, including meeting Surface Water Treatment Rule requirements. This water would likely require filtration, which increases the cost of infiltration galleries.

AQUIFER STORAGE AND RECOVERY WELLS

Aquifer storage and recovery (ASR) wells are wells that can inject water into and extract water from the aquifer. The same well is generally used for both injection and extraction, hence the term aquifer storage and recovery. This concept of dual-purpose wells resolves well plugging, an inherent limitation of injection wells. In the ASR setting, the pump used for extraction is also periodically used to redevelop the well, thus maintaining its capacity.

ASR wells are not water sources per se; they are tools available in some areas to allow water managers to improve the management of their water supplies. The benefit of ASR wells is that where the geology is favorable, the ASR wells can improve water basin management by storing water underground from periods of excess supply (flood season or wet hydrologic periods), and later allowing a portion of the stored water to be extracted during periods of demand or short supply (such as irrigation season or dry hydrologic periods). There is no evaporation in the aquifer, as would be the case in a surface reservoir, and in some ASR wells, the recovery is very high. Therefore, ASR wells can be a cost-effective means of aquifer recharge because of increasing land prices. Local conditions dictate success of the ASR concept. There are other benefits of ASR wells including storage for emergencies; reduction of disinfection by-products, reduction of the potential for land subsidence and saltwater intrusion; reduction in pumping costs resulting from a higher water table; and opportunities for conjunctive use of surface water and groundwater.

Because ASR wells have certain unique design and construction features that differ from single purpose wells, special skills may be required. Using professionals that have an understanding of the concept of injection wells and ASR technology is required to ensure that utility dollars are not misspent. AWWA and others have published books on the subject, however the number of publications is limited (but growing). An ASR program requires several steps. These include a preliminary understanding of the underground formations, including transmissivity, thickness and confinement, and water quality and formation type.

Successful use of the ASR process requires an aquifer that has a significant amount of storage capacity in the interstitial spaces between the sand and gravel particles. It also requires that there be sufficient transmissivity to allow the water injected into the formation to move away from the injection wells at a sufficient pace to continue to be injected, but not too much transmissivity as the water will tend to migrate away from the well. Where the formation has the appropriate transmissivity, the aquifer should be productive enough to permit extraction of the injected water by the same facilities that treated it. A test program should include permanent monitoring wells and logging of information.

Understanding the formation is important to predict interaction between the formation and native water, and the injected water. A variety of geochemical issues arise with the interaction of ground and surface waters (to be discussed later in this chapter). One major issue is that calcium carbonate precipitates can significantly reduce the capacity of the aquifer to accept the treated water. As a result, water stability and mixing models must be employed to ensure that the surface water mixing with the groundwater does not reduce the aquifer's transmissivity. In addition, in formations with a lot of pyrite, arsenic leaching is likely to be a problem.

Water rights must be dealt with to ensure that the facility that places the treated water in storage is able to pump that water at a later date. Most states now have a system of water rights that allows this to occur, but the necessary permits must be secured. A few states still use the right of capture to control groundwater, and in these states, anyone can pump the stored water without penalty, if they can show a need for it.

From a management perspective, a benefit of ASR wells is the ability to optimize treatment plants. The necessity to have significant infrastructure that sees limited maximum day usage is not cost effective. ASR can be a way to shave peaks, thereby reducing capital investment, the surface water must be captured in a short time during high flow situations. This demonstrates that ASR projects are not water sources because they must rely on some combination of water treatment plant capacity and temporary storage to accomplish their mission.

In addition to the water treatment plant infrastructure issues, the evaluation of ASR projects should consider the costs for installation and operation of the necessary piping to convey treated water to the injection wells, for the injection well pumps themselves, and for the production wells to return the recovered water back to the point of use. Because all of the water to be pumped is of potable quality, the transmission lines can carry both the water to be injected and the water to be recovered, in the associated, opposite directions.

Finally, many locales do not have the appropriate geology to use ASR wells successfully. Therefore, while a potentially useful tool, ASR should not be viewed as a panacea to solve all water supply problems for a utility.

Systematic Development of Groundwater

As mentioned earlier, some level of groundwater development normally takes place when needed before regulatory controls are imposed or planned development of groundwater is undertaken. The systematic development of groundwater as an alternative source of water supply can be thought of as a three-step process: (1) exploration, (2) quantification, and (3) sustainable development within the constraints of safe yield.

Groundwater Exploration

In the groundwater exploration phase, the primary activities are as follows:

- Identify potential water-bearing formations (i.e., aquifers).

- Determine the nature and origin of geologic deposits and geologic structures (alluvial deposits, quaternary deposits, fractured rocks, solution rocks, etc.).

- Identify recharge and discharge areas, as well as their extents.

- Locate static water level in each permeable layer of the underground aquifer.

- Identify groundwater flow directions.

- Determine the nature of groundwater occurrence (i.e., confined or unconfined aquifer).

- Drill test holes and sample representative penetrated formations.

- Sample representative water to determine water quality at each layer.

Groundwater exploration enables a resource planner to answer the following questions:

- Where (horizontally and vertically) is the groundwater?

- Which geologic formations contain groundwater?

- How deep is the groundwater level?

- How good is the groundwater quality?

The following investigative techniques are most commonly used for groundwater exploration:

- Hydrogeologic maps and reports compiled by federal, state, and local agencies

- Geophysical/geological reasoning

- Test hole drilling

- Geophysical/geological surveys

- Step-drawdown tests

- Geophysical logging

- Chemical analyses and geochemical classification

Groundwater Qualification

In the groundwater quantification and basin characterization phase, the primary activities are as follows:

- Identify groundwater basin boundaries, such as groundwater divides.

- Generally determine groundwater inflows into an aquifer, and determine recharge from rain, streamflows, subsurface inflows, seepage from surface reservoirs, irrigation applied water, and artificial recharge ponds.

- Generally determine groundwater outflows from the aquifer, such as natural outflows through springs, seepage into streams and lakes, and phreatophytic evapotranspiration, pumping by wells, and drainage through tile drains.

- Generally determine overall groundwater budget (inflow − outflow = change in storage) and average annual replenishment.

- Determine aquifer characteristics, such as homogeneity/heterogeneity; isotropy/anisotropy; preferential flow paths; hydraulic conductivity; porosity; storage coefficients; and transmissivity.

- Determine specific capacities of wells at various locations.

- Determine hydrogeologic characteristics of the unsaturated zone above the water table.

- Characterize water quality distribution in the aquifer and in the overlying land surface.

- Conceptually model groundwater basin.

Quantifying groundwater enables a resource planner to answer the following questions:

- How much water is coming into or leaving the aquifer?

- What are the depths and thicknesses of water-bearing formations?

- How much water is stored in each layer and how do layers interact?

- How fast is water moving naturally and how fast is a contaminant plume likely to move in the aquifer environment?

- How much drawdown will occur per unit volume of water extraction?

- What is the water quality of under-groundwater, and how may it be affected by groundwater pumping and overlaying land use practices?

- How is the aquifer likely to behave under various groundwater pumping and management scenarios?

- What is the potential for artificial recharge?

The following investigative techniques are most commonly used for groundwater quantification:

- Analyze hydrologic data for water budget (rainfall, streamflow, subsurface flows, boundary conditions, spring flows, land use, water use, irrigation-applied water, evapotranspiration).

- Correlate and integrate various sources of data, such as water-level maps, well hydrographs, geologic maps, well logs, geophysical logs, driller's logs, geochemical analyses, river flow analyses at various gauging stations in the groundwater basin, pumping tests, observations at monitoring wells, isotope methods, and observations from test holes.

- Conceptually model groundwater basin using standard modeling approach (see chapter 8).

Sustainable Groundwater Development and Management

The primary purpose of this phase of groundwater development is to determine the maximum safe yield of a groundwater basin and develop management strategies to protect the aquifer from overexploitation. Safe yield refers to the annual amount of water that can be withdrawn from an aquifer without producing any undesirable result (hence the term *safe*). The undesirable result can take any of the following forms or any combination thereof:

- Withdrawal in excess of natural recharge

- Lowering of water table below certain limits

- Interference with the groundwater rights of others

- Intrusion from saline or other low water quality areas

- Reduction of base flow to streams and other wetland impacts

- Degradation of groundwater quality

Most commonly, safe yield is considered as the average annual natural inflow to a groundwater basin on the basis of data from 30 to 40 years of hydrologic record. Because conditions change, a single value of safe yield is not a reliable measure. Any quantification is based on certain specified conditions or data assumptions. Any change, such as a change in pumping pattern, may change recharge. Changes in land use or urbanization can also cause a change in recharge and thus affect the *safe yield*.

The primary activities under a sustainable groundwater development and management phase are as follows:

- Specific computation of a hydrologic budget of each component of the groundwater basin

- Determination of safe yield

- Specific computation of interaction with stream flows and agricultural irrigation

- Specific computation of changes in flow patterns caused by well pumping

- Evaluation of land subsidence

- Determination of pumping lifts and costs of pumping

- Evaluation of legal (water rights), jurisdictional, and administrative constraints

- Development and calibration of mathematical models

- Evaluation of groundwater conditions under various alternative development scenarios

- Quantification of artificial recharge potential

- Evaluation of conjunctive use opportunities

- Evaluation of the impact of pumping on groundwater quality

- Determination of saltwater or poor-quality water intrusion from the neighboring water environment

- Determination of the potential for modifying the natural regimen of streamflow

- Monitoring groundwater wells for water levels and water quality

Groundwater management planning enables a resource planner to evaluate the following questions:

- How much water is entering and leaving the aquifer from each specific source (such as rainfall, streamflow, subsurface flow)?

- What are the response characteristics of the groundwater aquifer?

- What is the safe yield of the basin? What is the maximum amount of long-term sustainable pumping?

- What are the regional, as well as local, groundwater flow regimes and how are they affected under various alternative water development scenarios?

- What are the relationships between the streams and the aquifers and how they may change in the future?

- What is the relationship between land subsidence and pumping in the aquifer?

- What are the impacts on pumping costs caused by the lowering of groundwater levels by pumping?

- What water quality impacts have resulted from groundwater development?

- How may the aquifer recharge characteristics change because of over-pumping or artificial recharge?

- How does groundwater development interfere with other environmental parameters and constraints?

- How does groundwater development interfere with other regulatory constraints (such as water rights in aquifers and in surface streams that recharge the aquifers)?

The following investigative techniques are most commonly used for sustainable groundwater development and management:

- Develop and calibrate mathematical models for groundwater flow and water quality.

- Perform alternative analyses using mathematical models.

- Develop monitoring network for flow and water quality.

- Perform geohydrologic investigations combined with additional data collection programs.

- Conduct pump tests and geologic logging to determine the aquifer properties.

- Conduct economic analyses of alternatives for groundwater development and various management strategies.

- Optimize models.

CONJUNCTIVE USE OF GROUNDWATER AND SURFACE WELLS

The amount of surface water use for municipal and industrial purposes is generally restricted to water that still is available during a 100-year drought ensuring that water is present in ongoing years for such needs. In the same way, many aquifers are managed to produce only the amount of groundwater that is replenished annually. In this way, the resources are not depleted and the water needed is available every year. However, demands are continuing to grow while the potential sites for new surface water sources in the US are dwindling. At the same time, the potential sites that remain face ever-increasing environmental scrutiny with greatly increased costs and environmental mitigation needed, if they are to be developed.

As a result of all of the above factors, utilities are trying to maximize the use of all sources available to them. In the same way that operation of multiple reservoirs as a system produces a yield in excess of the firm yield of the individual components, conjunctive use of groundwater and surface water sources can maximize the yield of both under certain circumstances. In addition, at least in the case of confined aquifers, there is often a lesser effect of dry weather conditions on the aquifer because of the time lag and the relatively slow travel of water in a confined aquifer. Rainfall on the surface of the ground that actually infiltrates into the aquifer is often only a few inches per year. This is primarily caused by saturation of the aquifer outcrop during rainfall events. Once the pores of the aquifer outcrop (recharge area) are saturated, then the remainder of the rainfall runs off and appears as surface water. During dry weather conditions, what little rainfall does occur has a greater tendency to move directly into the aquifer, with the result that the ground water source is less affected by the dry weather than the surface water source. Where this is the case, over pumping of the groundwater during 100 year drought conditions may not cause significant reductions in the groundwater table as the shortages are made up in wetter years through the exclusive, or nearly exclusive, use of surface water instead.

Given the above background, there are a number of specific instances in which conjunctive groundwater and surface water use can expand the water supply available, or provide additional firm yield to a system that is utilizing water that is less then 100 percent reliable from one or another source. The first of these examples, Scenario 1 concerns water quantity. If an existing surface water right is less than the dry weather demand of the system, and if groundwater is available, then the groundwater can be used in the system to make up the difference needed. The preferred method of introducing groundwater into the system would be through mixing water from properly constructed groundwater water wells, which are capable of producing potable quality water, with treated surface water in existing storage facilities. This mixing is oftentimes needed to avoid taste and odors problems that might occur from mixing dissimilar waters. Mixing in a storage facility provides the necessary detention time for reactions to occur, and precipitates, if any, to settle out prior to being distributed to the systems' customers. Ideally, this mixing would occur at the site of the surface water treatment plant finished water storage to ensure uniformity of water quality in the distribution system. But these waters could also be mixed in distribution system storage tanks as well and still be adequate to reduce unwanted effects of mixing. The key element that would favor mixing at the point of the distribution storage tanks would be avoiding the cost of infrastructure to convey the groundwater to the treatment plant location.

Issues that must be considered for this application include the blending issues noted above, as well as the cost of the groundwater infrastructure and the limited amount of time that it would be used. The wells would have to be exercised on a regular basis, and the water either pumped to waste, used for irrigation, or if possible, blended into the system on a regular basis to provide more uniform water. In addition, the volumes of water needed may require spacing of the wells such that a considerable investment must be made in additional infrastructure to convey the groundwater to the desired mixing points.

A second instance of beneficial application of conjunctive use of surface and groundwater sources, Scenario 2, is the augmentation of an existing surface water supply source with groundwater of lesser quality if the blended product has a quality meeting current state and federal water quality regulations under the Safe Drinking Water Act. An example of this would be surface water with low amounts of arsenic that could be blended with a groundwater that has arsenic above the current limit. This type of conjunctive use requires additional controls on the output of the storage facilities where the blending occurs to ensure that the levels of contaminants are not exceeded. When the concentrations of the various contaminants vary in the surface water then the blending must be amended to increase or decrease the percentage of groundwater used to ensure meeting the necessary limitations. The ability to control the output of the groundwater source is critical to success in achieving the necessary water quality levels.

Issues that must be considered for this application include the same issues as noted in the first application, with the additional concern that there may be less usability of the water for irrigation. In addition, with lower demand, it may be more difficult to properly balance the constituent levels in the tank with smaller volumes of use.

A third common example of conjunctive use, Scenario 3, is the production of groundwater from less than potable quality wells, such as irrigation wells, infiltration galleries, or other groundwater sources that do not provide sufficient protection to the quality of the water to allow direct mixing with the treated surface water. In this instance, the groundwater is mixed with raw surface water prior to the treatment processes. This scenario has the advantage of being able to use wells that are less expensive to construct, and in some cases even existing wells that have adequate source water protection but are not constructed to potable water standards can be used to further reduce the expense. It also provides a more uniform water quality by treating all water with the same treatment processes. While the preferred arrangement is to have all of the needed groundwater enter into the system at the presedimentation facilities or storage ponds prior to the treatment process, the spacing of wells to avoid interference of draw down generally prevents this optimum arrangement from being feasible. Wells are often drilled along the sides of canals or other conveyance facilities, or discharge directly into raw water supply reservoirs.

In addition to the advantages and disadvantages noted above for the scenarios discussed so far, this third scenario has some potential environmental disadvantages and a potential for increased losses of groundwater as possible consequences. Most groundwaters are devoid of oxygen and must be introduced into natural water with either sufficient mixing to avoid dead zones around the mixing point, or oxygen must be added to the groundwater prior to mixing. If groundwater is added to the presedimentation basin or the storage ponds at the water treatment plant site, these concerns do not apply. If it is introduced to the natural environment, however, these issues must be addressed. Addition of oxygen to the water is conveniently done by causing turbulence of the water through weirs or dams that cause the water to tumble or splash and introduce oxygen from the atmosphere. The drawback is that the groundwater is being used under dry weather conditions and significant losses can occur through evaporation to the atmosphere or to percolation into the underflow of nearby streams or rivers. In excess of 20 percent of the original water produced may be lost using this technique, through evaporation and streamflow losses.

A fourth scenario for conjunctive use is through the storage of treated surface water in an aquifer for use during times of limited surface water availability—the concept of aquifer storage and recovery discussed previously.

To this point, all of the instances above have involved conjunctive use that is for direct consumption purposes. There is a final scenario to be discussed that is more indirect, but which still involves the use of multiple sources of supply. An example of such a process is the original Water Factory 21 in California. This project used wastewater treatment plant effluent and stormwater to recharge aquifers along the Pacific coast in Orange County, Calif. The water that was injected into the aquifer served initially as a barrier to salt-water intrusion that occurs in coastal areas as the fresh water is withdrawn from the aquifer to serve the needs of the population (as salt-water intrusion progresses inland, additional mixing with the fresh water supplies causes more and more water to be too salty to use). The injected water was used to stabilize the salt-water intrusion and create an additional water supply to meet the needs of the area as the demands continue to grow. To a lesser extent, each instance of a system using groundwater that converts some of their irrigation demand to be satisfied by wastewater treatment plant effluent represents a conjunctive use of different sources of water.

IDENTIFICATION OF TIMING AND MAGNITUDE OF NEW SOURCE DEVELOPMENT

Yield and Demand Forecasts

As discussed in chapter 3, demand forecasts are prepared to identify anticipated growth trends for potable water supply needs. These forecasts typically incorporate residential, commercial, and industrial potable water supply uses, and conservation and efficiency benefits.

To establish the need for additional sources of supply, reliable diversion rates must be established from water supply sources (safe yield) contributing to the water supply system. Most simply, safe yield is defined as the reliable withdrawal rate of acceptable quality water that can be supplied by available flows and/or storage releases from reservoirs and/or groundwater reserves throughout a critical drought period. Detailed discussion of hydrologic modeling for yield analyses is presented in chapter 8.

Surplus/Deficit Projections

The yield of a water system combined with demand forecasts identifying a reasonable range of future needs provides the basis for evaluating actions that will need to be considered over the planning period. Supplies are generally considered to be reasonably constant over time but may decline because of source degradation, reservoir siltation, changes in permit requirements, and other factors. The relationship between available supplies and projected demand levels defines the estimated time of onset of supply deficiency (e.g., from the year 2002 to 2005) and the extent of the projected deficit over the planning period (e.g., from about 8 to 15 mgd [0.03-0.06 m^3/d]). The level of defensibility of this relationship provides the basic justification for developing new sources of supply.

Factors Affecting Project Development

Several factors will affect decisions related to project size for expanding or adding a new source of supply. Typical factors include

- sources of capital and financing options
- regulatory issues (water allocations, 404 permitting, mitigation needs, etc.)
- competition for water allocations (if not spoken for now, will it be there later?)
- anticipated extent of additional growth beyond the planning period
- opportunities for staged (or incremental) project development
- technical, environmental, and economic size limits of some projects (especially reservoirs)
- rate impacts on customers

Each factor needs to be considered in the context of the water resources alternatives available for development. Short-listing and project selection can be a complex process that needs to give careful consideration such as

- environmental impacts
- capital and operations costs
- development step size
- water quality and contamination potential
- permitting concerns, constraints, and limits
- political issues and other local factors

Step Size Considerations

New source projects that will likely require extensive project development time and cost, and that cannot readily be phased in small increments, should be sized to provide about a 15- to 25-year deferment in the anticipated onset of a supply deficit. However, opportunities and constraints are unique to each situation and locale, so special circumstances may dictate a longer or a shorter time step for project development.

Investigations, planning, environmental studies, permitting, and other activities required for developing a new source of supply can be rigorous, time consuming, and costly endeavors that water utilities will not want to repeat often to accommodate stepped expansion of their water systems. Additionally, over the past several decades, permitting requirements have shown a clear trend toward being more rigorous and demanding, in terms of both time and cost. This trend should continue for the foreseeable future. Therefore, when the following four conditions are present, a longer term solution should be pursued:

1. Project permitting will be rigorous, costly, and time consuming.

2. Continued long-term growth beyond the planning period can be demonstrated.

3. An environmentally, technically, and economically viable large-yield project alternative (greater than or equal to the planning period shortfall) has been identified.

4. Financial resources are sufficient to accommodate a larger project step size.

In some cases, staged development can be a cost-effective and financially desirable means of meeting growing demand. Small increments of additional supply, such as incrementally developing wells in a well field, should be brought on line when economical. This prudent approach allows capital costs to be deferred to match the growing revenue stream. If a major, staged construction project is considered, permits should be obtained if possible for the entire project before the first stage of construction. When the initial phase of water supply development is shown to be economically attractive by itself, a greater level of risk related to permitting of subsequent phases can more readily be accommodated. However, permits and allocations for the ultimate level of project development should be obtained when possible.

In general, permits for reservoir projects that allow a later expansion date without triggering a new round of permitting activities are not allowed. Therefore, reservoir projects should be developed to their ultimate storage capacity in a single phase when economically feasible. Developing a reservoir project to accommodate the later addition of pumped diversions from an outside source will generally merit the construction of a larger and more costly reservoir than would be justified on the basis of natural recharge alone. In these cases, the added costs for a larger reservoir (beyond its economically viable size for on-stream use) will be at risk unless permits and diversion allocations for both the reservoir and the future diversion source are obtained before the reservoir is initially constructed.

Many individualized negotiations will likely need to be undertaken, and mitigation for the entire project may need to be included in the initial implementation phase. Jurisdictional differences preclude the development of a fully systematic approach that can be applied independent of the locale of the project.

REFERENCES

American Water Works Association (2002), *Survey and Analysis of Aquifer Storage and Recovery (ASR) Systems and Associated Regulatory Programs in the United States*, AWWA, Denver, CO.

American Water Works Association (2002), Manual M21–*Groundwater*, Denver, Colo.: American Water Works Association.

US Department of Interior. 1981. *Groundwater Manual*, Government Publications.

This page intentionally blank

Chapter **6**

Evaluation of Other Sources

In addition to the conventional sources of water described in the previous chapter, other sources should be evaluated. One of the most important steps in planning a new water supply is identifying and evaluating all possible sources.

- Conservation

- Reclaimed water

- Desalination

- Water marketing and transfers

This chapter provides guidance on evaluating these sources, including the cost of water supply, and issues specific to the source type.

CONSERVATION

Conservation may be viewed as a supplemental or even an alternative technology for meeting safe drinking water needs. Conservation should be implemented as part of a long-term strategy for providing safe and reliable drinking water. One of the chief purposes of conservation is to avoid, postpone, or reduce capital costs associated with new facilities. (*USEPA Water Conservation Planning Guidelines*).

Water conservation reduces demand for water through improvements in efficiency and diminishing water waste. A carefully planned and implemented long-term water conservation program can reduce water consumption 10–20 percent over 10–20 years. (*Journal AWWA*, November 1996). In addition, when droughts occur, short-term demand reduction measures—typically rationing, water use restrictions, and restrictive pricing schemes—can be implemented in addition to public information campaigns to achieve further reductions in water use.

Just as temporary supply shortages create a need for demand reduction, permanent shortages foreseen in water demand forecasts can be partially tempered through water conservation. Integrating long-term conservation with water supply planning involves the following basic steps:

- Forecasting water demand at the customer class level
- Identifying nonstructural alternatives, such as
    — Conservation
    — Reclamation
    — Exchanges-transfers
    — Compare costs and benefits with new supply cost
    — Seek balanced solution

The development of a detailed water use forecast is discussed in chapter 3. The balanced approach using economic feasibility and cost-effectiveness analysis to evaluate source alternatives, including conservation, is discussed in chapter 12. The following discussion highlights considerations for assessing and building long-term strategies and short-term contingencies during serious supply shortage into viable programs to meet water supply needs.

Long-Term Water Conservation Planning

The goal of long-term water conservation is simple-save water. The objective is to optimize demand management while acquiring additional water supply to increase overall system reliability. Numerous advantages exist in pursuing demand management alternatives. The two basic disadvantages—lower revenues and concerns over drought conditions—can be addressed through preventive measures, such as periodic rate adjustments and development of a drought contingency plan as described under the Short-Term Demand Reduction Planning section.

Advantages of Demand Management

The primary advantage to long-term water conservation is the quantifiable benefits to water utilities and equally important benefits to the local community and the environment. An overview of these categorized benefits is presented in Table 6-1. For additional details, see AWWA Manual M52, *Water Conservation Programs—A Planning Manual* (AWWA 2005).

Current and planned water systems are affected by reduced consumption in a variety of ways. Case studies for quantifying the effects of conservation on eight water utilities and one wastewater utility are developed in *Impacts of Demand Reduction on Water Utilities* (AwwaRF, 1996). The report assesses the impacts of conservation from the perspective of source of water type: surface water, groundwater, both, or purchased water. Further description of advantageous effects from conservation on water or wastewater utility system costs, operations, and design criteria is provided in the following paragraphs. For more detailed information on the energy cost savings for water and wastewater utilities, refer to *Energy Audit Manual for Water/Wastewater Systems* (EPRI, CEC, and AwwaRF, 1994). Guidelines for the actual implementation of energy audit recommendations are provided in the *Quality Energy Retrofits for Water Systems* (EPRI, CEC, and AwwaRF, 1997) and the *Quality Energy Efficiency Retrofits for Wastewater Systems* (EPRI, CEC, and AwwaRF, 1998).

Table 6–1   Overview of benefits

Recipient of Benefit	Type of Benefit	Description
Water utility	Supply system O&M	Short-term and long-term O&M costs reduced due to lower energy expenses because of less pumping and chemical use in water treatment and disposal.
Water utility	Supply system capital investment	Capital facilities can be deferred or downsized.
Water utility	System reliability	Less water purchased from wholesale water purveyors and more reliability of supply yield depending on capacity availability.
Wastewater utility	System O&M	Short-term and long-term O&M costs reduced due to lower energy expenses because of less volume pumping, aeration, and chemical use in wastewater treatment.
Wastewater utility	Disposal system capital investment	Capital facilities for land disposal can be deferred or downsized.
Environment	Quality enhancement	Decreased need for dams and reduced construction disturbance in natural waterways.
Environment	Quality enhancement	Higher in-stream flows for fish and wildlife habitat and lower withdrawals from supply sources.
Environment	Quality enhancement	Lower discharges of treated wastewater to receiving waters.
Environment	Quality enhancement	Reduced pollution due to less construction of capital facilities.
Community	Aesthetic quality	Diminished aesthetic effects on waterways from avoided capital projects.
Community	Environmental justice	Less social equity issues with facility siting concerns.
Community	Economic	Increased economy on the same resource, creation of water conservation jobs, and customer savings in utility bills.
Community	Economic/political	Fiscal savings from avoided or delayed new capital expenditures or bond indebtedness.

Water system operating costs. Water conservation reduces the volume of supply water, which in turn lowers pumping energy expended to acquire, treat, and distribute water. In addition, the volumes of chemicals used in water treatment that are dosed on a flow basis, such as chlorine, are reduced. Reductions in pumping energy and treatment chemicals directly lower O&M expenses. Estimated energy use to deliver various sources of water and significance in total O&M costs is presented in Table 6-2.

Water system design criteria. Water conservation can affect the design parameters of new water facilities. The opportunity to downsize or postpone expansions for facilities can only occur if the design of the facility is dependent on

Table 6–2   Energy used to deliver water

Type of Water	Energy Use, KW•h/1,000 gal	Electricity as Percent of Total O&M	Electricity as Percent of Total Cost
Groundwater	1.2	18	7
Surface water	0.7	11	4
Purchased water	0.6	4	3

Source: Water Industry DataBase, AWWA, 1991.

Table 6–3   How water system elements are affected by consumption

System Element	Design Criteria Based on			
	Average Day	Peak Day	Peak Hour	Fire Flow
Source water acquisition	✓			
Raw water storage	✓			
Water pipelines			✓	✓
Water treatment plants		✓		
Pumping stations			✓	✓
Treated water storage		✓		✓

Source: Maddaus, W., *Estimating Benefits from Water Conservation*, 1999.

water flows. Table 6-3 illustrates typical design criteria for water facilities that may be affected by reduced consumption.

Facilities based on average day flow or peak day flow design criteria may achieve significant capital investment savings. Reduction in average day affects how much water must be developed, or imported and stored, prior to treatment and use. Reduction in peak day demand affects the sizing and timing of water treatment plant expansions and treated water storage. Water pipelines and pumping stations are affected by peak hour pumping volumes. Peak hour is dependent on customer peak hour demands plus required fire flows. Water conservation will reduce customer peak hour demands. However, water conservation will have a relatively insignificant effect on the size of facilities based on fire flow design criteria. Fire flows are determined by the type of land use to be protected and therefore design criteria and the influence from water conservation efforts will vary based on local conditions.

Wastewater system operations.   Wastewater systems, similar to water systems, have O&M benefits in lower energy and chemical use from conservation. While the majority of wastewater collection systems are designed to flow by gravity, volume reductions from water conservation do lower pumping energy required in force mains, to lift the wastewater into treatment plants and to process the waste. Additionally, part of the energy use at treatment plants is dependent on flow; however, most of the energy is used for waste aeration or biological treatment. Disposal usually involves pumping and discharge fees of treated wastewater to receiving waters or to land disposal sites, and these costs may be reduced if dependent on flow volume. Each system is different and ascertaining the savings is calculated on a case-by-case basis. Wastewater is chlorinated at least once during the treatment process and sometimes dechlorinated. Use of these chemicals is flow-dependent.

Table 6–4   How wastewater system elements are affected by conservation

| System Element | Design Criteria Based on | | |
	Average Dry Weather Flow	Peak Wet Weather Flow	Solids Loading
Collection systems		✓	
Interceptors		✓	
Treatment plants		✓	✓
Disposal to receiving water		✓	
Land disposal	✓	✓	

Source: Maddaus, W., *Estimating Benefits from Water Conservation*, 1999.

Wastewater system design criteria.   The impacts of conservation (wastewater flow reduction) on design of new facilities are illustrated in Table 6-4. Design criteria for land disposal systems are volume-dependent. Most facilities are based on peak wet weather flow, which can benefit predominately from infiltration/inflow control programs, but remain relatively unaffected by conservation program water savings.

Target Largest Water Use Sectors and Categories of Use

An essential part of planning a conservation program is to take inventory of the types of customers, how many customers of each type, and review their associated water use patterns. The inventory can range in detail from a full-scale water audit to querying metered water consumption. Each community will have a different mix of customer types, which are commonly divided into four sectors: residential, commercial, industrial, and institutional. Within each sector, there are numerous subtypes; for example, schools are one subtype in the institutional sector.

To achieve desired conservation levels from a program, the selection of conservation measures should be based on the larger use sectors and categories while taking into account the ability to implement the measures and acceptability by customers. For example, the residential sector may be the largest use sector in the community, and literature suggests that toilet flushing is the largest category of use in the home. This may lead to the planning and implementation of a low-flush toilet installation program through rebates or direct install based on customers' acceptability. The following discussion provides some background information to assist in the ranking of conservation potential.

Once an inventory has been taken of the types of customers in the community, a review of the key categories of use (e.g., toilet flushing, cooling towers, laundry) for each sector is useful in identifying areas of maximum achievable water savings. Two important studies sponsored by the American Water Works Association Research Foundation (AwwaRF) provide some insight into the end uses of water by different customer types: *Residential End Uses of Water* (AwwaRF, 1999) and *Commercial and Institutional End Uses of Water* (AwwaRF, 2000). Conservation measures usually target one of the end uses of water.

Key Findings from AwwaRF Study: Residential End Uses of Water

Using 1,188 study homes in 12 different study areas mostly located in the western United States, the total average measured water use was 171.8 gallons per capita per day (gpcd [0.65 m^3 pcd]). The breakdown into subcategories of indoor uses is presented in Figure 6-1. The indoor use ranged between 57.1 and 83.5 gpcd (0.21 and 0.32 m^3 pcd) with a mean value of 69.3 gpcd (0.26 m^3 pcd).

The total outdoor use at a mean value of 100.8 gpcd (0.38 m^3) was approximated across the 12 study sites. Outdoor water use is derived by subtracting the average winter consumption (1- to 3-month average) from metered water consumption. In the Residential End Uses study, the outdoor use estimates were developed from historic metered billing data and data-logged indoor usage data for each of the households. Note that different climatic conditions that exist within different communities will result in variations in higher or lower per capita water use estimates. The outdoor use estimates presented in the Residential End Uses study were weather normalized.

The relative percentages of each category of indoor use are presented in Figure 6-2. From the results of the Residential End Uses study, fixtures with the highest average percentage of indoor water use are toilets (26.7 percent), clothes washers (21.7 percent), showers (16.8 percent), faucets (15.7 percent), and leakage (13.7 percent). These fixtures account for more than 90 percent of the water use inside homes. Note that 13.7 percent of average indoor use represents leakage; however, in the 100 data-logged homes with the highest average daily indoor water use, leaks accounted for 24.5 percent of average daily use.

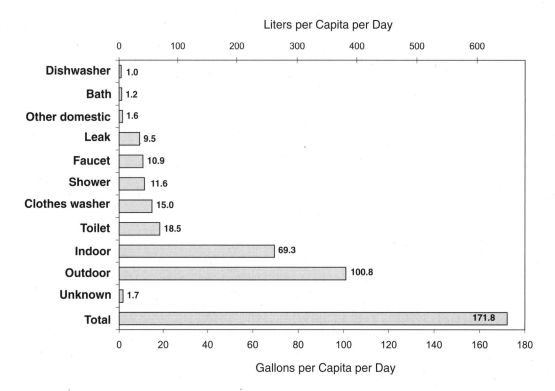

Source: Residential End Uses of Water, *AwwaRF, 1999.*

Figure 6–1   Mean daily per capita water use, 12 study sites

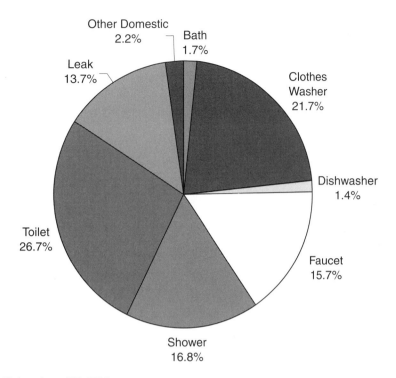

Source: Residential End Uses of Water, *AwwaRF, 1999.*

Figure 6–2   Indoor per capita use percent by fixture, 12 study sites

Key Findings from AwwaRF Study: Commercial and Institutional Uses of Water

Potential water savings in the commercial and institutional (CI) sector range between 15 and 35 percent (AwwaRF, 2000). In addition, many users do not need potable water for all their uses, and water use can be considered for on-site recycling or reclaimed effluent use from the wastewater utility. Conservation implemented in the CI sector can be cost-effective where conservation measures tend to have low payback periods of one to four years. Cooperation between different water, wastewater, and energy agencies can determine optimal demand management practices and allow for combined financial incentive packages (i.e., joint rebates) for CI customers.

Water use is highly variable even among similar types of CI customers. Within the CI sector, benchmarks for average daily use per account are infeasible because of the high variability among different user types and timing of use issues that make average values unreliable estimates of water use. Generally, each facility should be evaluated on an individual basis to determine its specific water conservation potential. However, during the conservation program design phase, useful information is gained from the study of CI customer types, and further investigation into a standardized classification practice and meaningful benchmarks is necessary.

Initially, in the AwwaRF CI *End Uses* study, eleven types of use were studied based on analysis of five water providers located in the southwestern United States. The eleven categories include

- urban irrigation

- schools/colleges
- hotels/motels
- laundries/laundromats
- office buildings
- hospitals/medical offices
- restaurants
- food stores
- auto shops
- membership organizations
- car washes

The results from a study of historical billing data for the eleven categories are presented in Table 6-5.

Further analysis, including field studies of 25 CI facilities, audits of data, and models of audited data, was performed for a subset of five categories exhibiting the types of highest users, which included schools, hotels/motels, office buildings, restaurants, and food stores. The AwwaRF CI *End Uses* study has additional descriptions of data analysis, assumptions, and results associated with assessing water conservation in the CI sector. Efficiency benchmarks developed from the field studies, audit data, and modeling results for schools are illustrated in Table 6-6.

Table 6–5   Characteristics of significant CI categories in five participating agencies

Customer Category Description	Average Annual Daily Use (gpcd)	Coefficient of Variation in Daily Use (gpcd)[*]	Percent of Total CI Use (%)	Percent of CI Customers (%)[†]	Percent Seasonal Use (%)[‡]	Scaled Average Daily Use (gpcd)[§]
Urban irrigation	2,596	8.73	28.48	30.22	86.90	739.0
Schools and colleges	2,117	12.13	8.84	4.79	57.99	187.0
Hotels and motels	7,113	5.41	5.82	1.92	23.07	414.0
Laundries/laundromats	3,290	8.85	3.95	1.38	13.35	130.0
Office buildings	1,204	6.29	10.19	11.67	29.04	123.0
Hospitals/medical offices	1,236	78.50	3.90	4.19	23.16	48.0
Restaurants	906	7.69	8.83	11.18	16.13	80.0
Food stores	729	16.29	2.86	5.20	19.37	21.0
Auto shops	687	7.96	1.97	6.74	27.16	14.0
Membership organizations	629	6.42	1.95	5.60	46.18	12.0
Car washes	3,031	3.12	0.82	0.36	14.22	25.0

*The ratio of standard deviation of daily use to average of daily use.
†CI customers in sites that have respective category only.
‡12 × minimum month use = total annual use.
§Average annual daily use in category × percent of total CI use attributed to the category.

Source: Commercial and Institutional End Uses of Water, AwwaRF, 2000.

Table 6–6   Efficiency benchmarks for schools

End Use/Benchmark Measure	N	Efficiency Benchmark Range[*]
INDOOR USE		
Gal/ft^2/year	142	8–16
Gal/school day/student	141	3–15
COOLING USE[†]		
Gal/ft^2/year	35	8–20
IRRIGATION USE[†]		
Inches per year	132	22–50
TOTAL WATER USE[†]		
Gal/ft^2/year	142	40–93

[*]Developed from combined methods (field studies, audit data, and modeling results.
[†]Appropriate benchmarks will depend on local climate.

Source: Commercial and Institutional End Uses of Water, AwwaRF, 2000.

Assess the Benefits and Costs of a Conservation Program

An integral part of the water resources planning process is to determine the benefits and costs of a conservation program. The first step is to define the needs and goals of the program. In order to optimize water conservation planning with other water supply alternatives, it must be based on the same planning assumptions (e.g., consistent demographic data and planning timelines) involved in the overall water resources planning effort.

The goals of a comprehensive conservation program determined through a public participation process will tailor the program to local needs. Effective program implementation requires a written plan that sets forth the goals, objectives, policies, tasks, implementation schedule, assumptions, expected results, and recommendations.

The overall objective of a conservation program is to identify the conservation measures that are best for a specific utility and then project the potential water savings and costs of water saved through the forecast period. The following ten basic steps outline the activities undertaken in a water conservation planning effort to most accurately assess the associated benefits and costs.

Step 1.   Review detailed demand forecast.
Step 2.   Review existing water system profile and descriptions of planned facilities.
Step 3.   Review existing conservation measures.
Step 4.   Define conservation potential.
Step 5.   Identify conservation measures.
Step 6.   Determine feasible measures.
Step 7.   Perform benefit–cost evaluations.
Step 8.   Select conservation measures.
Step 9.   Combine overall estimated savings.
Step 10.   Optimize demand forecasts.

Step 1. Review demand forecast.   Analysis begins with a baseline forecast of the product of the water use analyses and the demographic (customer account or population) projections. The impacts of current and selected additional conservation measures can then be superimposed on the baseline forecast.

Step 2. Review existing water system profile and descriptions of planned water supply facilities.   With the water demand increase, utilities need to maintain information necessary to develop and update a system profile from an inventory of resources and conditions. A review of this information is essential for accurately targeting water conservation measures when appropriate needs emerge, for example reductions in peak day water use.

Step 3. Review existing conservation measures.   If conservation measures are present in the water use analyses (which is usually depicted by a declining weighted mean average in historical billing data), the degree of current and prospective conservation stemming from these measures needs to be quantified. Some of this effect could be naturally occurring if it results from the Energy Policy Act of 1992, which requires that replacement fixtures and fixtures in new construction are water efficient. A typical response for a utility's residential customer base from these "naturally occurring conservation measures" is about 0.5 percent per year until saturation of the methods occurs.

Step 4. Define conservation potential.   A detailed assessment of the indoor and outdoor water use for existing and new customers is essential to determine the conservation potential. Comparison of the water use profile with AwwaRF assists in identifying relatively high water use areas.

Step 5. Identify conservation measures.   Even though many water conservation measures are transferable among locations, water conservation measures should be tailored on a case-by-case basis to develop the most effective program for local conditions within a given service area.

General conservation methods and measures that can be targeted in a conservation program include the following:

- Customer education
- Restriction programs
- Irrigation efficiency audits
- New home Xeriscaping
- Large landscape irrigation audits
- Residential home water audits
- Large commercial programs
- Small commercial programs
- Exterior city building retrofits
- Interior city building retrofits
- Low-flush toilet replacements
- Commercial landscape ordinances
- Landscape retrofits
- A conservation rate structure

Numerous water agencies around the country, particularly in the arid states of the southwest, have been implementing water conservation programs for more than 20 years. In California, the California Urban Water Conservation Council currently has a memorandum of understanding with 160 signatory wholesale and retail water agencies to voluntarily implement and report on fourteen cost-effective best management practices (BMPs), which are:

BMP 1   Water survey programs for single family residential and multifamily residential customers
BMP 2   Residential plumbing retrofit
BMP 3   System water audits, leak detection, and repair
BMP 4   Metering with commodity rates for all new connections and retrofit of existing connections
BMP 5   Large landscape conservation programs and incentives
BMP 6   High-efficiency washing machine rebate programs
BMP 7   Public information programs
BMP 8   School education programs
BMP 9   Conservation programs for commercial, industrial, institutional accounts
BMP 10   Wholesale agency assistance programs
BMP 11   Conservation pricing
BMP 12   Conservation coordinator
BMP 13   Wastewater prohibition
BMP 14   Residential ultra-low-flush replacement programs

Step 6. Determine feasible measures. Not all conservation measures will be practically, politically, or economically feasible for a given utility. For example, drought-tolerant landscaping is not suitable for Fargo, N.D.; an inclining block rate structure is not suitable for an unmetered area or where there is strong customer resistance; and capital-intensive reclamation facilities will not provide an economic return in smaller communities. To complete the feasibility analysis, the number of accounts that could and would use each measure and the specific savings over time that would accrue must be determined. In addition, legislative or institutional obstacles to implementation must be researched.

Estimates of market penetration are based on measure design and experience from similar measures implemented by other water utilities. The key factors influencing market penetration are illustrated in Figure 6-3.

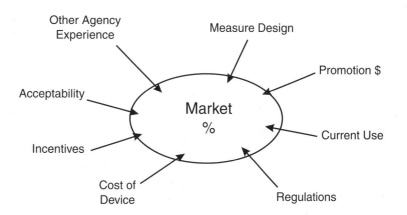

Source: Maddaus, W., *Estimating Benefits from Water Conservation*, 1999.

Figure 6–3   Determine market penetration

More than 100 individual conservation measures could be implemented among the residential, commercial, industrial, irrigation, agricultural, and public authority accounts in large metropolitan areas. The implementation of conservation programs usually includes a degree of education, sometimes financial assistance (toilet rebates), sometimes financial incentives (conservation rates), and sometimes legislation (ULFT replacements). Measures can be qualitatively screened to a short-list of the most promising measures. The short-listed measures can then be evaluated for water savings, benefits, and costs. Some of the more commonly implemented measures and associated unit water savings are presented in Table 6-7.

Step 7. Perform benefit–cost evaluations. If the water supply is at a critical level, the benefits of conservation are virtually priceless. Providing water for essential indoor residential and commercial needs is the most important concern. Under less extreme circumstances, however, it is necessary to conduct a basic benefit–cost analysis that relates the value of water saved to the cost of implementing the program over a useful program life. A basis for valuing conservation programs is through the benefits associated with the delay, downsizing, or averting of new facilities (Figure 6-4). Some communities engage in modest conservation efforts as part of public-spirited programs that link with ecological and environmental goals for a better world to live in. Benefits are often measured from the consumer's point of view, usually in terms of less water consumption to pay for and less energy cost for heating water. The factors considered in benefit–cost analysis are illustrated in Figure 6-5. Additional considerations for the benefits accrued based on different accounting perspectives are presented in Table 6-1.

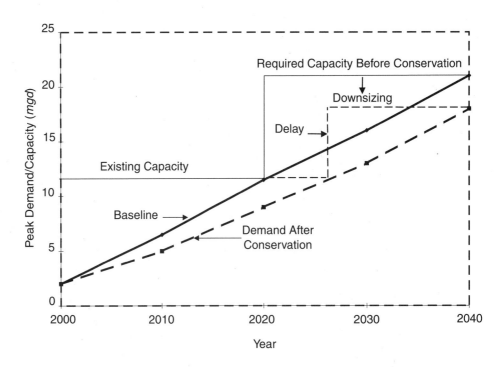

Source: Maddaus, W., *Estimating Benefits from Water Conservation*, 1999.

Figure 6–4   Example of delay downsize facility based on demand forecast accounting for conservation effects

Table 6–7   Unit water savings of conservation measures

Measure	Applicable Customer Classes	Water Use Reductions per End Use per Account	Applies to
Industrial facility audits	IND	10–50%	Indoor/outdoor
Industrial processes and operations (Recycled or reclaimed on-site water use)	IND	0–90%	Indoor/outdoor
Good Housekeeping Hotel/Motel Program	COM*	5%–10%	All hotels indoor/outdoor
Commercial cooling tower audits	COM	10%	All commercial cooling towers
Landscape water budget	IRR	10%	Outdoor
Landscape/irrigation codes	IRR	20%	Peak day outdoor
Irrigation audit	IRR	15%	Outdoor
Public education program	RSF	3%	Indoor/outdoor
Residential water audits	RSF	5%	Indoor/outdoor
Landscape use efficiency	RSF/RMF	10%	New irrigation outdoor
New home points program	RSF/RMF	0%–30%	Indoor/outdoor
Drip irrigation rebate	RSF/RMF	10%	Outdoor
Efficient use clothes washing machine rebate	RSF	23.4%–33.0%	Indoor
Toilet flapper rebate	RSF	8%	Indoor
Water reclamation facility (water reuse)	ALL	90%	Outdoor
Inverted block rate structure (increased differential)	ALL	1%–2.5%	Indoor/outdoor
Sliding-scale connection fee	ALL	0%–30%	Indoor/outdoor

*Targeted at new accounts only.

Customer Types:
    RSF: Residential single family
    RMF: Residential multifamily
    COM: Commercial
    IND: Industrial
    IRR: Irrigation
    ALL: All customer types

Maddaus, W., *Estimating Benefits from Water Conservation*, 1999.

When assessing benefits and costs of conservation measures, overlap of multiple benefits or double counting of costs should be avoided. Chapter 12 provides more detailed information on performing benefit–cost evaluations, and examples of spreadsheet models designed to estimate benefits and costs from capital project deferrals are provided in the *Impact of Demand Reduction on Water Utilities* (Bishop and Weber, 1996).

Step 8. Select conservation measures. Individual conservation measures should be packaged into a comprehensive program for implementation. The package will include an array of justifiable outdoor and indoor measures that meet the payback criteria and will achieve needed and targeted results. This package must

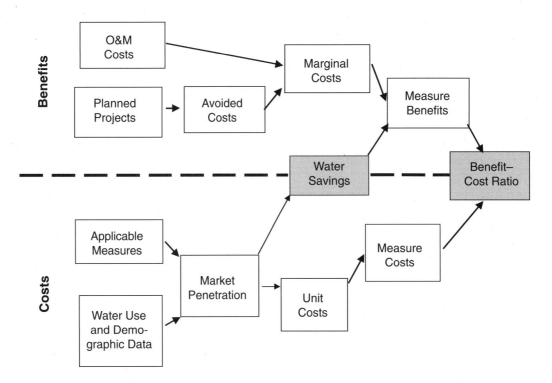

Source: Maddaus, W., *Estimating Benefits from Water Conservation*, 1999.

Figure 6–5   Benefit–cost analysis methodology

also be acceptable to the utility management and governing bodies included in long-range demand forecasts.

Step 9. Combine overall estimated savings.   Once the optimal mix of conservation measures has been determined, an estimate of program water savings can be developed with a cautious summation that avoids counting estimated water savings from individual measures more than once (i.e., residential water audit toilet water savings and ULFT replacement). Also, an overall program implementation schedule for the package of measures is necessary to determine the timing of conservation effects on the demand forecasts.

Step 10. Optimize demand forecasts.   The baseline demand forecast should be modified for quantification of demand reductions and graphical comparison of the water forecast with and without conservation. The optimization process involves integrating conservation performance into demand forecasts. Modification of demand forecasts may be done iteratively or simultaneously with different cost-effective packages of conservation measures to meet desired conservation targets. An example of a revised demand forecast is provided in Figure 6-6 and additional information is provided in *USEPA Water Conservation Planning Guidelines*.

Short-term Demand Reduction (Drought Contingency) Planning

Drought is a naturally occurring adverse component of normal meteorological variations just as are flood, tornadoes, hurricanes, and other storms. Drought is an abnormally dry period for a specific area. Drought differs from other adverse meteorological events such as storms in several ways. Storm events develop in a

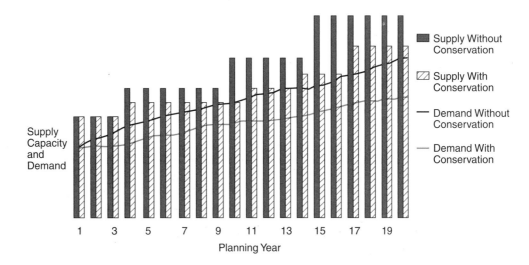

Source: Adapted and modified from *USEPA Water Conservation Planning Guidelines*, EPA-832-D-98-001, August 1998.

Figure 6–6   Demand forecast with and without water conservation

matter of minutes for tornadoes or days for hurricanes. By contrast, the first sign of drought is often a number of beautiful, sunny days. Droughts take months to develop and last for months and even years.

Drought cycles usually contain three phases:

1. First is the meteorological phase or period of below-normal rain. Significant impacts have not yet become manifest, but will if the dry conditions prevail.

2. The next phase is the agricultural/environmental phase in which soil moisture is depleted and small bodies of water begin to dry up. Crops die, terrestrial plants and animals become stressed, and runoff and aquifer recharge diminish. It is in this phase that most of the economic loss caused by crop damage occurs. Wildfires, dust storms, and abnormal animal movements and death often occur. Water demand increases as landscape and crop irrigation increase, and treatment and distribution systems are often stressed. During this phase, urban users' lawns dry up, plants become stressed, and cracks appear in yards. The result is increased water use for landscape irrigation by both commercial and residential users.

3. The third phase is the hydrological phase. Streams begin to dry, lake and aquifer levels fall, springs fail, and water supplies for human needs are stressed.

Droughts usually end in reverse order. Precipitation returns to normal; soil moisture is replaced so that normal runoff and aquifer recharge begin to recover; and then streams, lakes, and aquifers return to normal.

Drought Management and Water Resources Planning

What drought management is not. Drought management is often considered the same as water conservation, but the two are different. Drought management involves those strategies needed to temporarily reduce demand and find alternate water resources in response to drought or other conditions that require a quick response. Measures taken can involve those practices normally found in long-term water conservation programs, but also include mandatory water use restrictions and rationing in response to drought or other temporary water supply or water treatment and delivery system emergency conditions.

Coordinating drought planning with other water resources planning.   A primary function of water resources planning is to provide water for periods of drought. Most municipal water supply plans consider the drought of record when estimating the firm or safe yield of a water source, and most water treatment and distribution facility plans consider peak customer water demand when establishing design capacity. Firm yield calculations for surface water reservoirs and safe yield calculations for groundwater supplies are derived from the available hydrological record. These calculations also depend on the ability to correctly reflect the impacts that man has had on that supply when up-stream dams, diversions, and return flows are considered or aquifer recharge and pumpage models developed to reflect increased pervious cover and other factors.

Therefore, according to the plan, there should be adequate water supply and system capacity to meet increased demand under drought conditions. However, as the poet Robert Burns said, "the best laid plans of mice and men oft go astray." Nature does not always operate according to plan. From an integrated water resources planning approach, all demands on the resource such as agricultural and industrial water uses, and recreational and environmental water needs must also be considered. As a growing population strains the physical limits of providing water in some areas, shortages will reoccur. In these instances, drought planning may incorporate planned load or demand shedding as a planning tool.

Planning for these contingencies, and determining how much water can be temporarily conserved in times of shortage, is the function of a drought management plan. Three key words, supply, demand, and capacity, are used to describe drought management planning. The purpose of a drought management plan is to manage a period of declining supply and increasing demand so that demand does not exceed either supply or system capacity. It is a way of sharing a shortage or as one water resources planner put it, "sharing the pain." This is a key difference between drought planning and other water resources planning functions that have as their goal the provision of sufficient water supply and system capacity to meet all demands.

Drought management is a means for dealing with a temporary supply/demand imbalance. The magnitude and frequency of the shortages that should be dealt with by drought management is a policy decision.

Plan development.   Drought management plans, as well as other emergency plans, differ from overall water resource plans in another significant way. Drought and emergency demand management plans all contain specific mandatory and enforceable requirements and penalties that become effective when certain conditions are met. This section describes the components found in most drought management plans and provides a procedural guide for developing these plans. It is important to note that drought plan components are the same as other emergency plans that result in a limited water supply. These can include major water treatment and distribution equipment failure due to mechanical causes or power loss, or because of natural causes such as floods, or due to contamination of a water source, acts of war, etc. Therefore, many drought management plans contain trigger components that address these other issues as well. It must be remembered that the purpose of a staged response is to reduce demand before a major shortage develops. The ultimate goal is to protect health and safety of the community served, while providing for the most beneficial uses possible under adverse conditions. In the most severe cases this means providing drinking water and providing for basic sanitation and fire fighting ability.

Plan elements. Certain components are essential in drought or emergency demand management plans. It is helpful to list these components first so that the description of how to develop each of these components can be understood from the perspective of the desired product. Elements include

1. *Declaration of purpose and definitions.* This section should state the purpose of the plan, legally who is covered if restrictions are imposed, and a definition of terms used in the plan. The section should also define essential and nonessential water use that may be subject to different levels of imposed cutbacks.

2. *Public education.* This will include methods of informing the public about the existence and conditions contained in the plan. This should include basic knowledge about the sources of water available and their limits as well as design limits of the treatment and distribution system and the possible range of restrictions that may be imposed if these limits are approached. The purpose is to ensure that the public is aware that such a program exists before these measures have to be implemented.

3. *Trigger conditions.* This section should contain specific trigger conditions for initiating restrictions at different stages of severity. Plans with three to five stages are common. Examples would be mild, moderate, severe, and critical stages. Trigger conditions are important for two reasons. First, they provide specific written criteria that give the utility authority to impose specified legal restrictions once a trigger condition has been met. Second, trigger conditions provide set points of reference for the utility to watch for to determine when they are approaching drought conditions.

4. *Response measures.* These are the specific actions that are taken to reduce use, find alternate sources, and respond to other needs. A formal exemption procedure and list of exempted uses for each stage should also be developed.

5. *Implementation procedures.* Written implementation procedures that specify the following need to be included in the plan:

    a. Specific title or position with the authority to implement the program, such as the mayor, city manager, utility director, etc.

    b. Whom to notify including city officials, state or regional authorities, news media, law enforcement, and legal authorities.

    c. Means and methods of notifying the public in a manner needed to ensure they know what to do before enforcement begins.

    d. A list of other actions that need to be taken.

6. *Termination procedures.* Written procedures of the methodology of moving from a higher stage to a lower stage and for notification of the public (customers).

7. *Legal documents.* Implemented drought ordinances, contract modifications, emergency rate schedules, and other documents as needed.

8. *Procedures for periodic review and revision.* Provisions for, at least, an annual review of the plan and provisions to make changes as needed.

Drought management plan development procedure. Implementing the planning process establishes what reasonable temporary demand reductions can be expected (likely to be highly dependent on local conditions). Development of a drought management plan should involve the following procedures:

Step 1. Public involvement. Public input is an essential first step in development of a drought plan. By having public input, the utility is able to avoid major omissions, obtain customer buy-in, and greatly facilitate the public information process.

Step 2. Setting trigger criteria. The trigger conditions need to be set so that measures are implemented to slow demand and find alternate emergency water sources before the actual limits of the system are met. Trigger conditions provide the legal authority to initiate certain legal actions with criminal penalties. Therefore, trigger conditions need to be specific and precise. They also need to be worded so that authorities may choose not to begin enforcement if judgment warrants delay of implementation of the penalties. At a minimum, each stage should address supply, demand, and system capacity constraints. Supply includes firm yield of reservoirs, water contracts, water rights limits, and aquifer drawdown levels. Capacity sets triggers to address both the treatment and pumping capacity of the system. Demand is knowing how demand responds to excessively dry conditions.

Step 3. Establish drought response measures and goals. These should address

   a. curtailment of nonessential use,

   b. water allocation, watering restrictions, etc., for customers,

   c. identification of alternate emergency water supplies, and

   d. required modifications to utility operations, such as reduced or discontinued irrigation of public land, closing of public parks and pools, and modified main flushing.

Each response measure should contain a stated goal, such as a percent reduction in water use or reductions to a certain level.

Step 4. Design the plan. This should include all provisions listed under the plan elements above.

Step 5. Adopt the plan. No plan is enforceable until the governing political body or utility managing board has officially adopted it.

Step 6. Periodic review. Provide for periodic review and revision as needed.

What to expect. A primary purpose of drought planning is to develop and have ready a set of tools to reduce demand on a temporary, emergency basis. Next, how different measures will reduce demand must be determined. First, reduction must be defined. For example, most report a reduction from peak demand while others report a reduction from some other use rate such as maximum system capacity. Second, each individual measure and what type of use it will impact must be evaluated. For example, if your measure is to reduce outdoor water use by implementing a five-day watering cycle, but 80 percent of water use is for industrial purposes, that measure will not have much impact on peak. Table 6-8 states the typical ranges of reduction from peak use that one can expect based on experience of others.

Do's and don'ts. The following is a list of do's and don'ts that come from experience of utilities that have implemented drought measures.

- Do develop the plan before the drought occurs.

Table 6–8   Examples of drought plan conditions

Stage	Trigger	Goal	Response Measures
1 - Mild	Supply – Well drops to 355 feet	Awareness and 5% drop	Public notification of problem
	Demand – Use reaches 14 mgd for three consecutive days		Voluntary five-day watering schedule
	Capacity – Use reaches 85% of capacity		Articles for public media
2 - Moderate	Supply – Lake at 40% of capacity	Reduce peak use by 15%	Closing of outdoor ornamental fountains
	Demand – Use reaches 90% ability to refill elevated storage		Five-day watering schedule and time-of-day schedule imposed
	Capacity – Use reaches 90% of contract with City X		Waste of water ordinance implemented
3 - Severe	Supply – Lake at 6-month supply left	Reduce peak use by 25%	Hand watering only
	Demand – City not able to completely fill elevated storage		Close all pools, emergency rate imposed of $15/1,000 gal for residential use over 20,000 gal per month
	Capacity – City reaches 85% of annual water rights		Industry asked to cut back potable water use by 10%
4 - Critical	Supply – Lake at 6-month supply left	Reduce peak use by 40%	Outdoor use banned, home water use limited to 75 gal/person/day or pull meter
	Demand – City not able to completely fill elevated storage		Emergency rate imposed of $50/1,000 gal for residential use over 15,000 gal per month
	Capacity – City reaches 85% of annual water rights		Commercial car washes closed, industries asked to reduce potable water use by 20%
5 - Emergency[*]	Supply – The lake is dry	Reduce peak use by 60%–80%	Eliminate all uses not directly involved with health, sanitation, or fire fighting
	Demand – Use has caused pressure to drop and system failure		Close public schools and offices
	Capacity – The system has failed		Shut down industrial operations

*If the emergency stage has been reached, the drought management plan has failed and only total restrictions will work.

- Don't rely on odd–even watering. Many utilities have actually had water use go up with odd–even watering schedules. Most successful schedules call for watering every five to seven days.

- Do consult with legal staff when developing the regulatory components of the plan.

- Don't go in and out of stages if that can be avoided.

- Do coordinate with other utilities in the area to develop identical watering restriction schedules so that local print and broadcast news can help spread the information for all.

- Don't wait until the last minute to adopt ordinances.

In summary, drought management plans should be designed to move a community into ever more stringent water restrictions so that demand is slowed before system capacity or supply are exceeded, at which point very draconian measures would be necessary. Implementation of these plans places the enforcing entity in a policing mode of operation. If citations and fines are involved, the legal ramifications are similar to those of traffic tickets and must be able to stand up in court.

RECLAIMED WATER

An analysis of reclaimed water as a source begins with the raw wastewater from which it is derived and ends with its ultimate reuse. For various reasons, *recycled water* is preferred as a general label over *reclaimed water*. A more precise labeling recognizes the terms are related but not really equivalent: water is *reclaimed* from wastewater in order to be *recycled* for *reuse*. The first label speaks of derivation, the second of distribution, and the third of disposition. The following sections discuss issues relating to all of these three processes.

Water recycling usually implies intentional reclamation for beneficial reuse of the product water. Wastewater treatment for mitigating the discharge of otherwise untreated raw wastewater is usually termed *disposal*. This distinction is neither precise nor universally recognized. Water reclamation often provides both water supply and pollution control. Another way of characterizing this distinction is to consider wastewater disposal as reclamation without the direct supply benefit.

Water Quality

Recycled (or reclaimed) wastewater quality depends on raw wastewater quality, and the type and extent of treatment applied to produce recycled water. Raw wastewater quality depends on prevalent sources of wastewater generation, often lumped into the two broad categories of *municipal* and *industrial*. The type and extent of treatment are often simply combined as level of treatment, ranging from preliminary to tertiary or advanced.

Municipal wastewater. Municipal wastewater quality across the United States varies significantly, but as a category has become the primary benchmark for wastewater quality consideration and comparison. Industrial wastewater quality is often characterized by comparison with a quantified municipal standard. Common levels of treatment used for municipal wastewater include pretreatment (usually means type and extent of treatment sufficient to improve a particular raw wastewater quality to that of municipal wastewater), and primary and secondary treatments (generally treating wastewater to an improved level of quality as primarily characterized by removing the major constituents that distinguish municipal wastewater from potable water).

Municipal wastewater is characterized by wastes added during residential or domestic uses of potable water. As constituents in wastewater, these increments include about 200-300 mg/L biochemical oxygen demand (BOD), 200-300 mg/L total suspended solids (TSS), 10-15 mg/L phosphorus, 20-40 mg/L nitrogen, and 200-400 mg/L total dissolved inorganic solids. The most significant other constituent in municipal wastewater, not by mass per unit volume but by potential health effect, is pathogen concentration. This factor is usually expressed by concentration of coliform bacteria, a nonpathogenic indicator organism. For municipal wastewater, the total coliform concentration is about 10^6/100 mL.

Industrial wastewater. Industrial and commercial wastewater quality is more widely varied than municipal wastewater quality. An absolute characterization of industrial wastewater quality depends on the particular industry; however, a relative characterization is made by noting that the concentration of at least one (and usually more than one) constituent is much higher than the municipal wastewater average. For example, a wholesale bakery waste may have a BOD concentration of 1,000 mg/ L, compared with 250 mg/L for municipal wastewater. Table 6-9 lists representative BOD and TSS concentrations for several common industries.

Required treatment level. The level of treatment required to produce recycled water depends on both the quality of raw wastewater influent to the treatment plant and the quality of plant effluent required to satisfy the most constraining reuse. Definitions of treatment levels vary in common usage and even overlap. The following levels are guidelines and raw municipal wastewater is used as a standard of comparison.

- Pretreatment is the level of treatment required to produce raw municipal wastewater quality from a raw wastewater source substantially exceeding that quality in at least one major constituent, or containing at least one major constituent in a concentration that would negatively affect downstream treatment processes. An example of the former is TSS removal from brewery waste. An example of the latter is a simple grease trap applied to restaurant wastewater. Pretreatment is often a requirement imposed on a wastewater source through a sewerage agency's source control program.

- Primary treatment is the level of treatment required to produce effluent free of most settleable and floatable solids present in raw municipal wastewater. A substantial reduction in total but not dissolved oxygen demand is usually accomplished at the same time. Primary treatment is usually provided by the gravity sedimentation process, and its performance often assessed by the extent of TSS and BOD removal.

Table 6–9   Example industrial wastewater constituents*

Industry	Concentration, mg/L	
	BOD	TSS
Auto steam cleaning	1,150	1,250
Wholesale bakery	1,000	600
Hotel with dining	500	600
Industrial laundry	670	680
Market with garbage grinders	800	800
Professional office	130	80
Restaurant	1,000	600
Septage	5,400	12,000

*Data collected and published by California State Water Resources Control Board.

- Secondary treatment is the level of treatment required to produce an oxidized effluent in which organic matter has been stabilized, is nonputrescible, and contains dissolved oxygen. Secondary treatment is often characterized by an effluent with TSS and BOD concentrations of 30 mg/L or less. This level of treatment is usually provided by an aerobic biological process, such as activated sludge, performed on good-quality primary effluent.

- Advanced secondary treatment is the level of treatment required to produce an effluent with less than 5 mg/L TSS and BOD (about 97 percent removal). Advanced secondary effluent is often characterized by turbidities almost as low as those of a potable water supply. This level of treatment is usually provided, at minimum, by filtration and high level disinfection.

- Advanced or tertiary wastewater treatment (AWT) involves primary, secondary, and filtration treatments focusing on and progressively removing TSS and BOD concentrations from raw wastewater, plus the removal of nutrients (nitrogen and phosphorous) to low levels typically found in the ecosystem. For example, modifying conventional activated sludge to completely nitrify process water and then denitrify it is considered advanced treatment for nitrogen reduction or removal. Advanced treatment is also used to remove a constituent not present in raw wastewater. For example, dechlorination is advanced treatment to remove chlorine residual created by chlorine disinfection. In nitrogen removal, the constituent removed by denitrification is nitrate created by the activated sludge process from organic and ammonia nitrogen present in raw wastewater.

- Full treatment includes all of the above, plus chemical conditioning and reverse osmosis applied to AWT effluent that has been through advanced treatment for specific ion, pathogen, or total dissolved solids reduction or removal. Also, chemical augmentation of conventional primary sedimentation is advanced treatment for phosphorus reduction or solids treatment optimization.

For a given recycled/reclaimed wastewater water use, required wastewater treatment levels vary among jurisdictions in the United States, and more so among those around the world. In the United States, individual states promulgate specific requirements. Table 6-10 lists a range of recycled water uses and the minimum treatment level required, in order of increased recycled water quality. Because of state-to-state regulatory variation, categorizations are illustrative and not precise. As listed in the footnotes, level of disinfection varies with reuse requirement. Type of disinfection, as by chlorination or ultraviolet radiation, can also vary with reuse requirement as well as process water quality being disinfected.

Water Quantity

A critical issue in using recycled water is balancing supply and demand over time. If imbalances will occur, storage is generally required.

Supply variations. Wastewater flow generally varies seasonally and with weather conditions. The diurnal fluctuations seen on water systems are generally mitigated in the pipe and through detention time in the treatment process. Seasonal flow variation in municipal wastewater generated in a given service area can be substantial, depending on the fluctuations in population (resort communities), weather conditions (wet areas like Florida), and size of populations (smaller

Table 6–10   Reclaimed water use by treatment level

Use	Treatment Level
Fodder, fiber, seed irrigation	Primary effluent
Orchard, vineyard irrigation	Primary effluent
Pasture irrigation for milking animals	Disinfected[*] secondary
Controlled impoundment	Disinfected[*] secondary
Landscape irrigation with restricted public access	Disinfected[*] secondary
Food crop surface irrigation	Disinfected[†] secondary
Uncontrolled impoundment	Advanced Wastewater Treatment[†]
Landscape irrigation with unrestricted public access	Advanced Wastewater Treatment[†]
Food crop spray irrigation	Advanced Wastewater Treatment[†]
In-building toilet and urinal flushing	Advanced Wastewater Treatment[†]
Groundwater recharge for nonpotable supply	Advanced Wastewater Treatment[†]
Cooling tower supply	Advanced Wastewater Treatment[†] Plus[‡]
Groundwater recharge for potable supply	Advanced Wastewater Treatment[†] Plus[§]
Live-stream discharge (environmental enhancement)	Advanced Wastewater Treatment[†] Plus[**]

[*]A lower level of disinfection may be allowed.
[†]A higher level of disinfection may be required.
[‡]A demineralization process may be required.
[§]Demineralization and activated carbon processes may be required.
[**]Nutrient removal and dechlorination processes may be required.

communities generally have larger fluctuations). Substantial seasonal variation in individual discharger wastewater flows is also found, as in canning and certain product manufacturing. Industrial flow variations may be effectively reduced at the downstream treatment plant by a combination of several industries with different seasonality and in combination with flow generation by a larger municipal population base. Diurnal fluctuations are generally limited to small communities.

With industrial wastewater, diurnal variation can be significant (see Figure 6-7). In the extreme, an industrial wastewater hydrograph approaches a step function distribution: for parts of the day—when a plant has no staff and no process generation—there is no flow; for the balance of the day—when the process operates—the flow is relatively constant at the maximum rate. A large range of wastewater hydrographs is possible, depending on industrial processes involved, any on-site wastewater reclamation, number of work shifts per day, and other features of process design and staffing.

In larger communities, the pipe travel time, wet-well storage, and equalization of flow in the treatment process eliminates most diurnal variations. Where daily fluctuations are a problem, flow attenuations can be imposed upstream of the plant in the collection system as a predischarge requirement for a larger industrial wastewater discharger, thereby benefiting the entire downstream collection and treatment system.

Additional supply flow variations can result if potable, or some other nonrecycled supply, is used. Potable water can be used as a short-term contingency to recycled water quality problems or quantity shortfalls.

Demand variations. Recycled water demand variations depend on use, which include agricultural and landscape irrigation, commercial and industrial

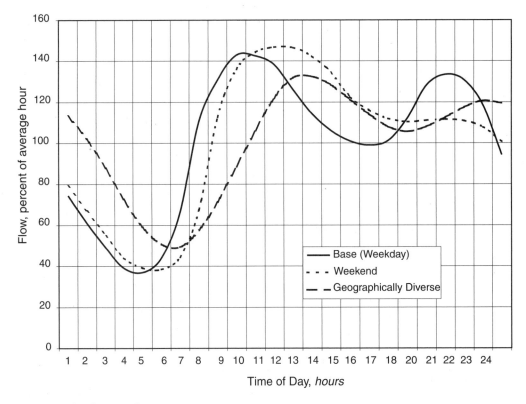

Figure 6–7   Wastewater hydrograph

processes, environmental applications such as marshes and live streams, and others. As with supply, demand may vary seasonally and diurnally.

Seasonal variation in irrigation and some environmental demands are substantial in a given year, and from year to year depending on prevailing weather. In both cases, the seasonal demand hydrograph tends to complement the associated annual precipitation hydrograph; i.e., irrigation and some environmental augmentation are largely providing needed water when precipitation does not occur. Seasonal variation among commercial and industrial process demands ranges from little to very substantial. As noted earlier in seasonal supply flow variations, industries that depend on agricultural production schedules for raw material often have large seasonal water demand variation. Industries that use raw materials generally available year-round, usually exhibit very little seasonal demand variation.

Diurnal variation of recycled water demands is often greater than seasonal variation on a percentage basis. Irrigation and many commercial or industrial demand hydrographs have a step-function distribution—off for much of the day, on for the balance. Most landscape irrigation with recycled water is regulated to hours when the public is generally absent from the site, as in a park, schoolyard, golf course, or residential greenbelt. A common daily *duty cycle* for such demands could be irrigation for nine hours at night and no irrigation for the remaining 15 hours.

Some uses are buffered from the recycled water distribution system with on-site storage. Such storage can be required by the recycled water purveyor to control demand variation for the sake of production or distribution facilities, or such storage can be required by the end user for its own purposes. Many golf courses use impoundments, which may double as visual amenities or water hazards, for receiving irrigation supply during the day and incurring irrigation withdrawal at night. Many commercial and industrial end users also maintain on-site storage tanks for supply-and-demand buffering. Provision for supply-and-demand buffering within recycled water transmission and distribution systems is discussed in the section on storage.

Storage.   Flow rate differences in the balance of recycled water supply and demand over time result in potentially needed storage volumes. As in the discussions for supply and demand, storage evaluations can be segregated into seasonal and diurnal. In all cases, volume of needed storage centers on particular time dependencies of supply and demand, and includes any defined contingency allotments and dead storage. Lack of adequate storage requires modulating supply production, or wasting potential recycled water supply and use of nonrecycled supplemental supply.

The relatively common balancing of recycled water supply derived from a relatively large municipality's wastewater and landscape irrigation demand illustrates several points. In this case, the supply is relatively constant over the year, and the demand is not. Maximum-month demands are often twice the average-month demands. If the reclamation plant's production capacity is sized for the maximum month, excess supply is potentially available. If the plant is sized for the average month, it will need seasonal storage, supplemental supply, or both.

A seasonal storage hydrograph is calculated as the difference between supply and demand, usually monthly, over the 12 months of the year. If average annual supply and demand are equal, cumulative excess supply equals cumulative supply deficiency, which in turn equals the seasonal storage volume to exactly buffer or balance supply and demand. Typically, several hundred acre-feet of seasonal storage are required for balancing each 1 mgd (m^3/d) of supply. Figure 6-8 illustrates a typical seasonal storage hydrograph.

Because relatively large storage volumes are needed for relatively small-capacity recycled water systems, seasonal storage is most often constructed in open-storage reservoirs. Because these usually require relatively large land areas, a particular range of elevations, a dam, and other appurtenances, such reservoirs are

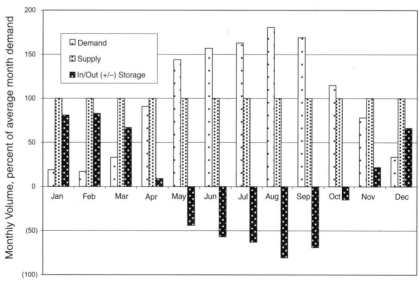

Figure 6–8   Supply sized for average month demand

often not constructed because of considerable expense and environmental impact. In foregoing seasonal storage, many systems provide recycled water supply to meet maximum-month demands. In California, where approximately 400,000 acre-feet $(4 \times 10^6 \text{ m}^3)$ of recycled water were used in 1995, only four seasonal storage reservoirs were in service.

Diurnal storage needs are illustrated in the same example. Recycled water supply derived from municipal wastewater has large variations throughout the day. Landscape irrigation with recycled water is often practiced at night. A diurnal storage hydrograph is calculated as the difference between supply and demand, usually hourly, over the 24 hours of the day. In this example, the bimodal supply peak is usually out of phase with the demand step-function distribution, and considerable diurnal storage is required. Typically about 1 million gallons $(3,785 \text{ m}^3)$ of diurnal storage are required for each 1 mgd $(3,785 \text{ m}^3/\text{d})$ of supply. Figure 6-9 illustrates a typical diurnal storage hydrograph.

Apart from fire demand storage, often not provided in recycled water distribution systems, recycled water diurnal storage volumes are similar to those in a potable water distribution system. Recycled water diurnal storage is most often provided in aboveground steel reservoirs and sometimes in belowground concrete reservoirs.

Environmental Factors

Water reclamation and reuse can have positive and negative environmental impacts. On the positive side, the quality of treated wastewater released to the environment is usually better when wastewater is reclaimed rather than disposed of. Also, the appropriate use of recycled water saves an equivalent volume of more naturally

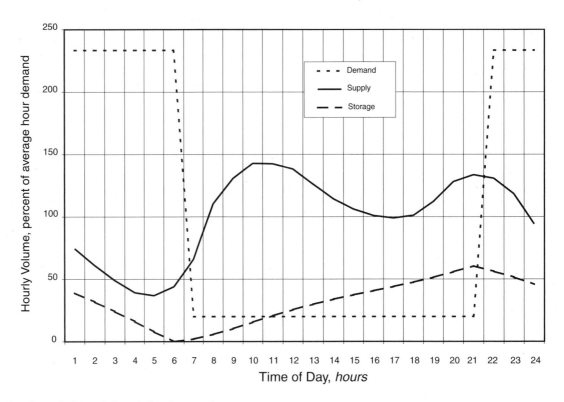

Figure 6–9   Supply sized for daily demand

pristine water, such as with potable quality, for higher and better use. In arid locations, such as much of California and Arizona, potable quality water has to be conveyed hundreds of miles to its end uses. Reclamation and recycling of locally generated wastewater can provide a net energy savings in its production and distribution to the end user versus the alternative imported potable water transmission.

Most potential negative environmental impacts from the application of recycled water to the environment come from recycled water's origin as wastewater. These impacts include other water resources, potential contamination of surface and groundwater sources, public health hazards, and other environmental impacts that may directly or indirectly affect the public. Fortunately, very few significant negative impacts have ever occurred.

Surface water impacts.   The potential impact of recycled water on surface water depends on several things: the surface water quality and volume, any plans for changes in quality or volume, and current and planned beneficial uses in situ or as a source of supply. The impact also depends on the recycled water: its quality, volume of particular reuses, and how these factors affect the surface water elements.

The effects of recycled water on surface water vary greatly by type of reuse. For many commercial and industrial applications, little or no recycled water is discharged to the environment. For well-managed irrigation applications, most of the applied water ultimately evaporates into the atmosphere, a lesser fraction percolates into the ground, and a still lesser fraction results in surface runoff. For environmental enhancement applications, such as a live-stream discharge, the extent of impact is usually considerable, but intentional.

Specific quality effects depend on type of reuse and elements of the surface water body. A common concern is excessive amounts of algal nutrients, nitrogen, and phosphorus. Another concern is excessive oxygen demand. Still another may involve one or more other specific constituents. Also, increased salinity above that of an alternative potable water supply is a concern.

Potentially negative impacts can be mitigated by preventing or controlling environmental discharges and by adequate treatment.

Groundwater impacts.   The effects of recycled water on groundwater are the same for surface water. The effects also vary greatly by the type of reuse. Again, little recycled water reaches groundwater from most commercial and industrial applications. The fraction of recycled water applied to irrigation that percolates into the ground represents a relatively lower volume but usually carries a higher concentration of salts. Some recycled water applied to surface water environmental enhancements may incidentally reach groundwater. Possibly the most significant concern for potential impacts is intentional groundwater recharge with recycled water. If the recharge is directly or indirectly to a potable groundwater supply, political and emotional impacts can be more significant than physical ones.

Specific quality effects on groundwater vary greatly, as with those on a surface water. A common concern is for organic contamination as generally characterized by the total organic carbon concentration. Another common concern, much like that for surface water, is for increased salinity. Increased nitrogen in the potable supply is a concern because of the infant disease methemoglobinemia, as well as other drinking water standards.

Potential negative effects can be mitigated by preventing or controlling discharges, performing adequate treatment at the reclamation source, or using adequate supplemental treatment through the ground before the recycled water reaches the water body.

Human health effects.   Health risks from water reuse are generally associated with exposure to particular chemical or microbial agents present in recycled water. Exposure can occur directly, such as through skin contact or aerosol ingestion, or indirectly, such as from eating food from an outdoor table surface sprayed with recycled water or food crops irrigated with recycled water. Health effects studies have been performed on many of the better known agents, but the number of potential pathogens is endless. Therefore, the potential remains for health effects from unstudied agents. Reuse regulations have been developed that minimize direct and indirect exposure, and guard against better known and unstudied agents.

Other environmental impacts.   Some of the most significant effects of recycled water other than on human health and water resources occur with plants and soils. The effects on plants and soils vary greatly and may depend on general recycled water salinity or specific water constituents. Mitigation may include specific constituent reduction or removal by treatment in combination with proper water application management.

PROJECT SITING

Most water recycling projects grow naturally out of wastewater treatment systems, coupled with requirements of water distribution. Project siting is therefore very sensitive to topography. Reclamation plants are most often sited with wastewater treatment at the downstream end of the raw wastewater collection system, and the distribution of recycled water must overcome the same terrain in reaching end users.

Plant locations.   Because raw wastewater flow is predominantly by gravity, most wastewater treatment plants are sited at lower elevations in the overall collection area. Plants are also sited, where possible, to mitigate concerns for aesthetics, potential odors, noise, light, and human safety.

Many water reclamation plants comprise advanced treatment processes added to a secondary treatment plant whose initial objective was pollution control. On average, the effects of water reclamation facilities on the environment are much less than conventional primary and secondary treatment and solids handling.

Distribution.   Besides the production source, a water recycling project site has the general features of a potable water distribution system. Recycled water must be delivered to end-use sites, requiring pumping, transmission, storage, and distribution. The sites for these facilities, and for potable water systems, depend on topography and demographics. Because water recycling projects have historically arisen after communities are substantially constructed, the optimal siting of pump stations and reservoirs may be difficult because land is not available. However, many recycling projects are being master planned as part of new or expanding communities, with greater opportunity for optimal site locations.

Typically, the cost of pumping recycled water to the elevations where it is needed is the highest cost after treatment. For larger collection and distribution areas that cover substantial elevation change, it may be more cost-effective to site a water reclamation plant well upstream of a terminal pollution control facility, especially if there is substantial demand for recycled water nearby or at higher elevations. A fraction of raw wastewater is then intercepted on its way downstream, treated, and the recycled water pumped to distribution. The largest version of such a *satellite* recycled water system has been constructed and operated by the County Sanitation District of Los Angeles County, California. Wastewater not reclaimed is given secondary treatment at the single downstream terminal plant whose effluent is conveyed to ocean disposal.

Supply Reliability

The reliability of recycled water supplies includes qualitative and quantitative factors. Production quality must remain equal to or better than the requirement for the least constraining reuse. Adequate volume must be available to satisfy demands. The two factors are closely interrelated.

Quality. The difference between the quality of many raw and treated potable water supplies is usually much more subtle than between raw wastewater and recycled water supply. This increased difference amplifies the magnitude of quality concerns related to possible failures in producing recycled water.

Quality reliability is achieved at three stages: facilities planning and design, construction, and O&M. Among other sanitary engineering considerations, good design must include proper process selection and adequate provision of flexibility and redundancy. Table 6-11 illustrates relevant treatment design requirements from Title 22, California Code of Regulations.

Construction and O&M must sustain the design goals of quality reliability. Properly specified and tested equipment and installations must be used in constructing water reclamation plants and system facilities. Adequate O&M procedures routinely conducted by properly qualified staff are essential to enduring recycled water quality.

Storage facilities contribute to supply quantitative reliability, and can provide occasion for quality degradation. For example, residual recycled water oxygen demand can cause anaerobic conditions in a poorly circulated operational storage reservoir. Open seasonal storage, as with a potable water supply, can significantly degrade quality from the level achieved in reclamation plant effluent. In some cases, partial retreatment is required; in other cases, such as with Santa Margarita Water District's Upper Oso Reservoir, no significant retreatment is required. This 4,000 acre-ft uncovered reservoir has been in service in Southern California since 1979 without major distribution system water quality problems, using only fish screens and a simple mechanical straining device, coupled with a multiple-port inlet and outlet works for selecting the best water stratum for outflow.

Quantity. Whereas recycled water's wastewater origins may challenge its ultimate water quality reliability, they tend to support its quantitative reliability. Unlike some potable water supplies, municipal wastewater usually exhibits little seasonal fluctuation in average daily flow volume. As noted earlier, exceptions to this occur when the municipality has a significant seasonal population influx or when dominant industrial wastewater discharges have seasonal dependency. Because of this inherent quantitative reliability, in the arid southwestern United States recycled water is typically considered a *drought-proof* irrigation supply source.

As with quality, quantitative reliability is achieved at three stages, but unlike qualitative considerations, quantitative reliability features differ with respect to maintaining an adequate volume over time. Over hourly time frames, reliability is achieved with standby pumps and adequate diurnal storage reservoir volumes. Over daily and monthly time frames, reliability is achieved with seasonal storage reservoir volumes. Standby supply sources, potable or nonpotable, can be used to provide both diurnal and seasonal reliability.

Facilities

Reclamation plants. Reclamation facilities are most often installed on the same site as secondary wastewater treatment facilities. Particular reclamation process selection depends on required treatment levels discussed earlier. Facility layout depends on process selection and overall site planning, whether or not it is

Table 6–11   Water reclamation plant flexibility and reliability requirements

Process	Alternative Requirements
Primary treatment	Multiple treatment units capable of producing primary effluent with one unit not in operation. Standby primary treatment unit process. Long-term storage or disposal provisions.
Biological treatment	Alarm and multiple treatment units capable of producing oxidized wastewater with one unit not in operation. Alarm, short-term retention or disposal provisions, and standby replacement equipment. Alarm and long-term storage or disposal provisions. Automatically actuated long-term storage or disposal provisions.
Secondary sedimentation	Multiple sedimentation units capable of treating the entire flow with one unit not in operation. Standby sedimentation unit process. Long-term storage or disposal provisions.
Coagulation	All coagulation unit processes shall be provided with certain mandatory features for uninterrupted coagulant feed. All coagulation unit processes shall be provided with certain reliability features.
Filtration	Alarm and multiple filter units capable of treating the entire flow with one unit not in operation. Alarm, short-term retention or disposal provisions, and standby replacement equipment. Alarm and long-term storage or disposal provisions. Automatically actuated long-term storage or disposal provisions. Alarm and standby filtration unit process.
Disinfection	All disinfection unit processes in which chlorine is used as the disinfectant shall be provided with features for uninterrupted chlorine feed. All disinfection unit processes in which chlorine is used as the disinfectant shall be provided with reliability features.

master planned for reclamation. A brief discussion of reclamation facilities follows in the categories of tertiary treatment, advanced treatment, and disinfection.

Tertiary treatment. Tertiary treatment facilities may include the following processes: chemical coagulation, flocculation, sedimentation, and filtration—essentially a complete water treatment plant. More cost-effective performance equivalents have been demonstrated over the past few decades, generally excluding tertiary sedimentation, which is capital cost and land intensive. Often flocculation is accomplished in-line, upstream of filtration, rather than in a more traditional flocculation chamber. The Pomona Virus Study, published in 1977, effectively demonstrated alternative tertiary treatment process configurations.

Advanced treatment. Advanced treatment may include vegetation nutrient removal processes, as for nitrogen and phosphorus, reverse osmosis, activated carbon, and dechlorination. Where tertiary treatment produces recycled water irrigation supply, some advanced treatment processes may enhance that objective, others may conflict with it. For example, reverse osmosis may be required to decrease general wastewater salinity for specific irrigation applications, yet beneficial vegetation nutrients, nitrogen, phosphorus, and potassium are substantially reduced as well. Similarly, specific vegetation nutrient removal required for environmental enhancement reuse conflicts with nutrient need for irrigation demands in a mixed-reuse project.

Disinfection.   Disinfection processes include traditional chlorination and other, more recent entries such as ultraviolet (UV) radiation. The effectiveness of both processes benefits from a low-TSS influent. Chlorination facilities include chemical storage and handling and a contact chamber. UV facilities are typically simpler and less site intensive. If residual disinfection capability is needed in the recycled water, some amount of chlorination may be unavoidable.

Distribution facilities.   Recycled water distribution facilities are essentially the same as their potable water counterparts. Several differences are worth noting. As previously discussed, facility sizing depends on recycled water supply and demand peculiarities. Also, facility layout will differ to the extent distribution system features are controlled by production source locations. For example, in a *satellite* recycled water system, pressure zoning may be significantly affected by the location of the *satellite* reclamation plant, whose siting was heavily constrained by wastewater collection requirements. Materials used may be different because the typically higher recycled water salinity increases corrosion potential. Material specifications for pumps, piping, valves, and other appurtenances should take this potential into account. Figure 6-10 illustrates an integrated/satellite system layout.

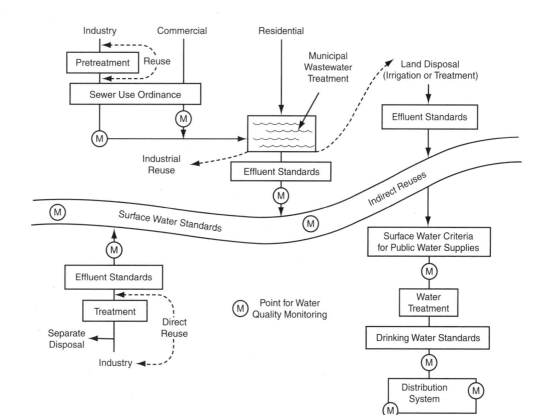

Figure 6–10   Integrated/satellite system layout

Connections to other supply sources.   Potable or potentially potable water supplies are often used to supplement recycled water sources. These and other nonwastewater sources must be protected from recycled water backflow or cross connection. A properly designed air gap at the point of connection, which may be a reservoir or pump station wet well, provides backflow prevention.

Economic Considerations

To determine the economic attractiveness of a given water recycling project, costs and benefits must be considered. Capital and operating costs should be included. Some benefits can be quantified; others may be nonmonetary.

Capital costs.   Table 6-12 provides representative water reclamation capital costs by process for several tertiary and advanced treatment and disinfection processes.

Operating costs.   Reclamation costs are highly dependent on the processes used to reclaim the water and on current costs of energy. This manual does not attempt to present current operating costs.

Benefits.   A water recycling project often provides benefits of both increased water supply and pollution control. More specific benefits may include

- water conservation
- water supply reliability
- surface water or groundwater enhancement
- wastewater disposal
- energy conservation
- nutrient conservation

One way of valuing a project's benefit is by the economic cost of the alternative water supply or wastewater disposal most likely otherwise required. A water recycling project is cost-effective when its unit cost, say, in dollars of total annual cost per acre-foot (m^3) of annual yield, is less than the unit cost of the alternative supply and disposal projects.

Table 6–12   Representative water reclamation capital costs[*]

Process	Cost[†] $/1-mgd[‡]
Coagulation[§]	283,000
Flocculation[§]	122,000
Tertiary sedimentation	585,000
Filtration	340,000
Granular activated carbon (GAC)	1,010,000
Reverse osmosis (RO)	2,385,000
Chlorination	270,000

[*]From *The Cost of Wastewater Reclamation in California*, 1992.

[†]Costs for process equipment and construction only, exclusive of general plant site development, process piping, electrical and instrumentation systems, and engineering services; based on a 20-cities average ENRCCI of 4,800 (January 1990).

[‡]Costs for higher flow capacities increase less than linearly with flow, i.e., there is an economy of scale.

[§]Coagulation includes 80 percent of the total cost of chemical handling, storage, and metering; flocculation, 20 percent.

DESALINATION

Historically, desalination processes were used to treat seawater. As more readily available and less costly water sources are no longer available because of increasing potable demands and environmental uses, less desirable water sources are being considered. These less desirable sources tend to have high total dissolved solids (TDS), synthetic and natural organic contaminants, and high concentrations of other undesirable minerals. Membranes are also useful for treating these other water sources. The reduction in operations costs is also encouraging communities to consider seawater as a larger component of new water sources.

Saltwater intrusion into coastal aquifers on both sides of the United States is a problem in coastal areas drained for human habitat. However, high TDS water contamination is not limited to coastal areas as upconing can contribute to saltwater migration. Within the Colorado River drainage area, as the river flows south to Mexico, agricultural runoff contributes to TDS levels as high as 2,600 ppm at the United States/Mexico border. In fact, the world's largest desalination plant located near Yuma, Ariz., produces up to 72 mgd (0.27 Mm^3/d) of desalted water. The plant was built to treat Colorado River water before it enters Mexico, to meet treaty requirements between the United States and Mexico limiting salinity to approximately 1,000 ppm.

In arid regions of the Southwest, greater water demands are driving water purveyors to spend more money treating lower quality water supplies, in part to meet these demands and in part because advanced treatment techniques are becoming more cost competitive. Membrane processes have been used in the United States since 1962 in Buckeye, Ariz., and are now found in Florida, California, Arizona, Texas, Oklahoma, and Washington. New water quality regulations are being promulgated for more contaminants. Quality standards are being raised for regulated constituents, and higher potable water treatment levels are required, including treatment of protozoa and viruses, color, and organic compounds such as trihalomethanes.

One reason membrane processes are receiving greater interest is that treated water could meet regulatory requirements of microbes and disinfection by-products with fewer treatment unit processes. Highly colored groundwater, due to organic compounds in the water, can also be treated using membrane processes. Thermal separation processes are used extensively in arid parts of the world and are now becoming more common in the United States. The first US city to use a thermal desalination process to treat seawater was Key West, Fla., in 1967.

Treatment Options

Current desalination techniques fall into two major categories: membrane separation processes such as electrodialysis reversal (EDR) and reverse osmosis processes (RO); and thermal processes such as multistage flash (MSF) distillation, multiple effect distillation (MED), and mechanical vapor compression (MVC). Each requires varying degrees of energy, either electric or heat, to convert seawater or brackish water into potable water for municipal use. EDR and RO are the preferred processes for treating brackish water that typically has a TDS range of 500 to 10,000 ppm. MSF and RO are the preferred processes for treating saline groundwater, or seawater with a TDS up to 35,000 mg/L.

Table 6-13 lists commercially viable desalination processes for typical water TDS concentrations in use worldwide. RO and EDR product water resulting from these processes is referred to as *permeate*. Approximately 1 to 2 percent of salt in the

Table 6–13   Desalination process chart

Source Water	Typical TDS Concentration, mg/L	Variable Process[*]				
		EDR	RO	MED	MSF	MVC
Potable	1,000	✓	✓	✓	✓	✓
Brackish	7,500	✓	✓	✓	✓	✓
Seawater	35,000	✓	✓	✓	✓	✓
Brine	60,000	No	No	✓	✓	✓

[*]Reverse osmosis (RO), electrodialysis reversal (EDR), multiple effect distillation (MED), multiple stage flash (MSF), and mechanical vapor compression (MVC).

Table 6–14   Pretreatment methods for desalination systems

Constituent	Problem	Potential Treatment Method
Dissolved gases (H_2S)	Fouling with colloidal sulfur, corrosion	Aeration, EDR only
Suspended matter (turbidity)	Fouling, clogging	Direct filtration Coagulation and sedimentation plus filtration
Color, organics, or bacteria	Fouling	Coagulation, sedimentation, filtration, and chlorination; activated carbon adsorption
Calcium, barium, and strontium[*]	Scale	Lime softening and filtration Lime–soda softening and filtration Chemical scale inhibitors
Residual chlorine	Membrane degradation	Activated carbon adsorption Sulfite reduction
Sulfate[*]	Scale	Barium precipitation and filtration Anion ion exchange Chemical scale inhibitors
Iron and manganese	Fouling	Low concentrations—aeration, oxidation, pH adjustment, filtration Moderate to high concentrations—aeration, oxidation, pH adjustment, chemical coagulation, and sedimentation, filtration Permanganate oxidation, chlorination
Silica	Scale	Alum/iron coagulation, sedimentation, filtration Lime or lime-soda softening
Alkalinity	$CaCO_3$ scale	Lime precipitation, sedimentation, filtration, acidification

[*]Sulfate will not be a problem if calcium, barium, and strontium are removed.

source, or feedwater, passes through a membrane process into the permeate. For example, RO can produce 350-ppm product water from 35,000-ppm seawater. The thermal processes MED, MSF, and MVC all produce distilled water. Typically, distillate is very pure with TDS ranging from 1 to 50 ppm. Table 6-14 illustrates the pretreatment methods for desalination systems.

Electrodialysis Reversal

Electrodialysis (ED) is a well-developed and a widely used membrane process for brackish water treatment. It has been in use since 1962, and can be used to treat brackish water from 5,000 to 10,000 ppm TDS. ED transfers ions through membranes to remove those ions from the brackish water source. Salts and minerals are dissolved in brackish water, forming cations and anions. For example, source water containing salt, or sodium chloride, ionizes in water to form a sodium cation (positively charged) and a chloride anion (negatively charged). Under an applied direct current electric field, positively charged sodium ions move toward negative electrodes (cathodes), and negatively charged chloride ions move toward positive electrodes (anodes).

Process description. By passing brackish water through alternatively arranged stacks of ion selective membranes, salts become separated from the source water. The source or feedwater flows tangential to the membrane and the ions flow perpendicular to the ion-selective membranes toward their respective electrodes. As positive ions migrate to the cathode, they pass freely through a positive ion permeable membrane. The next membrane in the stack is a negative ion permeable membrane that rejects the positive ion from passing through it. Typical selectivity is greater than 90 percent. As this migration process continues, product water compartments lose ions and concentrate compartments gain ions. Figure 6-11 shows a typical multiple compartment ED unit.

These membranes remain separate using plastic spacers that also act as guides for creating a more turbulent flow path for the feedwater. Typically, several hundred membrane pairs and spacers are placed between a single set of electrodes to form a single stack, or stage. Salt removal per stage ranges from 25 to 65 percent (CWC, 1986; USDI 1982). To achieve the level of treatment required for potable water, three or four stages are required, depending on the source water's salt concentration. An estimate of the required number of stages can be made by assuming 50 percent salt removal per stage. Removal efficiencies improve with higher feedwater temperature, as high as 100°F (38°C) or higher, turbulent water flow, and feedwater pretreatment to remove substances such as films of scale, slime, and other deposits that form on the membrane's concentrate side.

ED membranes periodically plug as ions accumulate on the charged membranes. Adding acid or polyphosphates can control insoluble salt precipitation on the concentrate side. However, in the early 1970s, the EDR process was developed to minimize or eliminate the need for pretreatment. Since 1974, most ED treatment systems use EDR technology. In the EDR process, the electrode polarity is reversed.

This polarity reversal begins converting the concentrate compartments to product water compartments by reversing the ion flow direction. For 1 to 2 minutes after this reversal is initiated, both compartment streams are wasted, allowing films, scale, and deposits to be removed from the membranes. This reversal process is timed to occur every 15 to 20 minutes. Therefore, the membranes tend to be self-cleaning.

Other advantages of an EDR system include less sensitivity to inlet concentration changes, lower operating and membrane replacement costs than other desalination processes, and high recovery of treated water from the source water. Disadvantages include high power consumption, relatively low TDS limit for efficient treatment, and lower efficiency at lower water temperatures.

The typical operating pressure for EDR is 30 to 45 psi (207-310 kPa). The typical product water recovery is approximately 80 percent. Total electrical demand of a large plant is estimated to be approximately 7.5 kW/kgal; the major power expense is the electricity required for charging the poles.

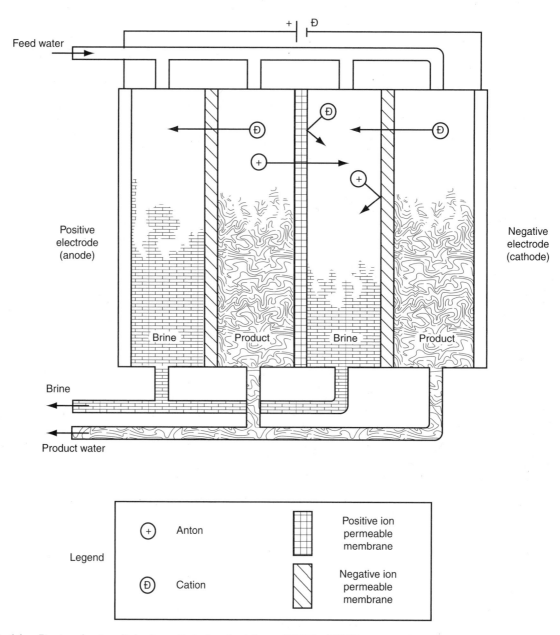

Figure 6–11   Basic electrodialysis unit (adopted from USDI, 1982)

Reverse Osmosis

Reverse osmosis processes use semipermeable membranes to treat fresh, brackish water, or seawater. The water source will dictate the type of membranes (for example, nanofiltration membranes are used to remove hardness/soften, while low pressure RO membranes are used for brackish water). In chemistry, the phenomenon of osmosis is essentially the flow of one constituent of a solution through a semipermeable membrane while other constituents are blocked. For example, water with a low salt concentration will flow to a solution with a higher salt concentration. The driving force for this phenomenon is the osmotic pressure induced by the solute concentration gradient across the membrane. Applying pressure greater than the osmotic pressure to the more concentrated solution can reverse this osmotic driving force—in this case high TDS water—thus forcing the water to diffuse from the feedwater solution through the membrane to the lower concentration solution, or potable water. The solute is *rejected*, or not allowed to migrate through the membrane. This concentrated solution is called the *reject solution*.

The more concentrated the salt solution, the higher the required applied pressure to reverse the osmotic pressure and drive *clean* water across the membrane. The salt solution concentrates until water will no longer pass through the membrane at the applied operating pressure, then the salt solution is discharged. The 72-mgd $(2.7 \times 10^5 \text{ m}^3/\text{d})$ RO plant in Yuma, Ariz., previously mentioned, is the largest reverse osmosis plant now in operation in the United States. This plant controls Colorado River water salinity by treating irrigation drainage flowing into the river.

Membranes. Several types of RO membrane materials are available. These include cellulose acetate (CA) and polyamide materials. The best membranes are thin-film composite polyamide membranes because of their superior operating pH range, resistance to biodegradation (a serious problem for CA membranes), and greater resistance to oxidizing agents. Three common, commercially available membrane systems are spiral-wound, hollow-fiber, and tubular. For municipal water treatment, the two most common configurations are spiral-wound and hollow-fiber; spiral-wound are the most popular because they are more resistant to fouling and can be effectively backwashed.

RO membranes may experience surface compaction and flow constriction with aging. This potential is insignificant at operating pressures lower than 400 psi (2,758 kPa) but may result in a significant loss of production at 400 psi (2,758 kPa). Fouling and biogrowth may also be significant problems as with any membrane process. These conditions result from concentration polarization of heavy metals, silica, and organic matter, as well as excessive turbidity in the feedwater. Fouling can be eliminated with pretreatment for removing suspended solids and excessive hardness, in addition to providing adequate scour velocities. Biogrowth, which may occur if the source water has high organic matter content, can be eliminated by disinfection with nonoxidizing biocides. Residual chlorine higher than 0.1 mg/L will damage all types of membranes.

Process description. Typical RO processes include 1-micron filters for pretreatment, high-pressure pumps, RO membranes, and disinfection. For some source waters, pretreatment using flocculation/sedimentation/filtration may also be required to remove suspended solids from the feedwater to protect the RO membranes. Chemical pretreatment is also often required to prevent biogrowth on the membranes. Chemical and physical treatment may also be required to oxidize and remove iron and manganese. Chemicals are also needed to adjust pH and prevent scale formation on the membranes, depending on the water's Langelier Index. RO will filter out microorganisms, but a disinfectant residual is still required to prevent biogrowth downstream of the process and in water distribution systems. To reduce operating costs, flow splitting after pretreatment and product water blending may be used to reduce the volume of RO treated water and therefore the electrical demand.

Process selection. The RO process has excellent removal characteristics for ionic and nonionic solutes, such as silica and many organics, has the ability to operate at low temperatures without loss of solute rejection, can be designed in modular units or stages, and has capital costs lower than those of other desalination processes. The primary disadvantage is the high operating pressure that results in high operating costs resulting from power consumption.

Typical operating pressures for RO are 150 to 400 (1,034-2,758 kPa) psi for brackish waters. The operating pressure is determined largely by feedwater TDS and percent solute removal required. The total plant electrical demand for a large plant is estimated to be 7.5 kW/kgal.

Both EDR and RO are well suited to treat brackish groundwater. The salt concentration and temperature of groundwater are typically more constant than a surface water source. Also, because the ground acts as a filter, pretreatment requirements may be less stringent than for surface water.

Distillation

Distillation is the oldest desalination process and is most commonly used for desalting seawater. Distillation is basically a heat transfer process. When a saline solution is boiled, dissolved salts remain in solution as the water vaporizes. The water vapor is then condensed on a cooler surface. Energy requirements are generally 1,000 Btu to vaporize 1 pound of water.

Process description. Various types of distillation systems have been developed to lower this high energy requirement and recover heat loss from the distillation process. Four major types currently used to distill seawater include MSF, vertical tube evaporation (VTE), vapor compression (VC), and multieffect multistage (MEMS).

MSF distillation consists of heating water under pressure in tubes and then allowing it to expand suddenly or *flash* into a chamber. As some of the water evaporates or flashes, the rest cools slightly and flows into another chamber at a lower pressure where it flashes again. The flashed vapor condenses on the outside of condenser coils cooled by raw water in each chamber. Condensed pure water drips into collecting pans and is pumped for use. Units are fabricated to treat as much as 10 mgd (0.04 Mm^3/d); naval ships typically use this technique to treat seawater for boiler feed and drinking water.

MSF operates at varying reduced pressures to lower the boiling point of the feed stream, thus reducing the energy input required for vaporization. Product water recovery is approximately 15 to 20 percent. As many as 40 stages are typically used to treat seawater. Electrical demand of a large plant is estimated to be approximately 60-90 kW/kgal. The major power expense is heat required to boil the water. Unless a waste heat source to supply steam is available, EDR or RO is generally preferred to MSF because of better energy efficiency and lower operating cost.

VTE allows water to flow by gravity down the inside of a long vertical tube while hot vapor or steam supplies heat on the outside. Design improvements include fluted-surface tubes and adding biodegradable detergent foaming agents on the insides of the tubes, improving heat transfer by a factor of four (USDI, 1982).

VC distillation uses mechanical means to compress the water vapor that has been evaporated at a tube surface or in a flash chamber. The pressure and vapor temperature are raised for use in vaporizing more water. This process uses mechanical or electrical energy rather than heat energy for distillation.

MEMS distillation is characterized by repeated reuse of vaporization heat. Heat used to produce vapor in the first effect can be carried over with the steam to the second effect. The second effect is operated at a lower pressure and temperature than the first effect. Consequently, the first-effect steam condenses inside the tubing of the second effect and becomes product water. The heat given up during condensation enters the concentrate of the second stage and evaporates close to the same amount of steam as in the first effect. This process is continued in each succeeding effect, the steam from the last effect giving up its heat to cooling water in the condenser (Boyle, 1991).

Source Water Quality

Salinity is a function of ions present in brackish water, seawater, and brine. Although the predominant ions are typically sodium and chloride, the regulated parameter in potable water is TDS, which include charged particles as well as noncharged particles such as silica.

When using a membrane process, source water will often require some pretreatment to reduce membrane-fouling potential. Generally, source water should be treated to remove suspended solids. Charged particles and high-molecular-weight complexes can block the membrane. Some organic materials, such as proteins and amino acids, may precipitate on the membrane surface. A phenomenon called *concentration polarization* occurs when a high salt concentration layer builds next to a membrane surface, causing salts to precipitate onto the membrane. Concentrations higher than 0.3 mg/L iron, 0.1 mg/L manganese, or 150 mg/L silica can also foul EDR membranes. Iron concentrations higher than 1.5 mg/L can foul RO membranes. Hydrogen sulfide, once oxidized, can cause sulfur particles to precipitate and severely foul EDR membranes (USDI, 1982). Microbial contaminants can foul RO membranes and should be pretreated with a bactericide. In low doses, chlorine is effective but must not be used with polyamide RO membranes.

Scaling and corrosion are the two major problems associated with most distillation plants. The most common scale-forming salts are calcium sulfate and calcium carbonate. Feedwater pretreatment through pH adjustment or scale inhibitor, and sometimes decarbonation, can prevent calcium carbonate scale. In a typical distillation process, the limiting temperature and brine concentration are usually determined by the calcium and sulfate concentrations in the concentrate. Calcium carbonate will precipitate when brine is flashed. The distillation processes must be operated such that scaling does not occur.

Concentrate Disposal

Concentrate disposal costs can be a substantial part of the total cost of desalting and must be considered in the initial planning and design. When using either membrane or thermal separation processes, highly concentrated reject water (concentrate) is produced along with high-quality potable permeate. The TDS of the concentrate depends on the source water characteristics. For example, reject water from a nanofiltration plant may have TDS concentrations lower than 2,000 mg/L. Such relatively low TDS concentrate can, in some cases, be used for spray irrigation if blended with reclaimed wastewater (for a total TDS less than 500 mg/L). For brackish and seawater treatment systems, reject water concentrations can be significantly higher, typically ranging as high as 30,000 mg/L. Concentrate waste can also typically be characterized by low dissolved oxygen, low pH, and may contain corrosion products and residual chemicals from pretreatment processes. Concentrate is also toxic to marine and freshwater organisms, which make surface disposal very difficult. Low recovery systems also create a large volume of concentrate that is also hard to dispose of.

Six common methods for waste concentrate disposal are surface water discharge, indirect ocean discharge from a regional concentrate interceptor to a wastewater treatment plant not producing reclaimed water, land application, injection well, evaporation, and direct ocean discharge through an outfall. One variation on well injection is oilfield flooding. In many cases, sewer discharge may not be an option because of reject water quality or quantity.

Disposal Regulations

Reject water disposal is also regulated by several federal requirements and may also be regulated by specific state and local agency requirements. As a result of the number of desalination plants in California and Florida, these two states have been most active in regulating reject water disposal. The following paragraphs highlight federal requirements that may apply to desalination plants.

Clean Water Act. The federal Clean Water Act (CWA) prohibits pollutant discharges into navigable waters from point sources without a National Pollutant Discharge Elimination System (NPDES) permit. USEPA generally administers the NPDES program; however, states may be delegated the responsibility, provided their programs are at least as stringent. All desalination plants discharging to surface waters or the ocean must therefore be granted an NPDES permit that sets reject water pollutant limits, operation, reporting, and monitoring requirements. Meeting NPDES requirements helps ensure water quality standards are met.

Desalination plants disposing reject water to publicly owned treatment works (POTWs) are exempt from NPDES requirements but must meet USEPA's National Pretreatment Standards as well as any state or local POTW requirements through permits and/or local ordinances.

Section 503 of CWA regulates sewage sludge disposal requirements. POTWs must comply with these requirements. Hence, they may indirectly affect desalination plant reject water disposal.

Safe Drinking Water Act. Groundwater discharges via well injection and possibly land application are subject to underground injection control (UIC) under the Safe Drinking Water Act (SDWA). The UIC program can be administered by USEPA or at the state level. Well disposal requires an individual permit or must be authorized by rule based on one of five well classifications that regulate certain types of well disposal. Concentrate injection is prohibited if it causes a potable groundwater source to exceed SDWA maximum contaminant levels or affect public health.

Resource Conservation and Recovery Act. The Resource Conservation and Recovery Act (RCRA) applies to hazardous and nonhazardous wastes. Reject water must be classified under one of these categories. To qualify as a hazardous waste, a residual must first be considered as a solid waste. Solid waste is broadly defined to include waste in liquid, semiliquid, and solid forms. Therefore, reject water wastes are generally considered solid wastes. The reject water must then be determined to be hazardous or nonhazardous. A solid waste is hazardous if it is on any published RCRA list or exhibits characteristics of ignitability, reactivity, corrosivity, or toxicity. If the reject water is determined to be hazardous, RCRA identification, transportation, record keeping, and reporting requirements must be followed.

Coastal Zone Management Act. The Coastal Zone Management Act (CZMA) requires activities affecting a state's coastal zone to comply with an approved program. The CZMA applies to states adjacent to the Great Lakes, as well as to states along the East and West coasts and the Gulf Coast.

Other federal regulations. Several other federal regulations should be reviewed to determine whether they affect desalination plant reject water disposal. These include the Solid Waste Disposal Act; Comprehensive Environmental Response, Compensation, and Liability Act; Hazardous Materials Transportation Act; Toxic Substances Control Act; Clean Air Act; and Occupational Safety and Health

Act. Although these regulations would probably apply to reject water disposal, the reject water must be classified as either hazardous or nonhazardous. This assessment depends on source water quality, pretreatment requirements, and types of chemicals added to the processes. Specific contaminants must then be compared with the specific regulatory requirements in terms of contaminant concentration and quantity discharged.

Disposal Options

Surface water discharge. Low TDS concentrate waste may be suitable for surface water discharge. However, the primary regulatory concern will be surface water quality degradation and toxicity (caused by an ion imbalance as compared to seawater) to organisms in the receiving water. Toxicity is difficult to resolve as it requires significant treatment, although blending with wastewater is helpful. Surface discharge will require an NPDES permit. Effluent limits will be required if deviation from state water quality criteria is anticipated. This could result in some post-treatment of concentrate waste before the surface water is discharged.

Direct ocean discharge. For desalination plants located near a coast, ocean discharge is possible, but the ion imbalance that causes the toxicity in fresh water may be more of an issue in the ocean. Blending with wastewater has been shown to be helpful (Hollywood, Fla. does this), and where the potential exists for disposal in this manner, a viable and cost-effective disposal method is created. Concentrate can be discharged by pipeline or outfall to the ocean. Regulations limiting both temperature and salt concentration are becoming more restrictive.

Specific states may implement additional rules that require treatment of the concentrate. For example, ocean discharges in California must comply with the California Ocean Plan that describes the principles for waste discharge management to the ocean and specifies detailed water quality standards. This plan requires utilities to maintain a healthy and diverse marine community, which means that potential adverse effects of waste concentrate on marine biota, primarily from toxicity and heavy metal and low dissolved oxygen concentrations, must be avoided. Ocean outfalls and diffusion systems must be designed for rapid initial dilution and adequate dispersion to minimize local contaminant concentrations. Outfalls should be far enough from areas of special biological significance to maintain natural water quality conditions in these areas. High dilution rates are also needed.

A recent draft Environmental Impact Statement and Management Plan prepared for establishing the Monterey Bay National Marine Sanctuary indicated that future regulations may prohibit the discharge of wastes into the designated boundary of the sanctuary without approval from the US National Oceanic and Atmospheric Administration (NOAA). The NOAA report addresses the significance of potential harmful effects of industrial and municipal waste discharge to the marine community. Alternative regulations were proposed in the report that would give NOAA the authority to review and certify all new and current NPDES permits for industrial and municipal discharges. Similar regulations are expected for potential marine sanctuaries along the coast of California (Boyle, 1991).

The Florida Department of Environmental Regulation has set standards (Class III criteria) for concentrate discharge into surface water bodies. In a Florida survey, 10 of 13 large (0.5-mgd [1,893 m^3/d] or greater) brackish water RO plants were discharging concentrate directly to the ocean. The survey results indicated that most plants exceeded the criteria considerations in dissolved oxygen, mercury, and radionuclides (Boyle, 1991).

Indirect ocean discharge. For inland desalination plants close to major drainage systems, waste concentrate disposal through regional interceptors to wastewater treatment plants, and then to the ocean, may be an attractive option especially for low-concentrate flows. In a wastewater treatment plant, the waste concentrate stream can be mixed with the sewage stream before going through primary, secondary, and tertiary treatment processes. Typically, a waste concentrate stream constitutes a small percentage of the total plant capacity. Salts in the waste concentrate stream are neither reduced nor converted during the treatment processes that generally treat for BOD, suspended solids, or organic removal.

Local concentration and evaporation. Inland desalination plants located away from coastlines and regional interceptors can consider concentration followed by evaporation as an applicable method for waste concentrate disposal. Evaporation ponding only, without preconcentration, may not be cost-effective unless large land areas are available at low cost. To reduce needed land area, the quantity of waste concentrate can be reduced by processes such as EDR or MVC that produce additional product water and minimize residual concentrate volume.

Concentration and evaporation is particularly applicable to inland areas where annual evaporation rates are relatively high and annual precipitation is low. In designing an evaporation pond, adequate linings should be provided if groundwater infiltration is not allowed. To minimize pumping costs, evaporation ponds should be close to, and down gradient of, the desalting plant. Pond depth will depend on the concentrate inflow rate and evaporation rate. Using darker colored lining can increase evaporation rates. Also, greater air circulation will result in more, drier air over the pond. Spraying concentrate through sprinklers can also increase the evaporation rate provided energy costs are not prohibitive and that sprinkler nozzle plugging is not a problem. Concentrate ponds must be protected against flooding and residual concentrate must be removed every few years and disposed of in an approved landfill. If toxic metals are concentrated in the sludge, the waste may be classified as hazardous.

Deep well injection. Deep well concentrate injection is common in the oil and gas industries. Such disposal is feasible only in locations with suitable underground formations for the concentrate. Each potential site must be evaluated for suitability. Deep well injection of waste concentrate requires a comprehensive geologic investigation and field testing of the disposal zone and underground reservoir areas to determine that the injected concentrate is chemically compatible with fluids in the reservoir, it does not pollute potable groundwater sources, and future natural resources will not be contaminated.

The waste concentrate may need to be post-treated before injection to prevent aquifer plugging by bacterial slimes or suspended materials. Deep well injection is common in southeast Florida, typically extending 3,000 ft (914.4 m) or more into geologic formations well below potable water sources.

Oilfield injection. Oilfield operators sometimes inject water or steam into oil-bearing formations to increase the amount of oil extracted. When water is used, it is called the *waterflood technique*. In a waterflood project the water is a combination of water separated from product oil, called *product water*, and *supplemental water*. Initially, a large amount of supplemental water is needed to pressurize the oil reservoir and start the oil moving. Then smaller amounts are needed as more water is extracted from the oil. Although potable water is generally used for a waterflood project, saltier water may have advantages. Concentrate causes less swelling of clay particles, and thus reduces blinding in the oil formation. It also mixes better with product water that is generally saline. In general, oilfield operators have found that the more similar the supplemental water is to the product water the fewer problems occur.

Compliance strategy. A comprehensive regulatory compliance strategy should be prepared early in the project planning process. Figure 6-12 illustrates suggested steps for preparing a regulatory compliance plan. Regulatory agency contacts and requirements should be solicited from federal, state, and local agencies that typically have jurisdiction in matters concerning waste disposal, and groundwater and surface water quality.

Seemingly unrelated agencies should also be contacted as a precaution. These include the US Army Corps of Engineers, state and federal animal and fishery agencies, US National Oceanic and Atmospheric Administration, US Coast Guard, US Department of Interior for historic preservation, state land commissions, boating commissions, federal or state environmental compliance, and state and local health agencies. Multiple studies and permits will often be required, and should be conducted concurrently. Studies may include hydrological and biological impacts on receiving waters, including bioassays, water quality tests, dye tracer and dilution

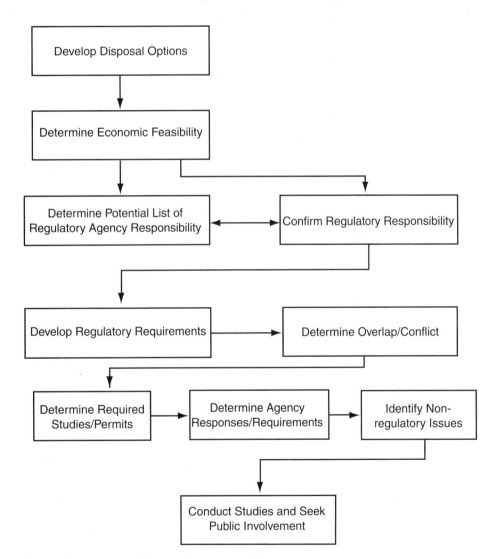

Figure 6–12 Typical regulatory compliance plan procedure

modeling, fisheries monitoring, benthic studies, impacts on navigation and structures; and impacts on other discharges to the receiving waters.

WATER MARKETING AND TRANSFERS

A tool that provides a supplemental water supply to meet short- and long-term water demands is water marketing. This method includes the transfer, sale, lease, and exchange of water or water entitlements from one water user to another. The methods can be temporary, such as when entitlement to the water is retained, but its use is transferred for a short time to another user. In a permanent transfer, water entitlements, gained through water rights or contractual commitments, are sold or transferred to another party.

The general types of water transfers, the issues related to each, and the procedures under which water has been transferred are discussed here.

Types of Water Transfers

Water has been exchanged among water entitlement holders throughout the United States for many years. Most transfers or exchanges, unless they are directly between adjoining water utilities, have taken place in the western United States. Most were intrabasin transfers, that is, exchanges of water by users situated within the same hydrologic water basin. An example would be one irrigation user transferring water, possibly temporarily, to another both being served by the same irrigation water district. In more recent years, water transfers have been developed to convey water from hydrologic basins with surplus supply, to basins where supplemental supplies are needed. The intrabasin transfers have been conducted rather informally, with little public scrutiny and regulatory oversight. Interbasin transfers, however, can have significant impacts and have been subjected to much more formal and rigorous review and approval procedures. Before discussing the issues related to water transfers, the types of transfers that have occurred and can be used to supplement limited water supplies shall be defined.

Fallowing. One of the most straightforward ways to create water for sale to others is for a farmer to fallow his ground (not plant a crop for which the water would normally be used to provide irrigation), and sell this increment of water, oftentimes to an urban user. Fallowing frees up water normally used for irrigation in one area for temporary use in another. This type of water transfer is normally used during drought years to provide a short-term supply to an area with restricted supply. In most states, a farmer who is willing to fallow his land must prove to the regulatory agencies that he would have otherwise planted a crop that would have used the water. The proof generally consists of a review of historical farming practices to establish the basis for the type of crop and water use that the farmer had established under similar conditions.

The seller must also be able to prove that entitlement to the water can be incontrovertibly established, and that the quantity of water created represents a reasonable level of consumptive use by the crops that have historically been grown with that water. In this type of transfer, the amount of water diverted for irrigation cannot be transferred for use by others, only the consumptive use portion. The water that would have returned to the system as agricultural runoff from the fields, or through infiltration into the groundwater and then into the surface water system, cannot be transferred. The portion of the original diversion that would have normally been available to other water rights or contractual entitlement holders in the basin remains for their use under normal farming practices.

Crop shifting. Water can also be transferred by shifting to a crop that requires a lower level of water use. This practice is more prevalent with farmers who grow row crops, where a high-water-using crop such as tomatoes can be replaced with a low-water-use crop such as safflower. Normally, this type of transfer is for one year; thus, a high-water-using crop such as alfalfa is not considered because it is more difficult and expensive to substitute. There are many examples of permanent shifts of cropping patterns to create water for transfer, such as shifting farmland used for permanent pasture to a vineyard.

A benefit of crop shifting is that it provides an alternative to fallowing, and the revenue and employment impacts on the local area are generally lessened. As with any transfer method, obtaining approval for the amount of water that can actually be transferred to another party requires proof that water is available that would normally have been used. This is discussed in more detail later in this chapter.

Groundwater substitution. Many water rights holders also have access to groundwater, and another popular method of water transfer is for the user (usually a farmer but could be any surface water user) to switch the source of supply from surface water to groundwater. For example, the farmer pumps groundwater to irrigate a crop, and transfers an equivalent amount of surface water that would normally have been used for irrigation, to another user. A number of issues must be resolved. For example, the groundwater pumping may adversely affect others, induce increased losses from the surface stream from which the farmer normally diverts, create overdraft in the groundwater basin, or represent practices that have not normally been used. These factors determine the amount of water that can be transferred.

Groundwater pumping. Another transfer method involving groundwater is pumping water from wells controlled by one user into a surface water body for transfer to others. This type of transfer poses the same questions as groundwater substitution and is very controversial in many areas. In some areas, restrictions on out-of-basin transfers of groundwater have been established. Legal and regulatory restrictions on groundwater transfers vary from state to state. Many states have the same types of regulations for groundwater as for surface water rights; groundwater transfers are thus subject to the same restrictions as surface water transfers.

Water conservation. Efficient use of water is important for all users. Because water used for agricultural irrigation in many states represents such a large portion of the surface water supply, conserving agricultural water creates significant supplemental supply without the need for construction of dams or other similar facilities. As the need for water transfers has increased, the potential for sale of the conserved water has been viewed by many agricultural users as a method to finance their conservation activities. An example of transfer of water created by conservation practices is the transfer from the Imperial Irrigation District (an agricultural user in the Imperial Valley of California) to the Metropolitan Water District of Southern California and the San Diego County Water Authority (two large urban users in Southern California).

Water conservation practices that can provide water for transfer are very specific to the hydrologic conditions of a given area. Although the need to conserve has been emphasized universally, the conserved water is viewed differently based on geographic location and the fate of the conserved water. In areas where the water lost from unlined canals and infiltration from irrigation enters the groundwater basin or surface streams, the loss may provide a supply for other users. In areas with direct interconnections between surface streams and groundwater basins, the water lost to groundwater may increase downstream surface flows, particularly during summer periods of low surface flow. In these cases, none or only a small portion of the conserved water has been allowed to be transferred.

Stored surface water. Excess reservoir storage can also be transferred. Short-term transfers can be made to provide an emergency drought supply, other transfers provide supply until a new source can be put on line, or permanently. The water rights issues related to sale of excess supply that would not have been released except to complete a transfer can be complex, and downstream water rights holders normally object to sale of this water. The withdrawal from storage creates capability for storage of water in a subsequent year. This water could not have been otherwise stored unless the volume transferred had been withdrawn. The transfer is thus viewed as an adverse impact on their ability to subsequently use the surface water stored in the reservoir. These types of transfers generally apply to western water use and are far less applicable to eastern practice.

Conjunctive use. Another way to create water for transfer is through the conjunctive use of surface water and groundwater to more efficiently manage the joint resource and create more yield. Water banking programs have been created in a number of areas through which excess surface water that is available during normal and wet years is stored in groundwater basins for extraction during years of limited supply. Banking of surface water includes in-lieu recharge, surface spreading and infiltration, and groundwater injection. In-lieu recharge programs allow users who normally rely on groundwater to irrigate crops with surface water provided from another area. By not using the groundwater reserves, surface water is banked and can then be pumped when needed.

Surface water can also be banked by directly recharging the groundwater basin through recharge basins or injection wells. This type of program has become very popular in California, where a number of entities in the Kern County area have established formal programs for banking others' excess surface water available in wet and normal years. These programs are providing a way for holders of water entitlements to better use the yield available during years of excess to provide supplies during restricted supply years.

Issues Related to Water Marketing

Water transfers can be very controversial and difficult to accomplish. The major issues that must be dealt with in most water transfers are discussed here.

Real or transferable water. Water is considered a public resource, and its use is permitted through water rights and contractual entitlements. Use must be reasonable and beneficial; thus, water that is being considered for transfer must not have been created by unreasonable use or excess to the needs of the water rights holder. In general, the ability to transfer water is based on the need to prove that the water rights or contract holder would otherwise have used the water, and because it was not used, it is available for transfer. Again, this issue generally applies to western water rights.

Numerous state and federal agencies are responsible for protecting water resources for the public benefit. As a result, water transfers are subjected to a process of review and approval with the primary emphasis placed on the need to prove that the transfer will not injure other water rights holders or adversely affect fish and wildlife. The amount of water that can be transferred has generally been based on proving the issue of *real water*, as opposed to *paper water*. Although a holder of water rights or contractual entitlements may have a written right to the use of the water, determination of transferable water includes the examination of how much of that water may be transferred. In general, this determination is based on how much water would have been used with and without the water transfer. The real water is the difference, and generally represents the water that would have been consumptively used by the entitlement holder if the transfer had not occurred.

For example, a holder of water entitlements (water rights or contractual entitlements) may have the right to divert 1,000 acre-ft (1.2×10^6 m^3) for use. Of the 1,000 acre-ft (1.2×10^6 m^3) of diversion, some of this water may have been returning to the surface stream as agricultural runoff. Some may also have infiltrated the groundwater basin, returning as underflow to the surface stream. The real water is the amount that would have been consumptively used by the entitlement holder and would not have been available for use by others. This amount of water can be transferred. Determination of this amount is complex and subject to review and approval by many regulatory agencies.

Third-party impacts.   Movement of water from one area to another through a water transfer can adversely affect the source area unless the transfer is properly planned and managed. Fallowing of cropland is an example of the potential for a transfer to adversely affect a local area's economy. Sales of agricultural products related to the growing and harvesting of the crops normally grown on the fallowed land, and the resulting impacts on jobs, business incomes, and taxes in the local areas must all be considered. This issue was the prime objection raised to water transfers coordinated by the State of California during the droughts of the early 1990s.

Measures that may mitigate third-party effects include limiting the number of acres in a given area that can be taken out of production, restricting the amount of water transferred by a given district or other large holder of water entitlements, and levying a fee on transfers to reimburse those affected for lost revenues or to pay for increased social costs. Methods to mitigate third-party impacts have been discussed and reviewed in detail in the many public hearings and meetings associated with the resolution of issues related to movement of water through the Sacramento-San Joaquin Delta in California, through a joint federal/state planning process called the CALFED Bay Delta Program.

Environmental impacts.   A major concern associated with any water transfer or exchange is a potential adverse impact on the environment. Water transfers can degrade surface and groundwater quality, affect aquatic and terrestrial flora and fauna, reduce recreational water uses, cause aesthetic problems, and subside the ground surface, affecting public infrastructure (such as drainage systems and flood control levees in the area of excessive groundwater pumping). Impacts can be local or regional, depending on the size and length of the transfer and the prior base environmental conditions. In general, short-term and intrabasin transfers have relatively minor potential environmental impacts and are therefore subjected to much less environmental scrutiny than long-term and interbasin transfers. Environmental analyses required to facilitate transfers varies among the states, and is highly dependent on the environmental compliance requirements of the agencies involved.

Area of origin.   Transfer of water from a given hydrologic water basin into another basin can be viewed adversely by many landowners and politicians in the area where the transfer originated. Many objections to the transfer are emotional and related to the desire to retain all resources within the local area for use by its residents. As a result, many local agencies have restricted transfer of water outside their hydrologic basin, unless the seller can prove that the transfer will not adversely affect other local water users or jeopardize local resources. Many landowners have refrained from participating in statewide water transfer efforts during droughts because they fear that participating in such a transfer will jeopardize their water rights or contractual entitlements.

Wheeling transferred water.   In many transfers, the water must be wheeled through conveyance facilities (such as pumping stations and canals) that are owned by others, often state or federal agencies. These agencies require that the parties to the transfer obtain an agreement with them to allow use of these facilities to move the water from its origin to the buyer's turnout. Because these facilities have been financed and constructed by the users contracting with these state or federal agencies, they also charge the parties to the transfer for the use of these facilities. These costs can be significant and can affect the economic feasibility of transfers.

By far the primary factor that has affected water transfers in California is for the parties in a transfer to gain access to these state or federal conveyance facilities. Because of the many restrictions on pumping of water created by concerns over the protection of fish as they migrate through the river system, state and federally operated pumping facilities that export water from the Sacramento-San Joaquin Delta in California do not have capacity to handle transfer water. In many years, they cannot wheel-transfer water except for very narrow windows of time in the late summer and early fall. As a result, transfer of water from areas with surplus in many years is not possible, if the water must be pumped out of the Delta.

Steps in completing a water transfer.   The procedures for developing and implementing a water transfer vary among the states because of the differences in water rights, the conditions of water conveyance in natural and/or man-made facilities, legislative and institutional differences, and the geographical distribution of water supply and areas of need. The length of the transfer and whether it is an intrabasin or interbasin transfer can also increase the complexity of a transfer. Some general steps that can be followed to implement a water transfer are described here. They generally apply to implementing a long-term transfer, but many are required for any transfer.

1. The first step in any water transfer is to put the buyer and seller in contact with each other to match water needs and available supplies. In some states, clearinghouses where buyers and sellers can make contacts to consider water sales may facilitate transfers. In most cases, however, the buyer and seller are connected through professional water brokers, water rights attorneys, or consulting engineers. A buyer or a seller could also independently identify another party with common interests who might be interested in a potential water transfer by contacting one of the state or federal agencies that has responsibility for water planning, regulation of water rights, or similar responsibilities. Staff in these agencies normally know the professionals who can provide assistance, or the buyers or sellers who might share common interests in pursuing a water transfer.

2. To successfully implement a water transfer requires both the buyer and seller to clearly understand each other's needs and objectives. An efficient way to facilitate the exchange of information is to prepare a memorandum of understanding that defines the basic terms the two parties agree to. This step determines rather quickly whether there are sufficient common interests and objectives.

3. After the parties have generally agreed on the potential terms of a water transfer agreement, the next step is to prepare a basic transfer proposal that describes the basic terms of the transfer and how it will be accomplished. This proposal should describe the amount of water to be

transferred, when it will be conveyed from the seller to the buyer, the basis of entitlement by the seller to the water to be transferred, the basis for determining the transfer amount, facilities that will be used to convey the water, and other similar information.

4. After the preliminary proposal has been developed, the parties should meet with the state, federal, and possibly local agencies or individuals that will review and approve the transfer. These could include

   • the state water rights agency, if the transfer requires modification of water rights or approval of differing use of water rights, or downstream water rights holders who may have concerns or objections to the transfer;

   • the agency that is a party to the contractual entitlements if the transfer involves use of water obtained through a contract;

   • federal and state fish and wildlife agencies that will review potential impacts or will determine whether, how, and when the water can be conveyed and diverted;

   • local landowners or special interest groups who may have concerns about the impacts of the transfer; and

   • the agencies or individuals who will be involved in permitting conveyance of the transferred water through their facilities.

5. The primary purpose of this series of contacts is to describe the basic transfer proposal and to surface any potential concerns that could affect its viability, feasibility, and costs. The need for environmental analyses and documentation, and the scope of any special studies that will be required to support the approval process, can also be defined.

6. Following this initial series of meetings, the parties to the transfer should meet to structure a final transfer proposal that considers input received in review of the preliminary proposal. Either party can withdraw from the agreement if it appears that the transfer will not meet their needs or expectations.

7. If the transfer parties decide to continue, the preliminary transfer proposal should be finalized and submitted to formal review and approval by the state, federal, and local regulatory agencies. This process can vary significantly in length and complexity, and the parties should define the approval process for each agency and the approximate schedule so the use of the water is based on a realistic schedule for approval of the transfer. In some states, a transfer that involves only use of the water for a year or less can generally be processed quickly, often with minimal environmental documentation. However, even with a short-term transfer, the primary issue of not damaging legal holders of water rights or adversely affecting fish or wildlife must always be considered. Long-term or permanent transfers can take as long as a year or more if significant environmental documentation or detailed technical studies are required.

8. Environmental requirements vary substantially among the states, and the need for and scope of environmental documentation will thus also vary significantly. If formal environmental analyses and documentation are required, the logical approach is to complete them while the review is

being completed by the regulatory agencies. Normally, certification of an environmental document is required as a condition of the approval of water rights modifications, wheeling agreements, and other transfer approvals needed to match state and local regulatory requirements.

9. After approval of the water rights modifications, completion of the environmental process and certification of the documents can take place, any other needed approvals can be obtained, and any needed wheeling agreements can be finalized, and the transfer of water can begin.

REFERENCES

A Guide to: Customer Incentives for Water Conservation, California Urban Water Agencies. 1994. California Urban Water Conservation Council and US Environmental Protection Agency. Sacramento, Calif.

A Water Conservation Guide for Commercial, Institutional, and Industrial Users. 1999. New Mexico Office of the State Engineer, Albuquerque, N.M.

American Water Works Association, 2000. M1, *Principals of Water Rates, Fees, and Charges.* Denver, Colo.: AWWA.

American Water Works Association. 1994. M24, *Dual Water Systems.* Denver, Colo.: AWWA.

American Water Works Association. 1992. *Drought Management Planning* (Water Conservation Committee-Water Shortage Subcommittee). Denver, Colo.: AWWA.

American Water Works Association. 1993. *Evaluating Urban Water Conservation Programs: A Procedures Manual.* Planning and Management Consultants, Ltd. Denver, Colo.: AWWA.

American Water Works Association. 1999. *Water Quality and Treatment*, Fifth Edition. American Water Works and McGraw Hill, Denver, Colo.: AWWA.

American Water Works Association Research Foundation. 2000. *Commercial and Institutional End Uses of Water.* Denver, Colo.: AwwaRF.

American Water Works Association Research Foundation, 1996. *Impact of Demand Reduction on Water Utilities.* AwwaRF, Denver, Colo.: AWWA.

American Water Works Association Research Foundation. 2000. *Long Term Effects of Conservation Rates.* AwwaRF, Denver, Colo.: AWWA.

American Water Works Association Research Foundation, 1994. *Energy Audit Manual for Water/Wastewater Facilities*, Electric Power Research Institute

(EPRI), Palo Alto, Calif.: 1994. Report No. CEC Report CR-104300, State of California Energy Commission, Sacramento, Calif. 1994. AwwaRF, Denver, Colo.

American Water Works Association Research Foundation, 1999. *Residential End Uses of Water.* AwwaRF, Denver, Colo.: AWWA.

Baumann, D., Boland, J., and Hanemann, W.M. 1998. *Urban Water Demand Management and Planning.* McGraw-Hill, New York City, N.Y.

Boyle Engineering Corporation Report to Metropolitan Water District of Southern California. 1991. Los Angeles, Calif.

California Urban Water Agencies. 1994. *Long Term Water Conservation & Shortage Management Practices: Planning that Includes Demand Hardening.* Sacramento, Calif.

California Urban Water Conservation Council. 1999. *Memorandum of Understanding Regarding Urban Water Conservation in California.* Sacramento, Calif.

California Urban Water Conservation Council. 1997. *Designing, Evaluating, and Implementing Conservation Rate Structures, A Handbook Sponsored by California Urban Water Conservation Council.* Sacramento, Calif.

Case Studies of Industrial Water Conservation in the San Jose Area. 1990. City of San Jose, Brown & Caldwell Consultants and Department of Water Resources, February. San Jose, Calif.

Clean Water Council. 1986. *Handbook Public Water Supply.* Washington, D.C.

Conlon, W.J. and Stuart A. McClellan. 1991. Membrane Softening: A Treatment Process Comes of Age. *Jour. AWWA*, Vol. __, No. 11, pp. ____.

Drought Response and Monitoring. 2000. Texas Water Development Board, Austin, Texas.

Estimating Benefits from Water Conservation, 1999. CONSERV99 Conference Proceedings, Monterey, California, February. Maddaus, W., Maddaus Water Management. American Water Works Association, Denver, Colo.: AWWA.

Maddaus, W. 1987. *Water Conservation.* American Water Works Association. Denver, Colo.: AWWA.

Maddaus, W., G. Gleason, and J. Darmody. 1996. Integrating Conservation into Water Supply Planning: How can water suppliers achieve an appropriate balance between capacity expansion and conservation? *Journal AWWA.* November 1996. Denver, Colo.

Nonresidential Water Conservation: A Good Investment. 1992. Ploeser, J.H., Pike, C.W., Kobrick, J.D. *Jour. AWWA*, Vol. 84:(10).

Policy for Implementing the State Revolving Fund for Construction of Wastewater Treatment Facilities. 1998. California State Water Resources Control Board. Sacramento, Calif.

Pomona Virus Study. 1977. County Sanitation Districts of Los Angeles County. Los Angeles, Calif.

Pontius, F.W. et al. 1996. Regulations Governing Membrane Concentrate Disposal. *Journal AWWA*, May 1996.

Quality Energy Efficiency Retrofits for Wastewater Systems, Electric Power Research Institute (EPRI), Palo Alto, CA: 1998. Report No. CR-109081, State of California Energy Commission, Sacramento, CA. 1998. Document No. P400-98-013, American Water Works Association Research Foundation, 1998. Call local Electric Service Provider or California Energy Commission (916) 654-4070.

Quality Energy Efficiency Retrofits for Water Systems, Electric Power Research Institute (EPRI), Palo Alto, CA: June 1997. EPRI-CEC Report No. CR-107838; State of California Energy Commission, Sacramento, CA. 1997. Document No. P400-97-003; American Water Works Association Research Foundation, 1997. Call local Electric Service Provider or California Energy Commission (916) 654-4070.

Richard, David, et al. 1992. *The Cost of Wastewater Reclamation in California.* University of California-Davis. Davis, Calif.

Rocky Mountain Institute. 1991. *Water Efficiency, A Resource for Utility Managers, Community Planners, and Other Decisionmakers.* Snowmass, Colo.

Urban Drought Guidebook, New Updated Edition. 1991. California Department of Water Resources, Sacramento, Calif.

Urban Water Conservation Programs. 1994. *Volume II: Topical Listings.* Planning and Management Consultants, Ltd. Sacrament, Calif.

Urban Water Conservation Programs, 1994. *Volume III: Experience and Outlook for Managing Urban Water Demands.* Planning and Management Consultants, Ltd. Sacramento, Calif.

US Department of Interior. 1982. *Evaluation of Desalination Techniques for Wastewater Reuse.* Washington, D.C.

US Environmental Protection Agency. 1993. *Designing a Water Conservation Program, An Annotated Bibliography of Source Materials*, Document No. 832-B-003. Washington, D.C.

US Environmental Protection Agency. 1998. *Water Conservation Plan Guidelines*, Document No. EPA-832-D-98-001. Washington, D.C.

This page intentionally blank

Chapter **7**

Water Quality

When planning water resources, the quality of potential sources is as important as the quantity of water each may provide. Ideally, source water should be free of microbial contamination from human and animal activities, of toxic natural and synthetic chemical contaminants, and be of adequate quantity to meet the needs of the population served. The quality of water sources in North America ranges from nearly pristine in some areas to very contaminated in others.

Pristine sources are rarely available. Increasing populations, increasing pollution from domestic and industrial activities, and other pressures cause many communities to use inferior quality source water. The poorer the source water quality, the greater the need to provide multiple-step treatment to remove microbial and chemical contaminants. Each increment of treatment increases the cost of the finished water.

This chapter introduces the main concepts of water quality and relates them to water resources planning. Topics covered include the hydrologic cycle and water quality, specific quality issues for surface water and groundwater sources, and the physical, chemical, and biological components of water quality. It also discusses the sources of water contaminant loading and sampling and monitoring water quality.

THE HYDROLOGIC CYCLE AND WATER QUALITY

Water supply sources are primarily surface water or groundwater. A region's surface water and groundwater resources are closely interconnected by the hydrologic cycle; however, US regulations are specific to surface water or groundwater. Chapter 9 discusses these regulations in more detail.

Many potential contaminants, whether natural or man-made, affect the quality of water supply sources. These contaminants can enter a water resource at any point in the hydrologic cycle. The following paragraphs introduce the components of the hydrologic cycle.

The hydrologic cycle is the continuous movement of water through the environment, above, on, and below the Earth's surface. When water evaporates, the moisture forms clouds and falls in the form of precipitation. The precipitation that does not evaporate falls onto land or surface water, or is intercepted by plants or structures. The water flows across the land, or stays in surface water until it evaporates or percolates into the ground. Trees and other plants also take up water through their roots and return it to the atmosphere in a process called *transpiration*.

Water that percolates into the ground can recharge groundwater aquifers. Excess infiltration percolates slowly, moving downward and laterally to sites of groundwater discharge, such as springs on hillsides, or seeps in the bottoms of streams and lakes or beneath the ocean. If the rate of precipitation exceeds the rate of infiltration, overland flows occur, carrying water into surface water bodies.

SURFACE WATER QUALITY

All the natural and human factors influencing water quality apply to surface waters either directly or through surface water and groundwater interconnections. The biological components of water quality that principally affect surface waters are dissolved oxygen, eutrophication, toxic substances, and temperature. These components affect the transmission of communicable diseases through consumption or contact. The dissolved oxygen concentration in a surface supply is an indicator of the general health of the aquatic ecosystem. Toxic substances can affect ecosystems and harm humans who consume contaminated water or contaminated food that contacts the water source. Temperature influences all biological and chemical reactions, and variations in temperature affect the density and transport of water.

Rivers, streams, lakes, and reservoirs are the four principal surface water sources. Estuaries, bays, and harbors are surface waters that connect streams or rivers with the ocean. A river or stream is a surface water source with a distinct downstream flow. A lake or reservoir is a surface water source distinguished by slow flow-through velocities and vertical temperature gradients.

Rivers and streams are rich and diverse ecosystems. The characteristics of the flow and the chemical components of rivers and streams are the principal factors that determine the biological components of water quality. The topography of rivers and streams affects the velocity, mixing characteristics, solids and sediment transport, and flow of the water. All these factors, in addition to the physical, chemical, and biological components, should be considered for their effects on the water quality of a river or stream source.

Lakes and reservoirs are sources for recreation and municipal and industrial uses, including agriculture, water quality control, and fisheries management. Lakes and reservoirs can become sinks for nutrients, toxicants, and other substances from incoming rivers; as a result, eutrophication is a significant water quality problem. The drainage area and length, depth, surface area, and volume of a lake or reservoir are significant factors affecting the extent to which the source will act as a sink.

Wetlands are flooded areas that are shallow enough to promote the growth of wetland plants. They can remove urban pollutants and raise the level of dissolved oxygen by decreasing the levels of oxygen-demanding substances.

GROUNDWATER QUALITY

All the natural and human factors influencing water quality apply to groundwater either directly or through surface water and groundwater interconnections. Groundwater is principally affected by dissolved contaminants (leachate) from landfills, by the seepage or leaching of contaminants through soils, and by pumping.

Iron, manganese, high hardness, radon, volatile organic chemicals, inorganics such as nitrate, and pesticides are frequently found in groundwater. Iron, manganese, other minerals, and radon originate in the geology of the groundwater; the other contaminants are transported to the groundwater. High chloride levels have been found near saltwater where groundwater is pumped faster than the water is recharged. If the water table lowers, salt water can intrude.

Geological and hydrological conditions, as well as the variety of contaminants, make each groundwater source unique. Groundwater flow is very slow laminar flow (compared to surface flow) with no mixing or dispersion of contaminants. The flow may be turbulent near wells and interconnections with surface water; in turbulent regions contaminants mix and disperse. By the time the water from a contaminated aquifer reaches the well and is recognized, the aquifer has generally been extensively contaminated. The contaminants are usually transported through the soils above the groundwater source from contaminant sources such as agriculture fields, landfills and other hazardous waste sites, and leaking underground storage tanks for chemicals and petroleum products. The movement of water through soils depends on soil characteristics such as permeability and moisture content. Other sources of movement include groundwater recharge and injection wells.

The transport of contaminants once in groundwater depends on the dilution and mixing characteristics; adsorption, permeability, precipitation, and hydrolysis properties; and the decay characteristics. Hydrocarbons such as methyl tertiary butyl ether or MTBE (a gasoline oxygenate additive) can move very quickly through groundwater sources. In general, quantifying the flow, recharge, chemical, and biological reactions is very difficult.

PHYSICAL, CHEMICAL, AND BIOLOGICAL COMPONENTS INFLUENCING WATER QUALITY

Pure water is tasteless, colorless, and odorless. Because water is a nearly universal solvent, organic and inorganic materials, including pollutants and gases, can become components of water as it moves through the hydrologic cycle. The quality of a source is measured by the kinds and quantities of these components found in the water. The components are generally categorized as physical, chemical, or biological.

Physical Characteristics

The principal physical characteristics of source water include total dissolved solids (TDS), turbidity, color, tastes and odors, and temperature.

Total dissolved solids.   TDS refers to the total inorganic and organic particulate material in water. TDS is often used as a measure of mineral content and can be estimated with electrical conductivity tests. Although it is not a regulated measure of water quality, USEPA has established a nonenforceable secondary standard of 500 mg/L. See chapter 8 in this manual for more information about secondary standards.

Turbidity.   Turbidity in water results from suspended matter that causes the water to be opaque or cloudy. The suspended matter is often soil runoff in water sources. By itself, turbidity has no health effects, but it can interfere with disinfection and provide a medium for microbial growth. Turbidity usually indicates the presence of microbes. The Surface Water Treatment Rule (SWTR) requires systems using surface water, or groundwater under the direct influence of surface water, to filter their water when certain water quality parameters are exceeded (see chapter 8). If turbidity goes above 5 nephelometric turbidity units (ntu), the system must filter the water. Systems that filter must ensure that the turbidity goes no higher than 1 ntu (0.5 ntu for conventional or direct filtration) in at least 95 percent of the daily samples of any two consecutive months.

Color. Color in water is caused by natural metallic ions, certain types of dissolved and colloidal organic matter leached from soil or decaying vegetation, and industrial wastes. USEPA has established a nonenforceable secondary standard of 15 color units. Because substances that cause color are usually in solution, the color generally cannot be removed by mechanical filtration.

Tastes and odors. Tastes and odors are caused by salts or TDS, decomposed or synthetic organic material, or volatile chemicals. Tastes and odors are usually more closely related with biological properties of water than chemical properties. Generally, dead organic matter can be broken down into taste- and odor-free compounds in water with adequate dissolved oxygen. Odor-producing chemicals include solvents, pesticides, and benzene compounds. A taste or odor threshold of a substance in water is the lowest concentration that can be tasted or smelled. For odor, USEPA has established a nonenforceable secondary standard of 3 threshold odor number.

Temperature. The temperature of water affects biological activity rates, oxygen saturation, and mass transfer coefficients (which describe how molecules of a substance move across an interface from one phase to another). In the case of groundwater, a significant or relatively rapid shift in temperature, which closely correlates with climatological or surface water conditions, likely indicates that the source is influenced by surface water and is subject to the SWTR (see chapter 8). Water temperature is also an important environmental consideration; for example, fish species generally thrive in a relatively narrow temperature range.

Chemical Characteristics

The principal chemical characteristics of source water include pH, alkalinity and acidity, dissolved cations and anions, hardness, conductivity, and levels of carbon dioxide. Specific elements or chemicals that affect water quality include nitrates and ammonia, phosphate, chloride, sulfates, iron and manganese, pesticides, solvents, and radioactive substances. Chapter 8 lists the maximum levels for regulated chemicals in finished water.

pH. pH is a scale measure of the acidic or basic (alkaline) nature of the water, which ranges from 0 to 14, with 7 being neutral. pH measures intensity, not capacity, in the same way temperature measures how hot or cold water is. (Technically, pH is the negative log of the concentration of hydrogen ions, and *pH* refers to the potential of hydrogen.) The pH of natural rainfall is about 5.6. Naturally occurring substances, such as carbon dioxide or minerals, and artificially occurring pollution such as sulfur dioxide from industrial emissions, can react with water to reduce the pH of rainfall to as low as 3. Closely related to pH are the characteristics of water called *alkalinity* and *acidity*. Alkalinity measures water's ability to neutralize acids, that is, its ability to react with H^+ ions. Acidity measures water's ability to neutralize bases, or its ability to react with OH^- ions. For finished water, USEPA has established a nonenforceable secondary standard for pH of 6.5 to 8.5.

Cations. Cations are positively charged ions in solution, and anions are negatively charged. Common cations found in water include calcium (Ca^{2+}), magnesium (Mg^{2+}), and iron (Fe^{2+}). Common anions include chloride (Cl^-), bicarbonate (HCO_3^-), and carbonate (CO_3^{-2}) Cations and anions indicate the level of, or potential for, certain kinds of pollution or harmful substances in water, and other characteristics such as hardness. A number of similar numerical scales for rating water hardness have been devised and published, including, for example, the following scale (AWWA, 2003):

Hardness Range mg/L of $CaCO_3$	Description
0–60	Soft
61–120	Moderately hard
121–180	Hard
More than 180	Very hard

Conductivity.   Conductivity is a measure of electrical resistance, the property of a substance to conduct (carry) heat or electricity. The unit of measure is the siemens (formerly called mho), which is the reciprocal of resistivity (1 divided by resistivity). Conductivity provides an estimate of the TDS, or can be used to verify the TDS results obtained in physical analyses of water.

Carbon dioxide.   Carbon dioxide, a minor gas in the atmosphere, is an end product of biological decomposition. In solution, it decreases pH (see previous discussion) and is a measure of the corrosiveness of water.

Biological Characteristics

Source water biological quality is extremely variable and depends on many factors. The factors include domestic and feral animal activity on the watershed; human activities on the watershed, including recreation, manufacturing and fabrication, and agricultural activities; municipal pollution inputs from raw sewage to primary and secondary wastewater treatment plant effluents; and storms over the watershed that wash natural and synthetic contaminants into the surface waters or that percolate into the groundwater aquifers. Microbial contaminants associated with these sources include bacteria, viruses, and protozoa, in pathogenic (capable of causing disease) and nonpathogenic forms. Larger animals, such as zebra mussels, can impair water supply facilities, though they are rarely as great a concern as microorganisms, except in areas such as the Great Lakes.

Bacteria.   Bacteria are unicellular and exist either as free-living organisms or parasites. Some bacteria are disease-causing (pathogens), some are not; however, professionals sometimes debate about what should be included in a list of pathogenic bacteria. In theory, any organism that can invade the human body and produce a toxic reaction in tissues or organs is a pathogen; in practice, outbreaks of waterborne pathogens must occur in two or more individuals and be spread by water. The major classifications of bacterial pathogens include *traditional, new or emerging, opportunistic,* and *socioeconomic environmental invaders.*

Major epidemics of typhoid fever and cholera resulting from contaminated water supplies have been documented from ancient civilizations, through the Middle Ages, and in the twentieth century. The traditional bacterial pathogens that cause these epidemics have been known for more than a century. Identifying the bacteria as the cause of disease led to the development of basic public health measures that reduce contamination of drinking water and food by human waste.

The new or emerging pathogenic bacteria are the results of improvements in laboratory methodology or of a species mutating into a more aggressive invader of humans. Pathogen *Escherichia coli* 0157:H7 (*E. coli*) is an example of the latter group.

Opportunistic pathogens are bacteria that can harm individuals with weakened immune systems, such as the elderly, individuals with compromised immune systems, and infants with underdeveloped immune barriers. Specific colonization sites may be the skin, respiratory system, eyes, ears, nose, or intestinal tract. Differences in socioeconomic environments caused by poverty, water scarcity, and political priorities over public health issues can increase the prevalence of certain waterborne pathogens. Some pathogens such as *Shigella* are often threats because of poor sanitation practices and nonexistent water treatment barriers.

Densities of bacteria, viruses, and protozoa vary widely because of wastewater effluents from domestic sewage treatment plants (raw wastewater bypass, primary or secondary treatment, septic effluents) and the frequency and intensity of storms that dilute and degrade the receiving water quality by contributing additional contaminants. The concentration of bacteria in water is typically measured with plate counts (the growth of bacteria on a culture medium) as colony-forming units (cfu) per milliliter. Bacterial counts may vary from less than 1 to 10 cfu/mL in groundwater to more than 1×10^7 cfu/mL in surface water badly polluted by municipal raw sewage or combined sewage and stormwater overflow effluents. The measurement of coliforms, bacteria that inhabit the intestines of warm-blooded animals, is used as an indicator that pathogenic bacteria may be present. Indicator bacteria (total and fecal coliforms, including *E. coli*) densities in source water can range from less than $^1/_{100}$ mL in good quality groundwaters to more than $1 \times 10^4/100$ mL in surface water badly polluted with municipal raw sewage or combined sewage and stormwater overflow. Few water systems treat surface water with more than 2×10^4 total coliforms/100 mL or 2×10^3 fecal coliforms/100 mL.

Viruses.   Human viruses found in source waters include rotavirus, enteroviruses (such as polio), reoviruses (which can infect the respiratory and gastrointestinal tracts), hepatitis A, and gastroenteritis viruses (including hepatitis E). All these organisms present significant health concerns and, if present in source water, must be removed or inactivated by water treatment processes. They are productive at lower temperatures but require a host to multiply or move.

Viruses occur more frequently and in greater abundance in surface source waters, but they may also be found in groundwater as a result of septic tank effluents, land application of sewage and sewage sludge, and other sources. Viruses can travel long distances as water percolates downward and flows through the soil; the distance of travel depends on the type of soil and the specific geology. Groundwater can no longer be considered pristine and safe for consumption without treatment. If a groundwater source is directly influenced by surface water intrusions, full conventional treatment may be necessary to ensure the treated water is safe for consumption. The US Safe Drinking Water Act (SDWA) established a maximum contaminant level goal (MCLG) (see chapter 9) of zero for enteric viruses in finished water.

Protozoa and parasites.   Waterborne parasites, such as *Giardia* and *Cryptosporidium*, are acknowledged as the leading identifiable agents of diseases acquired from drinking water. Bacteria have been generally cited as the major problem since Koch's 1836 observations; waterborne parasitic diseases date back many centuries.

Parasites causing waterborne diseases, such as giardiasis and cryptosporidiosis, were regarded as normal fauna of the human intestines. *Giardia lamblia* was first observed by van Leeuwenhoek in 1681, but not until the 1960s was *Giardia* recognized as a significant cause of human disease. The SDWA established an MCLG of zero for *Giardia lamblia* in finished water. *Cryptosporidium parvum* was first described by Tyzzer in 1912, but was not acknowledged as a significant threat to human health until the 1990s.

Worldwide, waterborne parasites continue to threaten health. For example, flatworms cause *swimmer's itch* in Africa, Asia, and Central and South America.

Close relatives of organisms responsible for swimmer's itch cause serious human disease.

Algae and fungi. Algae grow only in the presence of sunlight, and the presence of algae indicates eutrophication (the reduction of dissolved oxygen in water). Green algae and cyanobacteria (blue-green algae) impart color, taste, and odor to water. When algae die, the organic matter of the water increases the biochemical oxygen demand, the amount of oxygen taken up by microorganisms in decomposing the organic material in a water sample stored in darkness at 20°C. Some algae such as cyanobacteria can produce toxic substances. Fungi can grow without sunlight, impart taste and odor to water, and may clog water supply appurtenances.

Treatment of affected waters (typically with chemicals) is unreliable. Preventing algae growth by reducing the nutrient loading—especially phosphorus—is the best solution. The problem is worse in summer, when thermal stratification of reservoirs may lead to anaerobic conditions (an absence of free oxygen) in the lower layers. Blue-green algae are tolerant of such conditions. One method to reduce algae growth during the summer is to introduce river water upward by jets into a reservoir. The mixing will reduce the anaerobicity in the lower levels.

SOURCES OF CONTAMINANT LOADING IN WATER

Each type of water use has a unique set of water quality requirements or criteria. The main categories of water use are water supply (municipal and industrial), recreation (swimming, boating, and aesthetics), fisheries (commercial and sport), agriculture (irrigating fields or watering livestock), and ecological balance. Water used for potable supplies is regulated most stringently; it must be safe, that is, without risk of adverse health effects. Potable water has historically been classified as the "highest and best" use of a water source. Water used for recreation must be generally safe for ingestion or contact. Water used for fisheries must support aquatic species and be free from contamination that could pose a human health risk. Water used for agriculture must support the land and livestock and be free from contamination that could pose a human health risk. Water used to maintain ecological balance, such as minimum stream or river flows, is becoming a more prominent factor when evaluating water availability.

Natural and human factors influence the quality of a water source. Natural factors include climate, watershed characteristics, geology, microbiological growth, fire, saltwater intrusion, and density or thermal stratification. In general, natural factors cannot be controlled. Human factors are usually categorized as point or nonpoint sources. Point sources include wastewater treatment plant discharges, industrial discharges, hazardous waste facilities, mine drainage, and spills and releases. Nonpoint sources include agricultural and urban runoff, livestock, land development, landfills, erosion, atmospheric deposition (such as acid rain), and recreational activities (such as boating on reservoirs). Because of the larger areas involved and their diffuse nature, nonpoint sources of contamination are more complex and difficult to control than point sources. As point sources become more controlled or treated before release to a water source, nonpoint sources are increasingly being studied and regulated.

Natural Influences

Precipitation can affect water quality. Rain or snow can contain contaminants from air pollution. Storm runoff may dislodge soil particles and pollutants and carry them into surface water, increasing the turbidity, color, metals, or other contaminants. The natural flushing effect of storm flows also introduces particulate organic material and leaches dissolved ions from the contributing drainage area. Dry conditions can cause stagnation, increasing the likelihood of microbial activity and algal growth.

Watershed characteristics such as topography, vegetative cover, and wildlife can significantly affect water quality. Topography affects flow rates and the pattern of runoff and can lead to the introduction of sediment, debris, and nutrients into a water source. Natural decomposition of vegetation can affect water color and is a source of natural organics that contribute to formation of disinfection by-products. Vegetative cover can act as a natural filtering mechanism for runoff from nonpoint sources and can provide a barrier to human activities. Wildlife can affect the microbiological characteristics of surface waters.

The geology of a watershed directly affects the quality of surface water and groundwater. The weathering characteristics of the geologic parent material affect soil characteristics such as soil depth, texture, and structure, all of which affect natural erosion rates. Soils act as buffering agents for acidic precipitation that can adversely affect biological activity in lakes and reservoirs. Geologic formations in groundwater can release calcium and magnesium minerals, thus increasing the hardness of the water. Uranium may decay, releasing radon. Asbestos can also be leached into water from certain geologic formations in a watershed.

The state of a water body depends on nutrient levels and microbiological activity. Table 7-1 introduces the three states and their characteristics.

Eutrophic waters can deplete oxygen levels, increase microbiological activity, cause high turbidity and color levels, and form trihalomethane precursors.

Fires in watersheds are natural influencing factors and are usually caused by a combination of drought and lightning. The destruction of brush and forest reduces evapotranspiration, eliminates their function as natural filters, increases the likelihood of erosion caused by increased runoff, leaches nitrates, and creates taste and odor problems. Large quantities of water or chemicals used to extinguish fires can contribute to sediment, organic, and chemical loading in water sources.

Saltwater intrusion can be caused by the natural movement of saltwater into a freshwater source, or by pumping a groundwater source. Saltwater intrusion can result in increased salinity, which aggravates trihalomethane production.

Density stratification of surface waters can create an oxygen deficiency. When turnover of a lake or reservoir occurs, nutrients and anoxic water move from the lake bottom to the surface, feeding algae and degrading water quality.

Point Sources

Twenty-five years ago, sewage treatment plants served only 85 million people in the United States. Today the number of people served by modern wastewater treatment facilities has more than doubled to 173 million people. However, sewage discharges from municipal and community wastewater systems remain major sources of nutrients, bacteria, viruses, parasites, and chemical organic contaminants. Discharge

Table 7–1   Water states and qualitative characteristics

Water State	Nutrient Level	Microbiological Activity
Oligotrophic	Low	Minimal
Mesotrophic	Moderate	Moderate
Eutrophic	High	High

of poorly treated wastewater with high concentrations of nitrogen and phosphorus contributes to accelerated rates of algal activity and eutrophication.

Industrial discharges can affect the quality of water supplies by releasing contaminants into the air, water, and soil. Industrial facilities can also discharge directly into a water supply through a regulated discharge or accidentally, as in the case of a spill. Treatment and storage lagoons can contaminate groundwater through subsurface percolation. Figure 7-1 illustrates an example of point source pollution.

The operation of a hazardous waste facility in a water supply watershed or aquifer requires extensive precautions to prevent hazardous contamination to the water source. Hazardous substances may be flammable, corrosive, reactive, or toxic. Inactive facilities may require cleanup.

Mine drainage may cause a change in acidity and cause iron, manganese, and other contaminants to suspend in the water. Mining operations may also affect the topography of a watershed. Watersheds traversed by major highways and rail freight lines are subject to transportation accidents and chemical spills. Many spills and releases occur in conjunction with petroleum product storage installations. Leaks and spills from underground storage tanks and piping are of special concern because the release may go undetected for a long time.

Nonpoint Sources

Twenty-five years ago, agricultural runoff caused 2.25 billion tons of soil to erode and deposited large amounts of phosphorus and nitrogen into many waters. Since that time, the quality of rivers, lakes, and bays has improved dramatically as a result of the cooperative efforts of federal, state, tribal, and local governments and communities to implement the public health and pollution control programs. The amount of soil lost because of agricultural runoff has been reduced by 1 billion tons annually, but because more acreage is in production, the major reductions of phosphorus and nitrogen levels in water sources have resulted from point source reductions, not nonpoint reductions. Figure 7-2 illustrates an example of nonpoint source pollution.

Despite these gains, nonpoint contaminant sources continue to affect water quality. The application of pesticides, herbicides, and fertilizers degrades water

Figure 7–1   Point source pollution

Figure 7–2   Nonpoint source pollution

quality by contributing dissolved nutrients in runoff that accelerate eutrophication. Erosion caused by improper tilling techniques can cause increased sediment loading and increased color and turbidity in the receiving waters. Urban runoff, including runoff from highways, streets, and commercial areas, can contribute substantial loads of nitrogen, phosphorus, suspended solids, dissolved solids (salinity), coliform bacteria, heavy metals, and organic contaminants to the receiving waters. This type of contamination can be most severe during a "first flush" storm event that follows a prolonged drought during which pollutants accumulate. Agricultural areas are also major sources of pollution from endocrine disruptors and antibiotics, fed to livestock and fowl to keep them healthy and productive.

The presence of livestock in watersheds or aquifer recharge zones has a direct effect on bacterial contamination. Feedlots can contribute nitrates to wells and fecal coliform bacteria to surface supplies. Uncontrolled grazing or overgrazing can eliminate vegetative cover.

Land development on watersheds changes the topography and vegetative cover and results in new water uses. Impervious surfaces such as pavement decrease percolation into groundwater and introduce pollution associated with human activity.

Leachate from landfills can change water quality in many ways. If the landfill does not have effective barriers against precipitation or groundwater movement or a leachate collection system, leaching of any contaminants in the landfill can occur. The extent of contamination depends on the characteristics of the landfill.

Erosion is considered a nonpoint source of pollution because of its extent and diversity. It can cause sediment loading, containing soils and nutrients, through surface water runoff to water sources. Sediment loading increases the turbidity and color of a water source, may cause or exacerbate eutrophication, and can decrease the capacity of water sources and change the recharge characteristics of groundwater.

Airborne contaminants from industrial stack emissions, automobiles, or other similar sources can be transported great distances through the atmosphere. These contaminants may pollute water sources through precipitation (e.g., acid rain). The effects on water quality depend on the nature of the contaminant and the physical, chemical, and biological components of the water source. For example, more pristine water bodies having little buffering capacity can be drastically affected by acid rain.

The National Atmospheric Deposition Program (NADP) monitors wet atmospheric deposition at more than 220 National Trends Network (NTN) sites throughout the United States. NADP brings together the US Geological Survey (USGS) and more than 100 partners from federal, state, local, and private organizations. USGS supports 72 of the 220 NADP/NTN sites. A fundamental NADP objective is to provide scientific investigators worldwide with a long-term, high-quality database of atmospheric deposition for research support in the areas of air quality, water quality, agricultural effects, forest productivity, materials effects, ecosystem studies, watershed studies, and human health.

On Nov. 15, 1990, in response to mounting evidence that air pollution contributes to water pollution, Congress amended the Clean Air Act and included provisions that established research and reporting requirements related to the deposition of hazardous air pollutants to the "Great Waters." The water bodies designated by these provisions are the Great Lakes, Lake Champlain, Chesapeake Bay, and certain other coastal waters (identified by their designation as sites in the National Estuarine Research Reserve System or the National Estuary Program). In 1995, sulfur dioxide emissions from 445 power plants in the eastern United States were reduced by 3 million tons as mandated by Title 4 of the Clean Air Act Amendments. NADP/ NTN data formed the basis for a 1996 report showing that these emissions reductions have reduced the severity of acid rain in the eastern United States.

Recreational activities may affect the biological and chemical components of a water source. Recreational use of proposed water supply reservoirs has become a significant issue with new surface water sources. The biggest issues include swimming and boating (including sizes and types of motors).

WATER QUALITY SAMPLING AND MONITORING

Correct sampling of source water for quality is crucial for planning, just as monitoring of quality is critical when the source water is being used for supply. The frequency, duration, and intensity of water quality measurements depend on the designated use of the source as mandated by federal and state regulations. Appropriate agencies should be contacted for regulations once the use of a water source is defined. Statistics are generally used to quantify the quality of sampling results.

Sampling source water meets regulatory requirements and anticipates water treatment requirements. The numbers and types of samples collected and tested simply to meet regulatory requirements are generally considered a minimal effort in determining water quality. Increasing the numbers and types of samples collected and tested beyond what is specified by regulations provides data that may be more representative of water quality. These data help planners predict potential water quality and the treatment processes and maintenance programs to prevent deterioration of water quality.

The timing of taking samples is very important. If the sample collection misses a target event (such as a storm flush), information gained from the program may not reflect actual conditions. The best sampling techniques and laboratory quality control practices will not improve the meaningfulness of final results. Thoroughly understanding the water source being sampled is critical. This understanding requires developing an adequate history of water quality changes and identifying indicators that will predict changes.

Surface Water Sampling

Collecting meaningful samples from surface water sources or groundwater under the influence of surface water (subject to the same regulations as surface water) requires several considerations. Three important ones are (a) the design and intent of any sampling program must be defined clearly, (b) programs must be designed to represent average conditions, and (c) the timing of sample collection is critical to avoid results that may be biased or unrepresentative of true, overall water quality.

Designing a sampling program to represent average conditions may require collecting far more data than the minimum regulatory requirements. A realistic average history may require the sampling program to be in place for months or years. One approach is to collect samples at largely spaced intervals during times when water quality is relatively constant and to collect more samples at shortly spaced intervals when water quality fluctuates. USGS publishes a detailed manual on developing a water quality sampling program.

A sampling and monitoring program must consider the changing activities and conditions in the watershed. Agricultural, recreational, municipal, industrial, and other activities affect downstream water quality. The watershed should be assessed before a final comprehensive sampling and monitoring program is designed and implemented. Potential point and nonpoint sources of contamination should be inventoried. If a monitoring program has been established before such an assessment, the results of the data may be more difficult to interpret.

Point source discharges are regulated through National Permit Discharge Elimination System programs in which discharge limits are specified in a permit. Typically, routine point source discharges from these operations will not cause a sudden change in water quality. Most operations meet their limits during routine operations. The assumption that a waste treatment facility operating within its regulatory discharge limits will not be a major source of microbial contaminants appears sound. However, the atypical event may create a problem, such as discharges from combined sewers during periods of heavy precipitation and hydraulically overloaded wastewater treatment plants. Information about point source discharges is usually available through local state primacy agencies.

Nonpoint source discharges from upstream agricultural facilities may degrade water quality. Feedlots, dairy farms, stables, and commercial agricultural businesses, and the waste disposal practices of each operation are possible pollution sources. Local, county, or state agricultural extension or co-op agents are good starting points for obtaining this information.

The weather may be the most unpredictable influence on water quality. Precipitation, snowmelt, wind, drought, and temperature affect water quality. Overland flows of precipitation and snowmelt carry contaminants into receiving streams as nonpoint discharge. Precipitation runoff and snowmelt cause point source discharges from storm sewers, combined sewers, and treatment plants. The direction of the wind may cause a stream to discharge into a bay or a lake, changing course to flow over an intake. Drought conditions result in a reduced dilution factor and may attract wildlife and livestock to the major streams used by public water supplies. The influence of discharge from a waste treatment facility is magnified by a reduced dilution factor during droughts. Water temperatures affect the variety and viability of microbiological contaminants, although for some microbial contaminants, temperature may have little bearing on their survival in the water environment.

Developing a sampling and monitoring program to include other potential microbial contaminants beyond total coliforms in surface water or groundwater under the direct influence of surface water depends on the overall water quality expected. For source water in the Great Lakes not under the influence of inland streams or shoreline runoff, additional testing beyond total coliforms and heterotrophic (plate count) bacteria may be unnecessary. At the other extreme, for an inland river located downstream of urban areas or discharge from an overloaded waste treatment facility, routine tracking of microbial contaminants beyond total coliforms is crucial to demonstrate the effectiveness of potable treatment systems. In most situations between these extremes, a baseline understanding of the types of microbial contaminants should be established. Expanded monitoring to include contaminants other than total coliforms, *E. coli*, and fecal coliforms are based on past experiences and overall water quality. Bacteria counts may be useful in clean water conditions. Expansion of the monitoring program to *Giardia*, *Cryptosporidium*, or viral testing may yield critical information during nonroutine periods, especially during periods of high runoff.

An example of misleading data is routinely seen in northern inland streams subject to agricultural runoff. In some northern agricultural communities, manure is applied to the fields in December and January when the crops are off the fields and the frozen earth supports heavy farm equipment. Immediately following the application, little or no runoff occurs; however, near the end of February or early March, a combination of snowmelt and early spring rains carries contaminants into receiving streams.

Another surface water condition that may warrant increased sampling is reservoir turnover. Facilities that take water from surface water impoundments are subject to annual reservoir turnovers. Although site specific, turnover typically occurs once in the fall and sometimes in spring. Turnover is caused by the mixing of a formerly temperature-stratified reservoir. Cold oxygenated water drops to the bottom of the reservoir and replaces warmer water that was anoxic. This turnover can cause rapid changes in water quality.

Groundwater Sampling

The key to developing a sampling plan for a groundwater system is to obtain information about the aquifer and the wells in use. Performing a source water assessment or developing a wellhead protection program provides most of the information required to develop a sampling plan. Information regarding well construction practices is invaluable; a poorly constructed well cannot be expected to produce consistent water quality. Typical problem areas in construction include the wellhead, casing, or grouting. Holes, gaps, or other breaches in the systems allow contaminants access to a well.

To determine well construction problems, sampling may be required within the first few minutes or seconds of operating the well. The sample collector may need to determine water volume by measuring the static water level reading to the bottom of the screen or the open bore hole. The primary samples for examining well integrity generally need to be collected within the first two volumes contained in the well. A delay in collecting the sample may risk diluting the contaminants to below detection limits or losing contaminants by flushing the system with fresh water from the surrounding aquifer. A drop in microbiological counts from the initial samples to after the system has been adequately flushed generally indicates construction problems. Total coliform or heterotrophic bacteria counts, or both, can be used as indicators. Table 7-2 provides an outline of analyses that should be performed for groundwater in wells.

Sampling aquifer-related quality requires detailed knowledge of hydrogeological characteristics. For example, it may be necessary to temporarily seal portions of the

Table 7–2   Summary of the minimum parameters to be analyzed in water quality tests (Bloetscher, et al., 2005; AWWA, 2003)

Calcium (Ca)	Fluoride (F$^-$)
Magnesium (Mg)	Phosphate (PO$_4^-$) (total)
Sodium (Na)	Silica as silica dioxide (SiO$_2^-$) (total and dissolved)
Strontium (Sr)	Total Dissolved Solids (TDS)
Barium (Ba)	Total Organic Carbon (TOC)
Aluminum (Al) (total and dissolved)	Hydrogen Sulfide (H$_2$S)
Manganese (Mn) (total and dissolved)	Free Chlorine (Cl$_2$)
Iron (Fe) (totaled, dissolved, and ferrous)	Oxygen (O$_2$)
Potassium (K)	Carbon Dioxide (CO$_2$)
Bicarbonate (HCO$_3^-$)	pH
Sulfate (SO$_4^-$)	Temperature
Chloride (Cl$^-$)	Turbidity (nephelometric method)
Carbonate (CO$_3^-$)	Silt Density Index
Nitrate (NO$_3^-$)	

well with inflatable bladders to isolate one section of the aquifer from another. Alternatively, samples may have to be collected at specified intervals during a pumping test to detect variations in water quality. In general, an increase in selected indicator counts or values indicates aquifer problems. For example, a correlation between an increase in indicator microbial counts with some surface activities, such as precipitation, indicates direct recharge or groundwater under the influence of surface water. An observed increase in coliform counts over time may justify the expansion of the sampling program to include other possible microbial contaminants.

SUMMARY

The quality of water sources is as critical for resource planning as the quantity each may provide. The lower the quality the more expensive the source water will be to treat. A thorough understanding of the complex physical, chemical, and biological characteristics of any source water is important for effective water resources planning. Additional guidelines on groundwater monitoring are found in AWWA M21 *Groundwater.*

SUGGESTED ADDITIONAL READINGS

AWWA. 1990. *Water Quality and Treatment—A Handbook of Community Water Supplies*, 4th ed. Denver, Colo.: American Water Works Association.

AWWA. 2006. M48. *Waterborne Pathogens.* Denver, Colo.: American Water Works Association.

AwwaRF. 1991. *Effective Watershed Management for Surface Water Supplies.*

AwwaRF. 1995. *Electronic Watershed Management Reference Manual*, Version 1.0. Denver, Colo.: American Water Works Association and American Works Association Research Foundation.

AWWA. 2003. M21. *Groundwater.* Denver, Colo.: American Water Works Association.

Bloetscher, Frederick; Muniz, Albert, and Witt, Gerhardt M. 2005. *Groundwater Injection: Modeling, Risks and Regulations*, McGraw-Hill, New York, NY.

Cook, H.F. 1998. *The Protection and Conservation of Water Resources: A British Perspective.* Chichester, U.K.: John Wiley & Sons.

Driscoll, F.G. 1986. *Groundwater and Wells*, 2nd ed. Smyth Companies, Austin, Texas.

Driver, J.I. 1988. *The Geochemistry of Natural Waters*, 2nd ed.

Freeze, R.A. and J.A. Cherry. 1979. *Groundwater.* Prentice-Hall, Englewood Cliffs, N.J.

Frey, M.M., C.M. Hancock, and G.S. Logsdon. 1997. *Cryptosporidium: Answers to the Commonly Asked Questions by Drinking Water Professionals*. Denver, Colo.: American Water Works Association and American Water Works Association Research Foundation.

Geldreich, E.E. 1990. Microbiological Quality of Source Waters for Water Supply. In: *Drinking Water Microbiology: Progress and Recent Developments* (pp. 3- 31). G.A. McFeters, ed. New York: Springer/Verlag.

Geldreich, E.E. 1993. Microbiological Changes in Source Water Treatment: Reflections in Distribution Water Quality. In: *Strategies and Technologies for Meeting SDWA Requirements* (pp. 269-304). Edited by R.M. Clark and R.S. Summers. Lancaster, Pa.: Technomic Publishing Company.

Geldreich, E.E. 1996. *Microbial Quality of Water Supply in Distribution Systems*. Boca Raton, Fla.: CRC Press.

Hurst, C.J. 1991. Presence of Enteric Viruses in Freshwater and Their Removal by the Conventional Drinking Water Treatment Process. *Bull. World Health Org.* 69(1):113-119.

Linsley, R.K. and J.B. Franzini. 1979. *Water Resources Engineering*, 3rd ed. McGraw-Hill, New York City, N.Y.

Page, G.W. 1987. *Planning for Groundwater Protection*. Academic Press, Orlando, Fla.

Pontius, F.W. 1994a. Boiling Water Effective for Crypto and Other Microbes. *Opflow*, 20:10:10.

Pontius, F.W. 1994b. Surface Water Treatment Rule. In: *SDWA Advisor Regulatory Update Service*. Denver, Colo.: American Water Works Association.

Thomann, R.V. and J.A. Mueller. 1987. *Principles of Surface Water Quality Modeling and Control*. Addison-Wesley Publishing Co.

USEPA 1994, National Water Quality Inventory-Report to Congress.

USEPA, 2000. Water permitting 101. <http://www.epa.gov/owm/permits/pwcourse/101pape.htm>

This page intentionally blank

Chapter **8**

Hydrologic Modeling

This chapter introduces hydrologic modeling, which attempts to describe the movement of water in the natural environment. Groundwater models are often used as examples in this chapter, because they offer the most complex situations and special characteristics as outlined in chapter 5. However, all principles of modeling discussed in this chapter apply to surface water models, water quality models, reservoir operations, and optimization models, among others.

The quest to understand and manage water resources is as old as human civilization. The more that is understand about water and the environment, the better we will be able to manage this precious resource. Field measurements, experiments, and hydrologic modeling are all part of this quest. Hydrologic models are simplified mathematical representations of several complex physical processes and their interrelationships as they pertain to water in the natural environment. They are developed on the basis of our understanding of physical processes and are verified by field measurements and experiments. In short, hydrologic models provide insight into hydrosystems behavior. This knowledge helps water resource planners make intelligent decisions.

Discussing all the hydrologic models in this chapter is impossible; even discussing the principles of modeling in a few pages is difficult. As a result, this chapter provides an overview of hydrologic modeling. This chapter focuses on

- fundamental hydrologic processes for nonhydrologists,

- modeling tips for model developers,

- representative values of commonly used model parameters for model users, and

- general guidelines for conducting a modeling study for project managers.

This chapter is intended to broaden the reader's general understanding of the purposes and applicability of hydrologic modeling. For more detailed discussions, readers may consult numerous textbooks and monographs on hydrology and hydrologic modeling. Suggested references include the following:

- *Handbook of Applied Hydrology*, ed. by Ven Te Chow, McGraw-Hill

- *Handbook of Hydrology*, ed. by D.R. Maidment, McGraw-Hill
- *Hydrologic Modeling of Small Watersheds*, ed. by C.T. Haan, H.P. Johnson, and D.L. Brakensiek, American Association of Agricultural Engineers
- *Groundwater Management: The Use of Numerical Models*, P. van der Heijde, American Geophysical Union
- *Computer Assisted Floodplain Hydrology and Hydraulics*, D.H. Hoggan, McGraw-Hill

HYDROLOGIC MODELS: WHAT, WHY, HOW, AND WHEN ___

What Is a Hydrologic Model?

In its simplest term, a hydrologic model is a mathematical expression (usually an equation or a set of equations) describing a physical process of the hydrologic cycle of water and associated waterborne particles (sediments, chemicals, and biota). Multiple physical processes of the hydrologic cycle can be expressed in terms of multiple mathematical expressions that can be combined into one hydrologic model. A mathematical relationship devoid of physical basis has no place in modeling, regardless of the simplicity or complexity of that relationship. The danger of such indulgence was masterfully illustrated in a seminal paper by V. Klemes (1986). He argued that "For a good mathematical model, it is not enough to work well. It must work well for the right reasons. It must reflect, even if only in a simplified form, the essential features of the physical prototype."

In specific terms, a hydrologic model helps us estimate the responses of a hydrologic system to a given set of inputs. Field measurements and experiments can be prohibitively costly and time intensive; at times, field measurements are not available simply because the water management strategy being evaluated is not yet implemented. In such situations, hydrologic models, in some form or other, offer the only viable alternative to water resources planning.

Is Modeling Cost-Effective?

According to a 1982 congressional report (Office of Technology Assessment, 1982), the federal government spends about $50 million annually on water-related mathematical models that are used to plan and manage multibillion dollar water investments. Models are useful tools for evaluating alternative management strategies and for providing an objective basis for discussion among stakeholders who seek to identify and endorse a mutually acceptable resource management plan. Although some water resource plans may not need hydrologic modeling, evaluating a resource development impact with a good model can provide valuable information and may reduce costly dissent and litigation. In many cases, the costs of developing hydrologic models are insignificant compared to the value they add to the decision-making process, especially in light of the fact that the economic and environmental stakes of many water decisions are extremely high.

Why Hydrologic Models?

Water allocation and use decisions can be complex, as demonstrated by the following examples:

- Example 1: A reservoir manager may have the following competing goals:

— Retain sufficient water to ensure adequate future supply for agricultural and municipal users.

— Release enough water to maintain adequate empty storage in the reservoir for flood control.

— Maintain minimum instream flow requirements for fish and wildlife; release enough water to prevent saltwater from intruding into a delta.

— Maximize hydropower generation; maximize recreational opportunities by maintaining water stage in the lake.

— Release cold water from the lower levels of the reservoir to ensure a favorable temperature in the stream for fish and other aquatic life.

— Release enough water for navigation.

— Control discharge to maximize groundwater recharge from recharging streams.

The reservoir manager has planning procedures that range from using *best judgment* based on experience to sophisticated optimization models for reservoir operation. In such cases, a model that can be useful for short-term managerial decisions may not be appropriate for long-term water resources planning or for developing long-range reservoir operational criteria.

- Example 2: A water district manager is faced with an increase in nitrogen and total dissolved solids in the groundwater basin that is the primary water supply source for the district. A jurisdictional regulatory agency has also imposed a moratorium on further groundwater development until a water quality control plan is developed. The development of a water quality control plan for the groundwater basin includes the following steps:

  — Identify sources of groundwater pollution. (Was it caused by overlying land use practices, by pollutants migrating from the surrounding groundwater basins, or due to a reclaimed water recharge program or high-pollutant streamflow recharge?)

  — Characterize past and current groundwater flow and transport regimes.

  — Identify past and potential future impacts from the vadose (unsaturated) zone (Have all the pollutants been observed or does the vadose zone contain pollutants yet to appear in groundwater?)

  — Determine the effectiveness of mitigation measures.

A model that combines groundwater flow and transport factors with a vadose zone component will usually fare better than the *best judgment* approach for planning purposes.

The two examples illustrate that water decisions are often multifaceted and require evaluation of numerous issues and interrelationships among resources. Intelligent decision making involves balancing multiple sources of risks, dealing with multiple stakeholders, improving organizational efficiency, and handling increased complexity. Without a rigorous, methodical, and comprehensive approach, few resource and project managers would be equipped to handle these new challenges.

In general, a hydrologic model can help a water resource planner with these tasks:

1. Help the planner understand complex water management situations, because a hydrologic model requires that relationships be established among components of the problem.

2. Help compile pertinent data synergistically.

3. Help the planner examine the situation in more detail.

4. Develop an operational framework for solving a water management problem.

5. Provide insights into a water management problem.

6. Help identify the primary drivers and constraints of a system.

7. Allow simultaneous consideration of all processes and issues.

8. Enhance the information background of a decision.

9. Provide a tool for *what-if* scenario analysis.

10. Provide "look-ahead" capability.

11. Provide an objective basis for reconciling multiple interests.

12. Add technical credibility to the selected approach or project.

13. Help identify key issues, set priorities, and identify the common grounds for negotiation.

A simplified pictorial representation of model-related activities and their utilities is provided in Figure 8-1.

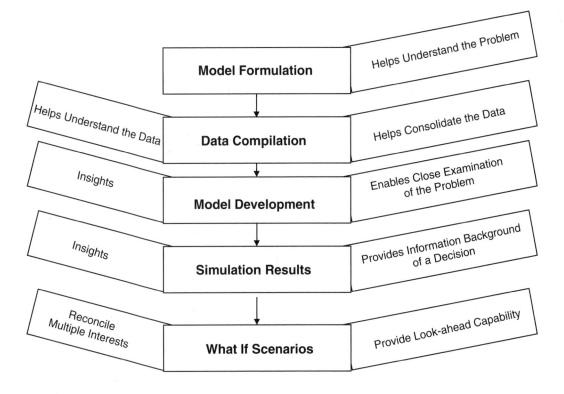

Figure 8–1   Model: activities sequence and utilities

When to Model?

This is one of the most important questions a project manager faces in a hydrologic investigation or water resources planning project. Good hydrologic models are almost always useful: they are excellent tools for exploring hydrologic characteristics of a watershed; they consolidate hydrologic data; they allow the data collection priorities to be identified. They enhance understanding of the hydrologic and environmental drivers of a watershed. A modeling study of a watershed integrates hydrologic data collected by various agencies. Good hydrologic models allow scenario planning and alternative analysis in an objective and quantitative framework. The benefits of modeling are building the knowledge base necessary to plan and manage water resources.

But there are studies and projects for which modeling is unnecessary or unproductive. For example, modeling is not productive when no model is available that addresses the specific project; or when there are no data to develop or validate a model; or when the physical process to be modeled is not well understood. Project scope, schedule, and budget especially preclude a modeling exercise; often conceptual modeling and expert judgment guide the decision-making process. Hydrologic modeling should not be recommended unless it is required to accomplish the study objective or adds value to the project.

HYDROLOGIC MODELS AND THEIR USE

Hydrologic models are best understood when their conceptual framework and key results are examined against the backdrop of hydrology principles and common sense. Models are best applied when one understands the purpose of the project; the hydrologic characteristics of the area under study; and the theories, assumptions, special features, and detailed inputs and outputs of the selected model. Models are best used when they strengthen the knowledge base that supports decision-making processes. Models should not be used to avoid making difficult decisions.

Role of Models in Decision Making

As good as a model may be for helping to make informed decisions, it should not be allowed to replace responsible decision makers. Instead, it should be used as a decision support tool. Decisions need to have a solid foundation built on data and analyses to be acceptable and defensible. This attribute of a decision process can be represented graphically as a decision pyramid, as shown in Figure 8-2. This figure shows the transformation of data to information to knowledge to decision, with rapidly increasing value from the bottom of a decision pyramid to the top. Data alone have little value; once they are processed, analyzed, and organized, they become information. Once the user processes the information to develop and enhance understanding of a situation or a problem, it transforms into knowledge. This knowledge can reduce the risk of undesirable consequences of a decision. An understanding of this decision hierarchy is crucial for determining a model's role in a decision-making process in today's complex environmental arena. Models straddle across all three bottom layers: in the data layer by providing a forum for synthesizing diverse sets of data; in the information layer by discovering interrelationships among data; and in the knowledge layer by providing a forum for understanding action–response characteristics of hydrosystems through alternatives analyses.

An understanding of the decision–data hierarchy is also important to help project managers allocate resources to the model development task in a hydrologic investigation project. Project managers can also exploit the opportunities for cost

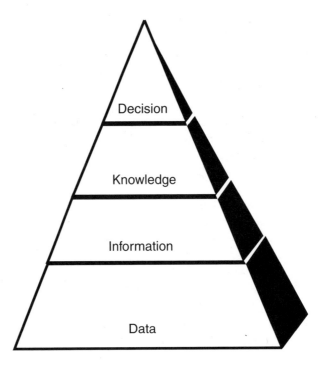

Figure 8–2   Data–decision hierarchy

savings in model development using the decision–data hierarchy. For example, in the conventional approach, a planner often starts at the bottom of the decision pyramid and moves upward by collecting data first; then processing those data; then performing a rigorous and all-encompassing (and often never-ending) data analysis and modeling phase before the planner can make a decision. This conventional approach lacks *a priori* consideration of the whole project, and limited project resources are often exhausted before one ever reaches the top of the pyramid. Thus, decisions are either not made or are made without benefit of proper scientific analyses.

A more effective approach is to start at the top of the decision pyramid and travel down to determine what subset of data and processing is essential for decision support on a specific set of decisions. This pragmatic approach can result in significant cost savings in data collection and model development because it ranks decision support needs. Not all modeling studies and model development efforts should be limited to supporting current and near-term decision-making needs. Models are excellent research tools for improving our understanding of hydrosystems behavior, which in turn helps utilities make better management decisions. Resource planners, public or private, may consider investing time and energy in developing very rigorous scientific models of the physical processes that characterize the hydrosystems behavior. However, the practicing engineers and hydrologists who are charged with solving a practical water resources problem at hand should focus on the purpose and extent of modeling that is needed to solve the problem most cost effectively.

How Much Modeling Is Enough?

Models are simplified mathematical representations of physical processes. Constructing a model that accounts for all the finest details of a process is not possible, nor is it useful or necessary. Simplification is the key to all successful hydrologic modeling, because too much physics or science can defeat its purpose. Also, too little physics or science can lead to oversimplification, which can also defeat the purpose of modeling. It is thus necessary to understand the level of accuracy that is needed and that can be obtained, and match that need with the right level of scientific detail.

For example, a model development task is proposed to predict the pollutant concentration at a water intake pipe in a river downstream of a waste discharge point. According to the physics of river flow, movement of water particles is three-dimensional and pollutant particles are dispersed in all three directions. However, developing a three-dimensional pollutant transport model for this purpose is not warranted; a one-dimensional transport model will be sufficient.

Another example can be made in groundwater. Groundwater flow systems are three-dimensional, but they are often accurately modeled by two-dimensional models in a horizontal direction with multiple layers in the vertical direction to represent the variability of flow dynamics along the third dimension. However, a one-dimensional regional groundwater model will contradict the physics of flow in groundwater aquifers. On the other hand, the flow of water in the vadose zone is predominantly vertical, and a one-dimensional model for vadose zone flow is often adequate. Elaborate soil moisture accounting and plant evapotranspirative process modeling at a 40-acre (16-hectare) land parcel scale for developing the water balance of a 100 mi^2 (256 km^2) watershed is meaningless when the rainfall data are available at only two or three rain gauges spread across the 100 mi^2 (256 km^2) watershed. Discretizing a 1,000 mi^2 (2,560 km^2) groundwater basin with a flat groundwater gradient to 10,000 cells or finite elements or setting a groundwater model convergence criterion to predict the water level with an accuracy of 0.001 ft (0.0003 m) is another example of overkill. In hydrologic modeling, elaborate physics in a model should not compensate for the deficiencies arising out of lack of data, a very common occurrence in the water resources field.

How much modeling is enough is a question that also arises while executing a modeling project. A modeler must decide what levels of accuracy are appropriate for comparative assessment of alternatives. A generalized model with limited accuracy does not provide the required level of confidence in the selection of a water management strategy; detail beyond that needed to provide a rational basis for comparing alternatives is wasteful. Examples of these situations are when modelers try to obtain accuracy of ±1 ft (0.3 m) in groundwater level predictions during model calibration, or when they try to evaluate a decision based on a 2 ft (0.6 m) difference in groundwater levels between two competing alternatives. In another instance, modelers waste effort trying to repeat all model runs used in alternative analyses because a 0.1 percent error in agricultural demand data was discovered just before the final report was submitted. In this case, it would have been more cost-effective and purposeful to assess the impact of this small error in demand data on modeling results or on conclusions of the alternative analyses.

This concept of suitability of models to solve real-world problems is beautifully illustrated by Harvard Business School Professor T. Levitt in a business context: "Excellent quality is not enough. Also required is suitability. In pursuit of wrong purposes, excellence is wrong. Employing gas spectroscopy is overkill when a simple microscope will accomplish the task. Using a simulation model to determine the optimal warehouse network may be excellent management science, but you'll realize it's ridiculous if you just stop to think. Common sense will suggest that you'll need a warehouse in the New York Metropolitan area, probably one between Washington and Philadelphia, one around Atlanta, around Chicago, around Houston–Dallas, in Los Angeles–San Francisco, in the Pacific Northwest, and somewhere on a line between Denver and Minneapolis. How much more scientific accuracy do you need? Your imagination can tell you in a moment a great deal more than scientific excellence would have told you at great expense and pretension in a year." (*The Marketing Imagination*, 1986)

Hydrologic Models and Common Sense

Numerous computer models with varying levels of sophistication and capabilities are now available to water resources professionals. As a result, selecting and using hydrologic models have become very challenging tasks. However, the contribution of these hydrologic models in understanding the governing natural processes of water flow and transport has been enormous. Models and model-derived knowledge have been successfully used to evaluate alternative water management strategies, resolve water disputes, and develop resource protection measures. This success has led to wide acceptance of models as an objective resource evaluation tool. However, success has its own peril: it often obfuscates the fact that hydrologic and transport models are based on mathematical simplification of very complex natural processes. Models are neither fictions nor absolute truths; at best, they are close representations of a physical system. Colorful graphical user interface (GUI) with very accurate graphics does not necessarily indicate the accuracy of the model results. Computer generated numbers and pictures from old and new models alike have often found a higher plateau of credibility than they deserve. As a result, hydrologic models have been misused and abused by unsuspecting practitioners, partly because of their lack of understanding of the models because of inadequate documentation of theoretical foundations and of the underlying assumptions of the models that may limit their applicability to particular situations. Most hydrologic models are developed for specific types of applications because of the prohibitive cost and resource constraints associated with developing an all-purpose, all-encompassing hydrologic model. Physical environments are replete with unique characteristics that may preclude transfer of a very successful model from one watershed or river basin to another. A poor hydrologic model often results when these facts are ignored.

One of the most important tasks of today's water managers and stakeholders is to maintain sight of the purpose and context of modeling. Hydrology is a science of common sense. Therefore, all hydrologic model results must conform to common sense derived from the principles of hydrology. If they do not, there is often something amiss in the input data or in the formulation of the problem that the model is solving. Historic data must support any model conclusions, whether about past hydrologic phenomena or about a future scenario. Any out-of-line model conclusions must be checked against model assumptions and scientific principles. Because of time and budget constraints, hydrologic modelers often make simplifying assumptions about complex natural processes that seem to be less important than others. Sometimes these assumptions are not valid because a specific model application is unique and thus produces results that are counterintuitive. A modeler should keep a watchful eye for such results that do not make sense and investigate reasons to support or discard those results.

Hydrologic Modeling Is Interdisciplinary

Water management is an evolving science; every day, more and more interdisciplinary issues extend the frontiers of this discipline. As a consequence, a modern-day water project involves hydrologists and ecologists, biologists and planners, civil engineers and environmental scientists, and the public. Hydrologists' expertise in water science has thrust them into the center of environmental planning and policy making because water is the primary driver of global ecosystems. As a consequence, the role of hydrologic models has been elevated from analytical tools to the last word in a decision-making process. Hydrologists and hydrologic modelers are no longer faced only with the traditional questions of water movement above and below the land surface, but also with the questions and issues related to the biological and chemical processes that depend on the storage and movement of water. In addition, more and more nonhydrologists are using or developing hydrologic models to estimate hydrologic inputs to their models. This overlap has led to confusion and chaos because they often do not understand the assumptions inherent in a hydrologic model. Hydrologic models are now used in environmental negotiations and in legal battles. The models are scrutinized by more and more interested parties; therefore, hydrologists must ensure that all hydrologic modeling and subsequent analyses are based on solid scientific foundation. Poor decisions can result from poor hydrologic models or from poor understanding of results of the best hydrologic models. On the other hand, good hydrologic models and their proper application can lead to good decisions that can have significant and beneficial effects on the ecosystem balance.

MODELS AND THE HYDROLOGIC CYCLE

All hydrologic models, in some form or other, are mathematical representations of components of the hydrologic cycle, in part or in full. A thorough understanding of the hydrologic cycle is essential to successfully develop and apply hydrologic models. The hydrologic cycle was introduced in chapter 6 as it relates to water quality issues. This chapter begins with a discussion of the aspects of the hydrologic cycle relevant to hydrological modeling.

The global hydrologic system is closed because the total quantity of water available on our planet is finite and nearly constant. Thus, water balance (the principle of conservation of mass) is the key concept of the hydrologic cycle. A pictorial representation of the global hydrologic cycle is shown in Figure 8-3. Annual volumes of water in various phases of the hydrologic cycle are relative to the volume of annual precipitation on the land surface (100 units for the purpose of relative comparison). About four times as much water falls on ocean surfaces as on land surfaces. Of the 100 units of precipitation, 61 return to the atmosphere through evapotranspiration and evaporation; the remaining 39 ultimately return to the ocean (primarily as river flow or streamflow—39 units). These 39 units combine with 385 units of precipitation on the ocean surface and ultimately return to the atmosphere as evaporation (424 units).

During the hydrologic cycle, the principle of conservation always holds true for water volume, heat energy, nutrients mass, sediments mass, dissolved gases, and other materials. As a result, the concept of a hydrologic cycle can be extended to include movement and phase changes of heat, sediments, gases, biota, and mineral matter. This extended definition enhances the value of the hydrologic cycle as an analytic framework for many problems in water resources planning and ecology.

There are many hydrologic subsystems in the global hydrologic cycle. Unlike the relatively closed global hydrologic system, these subsystems are open, that is, water

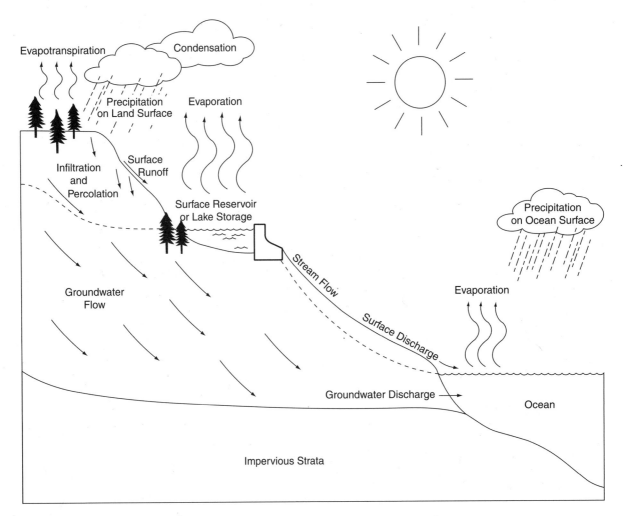

Figure 8–3   Hydrologic cycle

outflow from one subsystem becomes inflow to another, and so on. A hydrologic budget can be developed for each subsystem using the water balance equation 8-1:

$$\text{water inflow} - \text{water outflow} = \text{change in storage} \qquad \text{(Eq 8-1)}$$

A water budget analysis could be developed minute by minute or year by year for one watershed and for the entire Earth. However, the mix of the water budget components will vary depending on the choice of time and geographic scale. For example, equation 8-2 represents the long-term water budget for the entire globe:

$$\text{annual precipitation (inflow)} = \text{annual evaporation (outflow)} \qquad \text{(Eq 8-2)}$$

This equation does not hold month by month; the difference in monthly water input and output is equal to the monthly change in storage in all water bodies on Earth, as given in equation 8-3:

$$\begin{aligned}\text{monthly precipitation (inflow)} - \text{monthly evaporation (outflow)} \\ = \text{monthly change in storage in water bodies}\end{aligned} \qquad \text{(Eq 8-3)}$$

On a daily time scale, for example, a water balance equation for a surface water reservoir or lake requires several components of the hydrologic cycle, as given in equation 8-4:

[inflows]{daily stream inflows to the reservoir
    + daily groundwater inflows to the reservoir
    + daily precipitation to the reservoir}
− [outflows] {daily reservoir releases
    + daily groundwater outflows from the reservoir
    + daily evaporation of water}
= [change in storage] {volume of water in the reservoir
  at the beginning of the day
    − volume of water in the reservoir at the end
    of the day}   (Eq 8-4)

The primary purpose of all hydrologic modeling is to solve the water balance equation of the selected area or watershed. The model area can be hydrologically defined, such as a watershed or drainage basin; it can also be politically or arbitrarily defined, such as water district, county, or plot of land. Regardless of the time or geographic scale, a water balance equation should be developed as the first step of modeling to identify the components of the hydrologic cycle for a specific model area. The defining criterion for a model's reliability is how well it incorporates the water balance equation for the modeled hydrologic subsystem. A model that does not explicitly generate output showing water budget at the appropriate temporal and spatial scale should be used with extreme caution.

Human Influence on the Hydrologic Cycle

The hydrologic processes in a watershed are almost always influenced by human activities. Development of a water balance or pollutant mass balance for a watershed or hydrologic basin must consider human influences such as

- afforestation and deforestation that cause global climatic and local changes in runoff volume and timing;

- land development, urbanization, and mass construction of buildings and roads that affect volume and timing of surface runoff that affects flood and minimum streamflow conditions;

- surface water reservoirs and regulations for flood control and water storage that affect natural streamflow patterns, ecosystem habitats, migration of anadromous fish for spawning, and stream sediment loads;

- agricultural development and irrigation that affects interception, evapo-transpiration, return flows, infiltration, and percolation;

- groundwater pumping that affects groundwater hydraulics, natural recharge, aquifer water levels, and stream–aquifer interactions;

- surface water diversions and land applications that primarily affect streamflows, infiltration, and percolation;

- wastewater discharge to streams that affects streamflows, water quality, and biological characteristics of water bodies;

- interbasin transfers of surface water and groundwater that affect the hydrologic cycle of source and target watersheds;

- artificial recharge of groundwater that affects the groundwater hydraulics and recharge dynamics;

- irrigation practices, including use of fertilizers and pesticides, that affect the volume and quality of return flow to streams and aquifers;

- channel modifications, aggradation, and storm drains that affect streamflow patterns, seepage, and ecosystem habitats; and

- judicial and regulatory actions, and institutional agreements, such as minimum streamflows for aquatic resources or moratoria on groundwater development, that affect hydrosystems behavior and need to be considered as constraints in model development.

Models, Structured Programming, and Object-Oriented Programming

From a process point of view, the hydrologic cycle can also be presented as a flow diagram showing water pathways from precipitation to evaporation and back. Figure 8-4 can be used to develop a computational structure of a numerical hydrologic model. For example, the computational block for precipitation on the land surface may include four computational sub-blocks: interception, depression storage, runoff, and infiltration. Mathematical equations representing the physical processes associated with the corresponding components of the hydrologic cycle can be entirely coded within a computational block and necessary input or output for related

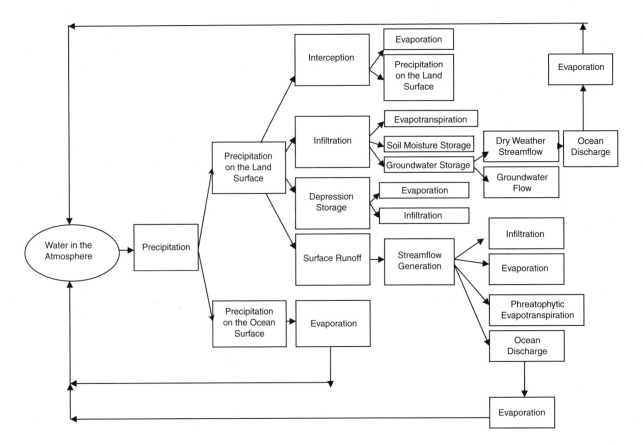

Figure 8–4   Schematic of hydrologic cycle

components can be accordingly exchanged across computational blocks or subroutines (a self-contained computational block performing specific functions). The best design for a model code (program instructions) is one that somehow incorporates this flow diagram in a structured programming or object-oriented programming context.

Structured programming evolved from procedural programming, in which a model code was thought of as a series of procedures with a given set of computational instructions. Structured programming helped organize these procedures by breaking this series of procedures into manageable self-contained subtasks or program modules. In comparison, object-oriented programming creates reusable program components or *objects* that have known properties, behaviors, functions, and features. Objects are combined to accomplish a computational task or program module. Although this chapter does not discuss the differences between the two programming approaches, a programming approach should not misrepresent proper hydrosystem behavior. For example, hydrologic objects might be created that oversimplify physical reality for the sake of ease of coding. In such a case, *reusability* becomes a liability because an inaccurate hydrologic object is used and reused throughout the model code, which, in turn, spreads and magnifies the errors from the original misrepresentation. The recommended course is to combine structured and object-oriented programming approaches to solve hydrologic problems.

Dominant Processes of the Hydrologic Cycle

A basic knowledge of the dominant processes of the hydrologic cycle is essential to successfully apply and evaluate any hydrologic model. A brief description of the components of the hydrologic cycle is presented here from a modeling perspective. For detailed descriptions of these physical processes, any standard textbook on hydrology may be consulted.

Precipitation

Precipitation is measured as accumulated depth of rainfall (in inches or millimeters) by rain gauges. Measurement errors can range from 5 to 30 percent depending on the intensity of the rainfall and the accompanying wind. Precipitation estimates are required for an entire watershed or for the geographical area under consideration. Often, only a few rain gauges are available in and around the model area. As a result, the validity and accuracy of the basinwide precipitation data used in the models depend on the density of the rain gauge network. The error variability of precipitation measurements is accounted for by adjustments of the model parameters during the calibration process.

The average precipitation for an area can be developed from a network of rain gauges via three methods: (1) arithmetic average method, in which a simple arithmetic average of all rain gauges is used as the areal average rainfall; (2) Thiessen method, in which polygonal influence areas for rain gauges are used as weights for calculating a weighted average areal rainfall; and (3) isohyetal method, in which precipitation contours are drawn using the gauge network and area between two contours and mean isohyetal values are used to develop average areal rainfall.

The arithmetic method is adequate for areas with uniform topography without strong precipitation gradients and where rain gauges are more or less uniformly distributed. The Thiessen polygon method is suitable for areas with nonuniform distribution of rain gauges with strong precipitation gradients; however, because of orographic influences, it is not suitable for mountainous regions. The isohyetal method is the most accurate for determining the average rainfall over an area and is applicable for mountainous terrains with strong precipitation gradients. Precipitation may increase uniformly with elevation even in areas of uniform meteorological conditions; hence, the elevation of precipitation gauges should always be noted and taken into consideration while combining precipitation data from two gauges or while using data from one gauge to estimate missing data for a neighboring gauge.

Precipitation data are available at 15-minute, hourly, daily, and monthly intervals. The choice of interval of precipitation data to be used in a hydrologic model depends on the purpose of modeling, the nature of the rainfall (storm versus mean monthly rainfall), and the time steps of the hydrologic model. If a monthly time step hydrologic model is being used, and aggregated monthly data are already available, hourly and daily rainfall data are not needed. Furthermore, estimates of missing data should be made on a time step consistent with the smallest time step of the model, not at the interval of the original data. Gaps in rainfall records are common and are filled by regression and correlation with neighboring rain gauges.

Precipitation data should be checked for consistency throughout the period of record by conducting double mass analysis. Rain gauge history can be useful in correcting inconsistency in rain data from a gauge. Relocation of a rain gauge, change in exposure, change in surrounding conditions such as growth of trees near the gauge site, urbanization and industrialization upwind of a site, and other factors can cause a marked change in the pattern of recorded precipitation at a gauge over time.

Precipitation data normally show wet and dry days in runs (wet days tend to follow wet days and dry days tend to follow dry days), and the annual volume of rainfall tends to occur in runs of wet and dry years. As a result, all models used in water supply planning should use a long period of record for precipitation data to capture the inherent variability of a precipitation pattern over a region.

The most commonly used precipitation models are rainfall runoff models. In these models, an actual or synthetic time series of rainfall amount is used to generate watershed runoff. Statistical methods are used to develop synthetic precipitation time series for water supply planning; autoregressive and Markov chain methods are used to describe persistence in a precipitation time series. Numerous deterministic and stochastic rainfall models are available, but very few have practical use outside the region for which they were originally developed. The rainfall generating mechanism of climatic systems varies from place to place and should be given due consideration in selecting a rainfall model.

Precipitation data can be obtained from national, state, and local government agencies. In the United States, the National Weather Service, National Oceanic and Atmospheric Administration, state water resources departments, local flood control districts, and local water agencies can provide information. The World Wide Web is also a good source of data or information about precipitation and other climatological data.

Interception

A certain amount of precipitation evaporates as it is intercepted by natural and artificial ground covers. In hydrologic modeling practice, interception is the most neglected significant component of the hydrologic cycle. It can account for a net loss of water of 10 to 30 percent of the gross precipitation volume. Interception loss depends on the nature and duration of rainfall; nature, distribution, and age of vegetative cover; frequency of rainfall; intervals between rainfall (because most interception occurs at the beginning stages of a storm); relative wetness of the vegetative cover; meteorological conditions; and the season of the year. Interception losses for various types of crops and forests are given in Table 8-1.

Table 8–1   Interception percentages for various crops and forests

Crop or Forest Type	Interception in % of Rainfall Growing Season	Interception in % of Rainfall Nongrowing Season
Alfalfa	36	22
Corn	16	3
Soybean	15	9
Oats	7	3
Deciduous forest	13	
Coniferous forest	27	
Pine	30	

Source: US Department of Agriculture.

Interception in hydrologic modeling is neglected because of three conflicting theories about its role in the overall water balance of a watershed. Until the early 1960s, the predominant view was that interception losses were not true losses from the land hydrologic cycle because they were compensated by a reduction in transpiration that would otherwise occur. It was argued that the total energy available for evaporation of water from vegetative cover was the same whether it was used to evaporate water from within the leaves of the plants (transpiration) or from leaf surfaces (interception). Experimenting on grasses, Burgy and Pomeroy (1958) proved this hypothesis under laboratory conditions. McMillan and Burgy (1960) and Rakhmanov (1958) verified this no-net-loss hypothesis of interception under field conditions.

During the late 1960s, field experiments and theoretical analysis contradicted the theory and hydrologists argued that interception losses are, at least partly, net losses from available water supply. Several field experiments (Thorud, 1967; Rutter, 1967; Leyton, 1967) and theoretical analysis (Murphy and Knoerr, 1975) indicated that although evaporation of intercepted water reduces transpiration, the rate of evaporation of intercepted water is two to five times greater than the transpiration rate under the same environmental conditions. Additional energy for a higher evaporative rate can be attributed to the differences in surface resistance and aerodynamic resistance under wet and dry vegetative cover. Water yield modifications by conversion of hardwood forest to pine forest (Swank and Miner, 1968) further support the net-loss hypothesis. Interception losses are more important in areas where nighttime rainfall predominates (such as maritime climates). When evapotranspiration losses are water limiting, that is, when amounts of evapotranspirative loss depend on the availability of water, interception will increase the net loss from the land hydrologic cycle by increasing the availability of water at the leaf surface. Interception losses are not important in hydrologic modeling associated with flood studies because they deal with large, intense rainstorms that occur over a relatively short period.

The third view about interception is the least known and the least common phenomenon. In forested areas of high relief, where fog and low clouds prevail, direct condensation of water on leaves and twigs can result in fog precipitation. This can be considered a net gain to the watershed water balance; however, the measurement methods are inadequate, and it is considered a negligible phenomenon of the land hydrologic cycle in most watershed areas.

Interception losses are accounted in hydrologic models in three ways: (1) an absolute abstraction amount (such as a percentage of gross precipitation); (2) a computed amount by regression-based empirical equations that relate interception losses to precipitation and vegetation characteristics (Horton, 1919; Merriam, 1960); and (3) a mathematical model that incorporates the physical processes (Rutter et al., 1975). Horton's empirical equation for interception for grasses is given below:

$$I \text{ (mm)} = 0.00042 \text{ H} + 0.00026 \text{ HP (clover and meadow grass)} \qquad \text{(Eq 8-5)}$$

Where:

$\quad$ I $\quad$ = $\quad$ interception
$\quad$ H $\quad$ = $\quad$ average grass height (mm)
$\quad$ P $\quad$ = $\quad$ precipitation (mm)

Evaporation and Evapotranspiration

Evapotranspiration is the largest component of the hydrologic cycle. According to equation 8-2, in global terms, total evaporation accounts for the disposal of 100 percent of precipitation. In humid regions, it accounts for 75 percent of water lost from the land hydrologic cycle; in arid regions, 100 percent.

Evaporation from free water surface is a very important factor in water supply planning because the increase in evaporation from a surface water reservoir can offset the gain in yield from a water storage project. For example, mean annual lake evaporation in the United States ranges from 20 in. (500 mm) in the Northeast to about 80 in. (2,000 mm) in Southern California.

Total evaporation is a function of meteorological conditions (e.g., solar energy, humidity, temperature, wind speed, difference in vapor pressure, atmospheric pressure), physical conditions (quality of evaporating water, water depth, surface area of water body), soil conditions (soil moisture content, soil color, soil capillary characteristics), and vegetation conditions (nature of vegetation, cropping pattern, albedo, stomatal control, aerodynamic resistance, rooting depth). As can be seen, modeling evapotranspiration is complicated by numerous process dependencies, difficulty in characterizing the dependent environment, and voluminous data requirements.

Total evaporation data on a watershed basis are most commonly used in hydrologic modeling. Evapotranspiration can be quantified by several methods such as the water budget method, pan evaporation method, energy budget method, and mass transfer method. The water budget method is based on the principle of conservation of mass and is given in equation 8-4. Although rainfall, stream inflow and outflow, and change in storage can be measured with reasonable accuracy, estimating groundwater inflow and outflow or net seepage is difficult and is subject to significant errors. As a result, accuracy in estimating evaporation depends largely on the accurate estimation of net seepage. Seepage estimates can be developed from estimates of aquifer hydraulic conductivity and changes in water levels in the surrounding groundwater area. Another technique for estimating net seepage can be applied if lake elevation data from periods of no net surface flow (zero surface inflow and outflow or surface flow equal to surface outflow) are available. In this case, a daily plot of change in elevation versus the mass transfer product, $u(e_o-e_a)$ is developed, where u is wind velocity, e_o is saturation vapor pressure, and e_a is air vapor pressure. The intercept of this line on the change in elevation axis is the net seepage rate. This method assumes that evaporation is proportional to the mass transfer product, $u(e_o-e_a)$. These estimates of seepage losses are very crude and can be used only for the long term for water balance purposes if net seepage losses do not change appreciably over an extended period.

Pan evaporation is perhaps the most commonly used method of determining evaporation. It involves developing a relationship between the evaporation from the lake and the evaporation from the standard US Weather Bureau class A pan. This relationship is called pan evaporation coefficient and normally ranges from 0.7 to 0.75. The class A pan is made of unpainted galvanized iron; it is 4 ft (1,220 mm) in diameter, 10-in. (254-mm) deep, and is mounted 12 in. (305 mm) above the ground on a wooden frame. Annual pan coefficients are consistent from year to year and from region to region, but monthly pan coefficients show greater variability. Average monthly and annual pan evaporation data are available from the US Weather Bureau. Energy budget and mass transfer methods for estimating evaporation are seldom used because of the high costs associated with instrumentation and data collection.

Evaporation from a soil surface depends on the availability of water in the near surface soil zone. Similarly, evapotranspiration from vegetation depends on the amount of water available in the root zone soil matrix. *Potential evapotranspiration* (PET) is a term used to define the maximum evapotranspiration from a vegetative surface that would take place with unlimited water. PET for the same crop varies with climatic zone. Evapotranspiration from the vegetative surface cannot exceed the potential evapotranspiration. Evapotranspiration can be directly measured by using a lysimeter in a block of soil and applying the water balance equation.

In hydrologic modeling, evapotranspiration estimates for a watershed are often obtained from empirical and semiempirical methods such as the Thornthwaite method, the Blaney–Criddle method, the Agricultural Research Service (ARS) method, and the Penman–Monteith combination method.

Selection of a method for evapotranspiration modeling depends on data availability and on the time scale of the model. The best results are provided by physically based models, in which the processes of soil–plant–atmosphere are simulated. For periods of 5 days or less, the combination method or other rigorous energy budget method provides the best accuracy. For monthly estimates of crop consumptive use, a crop coefficient-based method such as Blaney–Criddle is sufficient.

Part of the crop consumptive use requirement or crop evapotranspiration requirement is met by precipitation, which is called the *consumptive use of precipitation*. The rest of the crop consumptive use requirement is met by irrigation. The US Soil Conservation Service's handbook, *Irrigation Water Requirements* (SCS, 1970), discusses methods of estimation of the components of the soil–plant–atmospheric processes.

Hydrologic models developed for agricultural watershed management require that consumptive uses of applied water be determined. A simplified computer submodel at a monthly time step may consist of the following operations:

1. Read all data (rainfall, crop acreage, irrigation season, crop PET, or data for computing crop PET).

2. Estimate interception loss; the remainder is precipitation falling on the ground (P_g).

3. Estimate the consumptive use (CU) requirement of the crop.

4. Estimate the amount of water needed to maintain the desired soil moisture (SM) levels for crop growth.

5. Add estimates in steps 3 and 4 (CU + SM) and subtract the total from P_g in step 2. If the result is positive, no applied water is required for

irrigation. If the result is negative, the absolute value represents the volume of applied water required to meet the unmet portion of crop consumptive use demand. This amount represents the consumptive use of applied water, which is less than the amount of irrigation applied water. The ratio of the consumptive use of applied water and the amount of applied water is called the *field irrigation efficiency*.

Infiltration

Most precipitation that reaches the Earth's surface infiltrates the soil mantle. This infiltrated water replenishes the soil moisture, meets the crop consumptive use needs, and then moves downward through the unsaturated zone to recharge the deep groundwater aquifer. The remainder of the precipitation becomes overland flows or stays on the surface in depression zones for later evaporation or infiltration. The infiltrated water also may move laterally close to the soil surface as interflow and reappear on the surface as streamflow.

Quantification of infiltration is a major element in hydrologic modeling as it determines the amount of runoff to streams and channels, the amount of water supply to plants, and the amount of recharge water to groundwater aquifers. Knowledge of the infiltration process is also essential for understanding the movement and accumulation of contaminants (such as pesticides or nitrates) in the soil zone and in the underlying aquifer.

The most important factors that influence infiltration are soil type and moisture content. Infiltration involves three interdependent processes: water entering through the soil surface, water being stored in the soil matrix, and water moving through the soil matrix. The quantification of infiltration in hydrologic modeling is usually based on empirical equations developed from field measurements, or parameterized mechanistic equations developed from the understanding of the physical processes.

The flow of water through the soil surface is also affected by structural cracks and macropores in the soil. However, their explicit considerations are generally ignored in practical hydrologic modeling because more research is needed to understand associated physical processes and identify circumstances under which these processes need to be considered.

The terms *infiltration capacity* and *infiltration rate* are often used interchangeably in the literature, causing much confusion. The infiltration rate is the volumetric flow rate (flux) of water entering the soil per unit of surface area. The limiting factor on the infiltration rate could be either the rate of water supply at the surface (such as irrigation application rate or precipitation rate) or the capacity of the soil to absorb water.

The term *infiltration capacity* was coined by Horton in the 1930s to indicate the infiltration potential of a soil profile at any given time. Horton postulated that infiltration capacity varies with time, as given by equation 8-6:

$$f_p = f_c + (f_0 - f_c)e^{-kt} \qquad \text{(Eq 8-6)}$$

Where:

f_p =   the infiltration capacity at time, t
f_c =   a final or equilibrium capacity
f_0 =   the initial infiltration capacity
k   =   a constant representing the rate of decrease in infiltration capacity

Horton's definition implicitly assumed infiltration to be a soil surface phenomenon, as opposed to percolation, which is the vertical movement of water through the unsaturated zone to the groundwater table. Hillel (1971) coined the term *infiltrability* to describe the same concept, noting that capacity is an extensive aspect (one talks about storage capacity of a reservoir). In essence, infiltrability or infiltration capacity is the maximum infiltration potential of a soil surface profile at a given time. The infiltration rate is always less than this infiltration capacity. For example, at the beginning of a rainfall, the infiltration capacity is often higher than the rainfall rate; thus, the infiltration rate is equal to the rainfall rate. The infiltration capacity gradually decreases as the moisture content of the surface soil increases. If the rainfall rate exceeds the infiltration capacity, the infiltration rate equals infiltration capacity. As the rain progresses and more water enters the soil, the infiltration capacity decreases exponentially to an equilibrium rate equal to the saturated hydraulic conductivity of the soil profile because the underlying soil profile cannot transmit (or conduct) the water away faster. In simplistic terms, infiltration is a two-phase phenomenon: initially, a volumetric mechanism driven by available storage in the soil profile, and finally, a transmissive mechanism driven by ability to conduct water away from the lower zones. This concept is somewhat captured in the USDAHL-70 watershed model. Infiltration capacity is expressed in equation 8-7:

$$f = GI \times a \times S_a^{1.4} + f_c \qquad \text{(Eq 8-7)}$$

Where:

f = infiltration capacity (in./hr)

GI = growth index of vegetation in percentage of maturity

a = vegetation parameter

S_a = available storage in inches of water equivalent in the surface layer ("A" horizon in agricultural soils, i.e., about first 6 in. or 152 mm)

f_c = constant rate of infiltration after long wetting (in./hr)

The *GI* curves are expressed as a ratio of daily evapotranspiration rate as a percentage of the annual maximum daily rate. The value of vegetation parameter "a" ranges from 0.1 to 1.0; representative values are given in Table 8-2:

Infiltration capacity is an important parameter in rainfall runoff modeling. Representative infiltration capacity values for various soil textures are given in Table 8-3.

Table 8–2 Representative values of vegetation parameter "a"

Land Use or Cover	Vegetation Parameter "a"
Fallow	0.1 to 0.3
Row crops	0.1 to 0.2
Temporary pasture	0.4 to 0.6
Permanent pasture	0.8 to 1.0
Woods and forests	0.8 to 1.0

Table 8–3   Representative values of infiltration capacities

Soil Texture	Infiltration Capacity, *in./hr* (*mm/hr*)
Sandy	1 to 10 (25 to 254)
Sandy loam	0.5 to 3 (13 to 76)
Loam	0.3 to 0.8 (8 to 20)
Clay loam	0.1 to 0.6 (3 to 15)
Silty clay	0.01 to 0.2 (0.2 to 5)
Clay	0.05 to 0.4 (1 to 10)

Infiltration capacities of soils are indicators of their runoff potential during a rainfall. The higher the infiltration capacity, the lower the runoff potential. In watershed modeling, the soils are classified in order of infiltration rates (after thorough wetting) or equivalently in order of runoff potential. These hydrologic soil groups are

Group A (low runoff potential, high infiltration rate): consists primarily of deep sands and gravels that are well drained.

Group B (low to moderate runoff potential, moderate infiltration rate): consists primarily of shallow loess and sandy loams.

Group C (moderate runoff potential, low infiltration rate): consists primarily of clay loams, shallow sandy loams, and soils low in organics.

Group D (high runoff potential, very low infiltration rate): consists primarily of soils of high swelling potential, soils with permanent high water tables, heavy plastic clays, and saline soils.

In the United States, soil surveys that identify soil types and their characteristics are available for each county. The corresponding hydrologic soil groups for major soil types in the entire United States is published in National Engineering Handbook–Section 4–Hydrology.

Groundwater

Groundwater is the subsurface water in soils and rocks that are fully saturated. Some of the water that infiltrates into the soil surface moves down through the soil matrix to reach the water table, the defining boundary of the groundwater zone. The soil matrix between the land surface and the groundwater table is partially saturated, and is called the *vadose* or *unsaturated zone*.

Groundwater terms and definitions used in hydrology do not have universal consensus; however, an understanding of commonly used terms in groundwater is essential for conducting and evaluating a groundwater modeling study. Model developers sometimes use common groundwater terms differently; as a result, make sure that the definitions used in the model code are consistent with the input data. For example, if a model developer used "permeability" synonymously with hydraulic conductivity, it should be so noted when calibrating a model and used during the calibration to ensure the accuracy of model results. A selected list of terms and definitions related to groundwater is provided in Table 8-4.

Table 8–4 Groundwater terms, definitions, and representative values of parameters

Term	Definition and Representative Values
Aquiclude	A geologic formation that may contain water (often in appreciable quantities) but has very little or no transmissive capability
Aquifer	A water-bearing geological formation that is transmissive enough to yield significant quantities of water for groundwater development
Aquifuge	An absolutely impermeable formation that neither contains nor transmits any water
Aquitard	A saturated geologic formation that is semipervious in nature and transmits water at a very slow rate
Confined aquifer	An aquifer that is bounded by impervious formations from both above and below
Elevation head	The potential energy per unit weight of water, measured in feet of water
Homogeneity/ heterogeneity	A porous medium domain is called *homogeneous* if its hydraulic conductivity and other properties are the same at all points; in *heterogeneous* formations, hydraulic properties change in space. In models, assumption of homogeneity over a small scale (a finite difference cell or a finite element or a group of cells or elements) is commonplace. Also see definition of isotropy/anisotropy.
Hydraulic conductivity— saturated (K_s)	The discharge per unit area per unit hydraulic (piezometric) gradient. It measures the ease with which a fluid is transmitted through the aquifer material and is expressed as a scalar (dimensions: length/time; e.g., ft/d). The hydraulic conductivity is a property of both the soil matrix and the fluid passing through the matrix. See also definition of permeability. Hydraulic conductivity values in aquifers vary over a wide range from as low as 0.01 μm/d for clay to 10,000 m/d for clean gravels. Here are some representative values: silt, –0.0001 to 1 m/d; fine sands, 0.01 to 10 m/d; medium to coarse sands, 10 to 3,000 m/d; dune sand, 5 to 20 m/d; gravels, 1,000 to 10,000 m/d; sand and gravel, 0.2 to 10 m/d. Sometimes the hydraulic conductivity is expressed in units of $gal/d/ft^2$, which can be converted to ft/d by multiplying by a factor of 0.134.
Hydraulic conductivity— unsaturated (K_u)	Measures the ease with which a fluid is transmitted through a partially saturated soil matrix. The unsaturated hydraulic conductivity depends on the moisture content of the soil and is subject to hysteresis; i.e., has different values during drying and wetting cycles of the porous matrix. The maximum value of K_u is saturated hydraulic conductivity at saturation (i.e., when all pores are filled with water). It can vary over a wide range at different levels of saturation; e.g., at 50% saturation, it could be one-fifth to one-tenth of saturated hydraulic conductivity; e.g., at 25% saturation, it will be even less.
Isotropy/anisotropy	Variability of flow conditions (or hydrogeologic properties that affect flows such as hydraulic conductivity) with geographic direction. If flow conditions are the same in all directions, the aquifer is called *isotropic*; otherwise, it is *anisotropic*. Most aquifers are anisotropic because horizontal hydraulic conductivities are almost always higher than the vertical conductivities. However, in modeling, assumption of horizontal isotropy (no variations in flow properties in x and y directions) is commonplace.
Perched aquifer	A special case of a saturated soil layer of limited areal extent, located between the water table and the ground surface.

Table continued next page.

Table 8–4   Groundwater terms, definitions, and representative values of parameters *(continued)*

Term	Definition and Representative Values
Permeability	Often used synonymously with hydraulic conductivity. In the purest sense, it is the intrinsic property or the capacity of the porous matrix or soil for transmitting a fluid. Also called *intrinsic permeability*. Unlike hydraulic conductivity, this is a property of the porous medium alone. Hydraulic conductivity and permeability are related by the following formula: Hydraulic Conductivity = Permeability × (specific weight of fluid/dynamic viscosity of fluid). Units of permeability can be ft^2 or cm^2; in the petroleum industry, units of darcy are used. 1 darcy is equal to 9.87×10^{-9} cm^2.
Piezometric head	The sum of the pressure head and elevation head. Darcy's law states that the flow takes place from a higher piezometric head to a lower one, not from a higher pressure head to a lower one.
Porosity	The percentage of the rock or soil that is void of material; these voids may or may not be connected. In aquifers water normally occupies these voids. The porosity is also equal to the sum of specific yield and specific retention. Representative values of porosity are: clay, 0.40 to 0.60; silt, 0.35 to 0.50; soils, 0.3 to 0.5; coarse sand, 0.30 to 0.35; fine sand, 0.30 to 0.50; gravel, 0.25 to 0.40; sand and gravel, 0.20 to 0.30.
Potentiometric surface (also called piezometric surface)	Applies only in a confined aquifer. It is the surface representative of the level to which water will rise in a well cased to the aquifer.
Pressure head	The pressure energy per unit weight of water.
Safe yield	The safe yield of a groundwater aquifer can be defined in numerous ways. In the purest sense, it refers to the annual amount of water that can be withdrawn from an aquifer without producing an undesirable result (that is the source of the term "safe"). The undesirable result can take any of the forms listed here or any combination thereof: withdrawal in excess of natural recharge; lowering of the water table below certain limits, interference with the groundwater rights of others, saltwater intrusion from the sea or other low water quality areas, reduction of baseflow to streams, degradation of groundwater quality, etc. Most commonly, safe yield is considered as the average annual natural inflow to a groundwater basin on the basis of data from 30 to 40 years of hydrologic record. In this sense, it is also equal to the average annual groundwater pumping minus the average annual overdraft. Long-term changes in land and water use in a groundwater basin will change the safe yield of the basin.
Specific capacity	The rate of discharge of water from a well per unit of drawdown, commonly expressed in gal/min/ft or m^3/d/m.
Specific retention	The quantity of water retained in the soil against gravity by capillary forces per unit area and per unit drop of water table.
Specific yield (effective porosity)	The quantity of water that a unit area of unconfined aquifer gives up by gravity for per unit drop in the water table. It applies only to unconfined aquifers and is expressed as a decimal fraction; e.g., specific yield of clay ranges from 0.01 to 0.05, and sand ranges from 0.10 to 0.30. Representative average values are: clay, 0.03; silt, 0.15; fine sand, 0.20; coarse sand, 0.25; gravel and sand, 0.25.

Table continued next page.

Table 8–4 Groundwater terms, definitions, and representative values of parameters *(continued)*

Term	Definition and Representative Values
Storage coefficient (storativity)	Applies to confined aquifers only. It represents the volume of water released from storage per unit horizontal area of aquifer and per unit drop of piezometric head. In contrast to unconfined aquifers, where water is drained from the storage, the water released from a confined aquifer storage comes from compressing the aquifer and expanding the water when pumped. As a result, the value of storage coefficients for a confined aquifer is very low, ranging from 0.001 to 0.00001.
Transmissivity	A property of an aquifer. It represents a measure of the amount of water that can be transmitted horizontally by the full saturated thickness of the aquifer under a hydraulic gradient of 1. It is the product of hydraulic conductivity, K, and the saturated thickness of the aquifer, b. It is measured in ft^2/d or m^3/d. It is also measured in gal/ft/d, which can be converted to ft^2/d by multiplying with a factor of 0.134.
Unconfined (phreatic or water table) aquifer	An aquifer that is bounded on top by a free water surface under atmospheric pressure, i.e., the aquifer is connected with the atmosphere through open pores. The free water surface of unconfined aquifer is called the water table.

Groundwater flows are essentially three-dimensional; however, in most cases the assumption of two-dimensional flow is satisfactory because the dependency in vertical (downward) direction is very slight. Groundwater flow follows Darcy's law, as given by

$$Q = AK(dh/dl) \qquad \text{(Eq 8-8)}$$

Where:

Q = rate of flow
A = cross-sectional area of flow
K = saturated hydraulic conductivity
dh = difference in piezometric head between two measurement points
dl = distance between two measurement points

The ratio dh/dl is also called the hydraulic gradient.

Groundwater flow systems are a type of open subsystem in the hydrologic cycle. If recharge to a groundwater basin is exactly equal to the discharge from the basin, there will be no change in the amount of water stored in the aquifer; if recharge exceeds discharge, there will be a net gain in storage; if discharge exceeds recharge, there will be a net depletion in the aquifer storage.

A groundwater balance equation can be written as

change in storage in the aquifer = end storage – beginning storage   (Eq 8-9)
 = change in water table elevation × specific yield (unconfined aquifer) or change in piezometric head × storage coefficient (confined aquifer)
 = deep percolation + gain from stream – loss to stream + artificial recharge + subsurface inflows from neighboring areas or basins – subsurface outflows to neighboring areas or basins – groundwater pumping – evapotranspiration from plants with roots in the saturated zone

Runoff and Streamflow

Streamflows are very important for municipal and industrial water supply planning, flood control, surface water reservoir design and operations, hydroelectric power generation, agricultural irrigation, water-based recreation in reservoirs and rivers, fish and wildlife management, and navigation.

Key terms that are essential for understanding the runoff and streamflow include

Hydrograph. A graph of stream outflow or discharge plotted against time. A hydrograph at the watershed outlet combines the physical, geographic, and meteorological characteristics of the watershed. The area under a discharge hydrograph represents the volume of discharge water.

Unit hydrograph. A discharge hydrograph that produces 1.0 in. (2.54 cm) depth of runoff over a drainage area by a storm of uniform intensity occurring over a specific period. The storm duration is an essential part of the definition. For example, a 1-hr unit hydrograph for the same area is different from a 6-hr unit hydrograph for the same area. The unit hydrograph method has been successfully used to predict flood peaks for the past 50 years, with a ±25 percent accuracy. In this method, the runoff ordinates for a given duration of storm are assumed to be directly proportional to rainfall excess. For example, the discharge rates for a 2-hr storm producing 3 in. (7.62 cm) of rainfall excess would be 3 times the values of the runoff ordinates of 2-hr unit hydrograph.

The quality and quantity of streamflow generated in a watershed depend on its climatic and landscape (natural and human-made) features. For example, removing vegetation from a forested area may modify its infiltration characteristics to substantially change the amount and timing of storm runoff from the area, which can exacerbate downstream flooding conditions. Other human activities, such as land development, urbanization, agricultural diversions, and wastewater discharges can also significantly alter the quantity and quality of streamflow. As a result, an understanding of the runoff-generating mechanisms from the land surface is essential to effectively manage water resources.

The Hortonian description of runoff-generating mechanism provides the simplest conceptual framework. According to Horton's model, when rainfall rate exceeds the infiltration capacity of the soil, water accumulates on the soil surface in puddles, called *depression storage*. Once these tiny surface reservoirs are full, water spills over to flow downslope as overland flow. Numerous other pools of water storage, called *detention storage*, also build up during downslope flow; this stored water combines with overland flow in progressively larger channels, ultimately to appear as channel flow at the watershed outlet.

Horton's conceptual model is valid in arid and semiarid regions and in urbanized areas where infiltration capacity may be the limiting factor. However, in humid regions, where infiltration capacities are relatively high, the variable source area concept of runoff generation is more applicable. In this concept, two mechanisms can dominate the runoff generation, depending on the topography and soil characteristics of the watershed. In steep, straight hillslopes with deep highly permeable soils, runoff generation is dominated by subsurface stormflow, where an increase in subsurface outflow occurs because of a steepening of the water table near the stream. On the other hand, in thin soils with low permeability and gently concave slopes and wide valley bottoms, saturation overland flow dominates the runoff generation. In this process, the water table near the channel rises to the surface, and subsurface water escapes from the soil to flow into the channel as overland flow.

Urbanization has the greatest impact on the magnitude and timing of the natural runoff generation process. It replaces pervious surfaces with impervious roofs, roadways, parking lots, and paved sidewalks. As a consequence, the infiltration capacity can approach zero, resulting in Hortonian overland flow into gutters, drains, and storm sewers. These modifications of the natural runoff volumes and timing increase downstream flood peaks. In addition, urbanization reduces the groundwater recharge, which affects the dry weather streamflow and water quality in streams because of reduced baseflow supply.

Quantifying runoff from a watershed is a key element in hydrologic modeling. The unit hydrograph method is extensively used in flood hydrologic analysis. Many empirical and semiempirical equations predict peak flows.

For watershed modeling, a volumetric estimate of direct runoff over a specified period can be developed using the Soil Conservation Service's Curve Number method. The procedure was empirically developed from studies of small agricultural watersheds for areas as large as 2,000 acres.

Streamflow systems can also be considered open subsystems of the hydrologic cycle. A water balance equation can be developed as follows:

$$\text{change in storage in stream} = [\text{inflows}] - [\text{outflows}] \qquad \text{(Eq 8-10)}$$
$$= [\text{upstream inflows} + \text{tributary inflows} + \text{wastewater discharges} +$$
$$\quad \text{direct runoff} + \text{irrigation return flows} + \text{gain from groundwater aquifer}]$$
$$- [\text{downstream outflows} + \text{streamflow diversions} + \text{evaporation}$$
$$\quad \text{loss to phreatophytes} + \text{loss to groundwater aquifer}]$$

Field measurements of streamflow are kept by many organizations, including state and federal water agencies. The US Geological Survey (USGS) measures streamflows at numerous locations in the nation's streams. These data are available at the USGS Web site: http://waterdata.usgs.gov/nwis/rt.

Surface Reservoirs

Streamflows are often intercepted by surface reservoirs (or lakes) for flood control, water supply, irrigation, and hydropower generation. The main function of a reservoir, regardless of its size or the ultimate uses of the stored water, is to stabilize the streamflow, either by regulating the seasonal inflows in a natural stream or by satisfying a seasonal demand of the ultimate water use. A key concept of the surface reservoir systems is safe yield (or firm yield). Safe yield is the maximum quantity of water that can be guaranteed to be available from the reservoir during a critical dry period. A critical dry period is often taken as the lowest natural flow on record for the natural stream. As a result, the actual reservoir yield may be less than the reservoir safe yield if a drier period of natural flow, compared to the historic record, occurs. Linsley and Franzini (1979) provide a more detailed discussion on reservoir yield and reliability of supply.

HYDROLOGIC MODELS: DATA, CALIBRATION, SENSITIVITY, AND ERRORS

Models and Data

No matter how sophisticated a model is, the results are no better than its input data. As a result, data collection, compilation, and quality control play very important roles in modeling studies. Four primary aspects of data should be carefully addressed for a model:

1. How many data are required? (quantity aspect)

2. How accurate and how representative must the data be? (quality aspect)

3. What time intervals are essential for various types of data? (time-scale aspect)

4. What geographic area is to be covered? (space aspect)

The purpose and scope of the modeling study normally determine answers to all four questions. All sources of raw data and the data processing steps taken to prepare the input data for models must be documented. A well-defined model could also be used to identify data gaps and evaluate the relative importance of various types of data.

Models and Calibration

Calibration uses a model to achieve a match between the recorded (i.e., historic) and simulated distributions of dependent variables by choosing a range of possible values of the independent variables. In a hydrologic modeling situation, a modeler is confronted with the inverse problem: the distribution of dependent variables (such as groundwater elevation) is known and measurable; the distribution of independent variables (such as hydraulic conductivity of an aquifer) is unknown or can be estimated only within a range of possible values. The independent variables that are manipulated for model calibration are often called model *parameters*. For example, in a groundwater model, the most commonly used model parameters are the aquifer properties, such as hydraulic conductivity, specific yield, and storativity. A calibrated groundwater model provides *best* or *most reasonable* estimates of such model parameters, which are then used to predict the response of a dependent variable (such as groundwater elevation) under a changed land use or water use plan.

Some hydrologists maintain that models should also be verified by dividing the available historic data into two periods: (1) a calibration period, in which the independent variables or model parameters are manipulated to obtain a match between the observed and recorded values; and (2) a verification period, in which the model is run with the calibrated parameters and its performance in matching the recorded values is evaluated. If the performance during the verification period is favorable, the model is called verified. Unfortunately, this approach of strict calibration and verification periods is rarely followed, and often the model parameters are further manipulated to obtain a favorable verification. Thus, the verification process merely becomes part of the calibration.

The purpose of calibration is to evaluate the empirical adequacy of the model in representing a physical system and to corroborate scientific hypotheses that are already established through other means. Calibration is often given more weight by the modelers than it deserves. A well-calibrated model is no indication of its predictive ability since the natural system is dynamic and may change in unanticipated ways. However, calibration confirms historic observations and thus increases the probability that the model represents the physical environment and is not flawed in any obvious manner.

Understanding the purpose and limitations of model calibration is crucial to properly allocate resources in a modeling study. Relatively large amounts of time and resources are often spent in achieving the last 5 percent of improvement in model calibration. The following six calibration steps provide some general cost saving guidelines for model calibration:

Step 1. Set agreed-on calibration goals (e.g., in case of a groundwater model, an overall ±5 feet [1.5 m] of closure in measured water levels at wells could be an acceptable calibration goal).

Step 2. Set measurement criteria (e.g., How will this 5-ft [1.5 m] closure be measured? Does it have to be less than 5 ft [1.5 m] at all calibration wells all the time, or 5-ft [1.5 m] closure need to be met only 90 percent of the time?).

Step 3. Select and screen historic data (e.g., select wells at which comparisons will be made and screen the data for any anomalies, such as pumping water levels versus static water levels).

Step 4. Understand the error range of the historic data (e.g., the calibration goal should not be less than the possible margin of errors in the data).

Step 5. Limit the model parameters to a select few for calibration, then research and understand their possible range of values in the model area (good calibration [data match] can be obtained from unrealistic parameter values because of inherent weaknesses in model formulation).

Step 6. Stop calibration when it makes sense (use common sense).

Models and Sensitivity Analysis

Sensitivity analysis is the study of the distribution of dependent variables (e.g., groundwater elevations in a groundwater model) in response to changes in the distribution of independent variables, initial conditions, boundary conditions, physical parameters, and other factors. The analysis measures how sensitive the model output is to which variables or parameters. Specifically, the purpose of sensitivity analysis is fourfold:

1. Establish tolerances within which the physical system parameters can vary without significantly changing the model results or conclusions (a test for the robustness of the model).

2. Explore *what-if* scenarios under various input conditions.

3. Understand the impact of input data errors on model results (e.g., how model results and any decision based on those results can change because of errors in estimating agricultural pumping).

4. Understand which aspects of the system need to be studied most and studied further, what data are needed most and where, which input data collection and compilation should be given the most attention.

Similar to calibration, results of sensitivity analysis need to be presented in terms of a well-defined measure or metric. Simple metrics are best liked by senior managers as they provide the most *big picture* insight. Two simple metrics for expressing the sensitivity of a groundwater model to model parameters or to independent variables are given here as examples; more complex ones are available in modeling literature. The degrees of variation of these metrics with changes in parameters or independent variables are used as indicators of sensitivity of a model.

1. Average groundwater elevation over a model area, subregion, or water district. This average can be taken over all model nodes (point locations where groundwater elevations are calculated) within the area across all layers and over the entire period of simulation. This can be mathematically expressed as

$$\overline{H} = \frac{1}{M} \sum_{k=1}^{M} H_k \qquad \text{(Eq 8-9)}$$

$$H_k = \frac{1}{N} \sum_{i=1}^{N} \left[\frac{1}{L} \sum_{j=1}^{L} h_j \right]_i \qquad \text{(Eq 8-10)}$$

Where:

H = the average groundwater elevation
M = the total number of simulation months
H_k = the average head in the model area at k-th time step
N = the number of model nodes
L = the number of layers in an aquifer
h_j = the groundwater elevation at layer j at node i at k-th time step

2. Average root mean square error at the calibration wells is defined as the average of the individual root mean square errors at each calibration well. This can be mathematically expressed as

$$RMS \ k = \sqrt{\left\{ \frac{1}{N} \sum_{i=1}^{N} [h_i^o - h_i^s]^2 \right\}} \qquad \text{(Eq 8-11)}$$

Where:

N = the number of observations at all calibration wells
h_i^o = the observed groundwater elevation at month i at well k
h_i^s = the simulated groundwater elevation at month i at well k

Models and Error Analysis

All model results contain errors. An understanding of the source, nature, and magnitude of errors is essential to evaluate and use model results. For example, a groundwater model has three common sources of errors:

1. Modeling errors. A model represents physical processes occurring in nature by a series of mathematical approximations. Because of uncertainties associated with the governing physical processes, both in their phenomenological description and in their quantification, a mathematical representation is not possible without introducing certain simplifying assumptions. These assumptions lead to errors in model results. In addition to these sources of errors, there are limitations in the level of spatial discretization (element or cell spacing) and in the level of time discretization (time stepping). As a result, certain discrepancies between simulated and observed groundwater elevations are expected.

2. Input data errors. Even with no data entry errors, input data used in a model represent at best the most reliable information available at the time of model development. Often missing data were estimated by (a) statistical methods, (b) engineering judgment, and (c) inference from other sources. All introduce errors in model results. For example, groundwater pumping is one of the most critical sets of input data that affect the response of a

groundwater model. Historical groundwater pumping records over a large model area are often incomplete. As a result, pumping estimates are made on the basis of crop water requirements and other related information. These estimates are used in refining the model parameters during calibration. Hence, estimation errors in pumping data indirectly introduce proportional errors in model results through calibrated values of parameters, even for a future condition scenario when pumping is known or regulated.

3. Measurement errors. Data used in a model come from field measurements that can contain errors. For example, observed water levels are influenced by nearby pumping and do not represent regional groundwater conditions. As a result, changing model parameters to calibrate a regional groundwater model to match such field measurement will be erroneous. Another example may be cited from water quality models in which water quality data are subject to many types of errors, such as: sampling errors, laboratory errors, errors inherent in field methods, errors inherent in laboratory methods, errors caused by storage and transport, and reporting and data entry errors.

If a hydrologic model is necessary to meet the project goals, a project manager should continuously monitor and assess the modeling task in relation to the predefined set of objectives of the modeling and the project. Some general guidelines for conducting a modeling study and developing successful models are presented in the following sections.

How to Conduct a Modeling Study

1. Establish scope (breadth and depth) of inquiry and investigation.

2. Understand the purpose of the project and the place of modeling in the overall project.

3. Discuss relevant issues and goals of the modeling task.

4. Develop a data management plan and discuss hardware and software compatibility with the client.

5. If possible, involve the client in the model selection process, or at least educate the client on your selection criteria and process.

6. Discuss assumptions and limitations of the model with the client.

7. Consider the costs of needed or desired refinements of a model.

8. Start compiling and collecting data as early as possible in the model development process.

9. Develop a communications plan (i.e., determine what raw model results will be post-processed and presented in graphical or tabular forms and in a format that is understandable by decision makers, what level of reporting will be published; if possible, prepare a report outline with key details as early in the project as possible).

10. Define project milestones, for example:

    • Complete data collection.

    • Complete input data preparation.

- Develop a preliminary hydrologic budget.

- Initially test the model with input data and review the first round of results.

- Finalize the hydrologic budget and first round of calibration.

- Identify the second and third rounds of calibration and reassess calibration goals.

- Finalize the model calibration and customer buy-in of the model.

- Formulate alternatives to be studied using the model.

- Develop a modeling approach for alternatives and prepare input data.

- Present and have client review results of alternatives analyses.

- Submit draft report.

- Respond to client comments, submit a final report, and close out the project.

As a rule, a project manager should try to submit the draft report at 65 to 70 percent of the total project budget and reserve 30 to 35 percent of the budget for revisions and responding to client's comments and requests.

Types of Models

Many hydrologic models are available, including surface water and groundwater models, small- and large-scale models, and empirical, analytical, and numerical models. Besides these mathematical models, there are conceptual, graphical, and physical models. Conceptual and graphical models are visual representations that can help planners understand the parameters involved and better communicate all aspects of the project. Physical models, such as scale models of a reservoir project, can also be beneficial. A model can address one small component of the hydrologic cycle or the entire hydrologic cycle for a closed area or watershed; it also can address the water quality in natural environment or the sediment transport in water. Major functional classifications of hydrologic models are listed here with example model names; an Internet search on the basis of model names will provide additional information. Also, a search through the Web pages of the organizations (discussed in the next section) that develop hydrologic models would be very useful.

1. Surface water flow models (HSPF)

2. Groundwater flow models (MODFLOW, IGSM, PLASM, MICROFEM, WHPA)

3. Vadose zone models (RITZ, PRZM2, SESOIL, CMLS, HYDRUS, MOFAT, VLEACH)

4. Integrated groundwater and surface water models (IGSM, SHE, MIKE-SHE)

5. Watershed runoff models (HEC-1, SSARR, TR-20, SWMM)

6. River and reservoir operations and planning models (HEC-5, PROSIM, MODSIM, HEC-PRM, RIVERWARE)

7. Stream hydraulics models (HEC-2 or HEC-RAS, WSPRO, UNET, HEC-6)

8. River and reservoir water quality models (QUAL2E, WASP, CE-QUAL-RIV1, CE-QUAL-R1, CE-QUAL-W2, HEC-5Q)

9. Groundwater quality models (MOC, SUTRA, IGSM, SWIFT-II)

10. Hydrodynamics and estuarine models (Fischer Delta, DSM-2, RMA-10, TABS2)

11. Natural resources models (biological and ecological models such as PHABSIM, CROP-W, CROP-2, CRiSP)

12. Hydropower models (HEC-5Q, HYSSR, HYDROSIM, HYDREG, PM-DAM, CVPOWER)

13. Wetland models (DRAINMOD)

Selected Model Development and Distribution Organizations

In the United States, federal and state agencies, universities, research organizations and laboratories, local water districts and governing bodies or agencies, and commercial enterprises are involved in developing and distributing hydrologic models. State and local agencies are mostly involved in developing models that are specifically suited to solve a specific problem for the specific state or locality. Internationally, the United Nations' Water Resources and Environmental Branch catalogs and distributes hydrologic models. A select list of agencies with their Web page addresses is given here for reference without implying any endorsement or authenticity. An Internet search of the Web pages of these organizations will provide valuable information on the latest developments of water-related models.

1. Hydrologic Engineering Center (HEC): <http://hec.usace.army.mil/>

2. US Bureau of Reclamation (USBR): <http://www.usbr.gov/main/>

3. US Environmental Protection Agency (USEPA): <http://www.epa.gov/epahome/Data.html>

4. Center for Subsurface Modeling Support (USEPA): <http://www.epa.gov/ada/csmos.html>

5. Center for Exposure Assessment Modeling: (USEPA) <http://www.epa.gov/epa_ceam/wwwhtml/ceamhome.htm>

6. International Groundwater Modeling Center: <http://igwmc.mines.colorado.edu:3851/>

7. US Geological Survey (USGS): <http://www.usgs.gov/themes>

8. Waterways Experiment Station: <http://www.usace.army.mil/>

9. US Army Corps of Engineers: <http://www.usace.army.mil/>

10. National Resource Conservation Service (NRCS): <http://www.nrcs.usda.gov/AboutNR2.html>

11. California State Department of Water Resources: <http://elder.water.ca.gov/models.html>

12. World Meteorological Organization (WMO): <http://www.wmo.ch/web/homs/hwrphome.html>

13. United Nations (UN): <http://www.un.org/esa/sustdev/watbase.htm>

14. Danish Hydraulic Institute, Denmark: <http://www.dhi.dk/>

15. Institute of Hydrology, United Kingdom: <http://www.nwl.ac.uk/ih/>

Six Golden Rules of Cost-Effectiveness

The best cost-cutting measure is not to develop or use a model unless you have to. If you can answer the questions you are looking for objectively and reliably without the help of a model, do not develop one. Often the complexity of the questions and interrelationships among natural components may require a model. In that case, the following cost-efficiency measures may be helpful.

1. Research information; know the model area, its hydrology, hydrogeology, water use, and land use.

2. Develop a hydrologic budget without a model.

3. Document data sources, collections, and estimation methods, and perform quality control checks on input data.

4. Choose a well-documented and well-established model.

5. Ensure the model output not only meets your needs but also can be communicated to the stakeholders effectively.

6. Hire experienced modelers who understand water and mass balance, the purpose of modeling, the basin, and the theory behind the chosen model. They must also be able to communicate well.

Steps for Developing Successful Models

Developing models is only part of the overall objective of a study or investigation. To develop successful hydrologic models, utilities must understand the study objective and apply sound hydrologic principles and common sense. A stepwise approach to developing successful models is provided in Figure 8-5, using groundwater model as an example. The choice of a groundwater model as an example is based on the fact it is by far the most complex type of hydrologic models. This stepwise approach to successful modeling can be equally applied to any other type of modeling with appropriate customization.

Conclusion

Hydrologic modeling is a very significant component of water resources planning and management. However, a lack of knowledge of the underlying physical processes along with a lack of understanding of the practical issues at hand often lead to failures of modeling projects.

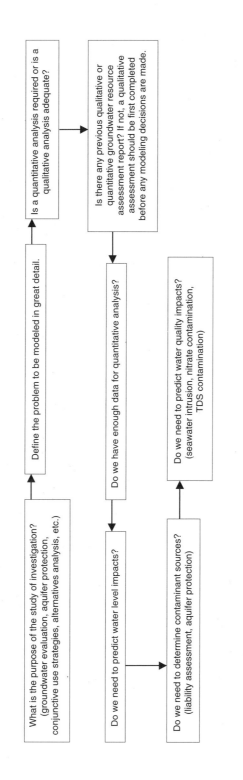

Figure 8–5.1   Developing successful models, step 1: Determine need for a model (Is a model needed?)

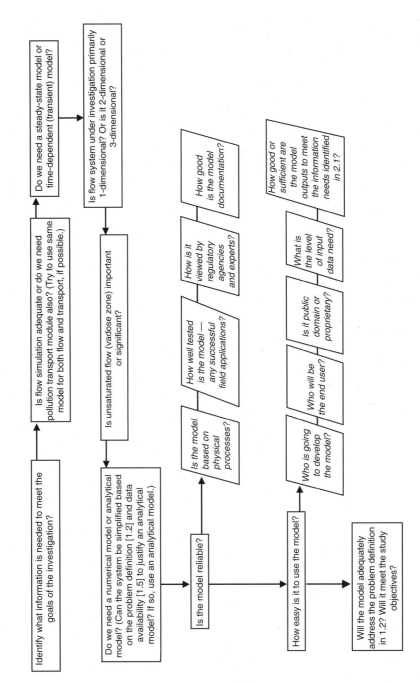

Figure 8–5.2   Developing successful models, step 2: Select a model

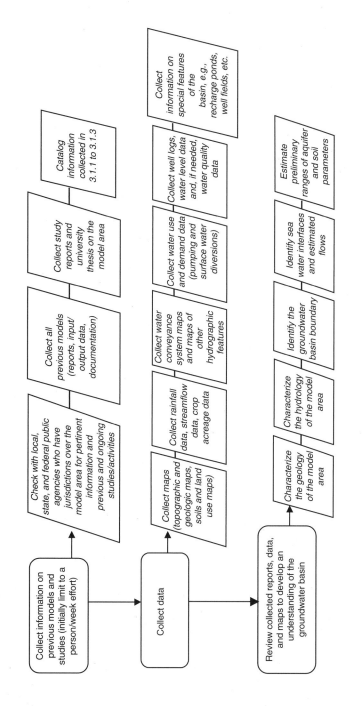

Figure 8–5.3a   Developing successful models, step 3: Build a model

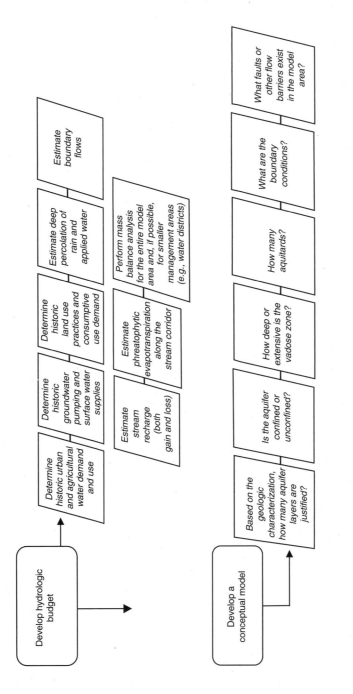

Figure 8–5.3b Developing successful models, step 3: Build a model (continued)

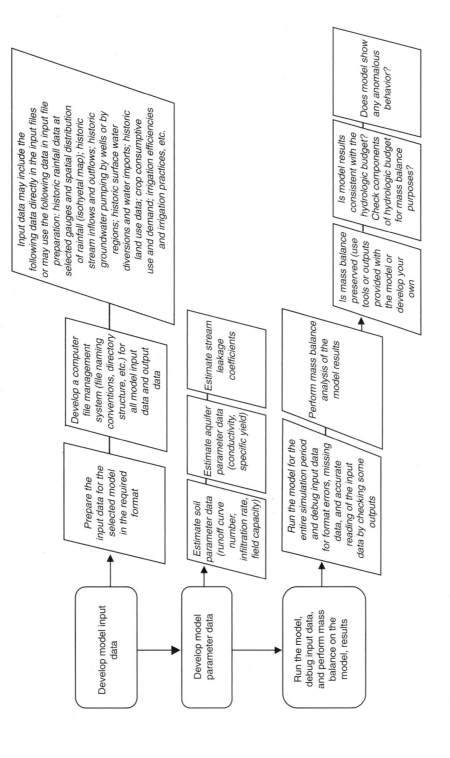

Figure 8–5.3c   Developing successful models, step 3: Build a model *(continued)*

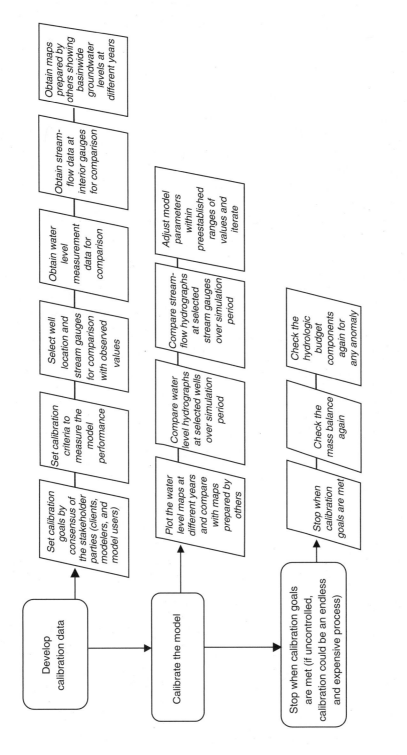

Figure 8–5.4   Developing successful models, step 4: Calibrate the model

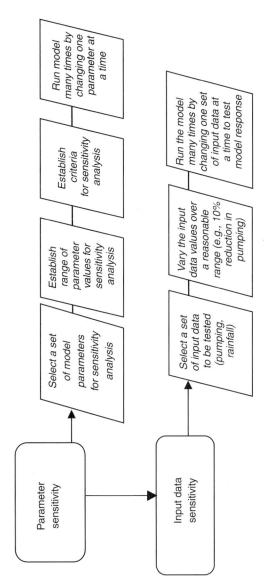

Figure 8–5.5   Developing successful models, step 5: Perform sensitivity analysis

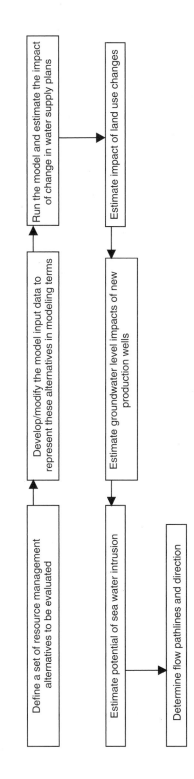

Figure 8–5.6   Developing successful models, step 6: Use a model

SUGGESTED ADDITIONAL READINGS

Burgy, R.H. and C.R. Pomeroy. 1958. Interception losses in grassy vegetation. *Transactions of American Geophysical Union*, 39:1095–1100.

Hillel, D. 1971. *Soil and Water: Physical Principles and Processes*. New York: Academic Press.

Horton, R.E. 1919. Rainfall interception. *Monthly Weather Reviews*, 47:603–623.

Klemes, V. 1986. Dilettantism in hydrology: Transition or destiny? *Water Resources Research*, 22:177S–188S.

Leyton, L., E.R. Reynolds, and F.B. Thompson. 1967. Rainfall interception in forest and moorland. *Forest Hydrology* (W.E. Sopper and H.W. Lull, eds.). Oxford: Pergamon Press.

Linsley, R.K. and J.B. Franzini. 1979. *Water Resources Engineering*, 3rd edition. New York: McGraw-Hill.

McMillan, W.D. and R.H. Burgy. 1960. Interception loss from grass. *Jour. of Geophysical Research*, 65:2389–2394.

Merriam, R.A. 1960. A note on the interception loss equation, *Jour. of Geophysical Research*, 65:3850–3851.

Murphy, C.E. and K.R. Knoerr. 1975. The evaporation of intercepted rainfall from a forest stand: An analysis by simulation. *Water Resources Research*, 11:273–280.

Office of Technology Assessment. 1982. Use of Models for Water Resources Management. *Planning and Policy, Congress of the United States*, Washington, D.C.

Rakhmanov, V.V. 1958. Are the precipitations intercepted by the tree crowns a loss to the forest? *Botanicheskii Zhurnal*, 43:1630–1633 (Trans. PST Cat. No. 293), Office Tech. Serv. Washington, D.C.: US Dept. of Commerce.

Rutter, A.J. 1967. An analysis of evaporation from a stand of Scots Pine. *Forest Hydrology* (W.E. Sopper and H.W. Lull, eds.). Oxford: Pergamon Press.

Rutter, A.J., A.J. Morton, and P.C. Robins. 1975. A predictive model of rainfall interception in forests, II. Generalization of the model and comparison with observations in some coniferous and hardwood stands. *Jour. Applied Ecology*, 12:367–380.

Swank, W.T. and N.H. Miner. 1968. Conversion of hardwood-covered watersheds to white pine reduces water yield. *Water Resources Research*, 4:947–954.

Thorud, D.B. 1967. The effect of applied interception on transpiration rates of potted ponderosa pine. *Water Resources Research*, 3:443–450.

US Soil Conservation Service. 1957. Hydrology. *National Engineering Handbook*. Washington, D.C.: US Soil Conservation Service.

Chapter 9

Regulatory Issues

This chapter introduces the main water quality regulations that affect water resources planning. As discussed in chapter 7, the quality of source water determines the level of treatment required to meet regulations. This chapter discusses the applicable US water quality standards as found in the Clean Water Act (CWA) and the Safe Drinking Water Act (SDWA) and its amendments.

The importance of water to public health, the environment, and the economy has long been recognized. Consequently, water policies, programs, laws, and regulations have been developed to address water quantity and quality. Water resources management must comply with many regulations involving groundwater and surface water use, land use planning and development, water supply and wastewater disposal, environmental and wildlife habitat quality, as well as hydropower generation, navigation, recreation, industrial, and agricultural water needs.

For example, in 1984, USEPA's Ground Water Protection Strategy focused on the need for joint state and federal initiatives to protect groundwater as a drinking water source. Since 1984, water resource planners and managers have regarded groundwater and surface water as interrelated in the hydrologic cycle and the watershed (or groundwater recharge zone) as the logical physical unit for planning and management.

The current strategy is to implement integrated, watershed-based resource management by establishing collaborative efforts among individuals, groups, and agencies with local, regional, state, and federal interests and responsibilities in each watershed. The watershed is the primary focus for coordinating and resolving resource management issues such as local or seasonal water supply shortages, streamflow levels, fisheries and wildlife habitat protection, and wastewater assimilation. In many states, water supply withdrawal requests have become core components of the basinwide assessment and permitting phase of the watershed approach, requiring watershed management decisions to consider water quality and quantity issues simultaneously.

Another example of how regulations address water quality and quantity is the regulation of stormwater. The impact of stormwater runoff as a diffuse source is regulated by USEPA's stormwater control rule, which requires best management practices for discharges from municipalities, industries, and construction sites larger than 5 acres (2 hectares). The link between surface water and groundwater is regulated through several rules, including the federal underground injection policy, groundwater as a surface water (under SDWA if shown to be "under the influence of the surface water"), and many that pertain to wetlands where major groundwater recharge occurs.

CLEAN WATER ACT

CWA's primary objective is to restore and maintain the integrity of the nation's waters. The two fundamental national goals of CWA are to eliminate the discharge of pollutants into the nation's waters and to achieve water quality levels that support fishing and swimming.

CWA provides a comprehensive framework of standards, technical tools, and financial assistance to address the many causes of pollution and poor water quality, including municipal and industrial wastewater discharges, polluted runoff from urban and rural areas, and habitat destruction. For example, the CWA

- requires major industries to meet performance standards to ensure pollution control;

- charges states and tribes with setting specific water quality criteria for their waters and developing pollution control programs to meet them;

- provides funding to states and communities to help them meet their clean water infrastructure needs; and

- protects valuable wetlands and other aquatic habitats through a permitting process that ensures development and other activities are conducted in an environmentally sound manner.

One of the most significant federal regulations affecting water suppliers is Section 404 of CWA. Section 404 regulates all waters of the United States, especially wetlands. It also regulates the discharge of dredged or fill materials into all waters of the United States, including wetlands.

Wetlands can be permanently inundated areas or may be water-saturated soils present within one foot (0.3 m) of the surface for as briefly as one week during the growing season. Therefore, wetlands are not always easily recognized and can occur across a broad spectrum of hydrologic regimes.

Federal wetland protection has evolved slowly over the past 30 years. The Rivers and Harbors Act of 1899 excluded more than 60 percent of all wetlands in the United States. Even after the CWA was enacted, Section 404 was interpreted by the US Corps of Engineers (Corps) to apply only to traditional navigable waters. Only after two major court rulings did the Corps radically alter the definition of waters of the United States. These two court cases led to a drastic alteration to the statute to encompass adjacent wetlands, man-made, seasonal, and isolated wetlands. The extent of jurisdiction of the Corps under Section 404 has grown such that practically any body of water in the United States could now arguably be regulated under the jurisdiction of the Corps and require a Section 404 permit before being filled or dredged. Since 1993, the program has been interpreted to regulate activities such as draining, dredging, and mechanized clearing of vegetation with minimal incidental discharges that result in the destruction or degradation of aquatic resources.

Section 404 is especially important to water suppliers because the criteria for which a permit is considered include evaluating numerous factors such as navigation, fish and wildlife, conservation, pollution, aesthetics, ecology, and public interest.

These broadened criteria have been sustained by court decisions, most notably the Two Forks Dam project in Colorado and the Ware Creek Reservoir project in Virginia. The Two Forks Dam project was a lengthy, complex, and expensive process culminating in a USEPA veto of a Corps Section 404 permit to build a dam. The veto was based on whether there were reasonable, practicable alternatives to the project. In the Ware Creek Reservoir project, a USEPA veto of a Corps permit to construct the reservoir was based solely on adverse environmental effects.

The critical issue facing water resource planners is the need to balance environmental concerns, including maintaining minimum streamflows to protect fish, wildlife, aesthetic, and recreational needs, with more traditional needs of water demand by people and industry. Water suppliers wanting to develop additional supply sources must consider the following:

- Various alternative sources

- Active promotion and practice of water conservation

- Feasibility of water marketing

- Use of salvaged water sources

- Hiring experts who understand Section 404

- Planning early and including wetland concerns in the site development process

- Actively communicating with the relevant regulatory agencies

- Ensuring that permit applications are complete and include supporting material

- Identifying the merits of the project and wetland avoidance and mitigation efforts

- Including the public in the process from the beginning

The permit program is jointly administered and enforced by the Corps and USEPA. However, other agencies, including the US Department of Interior's Fish and Wildlife Service (USFWS), the National Marine Fisheries Service, and the US Justice Department, are also involved in the water resources planning through Section 404.

One of the first and most important steps in the Section 404 permitting process is to identify the presence of wetlands on the land that is to be modified by source development. The Corps, the Soil Conservation Service, and the USFWS each define wetlands differently, although USEPA's definition agrees with the Corps' definition. The Corps and USEPA define wetlands as areas that are inundated or saturated by surface water or groundwater at a frequency and duration sufficient to support, and under normal circumstances do support, a prevalence of vegetation typically adapted for life in saturated soil conditions. Currently, wetlands are delineated according to the *Wetlands Delineation Manual*. The manual was prepared in 1987 and clarified and modified in 1991, 1992, and 1997. See http://www.wetlands.com/regs/tlpge02e.htm. The manual identifies three key provisions for defining a wetland:

1. Inundated or saturated soil conditions resulting from permanent or periodic inundation by groundwater or surface water

2. Prevalence of vegetation typically adapted for life in saturated soil conditions (hydrophytic vegetation)

3. Presence of normal conditions or circumstances (hydrology)

The Corps is the primary permit-issuing agency, and USEPA has veto authority. The Corps applies a broad-based public interest review test that must balance a variety of factors while ensuring that its actions comply with USEPA detailed Section 404(b)(1) guidelines. The Corps' public interest review process is used to decide whether to issue a permit and is based on navigation, wildlife, conservation, pollution, aesthetics, ecology, economics, historic values, flood controls, and any issues involving the National Environmental Policy Act (NEPA).

The regulations identify 24 specific factors as well as several general factors that the Corps must consider and weigh the benefits of the proposed action against any reasonably foreseeable detrimental impacts. The Corps must also ensure compliance with state water quality certifications.

A schematic flow diagram of the Section 404 permitting process is shown in Figure 9-1. The detailed individual permit review process may not always apply, and in some cases, a national or general permit process may apply. The permit review process may also involve the application of the NEPA review process. This would require a detailed environmental impact statement and could apply whenever a proposal for federal action could have significant environmental impacts. As shown in Figure 9-1, a preapplication consultation meeting is strongly recommended to identify the probable permit process facing the applicant.

In many states where water resources are being stressed, stringent requirements are being formulated to discourage interbasin transfers; therefore, drinking water supply sources in the basin must be developed before water can be imported. Likewise, wastewater discharges must occur within the basin to recharge local groundwater and surface waters. The important theme in water resources management is to view projects holistically from a watershed viewpoint, to consider quantity and quality simultaneously, and to consider all related regulations and policies.

In summary, water resource planners must implement a thorough and proactive program to address CWA regulations, particularly those that deal with wetlands. The planning team should include Section 404 experts and must address all relevant environmental considerations, including public participation of all interested parties.

DRINKING WATER QUALITY STANDARDS

The history of setting US water quality standards is just over 100 years old. In the 1890s, the American Public Health Association began the first push for quality criteria. But currently the question, "What is safe drinking water?" has not been fully answered. In the early 1900s, typhoid fever was a major health concern and the declining death rates were used as a measure of drinking water quality improvement in the United States. By the 1930s, typhoid death rates fell dramatically, chiefly because most water utilities provided adequate disinfection. However, just as typhoid was being conquered, other waterborne disease outbreaks, such as amoebic dysentery, continued.

In a 1938 to 1945 waterborne disease assessment, Rolf Eliassen and Robert Cummings stated: "Control [over waterborne disease] is seldom publicized in a positive manner, such as the number of consumer days without a serious outbreak. If presented in this fashion, the score of the waterworks personnel would be 99.99+ percent successful." Seemingly not much has changed in the past 50 years. Data taken in 1993, a year with a particularly high waterborne disease outbreak, show more than 404,000 reported cases of illness and deaths associated with drinking water. This number seems large, but compared to almost 241,000,000 people served by community water systems throughout the year, it amounts to a 0.17 percent case incidence. Stated as Eliassen and Cummings suggested, public water supply systems

Flowchart 1—Corps of Engineers Processing Flowchart

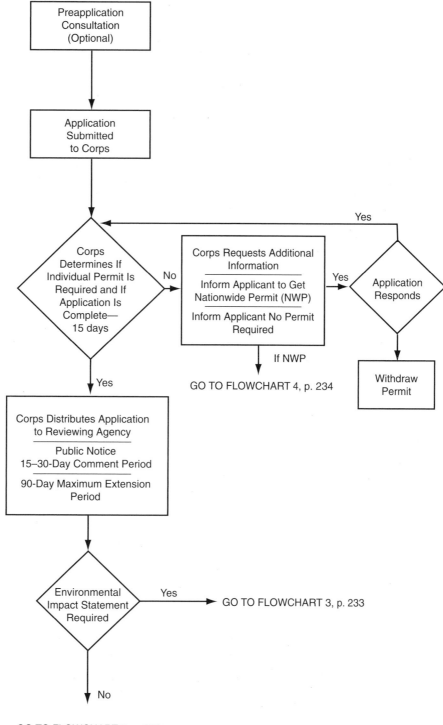

Figure 9–1   Permit process flowcharts

Flowchart 2—Environmental Impact Statement Not Required

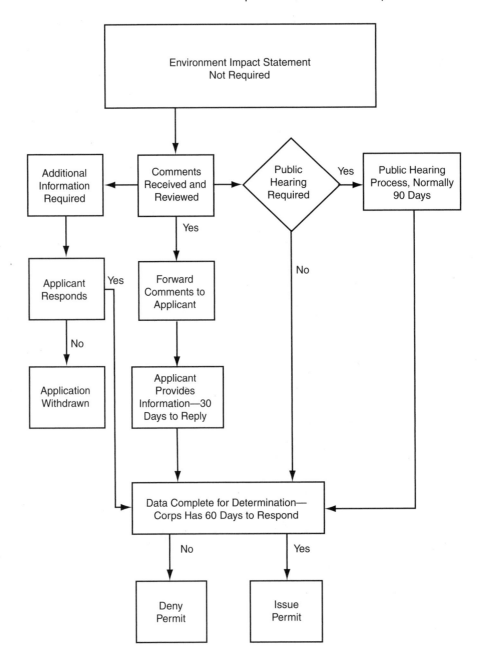

Figure 9–1   Permit process flowcharts *(continued)*

Flowchart 3—Environmental Impact Statement Required

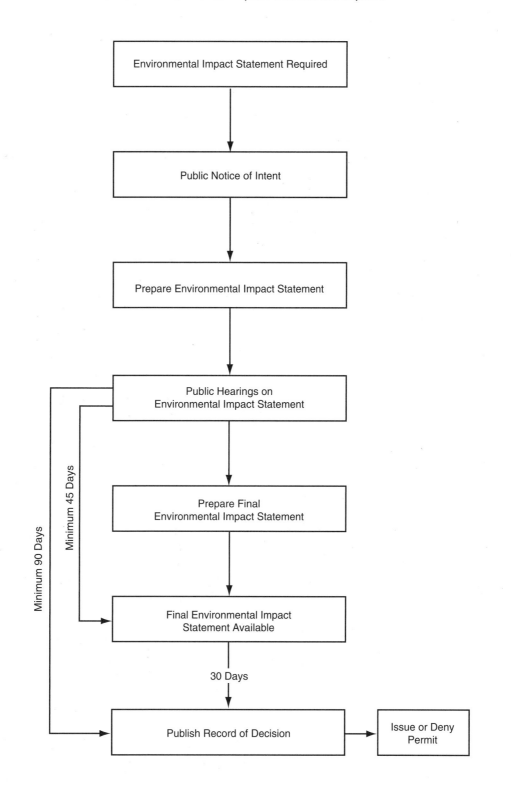

Figure 9–1   Permit process flowcharts *(continued)*

Flowchart 4—Nationwide Permit

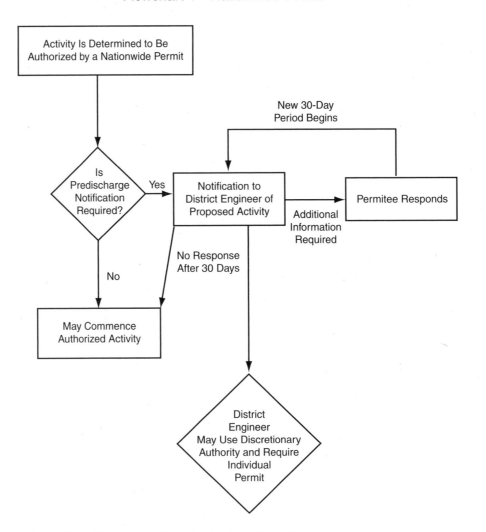

Figure 9–1   Permit process flowcharts *(continued)*

were 99.83 percent successful based on numbers of reported cases, and even more successful based on consumer days.

One undeniable change is that science seems to have outpaced technology. In 1914, the first US water quality standards were developed and focused on limiting bacterial contamination to 2 coliforms per 100 mL. By 1925, the coliform limit was reduced to 1 per 100 mL, and most large cities were filtering or chlorinating their water supplies. Standards were also set for physical and chemical constituents. By 1962, with increasing concern over chemical and industrial pollutants entering surface waters, the US Public Health Service (USPHS) set mandatory limits for 12 constituents and set recommended requirements for 19 more.

In 1974, two significant water quality events occurred. Trihalomethanes (THMs)—potentially carcinogenic chlorination by-products—were first discovered. This brought into serious question the continued use of chlorine, the most widespread drinking water disinfectant of the century. Then, in November 1974, USEPA published results of an epidemiological study documenting the presence of 66 trace organics in New Orleans tap water. Thus began the current trend of adopting ever-smaller constituent limits in drinking water. Currently, contaminants are measured in the parts per billion and parts per trillion. Put in perspective, 1 part per billion is equal to 1 second every 31.7 years.

Safe Drinking Water Act

Results of the New Orleans study prompted Congress to pass the SDWA on Dec. 16, 1974. Consider the far-reaching significance of this act as it empowered the USEPA administrator to "… conduct a comprehensive study of public water supplies and drinking water sources to determine the nature, extent, sources of, and means of control of contamination by chemicals or other substances suspected of being carcinogenic. Not later than six months after the enactment of this title, he shall transmit to the Congress the initial results of such study together with such recommendations for further review and corrective action as he deems appropriate."

Regulations were to be set in two steps. First, in 1975, the National Interim Primary Drinking Water Regulations were proposed, based on the 1962 USPHS guidelines. These standards consisted of 18 constituents, including organic and inorganic compounds, microbials, and turbidity. They applied to all "public water systems" defined as having at least 15 service connections or regularly serving at least 25 persons. In the second step, these regulations were to be revised and adopted by September 1977. This later deadline was never met. Fluoride was the only listed chemical to have a final maximum contaminant level (MCL) established. Fluoride primary and secondary MCLs were promulgated April 2, 1986, and became effective October 1987. Thus began the federal government's process of severely underestimating the time required to set meaningful drinking water standards—a process that is still used.

The 1975 interim regulations were amended four times between 1976 and 1983 to include radionuclides, THMs, and special monitoring requirements for corrosion and sodium. The fourth amendment identified the best generally available means to comply with THM regulations and was a landmark in that it was USEPA's first attempt to regulate a suspected human carcinogen in the parts per billion range.

Because of the complex issues affecting organic chemical contaminant regulations such as THMs, in 1982 USEPA announced a phased approach to future standards setting. More than 1,000 synthetic organic chemicals (SOCs) have been found in drinking water as a result of industrial contamination. Some are suspected human carcinogens, and the Phase I standards focused on some of the more widespread volatile organic chemicals (VOCs). Phase II standards focused on SOCs and other inorganic chemicals and microbials. Phase IIA dealt with regulating fluoride, Phase III with additional radionuclides, and Phase IV with disinfection by-products.

1986 AMENDMENTS

In 1986, several significant amendments were added to SDWA that directed USEPA to set MCLs and recommended maximum contaminant levels, known as maximum contaminant level goals (MCLGs). An MCLG is an unenforceable health goal and is required to be set at a level that no known or anticipated human health effects will occur, allowing an adequate margin of safety. An MCL must be set as close to an MCLG as feasible. *Feasible* was defined as using the best available technology (BAT), treatment, or other means that USEPA finds, after pilot testing, are available. An MCLG for a known or suspected carcinogen is automatically set to zero.

The 1986 amendments listed 83 contaminants to be regulated, in phases, by 1989. The amendments also allowed USEPA to substitute as many as seven contaminants, if they seemed to pose a greater risk to the public than contaminants already listed. The amendments further allowed USEPA to mandate, in lieu of an MCL, certain treatment techniques if a technologically or economically feasible method to monitor a given contaminant were not available. In addition, on Jan. 1, 1988, and every three years thereafter, USEPA was to publish a list of contaminants for possible regulation. Within two years of publishing these lists, USEPA was required to propose MCLGs, and one year later, to promulgate regulations for listed contaminants.

Secondary MCLs were developed for a number of constituents that do not pose a health risk, but because of aesthetic qualities, cause customer complaints. A few constituents addressed by secondary MCLs were turbidity, color, odor, iron, and manganese.

Since the 1974 SDWA was passed, 54 states and territories have been granted primary enforcement responsibility, or primacy, over setting, monitoring, and enforcing water quality regulations under federal laws. Each state or territory is required to adopt regulations that are at least as stringent as those set by USEPA. The 1986 amendments expanded primacy to Indian lands. Now Indian tribes that meet the same criteria as states can assume primary enforcement authority.

VOC Rule

On Jan. 9, 1989, the Phase I VOC Rule became effective, setting standards for eight VOCs: benzene, carbon tetrachloride, p-dichlorobenzene, 1,2-dichloroethane; 1,1-dichloroethylene, trichloroethylene, 1,1,1-trichloroethane, and vinyl chloride. The Phase I VOC Rule affected many groundwater supplies nationwide. Industrial contaminants from activities during World War II and cleaning solvents that migrated into groundwater sources now required treatment to remove them.

Surface Water Treatment Rule

The 1986 SDWA Amendments directed USEPA to establish minimum water quality criteria that, if not met, would require filtration for surface waters. USEPA addressed the filtration issue and fulfilled the requirement to regulate *Giardia* cysts, viruses, *Legionella*, turbidity, and heterotrophic plate count by promulgating the Surface Water Treatment Rule (SWTR) on June 29, 1989. The rule became effective Dec. 31, 1990. USEPA had estimated the SWTR would affect nationally about 2,800 unfiltered water systems and 6,900 systems then filtering their water.

All utilities served by surface water or groundwater under the direct influence of surface water must comply with this rule. Direct influence is defined as "any water beneath the surface of the ground with significant occurrences of insects or other macroorganisms, algae, or large-diameter pathogens such as *Giardia lamblia*, or significant and relatively rapid shifts in water characteristics such as turbidity, temperature, conductivity, or pH, which closely correlate to climatological or surface water conditions." A groundwater recharged by surface water may or may not be considered under direct influence according to this definition.

According to SWTR, systems meeting certain source water quality, disinfection, and site-specific criteria could be exempt from SWTR's filtration requirement. However, some state regulations were more restrictive. California, for example, did not exempt any public water system from the filtration requirement. For exemption, coliform and turbidity levels must not exceed specific limits; ongoing water quality monitoring and sampling are required; specific disinfection dosing and residual monitoring are required; and a watershed control program to minimize potential source water contamination by *Giardia lamblia* cysts and viruses is required.

SWTR's key requirements were that water suppliers provide multibarrier treatment, including filtration and disinfection, and achieve an overall 99.9 percent (3 log) removal–inactivation of *Giardia* cysts and 99.99 percent (4 log) removal–inactivation of viruses. *Giardia* cysts are the disinfectant-resistant form of the parasitic *Giardia lamblia* protozoan, the infectious agent of the intestinal disease giardiasis. Most occurrences in surface water are assumed to come from cyst shedding in the feces of infected wild and domestic animals in the watersheds. However, some research indicates this may be less common than first suspected. Viruses are those of fecal origin that can infect humans by waterborne transmission.

SWTR assumes that some cysts and viruses are removed by the filtration process, and some are inactivated by chemical disinfectants in the treatment process and in the water transmission and distribution systems. The regulation goes on to specify acceptable treatment technologies, performance criteria, and design and operating criteria to ensure that these levels of reduction can be reliably met through a combination of filtration and disinfection processes.

Although only the 3-log/4-log removal–inactivation limits are required by SWTR, primacy agencies may raise these limits based on the level of source water contamination, if such contamination exceeds a concentration of 1 *Giardia* cyst per 100 milliliters. Table 9-1 lists these greater removal–inactivation limits.

Filtration.   To determine the number of *Giardia* cysts and viruses physically removed by a treatment process, USEPA developed a credit system for various "currently used" filtration technologies. However, these credits are valid only if the physical treatment system meets specific performance criteria. USEPA has approved four physical treatment technologies based on data from numerous full-scale and research facilities demonstrating their ability to reliably remove *Giardia* cysts and viruses. The four acceptable filtration technologies "currently used" when the rule was adopted included the following, along with their respective cyst and virus removal credits listed in parentheses.

1. Conventional treatment (2.5-log/2-log)—coagulation, flocculation, sedimentation, and filtration.

2. Direct filtration (2-log/1-log)—coagulation (with or without flocculation) and filtration.

3. Slow sand filtration (2-log/2-log)—passing raw water through a sand filter at low velocities, generally less than 1.2 ft/hr.

4. Diatomaceous earth filtration (2-log/1-log)—a precoat cake of diatomaceous earth filter media on a support membrane, plus continuous addition of filter media to the feedwater.

Table 9–1   Removal–inactivation as a function of raw water contamination

Average Daily Cyst Concentration per 100 mL (Geometric Mean)	Required Removal–Inactivation	
	Giardia Cyst	Virus
≤1	3-log	4-log
>1–10[*]	4-log	5-log
>10–100[*]	5-log	6-log

[*]Advisory limits only.

Alternative technologies, including package treatment plant systems and cartridge filters, are also allowed under SWTR. Based on plant performance observations or pilot-plant studies, primacy agencies may categorize these technologies as one of the four listed earlier for determining removal credits.

Regardless of the technology employed, a public water system must meet turbidity removal performance criteria because turbid water "shelters" cysts and viruses from the inactivation effects of disinfectants. For all approved methods of filtration except slow sand, the filtered water turbidity was set at less than or equal to 0.5 nephelometric turbidity units (ntu) in 95 percent of the samples taken in a month. Slow sand filtration, if used, could not exceed 1.0 ntu, or exceed 1.0 ntu in more than two consecutive samples while the plant operates.

Monitoring frequency was set at intervals of no longer than four hours, whether by grab sample or by picking points off the chart of a properly calibrated continuous reading turbidimeter during plant operation. However, if performance criteria are met and the primacy agency approves, small systems (fewer than 500 persons) may reduce their turbidity monitoring to one grab sample per day.

Disinfection. Disinfection must inactivate *Giardia* cysts and viruses to supplement the filtration removal credit, such that the total treatment process achieves a 3-log/4-log reduction. The measure of effective disinfection is calculated by the contact time (CT) concept. CT is the product of the residual disinfectant concentration (C) measured at the first customer of the distribution system and the contact time (T) between the point of disinfectant addition and the first customer. Usually the first customer is the water treatment plant's potable water system connection. Some treatment plants add disinfectant at various treatment process stages, and the total CT value becomes the sum of multiple plantwide CT values.

In pipelines and pipelike structures, CT is measured by dividing the volume of pipe between two points, such as a disinfectant application point and a disinfectant measuring point, by the maximum flow rate past those two points. This contact time is the T value in minutes. For tanks or nonpipeline (and hence nonplug flow) structures, T is calculated as the time that 90 percent of the flow remains in the structure. This value is typically determined by a tracer study, or may be determined by using more conservative USEPA guidelines. The value of T is summed for all structures between disinfectant injection and measurement points, thus giving a T value for a known concentration of disinfectant.

To determine C for a disinfectant, tables provided in the USEPA Guidance Manual are used. The disinfectant concentration C is measured at the exit point of the structure being considered. Where different disinfectants are used, such as chloramine with ozone, in specific areas of the treatment and storage system, a C value is calculated for each area treated by the particular disinfectant. This is because each disinfectant has a greater or lesser capacity to inactivate *Giardia* and viruses, under given conditions of pH and temperature. The CT value is then calculated as the product of the detention times T and the disinfectants C, based on the disinfectant used, the water temperature and pH, and the amount of inactivation required.

In addition to meeting the CT requirement, a disinfectant residual entering the distribution system must be maintained at not less than 0.2 mg/L for more than four hours in any 24-hour period. Also, the residual disinfectant throughout the distribution system must be detectable in at least 95 percent of each month's samples. The presence of heterotrophic plate counts (HPC) at less than 500 colony-forming units (cfu) per milliliter is considered equivalent to a disinfectant residual.

Total Coliform Rule

The Total Coliform Rule (TCR) is structured quite differently from previous regulations covering microbiological contaminants. USEPA promulgated the TCR on the same day as the SWTR, on June 29, 1989. It is based on the presence–absence concept, rather than on the traditional determination of coliform density. Compliance is based on the number or percentage of samples testing positive (coliforms present) during a given month, not on the average concentration of coliform bacteria.

Samples are taken monthly with the number of samples a function of population served. Samples range from one for populations of 25 to 1,000, to as many as 480 for populations larger than 3,960,001. If any sample is determined to be coliform-positive, three repeat samples must be collected and analyzed within 24 hours, one at the original sampling location and at least one within five service connections upstream and downstream of the original site. Additional sets of three samples are to be taken until all three are negative, or the monthly MCL is met.

Whenever the MCL is exceeded, the primacy agency must be notified within 24 hours, followed by a report from the supplier identifying the cause of the problem. The TCR also requires proper public notification, using standard language as published in the federal regulation. The method and frequency of public notification is addressed in a separate regulation, and includes publication in a newspaper or posting within 14 days, mail or hand delivery within 45 days, and notification of electronic media (radio or TV) within 72 hours for acute violations.

Lead and Copper Rule

The final Lead and Copper Rule was promulgated on June 7, 1991. Compliance monitoring for large systems, those serving more than 50,000 people, began in 1992. Correction notices were issued on July 15, 1991, June 29, 1992, and June 30, 1994. This regulation required certain treatment techniques to reduce the presence of lead in drinking water. Typically, high levels of lead or copper are not present in source water. Rather, they are leached from customer service piping or compounds used to join water system piping several decades ago. The rule specifies optimal corrosion control techniques, along with treating levels of pH in raw water supplies and replacing service connections made of lead pipe or lead-based solder.

An action level (AL) of 0.015 mg/L measured at the consumer's tap was set for lead, along with an MCLG of zero. ALs must be met in 90 percent of the samples. The secondary MCL of 1.0 mg/L for copper was eliminated. In its place, an AL of 1.3 mg/L was set. The MCLG for copper was also 1.3 mg/L. All systems exceeding either the lead or copper ALs must provide corrosion control treatment and public education. Systems larger than 50,000 must optimize corrosion control.

Changes in the Lead and Copper Rule have been under USEPA review for several years. Additional changes were proposed on April 12, 1996. Final revisions and final rule were made in January 2000. Further revisions to sample collection and monitoring frequency are currently being proposed.

Disinfectant/Disinfection Byproducts Rule

Drinking water disinfection was one of the most significant public health advances of the 20th century. While disinfection is an effective method of controlling many microorganisms, the most common disinfectants, such as chlorine and ozone, are now known to react with naturally occurring materials in water to form undesirable organic and inorganic disinfection by-products (DBPs).

As previously discussed, the first DBPs to be regulated were total trihalomethanes (TTHMs), a group of four chlorinated organics formed when chlorine reacts with organic matter in water. These chlorinated organics are chloroform, bromoform, dibromochloromethane, and bromodichloromethane. In 1979, USEPA set an interim TTHM MCL of 100 mg/L as a running annual average of all samples collected quarterly at representative locations in the distribution system.

Expanding on the interim TTHM standard, in September 1989, USEPA distributed a preliminary "Strawman" Disinfectant/Disinfection Byproducts (D/DBP) Rule outlining the proposed rule's general structure and scope. Significant issues to be addressed by this regulation included TTHMs, other DBPs, and available treatment techniques for removing DBP precursors and eliminating by-product formation. This Strawman D/DBP rule sparked major criticism throughout the water industry in its attempt to balance acute risks of microbial contamination caused by inadequately disinfected water, with chronic risks of possible cancer-causing disinfection by-products.

As a result of critical reaction by the water industry to the proposed TTHM standards, USEPA initiated a process of negotiated rulemaking in September 1992, under the Negotiated Rulemaking Act of 1990. Called the reg/neg process, short for regulation/negotiation, USEPA, water industry leaders, and environmental interest groups conducted a series of meetings to reach negotiated regulatory limits acceptable to all stakeholders.

The stakeholders concluded that the existing SWTR needed revision to address health risks of high densities of pathogens in poorer quality source waters, as well as the health risks of *Cryptosporidium*. The group recommended three sets of rules: an Information Collection Rule (ICR), a two-staged D/DBP rule, and an Interim Enhanced Surface Water Treatment Rule (IESWTR) for systems serving more than 10,000 persons and a Long Term Enhanced Surface Water Treatment Rule (LT1ESWTR) for systems serving less than 10,000 persons.

The ICR was proposed in February 1994 and called for large water utilities to collect data on the presence and levels of microbial contaminants and disinfection by-products in their drinking water as well as on the effectiveness of different treatment technologies to reduce these levels. This included monitoring for bacteria, viruses, and protozoa over an 18-month period, as well as measuring the levels of organic materials in water that react with disinfectants to form by-products, the level of disinfectants, and the level of disinfection by-products.

ICR data would be used to further develop the Stage 1 D/DBP rule proposed in July 1994. However, the D/DBP rule's complexity and delays in starting the ICR further delayed the D/DBP rule-making process. The 1996 SDWA Amendments, in part, addressed these delays and established new regulatory deadlines for a number of contaminants.

1996 AMENDMENTS

In August 1996, Public Law 104-182 was enacted, amending the SDWA. Receiving bipartisan support in Congress as well as support by USEPA and the water supply industry, it provided significant changes in the regulatory process and added provisions for federal funding for infrastructure improvements and research. Notable highlights of the 1996 amendments included a more flexible process involving more public input, more risk-based standards, and more emphasis on small systems and on preventing contamination by protecting source water. The amendments replaced a "one size fits all" regulatory driven approach with one that provides more stakeholder input.

Because of the significant rule-making delays, USEPA had to rethink its schedule for promulgating the Stage 1 DBP Rule and IESWTR, as well as the time frame for National Primary Drinking Water Regulations (NPDWRs) becoming effective 18 months after promulgation. In the 1996 amendments, Congress lengthened the compliance time frame to three years, in consideration of the potential sizable capital investments utilities would likely be required to make. There was also a possible two-year extension if needed for capital improvements—which were necessary, especially for the small water systems.

The 1996 amendments also brought a more commonsense approach to rulemaking and provided states with greater flexibility when setting standards. They also allowed more focused financial resources on contaminant issues that threatened statewide, as opposed to national, public health. USEPA is now required to weigh the costs of a proposed water quality regulation against its possible benefits to more cost-effectively protect drinking water quality. The 1996 SDWA Amendments also retained USEPA's authority to promulgate secondary, aesthetic-based drinking water standards, although these secondary standards are not federally enforceable.

A new process for selecting contaminants requires USEPA to publish a list of contaminants that may require regulation. The first list was published in February 1998, and every five years thereafter USEPA is required to update the list. This list is known as the Drinking Water Candidate Contaminant List (DWCCL), and replaces the Drinking Water Priority List. Within three and one-half years after a DWCCL is published, USEPA must publish a decision whether to regulate at least five contaminants from that list. The agency can also decide to regulate a contaminant not on the list, if the contaminant meets the criteria for regulation.

USEPA now has authority to regulate contaminants based on several criteria, including whether a contaminant occurs or is substantially likely to occur in a public water system. It must choose contaminants that pose the greatest public health concern, and must publish an analysis of health concerns and an analysis of health risk-reduction benefits and costs with each standard. MCLs must maximize health risk-reduction benefits at justifiable costs.

USEPA was given three years to build a national occurrence database that includes detected levels of regulated contaminants and unregulated contaminants of concern. Regulations must be based on best available, peer-reviewed science and data from the best available methods. Scientific community review includes the Scientific Advisory Board.

Unregulated contaminants considered for listing include but are not limited to substances in Section 101(14) of the Comprehensive Environmental Response, Compensation, and Liability Act of 1980, and pesticides under the Federal Insecticide, Fungicide, and Rodenticide Act. Contaminant selection by USEPA must consider public health factors, specifically the contaminant's effect on subgroups comprising a meaningful portion of the general population, including infants, children, pregnant women, the elderly, and others with greater health risks than the general population.

When proposing an MCL, USEPA must seek public comment and publish a determination as to whether an MCL's benefits justify estimated compliance costs. In another departure from traditional regulation setting, USEPA may now establish an MCL at a level other than as close to the MCLG as feasible, if the feasible level results in increased overall risk by elevating other contaminant levels or by interfering with other treatment processes. MCLs and treatment techniques must be based on minimizing overall risk. This approach may help balance chronic illness concerns over known or suspected carcinogens such as DBPs, with acute illness concerns caused by pathogens and viruses. USEPA may, in certain cases, adopt an MCL that maximizes risk-reduction benefits at justifiable costs.

Federal Funding

In recognition of the tremendous financial burden SDWA compliance can have on utilities, for the first time the 1996 Amendments authorized federal funds for grants to capitalize state revolving loans to help finance drinking water infrastructure costs via the Drinking Water State Revolving Fund (DWSRF). This DWSRF authorized $9.6 billion from fiscal years 1994 through 2003 and allows states to fund source water protection, capacity development, and operator certification programs. A total of $1.275 billion was appropriated for fiscal year 1997. This includes $725 million of replacement funding when Congress failed to reauthorize the SDWA in 1995. To receive funds, states must match 20 percent of funding. States can also transfer as much as one third of any year's SDWA or CWA State Revolving Fund between the two accounts.

Microbial/Disinfection By-products Cluster

As noted earlier, delays in evaluating ICR data caused several related rule schedules to be revised. As required under the 1996 SDWA Amendments, USEPA was to promulgate an IESWTR, a final LT1 ESWTR, a Stage 1 DBP rule, and a Stage 2 DBP rule on specified schedules. These rules together with the Ground Water Rule (GWR), discussed later, are now known as the Microbial/Disinfection By-products (M/DBP) cluster. According to the 1996 Amendments, if a delay occurs in any one rule's promulgation, all other rules are to be completed as quickly as possible but no later than a revised date that would have the same interval schedule for the rule.

In December 1998, USEPA promulgated the Stage 1 DBP rule along with the IESWTR, both became effective in January 2002. Several DBPs and the most common disinfectants are regulated in the Stage 1 DBP Rule. This rule applies to community water systems and nontransient, noncommunity systems, including those serving fewer than 10,000 people that add a disinfectant to the drinking water during any part of the treatment process.

The final Stage 1 DBP Rule includes maximum residual disinfectant levels (MRDL) for disinfectants including chlorine and chloramines at 4 mg/L, and chlorine dioxide at 0.8 mg/L. MCLGs for individual DBPs are:

Bromodichloromethane	0
Bromoform	0
Chloroform	0
Dibromochloromethane	60
Dichloroacetic Acid	0
Trichloroacetic Acid	300
Bromate	0
Chlorite	800

An MCL for a group of five related chlorination DBPs called *haloacetic acids* (HAA5), was set at 60 mg/L, and at the same time the TTHM MCL was reduced to 80 mg/L. An MCL for bromate, an ozone DBP, was set at 10 mg/L; and for chlorite, a chlorine dioxide DBP, an MCL was set at 1,000 mg/L.

The IESWTR applies to water systems serving 10,000 or more people. Key provisions of the IESWTR included an MCLG of zero for *Cryptosporidium* and a 2-log *Cryptosporidium* removal requirement for systems that filter. The rule also required stronger combined filter effluent turbidity performance standards and individual filter turbidity provisions; disinfection benchmarking; and including the presence of *Cryptosporidium* in groundwater as an indication of groundwater under direct influence of surface water (GWUDI). Finished water reservoir covers and sanitary surveys for all surface water and GWUDI, regardless of size, were also required.

The LT1ESWTR became effective February 13, 2002, for systems serving less than 10,000 people. Compliance started March 15, 2002. The LT1ESWTR controls a wide range of pathogens in public water systems, and specifically addresses *Cryptosporidium* in systems serving less than 10,000 people with similar filter performance and turbidity requirements as established in the IESWTR.

Future M/DBP Rules

A second, more stringent Stage 2 DBP rule, and a Long Term 2 Enhanced Surface Water Treatment Rule (LT2ESWTR), born out of the 1996 ADWA Amendments are designed to further address the risk trade-offs between pathogen control and exposure to disinfections byproducts. The goals of both are to reduce exposure to DBPs in drinking water while maintaining public health.

USEPA began discussions with a Federal Advisory Committee (FACA) of stakeholders in December 1998 on the direction for the Stage 2 DBP Rule. As a regulatory option, FACA recommended maintaining 80 mg/L and 60 mg/L as the appropriate MCLs for TTHMs and HAA5, respectively. However, FACA also recommended a major change in the procedure for determining compliance with TTHM and HAA5 MCLs. USEPA proposed a location running annual average (LRAA) as the method by which compliance is attained. Under the LRAA, each DBP sampling location in the distribution system would still be monitored quarterly, but the running annual average of each individual location would have to comply with the MCLs, as opposed to the previous procedure of calculating the running annual average of all sampling locations collectively and comparing this level to the MCL.

In December 2002, USEPA announced that it planned to formally propose both the Stage 2 DBP and LT2ESWTR rules in 2003. The two rules were published/finalized in the *Federal Register* of January 4, 2006, and January 5, 2006, respectively. LT2ESWTR rule had a correction published in the *Federal Register* on January 30, 2006.

First Contaminant Candidate List

As previously discussed, within three and one-half years after the DWCCL was published, on August 2001, USEPA must publish a decision to regulate at least five contaminants. For those contaminants that USEPA determines to regulate, the agency has 24 months to propose MCLGs and NPDWRs and has 18 months following proposal to publish final MCLGs and promulgate NPDWRs.

According to SDWA, USEPA shall publish an MCLG and promulgate a NPDWR for a contaminant if the Administrator determines that three criteria are satisfied. The first is that the contaminant may have adverse effects on the health of persons. The second is that the contaminant is known to occur, or there is substantial likelihood that the contaminant will occur, in public water systems with a frequency, and at levels of public health concern. The third is, in the sole judgment of the Administrator, regulation of such contaminant presents a meaningful opportunity for health risk reduction for persons served by public water systems.

On June 3, 2002, USEPA made preliminary regulatory determinations for the nine CCL contaminants together with the determination process, rationale, and supporting technical information for each. The contaminants included: three inorganic compounds (IOCs) (manganese, sodium, and sulfate); three synthetic organic compounds (SOCs) (aldrin, dieldrin, and metribuzin); two VOCs (hexachlorobutadiene and naphthalene); and one microbial contaminant, Acanthamoeba. On

July 18, 2003, USEPA announced that no regulatory action was necessary for the nine contaminants on the first list. On February 23, 2005, the second CCL consists of nine microbial and 42 chemical contaminants or contaminant groups.

Arsenic Rule

Until January 2001, an interim standard for arsenic was set at 0.05 µg/L. In the early 1990s, USEPA, originally under a court-ordered deadline, considered lowering the arsenic standard to 0.5 to 20 µg/L based on studies showing quantities of arsenic in drinking water present a much higher cancer risk than previously thought. However, uncertainties concerning the health benefits of a lower standard led to delays in promulgation. Under the 1996 Amendments, USEPA was required to develop a comprehensive plan for studying health risks associated with low-level exposure to arsenic.

On June 22, 2000, the *Federal Register* published USEPA's proposed arsenic regulation for community water systems and nontransient noncommunity water systems. The agency proposed an MCLG of zero and an MCL of 5 µg/L. The agency also requested comment on alternate MCL levels of 3, 10, and 20 µg/L. Based on further agency analysis and significant public comment, the final arsenic limit was promulgated on January 22, 2001 with an MCL of 10 µg/L, effective January 23, 2006.

Radon Rule

In July 1991, USEPA proposed a rule governing radon, with an MCL of 300 pCi/L. There was much debate in the water industry to raise the proposed limit to 1,000 pCi/L or higher. Similarly, some regulators and environmental groups argued to set the limit even lower than 300 pCi/L. This debate stemmed from a suggested link of airborne radon levels in homes with cancer cases. However, no conclusive correlation linked levels of waterborne radon being transferred into the air and hence, inhaled.

The 1996 Amendments required USEPA to withdraw the July 1991 proposed radon NPDWR. USEPA arranged for the National Academy of Sciences (NAS) to prepare a risk assessment using the best available science and a study of risk-reduction benefits associated with radon exposure from drinking water and consider conditions likely to be experienced through residential exposure. Methods to reduce indoor air radon exposure were also to be evaluated. The latest proposed radon MCL was published November 2, 1999.

The November 1999 proposed rule provides states with flexibility in how to limit exposure to radon by allowing them to focus their efforts on the greatest radon risks—those in indoor air—while also reducing the risks from radon in drinking water. To accomplish this, USEPA proposed a multimedia approach to reducing radon risks in indoor air, while striving to protect public health from the highest levels of radon in drinking water. In recognizing that most radon enters indoor air from soil under homes and other buildings, and that only approximately 1-2 percent comes from drinking water, the agency proposed an MCLG and NPDWR for radon-222 in public water supplies. Under the framework set forth in the 1996 SDWA Amendments, USEPA also proposed an alternative maximum contaminant level (AMCL) and established requirements for multimedia mitigation (MMM) programs to address radon in indoor air.

Under the proposed rule, community water systems (CWSs) may comply with the AMCL if they are in states that develop a USEPA-approved MMM program or, in the absence of a state program, develop a state-approved CWS MMM program. The agency is also proposing a radon-222 MCL to apply to CWSs in non-MMM states that choose not to implement a CWS MMM program.

It is USEPA's expectation that most states will develop statewide multimedia mitigation programs as the most cost-effective approach. Most states currently have indoor radon programs that are addressing radon risk from soil and that can be used as the foundation for developing MMM program plans. The regulatory expectation of CWSs serving 10,000 persons or less is that they meet the AMCL and be associated with an approved MMM program plan—either developed by the state and approved by USEPA or developed by the CWS and approved by the state. USEPA will approve tribal CWS MMM programs, as well as those programs in states and territories that do not have drinking water primacy.

With a state-adopted or state-approved MMM program, the AMCL is proposed to be 4,000 pCi/L, and CWSs may comply with the AMCL. If an approved MMM program is not developed, CWSs must comply with a 300 pCi/L MCL. The AMCL/ MMM approach is USEPA's regulatory expectation for most CWSs because an MMM program and compliance with the AMCL is a more cost-effective way to reduce radon risk than compliance with the 300 pCi/L MCL.

Under proposed requirements, a MMM program plan must address four criteria:

1. Public involvement in developing the MMM program plan

2. Quantitative goals for existing home to be fixed and new homes to be built radon-resistant

3. Strategies for achieving goals

4. Plan to track and report results

Final approval for the Radon Rule may be in late 2007 or 2008.

Ground Water Rule

Groundwater quality depends on the water character entering an aquifer, the chemical nature of water-bearing formations, exposure to man-made contaminants, and the residence time in the aquifer. Historically, groundwater quality issues were concerned mainly with hardness and mineral content. However, issues of chemical and bacteriological contamination continues to raise concern.

Under the 1996 SDWA Amendments, USEPA must adopt a rule requiring disinfection of certain groundwater systems and provide guidance on determining which systems must be disinfected. This rule was to be adopted at any time after August 1999, but no later than the date USEPA adopted for the Stage 2 DBP Rule. As previously stated, the Stage 2 DBP Rule was published in the *Federal Register* on January 4, 2006. In May 2000, USEPA proposed the latest Ground Water Rule (GWR), which would establish protection against bacteria and viruses in drinking water from groundwater sources and would establish a targeted strategy to identify groundwater systems at high risk for fecal contamination.

The proposed strategy addresses risks through a multiple-barrier approach that relies on several major components. They include periodic sanitary surveys of groundwater systems requiring evaluation of eight elements and identifying significant deficiencies; hydrogeologic assessments to identify wells sensitive to fecal contamination; and source water monitoring for systems drawing from sensitive wells without treatment or with other indications of risk. They also include a requirement to correct significant deficiencies and fecal contamination through the following actions:

- Eliminate the source of contamination.

- Correct the significant deficiency.

- Provide an alternative source water, or provide a treatment that achieves at least 99.99 percent (4-log) inactivation or removal of viruses.

- Provide compliance monitoring to insure disinfection treatment is reliably operated where it is used.

This rule will apply to public groundwater systems that have at least 15 service connections or that regularly service at least 25 individuals at least 60 days of the year. This rule will also apply to any system that mixes surface and groundwater if the groundwater is added directly to the distribution system and provided to consumers without treatment. The final rule was published November 8, 2006.

SUMMARY

Current regulated and proposed contaminants are listed in Table 9-2.

Nonenforceable secondary standards are guidelines regulating contaminants that may have cosmetic effects such as skin or tooth discoloration, or aesthetic effects such as taste, odor, or color in drinking water. A list of secondary standards are shown in Table 9-3. USEPA recommends secondary standards to the water system but does not require systems to comply. States, however, may choose to adopt them as enforceable standards.

Meeting the myriad regulations that seem to be ever changing or evolving is a daunting challenge to all water supply professionals. In addressing this challenge, a broad perspective often is needed. This perspective can be best summed up in the following excerpt from Abel Wolman's 1982 keynote address at the New England Water Works Association meeting and reprinted in the June 1989 issue of *Journal AWWA*:

> Many people view published standards as acts of some remote supreme being that become engraved in granite when published. Any later examination or change in them takes on the semblance of sacrilege. Reminders that standards are man-made, empirical in nature, and subject to developing criteria are viewed with suspicion.
>
> As a result of remarkable advances in instrumentation, there are more than one hundred standards that address detection of contaminants in parts per trillion. Regulators, sensitive to the generated fears of the public, suggest that utilities make prompt public announcements if a particular standard is exceeded. Deviations from the values now dignified by the *Federal Register* simulate earthquakes or volcanic eruptions in the water supply field. Yet many of the standards are not firmly grounded insofar as their alleged public health effects are concerned. The manager, as always, must protect the consumer and maintain a balance between choice of treatment, cost, and preventing disease that is often nonapparent or lacking scientific basis.
>
> The list of potential problems, issues, and dilemmas that water supply professionals face today can be intimidating. Nevertheless, many of the problems of the past century have been equally intimidating. In reality, however, water supply professionals must correct, investigate, debate, and implement innovations. The degree of success depends on skill and intuition, both of which must be consciously created and nourished.

Our successors will inherit a better world than we did. Our successors are better trained, enthusiastic, and knowledgeable. Their world will have problems, but a universe with no problems would be a bore. I shall lose no sleep worrying about their future.

Table 9-2   National Primary Drinking Water Regulations (current contaminant listings can be found at http://www.epa.gov/safewater/contaminants/index.html)

Contaminant	MCLG* mg/L§	MCL† or TT‡ mg/L§	Potential Health Effects From Ingestion	Contaminant Sources in Drinking Water
Inorganic Chemicals				
Antimony	0.006	0.006	Increase in blood cholesterol; decrease in blood glucose	Discharge from petroleum refineries; fire retardants; ceramics; electronics; solder
Arsenic	none**	0.05	Skin damage; circulatory system problems; increased risk of cancer	Runoff from orchards; runoff from glass and electronics production waste; erosion of natural deposits
Asbestos (fiber >10 micrometers)	7 million fibers per liter (MFL)	7 MFL	Increased risk of developing benign intestinal polyps	Decay of asbestos–cement in water mains; erosion of natural deposits
Barium	2	2	Increase in blood pressure	Discharge of drilling wastes; discharge from metal refineries; erosion of natural deposits
Beryllium	0.004	0.004	Intestinal lesions	Discharge from metal refineries and coal-burning factories; discharge from electrical, aerospace, and defense industries
Bromate	zero	0.010	Increased risk of cancer	Byproduct of drinking water disinfection
Cadmium	0.005	0.005	Kidney damage	Corrosion of galvanized pipes; erosion of natural deposits; discharge from metal refineries; runoff from waste batteries and paints
Chromium (total)	0.1	0.1	Allergic dermatitis	Discharge from steel and pulp mills; erosion of natural deposits
Chlorite	0.8	1.0	Anemia; infants and young children: nervous system effects	Byproduct of drinking water disinfection

Table continued next page.

Table 9–2 National Primary Drinking Water Regulations (current contaminant listings can be found at http://www.epa.gov/safewater/contaminants/index.html) (continued)

Contaminant	MCLG,* mg/L§	MCL† or TT,‡ mg/L§	Potential Health Effects From Ingestion	Contaminant Sources in Drinking Water
Copper	1.3	Action Level = 1.3 TT††	Short-term exposure: Gastrointestinal distress. Long-term exposure: Liver or kidney damage. Those with Wilson's Disease should consult their doctors if their water systems exceed the copper action level.	Corrosion of household plumbing systems; erosion of natural deposits
Cyanide (as free cyanide)	0.2	0.2	Nerve damage or thyroid problems	Discharge from steel/metal factories; discharge from plastic and fertilizer factories
Fluoride	4.0	4.0	Bone disease (pain and tenderness of the bones); children may get mottled teeth	Water additive that promotes strong teeth; erosion of natural deposits; discharge from fertilizer and aluminum factories
Inorganic Mercury	0.002	0.002	Kidney damage	Erosion of natural deposits; discharge from refineries and factories; runoff from landfills and cropland
Lead	zero	Action Level = 0.015; TT††	Infants and children: Delays in physical or mental development. Adults: Kidney problems; high blood pressure.	Corrosion of household plumbing systems; erosion of natural deposits
Nitrate (measured as nitrogen)	10	10	"Blue baby syndrome" in infants younger than six months—life-threatening without immediate medical attention. Symptoms: Infant looks blue and has shortness of breath.	Runoff from fertilizer use; leaching from septic tanks, sewage; erosion of natural deposits

Table continued next page.

Table 9–2   National Primary Drinking Water Regulations (current contaminant listings can be found at http://www.epa.gov/safewater/contaminants/index.html) (continued)

Contaminant	MCLG,[*] mg/L[§]	MCL[†] or TT,[‡] mg/L[§]	Potential Health Effects From Ingestion	Contaminant Sources in Drinking Water
Nitrite (measured as nitrogen)	1	1	"Blue baby syndrome" in infants younger than six months—life-threatening without immediate medical attention. Symptoms: Infant looks blue and has shortness of breath.	Runoff from fertilizer use; leaching from septic tanks, sewage; erosion of natural deposits
Selenium	0.05	0.05	Hair or fingernail loss; numbness in fingers or toes; circulatory problems	Discharge from petroleum refineries; erosion of natural deposits; discharge from mines
Thallium	0.0005	0.002	Hair loss; changes in blood; kidney, intestine, or liver problems	Leaching from ore processing sites; discharge from electronics, glass, and pharmaceutical companies
Organic Chemicals				
Acrylamide	zero	TT[‡‡]	Nervous system or blood problems; increased risk of cancer	Added to water during sewage/wastewater treatment
Alachlor	zero	0.002	Eye, liver, kidney, or spleen problems; anemia; increased risk of cancer	Runoff from herbicide used on row crops
Atrazine	0.003	0.003	Cardiovascular system problems; reproductive difficulties	Runoff from herbicide used on row crops
Benzene	zero	0.005	Anemia; decrease in blood platelets; increased risk of cancer	Discharge from factories; leaching from gas storage tanks and landfills
Benzo(a)pyrene	zero	0.0002	Reproductive difficulties; increased risk of cancer	Leaching from linings of water storage tanks and distribution lines
Carbofuran	0.04	0.04	Problems with blood, nervous system, reproductive system	Leaching of soil fumigant used on rice and alfalfa

Table continued next page.

Table 9-2   National Primary Drinking Water Regulations (current contaminant listings can be found at http://www.epa.gov/safewater/contaminants/index.html) (*continued*)

Contaminant	MCLG,* mg/L§	MCL† or TT,‡ mg/L§	Potential Health Effects From Ingestion	Contaminant Sources in Drinking Water
Carbon tetrachloride	zero	0.005	Liver problems; increased risk of cancer	Discharge from chemical plants and other industrial activities
Chlordane	zero	0.002	Liver or nervous system problems; increased risk of cancer	Residue of banned termiticide
Chlorobenzene	0.1	0.1	Liver or kidney problems	Discharges from chemical and agricultural chemical factories
2,4-D	0.07	0.07	Kidney, liver, or adrenal gland problems	Runoff from herbicide used on row crops
Dalapon	0.2	0.2	Minor kidney changes	Runoff from herbicide used on rights of way
1,2-Dibromo-3-chloropropane (DBCP)	zero	0.0002	Reproductive difficulties; increased risk of cancer	Runoff/leaching from soil fumigant used on soybeans, cotton, pineapples, and orchards
o-Dichlorobenzene	0.6	0.6	Liver, kidney, or circulatory system problems	Discharge from industrial chemical factories
p-Dichlorobenzene	0.075	0.075	Anemia; liver, kidney or spleen damage; changes in blood	Discharge from industrial chemical factories
1,2-Dichloroethane	zero	0.005	Increased risk of cancer	Discharge from industrial chemical factories
1-1-Dichloroethylene	0.007	0.007	Liver problems	Discharge from industrial chemical factories
cis-1,2-Dichloroethylne	0.07	0.07	Liver problems	Discharge from industrial chemical factories

Table continued next page.

Table 9–2 National Primary Drinking Water Regulations (current contaminant listings can be found at http://www.epa.gov/safewater/contaminants/index.html) (continued)

Contaminant	MCLG,* $mg/L^\S$	MCL[†] or TT,[‡] $mg/L^\S$	Potential Health Effects From Ingestion	Contaminant Sources in Drinking Water
trans-1,2-Dichloroethylene	0.1	0.1	Liver problems	Discharge from industrial chemical factories
Dichloromethane	zero	0.005	Liver problems; increased risk of cancer	Discharge from pharmaceutical and chemical factories
1-2-Dichloropropane	zero	0.005	Increased risk of cancer	Discharge from industrial chemical factories
Di(2-ethylhexyl) adipate	0.4	0.4	Weight loss, liver problems or possible reproductive difficulties	Discharge from chemical factories
Di(2-ethylhexyl) phthalate	zero	0.006	Reproductive difficulties; liver problems; increased risk of cancer	Discharge from rubber and chemical factories
Dinoseb	0.007	0.007	Reproductive difficulties	Runoff from herbicide used on soybeans and vegetables
Dioxin (2,3,7,8-TCDD)	zero	0.00000003	Reproductive difficulties; increased risk of cancer	Emissions from waste incineration and other combustion; discharge from chemical factories
Diquat	0.02	0.02	Cataracts	Runoff from herbicide use
Endothall	0.1	0.1	Stomach and intestinal problems	Runoff from herbicide use
Endrin	0.002	0.002	Liver problems	Residue of banned insecticide
Epichlorohydrin	zero	TT[‡‡]	Stomach problems; increased risk of cancer over a long period of time	Discharge from industrial chemical factories; on impurity of some water treatment chemicals

Table continued next page.

Table 9–2 National Primary Drinking Water Regulations (current contaminant listings can be found at http://www.epa.gov/safewater/contaminants/index.html) *(continued)*

Contaminant	MCLG,* mg/L§	MCL† or TT,‡ mg/L§	Potential Health Effects From Ingestion	Contaminant Sources in Drinking Water
Ethelyne dibromide	zero	0.00005	Stomach, liver, or kidney problems; reproductive difficulties; increased risk of cancer	Discharge from petroleum refineries
Ethylbenzene	0.7	0.7	Liver or kidney problems	Discharge from petroleum refineries
Glyphosate	0.7	0.7	Kidney problems; reproductive difficulties	Runoff from herbicide use
Haloacetic acids (HAA5)	n/a‡‡‡	0.060	Increased risk of cancer	Byproduct of drinking water disinfection
Heptachlor	zero	0.0004	Liver damage; increased risk of cancer	Residue of banned termiticide
Heptachlor epoxide	zero	0.0002	Liver damage; increased risk of cancer	Breakdown of heptachlor
Hexachlorobenzene	zero	0.001	Liver or kidney problems; reproductive difficulties; increased risk of cancer	Discharge from metal refineries and agricultural chemical factories
Hexachlorocyclo-pentadiene	0.05	0.05	Kidney or stomach problems	Discharge from chemical factories
Lindane	0.0002	0.0002	Liver or kidney problems	Runoff/leaching from insecticide used on cattle, lumber, gardens
Methoxychlor	0.04	0.04	Reproductive difficulties	Runoff/leaching from insecticide used on fruits, vegetables, alfalfa, livestock
Oxamyl (Vydate)	0.2	0.2	Slight nervous system effects	Runoff/leaching from insecticide used on apples, potatoes, and tomatoes

Table continued next page.

Table 9–2 National Primary Drinking Water Regulations (current contaminant listings can be found at http://www.epa.gov/safewater/contaminants/index.html) (continued)

Contaminant	MCLG,* mg/L§	MCL† or TT,‡ mg/L§	Potential Health Effects From Ingestion	Contaminant Sources in Drinking Water
Polychlorinated biphenyls (PCBs)	zero	0.0005	Skin changes; thymus gland problems, immune deficiencies; reproductive or nervous system difficulties; increased risk of cancer	Runoff from landfills; discharge of waste chemicals
Pentachlorophenol	zero	0.001	Liver or kidney problems; increased risk of cancer	Discharge from wood-preserving factories
Picloram	0.5	0.5	Liver problems	Herbicide runoff
Simazine	0.004	0.004	Problems with blood	Herbicide runoff
Styrene	0.1	0.1	Liver, kidney, or circulatory problems	Discharge from rubber and plastic factories; leaching from landfills
Tetrachloroethylene	zero	0.005	Liver problems; increased risk of cancer	Discharge from factories and dry cleaners
Toluene	1	1	Nervous system, kidney, or liver problems	Discharge from petroleum factories
Total trihalomethanes (TTHMs)	none**	0.1	Liver, kidney, or central nervous system problems; increased risk of cancer	Byproduct of drinking water disinfection
Toxaphene	zero	0.003	Kidney, liver, or thyroid problems; increased risk of cancer	Runoff/leaching from insecticide used on cotton and cattle
2,4,5-TP (Silvex)	0.05	0.05	Liver problems	Residue of banned herbicide
1,2,4-Trichlorobenzene	0.07	0.07	Changes in adrenal glands	Discharge from textile finishing factories
1,1,1-Trichloroethane	0.20	0.2	Liver, nervous system, or circulatory problems	Discharge from metal degreasing sites and other factories

Table continued next page.

Table 9–2   National Primary Drinking Water Regulations (current contaminant listings can be found at http://www.epa.gov/safewater/contaminants/index.html) (continued)

Contaminant	MCLG,* mg/L§	MCL† or TT,‡ mg/L§	Potential Health Effects From Ingestion	Contaminant Sources in Drinking Water
1,1,2-Trichloroethane	0.003	0.005	Liver, kidney, or immune system problems	Discharge from industrial chemical factories
Trichloroethylene	zero	0.005	Liver problems; increased risk of cancer	Discharge from petroleum refineries
Vinyl chloride	zero	0.002	Increased risk of cancer	Leaching from PVC pipes; discharge from plastic factories
Xylenes (total)	10	10	Nervous system damage	Discharge from petroleum factories; discharge from chemical factories
Radionuclides				
Alpha particles	none**	15 picoCuries per liter (pCi/L)	Increased risk of cancer	Erosion of natural deposits
Beta particles and photon emitters	none**	4 millirems per year	Increased risk of cancer	Decay of natural and man-made deposits
Radium 226 and Radium 228 (combined)	none**	5 pCi/L	Increased risk of cancer	Erosion of natural deposits
Uranium	zero	30 µg/L as of 12/08/03	Increased risk of cancer—kidney toxicity	Erosion of natural deposits
Microorganisms				
Giardia lamblia	zero	TT§§	Gastrointestinal illness (e.g. diarrhea, vomiting, cramps)	Human and animal fecal waste

Table continued next page.

Table 9–2 National Primary Drinking Water Regulations (current contaminant listings can be found at http://www.epa.gov/safewater/contaminants/index.html) (continued)

Contaminant	MCLG,* mg/L§	MCL† or TT,‡ mg/L§	Potential Health Effects From Ingestion	Contaminant Sources in Drinking Water
Heterotrophic plate count (HPC)	N/A	TT§§	HPC has no health effects, but can indicate how effective treatment is at controlling microorganisms	HPC meaures a range of bacteria that are present in the environment
Legionella	zero	TT§§	Legionnaire's Disease, a type of pneumonia	Found naturally in water; multiplies in heating systems
Total coliforms (including fecal coliform and E. coli)	zero	5.0 percent***	Used as an indicator that other potentially harmful bacteria may be present†††	Coliforms are naturally present in the environment; as well as feces; fecal coliforms and E. Coli only come from human and animal fecal waste
Turbidity	N/A	TT§§	Turbidity is a measure of the cloudiness of water, and has no health effects but can interfere with disinfection and provide a medium for microbial growth. It may indicate the presence of microbes.	Soil runoff
Viruses (enteric)	zero	TT§§	Gastrointestinal illness (e.g., diarrhea, vomiting, cramps)	Human and animal fecal waste
Disinfectants				
Bromate	zero	0.01	Increased risk of cancer	By-product of drinking water disinfection
Chloramines (as Cl_2)	4	4.0	Eye/nose irritation; stomach discomfort, anemia	Water additive used to control microbes
Chlorine (as Cl_2)	4	4.0	ibid	ibid
Chlorine dioxide (as ClO_2)	0.8	0.8	Anemia; infants & young children: nervous system effects	ibid

Table continued next page.

Table 9–2 National Primary Drinking Water Regulations (current contaminant listings can be found at http://www.epa.gov/safewater/contaminants/index.html) (continued)

Contaminant	MCLG,* mg/L§	MCL† or TT,‡ mg/L§	Potential Health Effects From Ingestion	Contaminant Sources in Drinking Water
Haloacetic acids (HAA5)	n/a‡‡‡	1	Anemia; infants & young children nervous system effects	By-product of drinking water disinfection
Total Trihalomethanes (TTHMs)	0.8§§§	1	Anemia; infants & young children nervous system effects	By-product of drinking water disinfection

*Maximum contaminant level goal (MCLG)—The maximum level of a contaminant in drinking water at which no known or anticipated adverse effect on the health effect of persons would occur, and which allows for an adequate margin of safety. MCLGs are nonenforceable public health goals.

†Maximum contaminant level (MCL)—The maximum permissible level of a contaminant in water that is delivered to any user of a public water system. MCLs are enforceable standards. The margins of safety in MCLGs ensure that exceeding the MCL slightly does not pose significant risk to public health.

‡Treatment technique (TT)—An enforceable procedure or level of technical performance that public water systems must follow to ensure control of a contaminant.

§Units are in milligrams per liter (mg/L) unless otherwise noted.

***MCLGs were not established before the 1986 Amendments to the SDWA. Therefore, there is no MCLG for this contaminant.

††Lead and copper are regulated in a treatment technique that requires systems to take tap water samples at sites with lead pipes or copper pipes that have lead solder or are served by lead service lines. The action level that triggers water systems into taking treatment steps, if exceeded in more than 10 percent of tap water samples, is 1.3 mg/L for copper, and 0.015 mg/L for lead.

‡‡Each water system must certify, in writing, to the state (using third-party or manufacturer's certification) that when acrylamide and epichlorohydrin are used in drinking water systems, the combination (or product) of dose and monomer level does not exceed the levels specified, as follows:

    Acrylamide = 0.05 percent dosed at 1 mg/L (or equivalent)

    Epichlorohydrin = 0.01 percent dosed at 20 mg/L (or equivalent)

§§The Surface Water Treatment Rule requires systems using surface water or groundwater under the direct influence of surface water to (1) disinfect their water, and (2) filter their water to meet criteria for avoiding filtration so that the following contaminants are controlled at the following levels:

    Giardia lamblia: 99.9 percent killed/inactivated

    Viruses: 99.99 percent killed/inactivated

    Legionella: No limit, but USEPA believes that if Giardia and viruses are inactivated, Legionella also will be controlled.

    Turbidity: At no time can turbidity (cloudiness of water) go above 5 ntu; systems that filter must ensure that the turbidity goes no higher than 1 ntu (0.5 ntu for conventional or direct filtration) in at least 95 percent of the daily samples for any two consecutive months.

    HPC: No more than 500 bacterial colonies per milliliter.

    Long Term 1 Enhanced Surface Water Treatment (Effective 01/14/05); Surface Water or groundwater under direct influence of surface water (GWUDI) systems serving fewer than 10,000 people must comply with the applicable Long Term 1 Enhanced Surface Water Treatment Rule provisions (e.g., turbidity standards, individual filter monitoring, cryptosporidium removal requirements, updated watershed control requirements for unfiltered systems).

    Filter Backwash Recycling; The Filter Backwash Recycling Rule requires systems that recycle to return specific recycle flows through all processes of the system's existing conventional or direct filtration system or at an alternate location approved by the state.

***No more than 5.0 percent samples total coliform positive in a month. (For water systems that collect fewer than 40 routine samples per month, no more than one sample can be total coliform positive.) Every sample that has total coliforms must be analyzed for fecal coliforms. There cannot be any fecal coliforms.

Table footnotes continued next page.

†††Fecal coliform and *E. coli* are bacteria whose presence indicates that the water may be contaminated with human or animal wastes. Microbes in these wastes can cause diarrhea, cramps, nausea, headaches, or other symptoms.

‡‡‡Although there is no collective MCLG for this contaminant group, there are individual MCLGs for some of the individual contaminants:
- Trihalomethanes: bromodichloromethane (zero); bromoform (zero); dibromochloromethane (0.06 mg/L). Chloroform is regulated with this group but has no MCLG.
- Haloacetic acids: dichloroacetic acid (zero); trichloroacetic acid (0.3 mg/L). Monochloroacetic acid, bromoacetic acid, and dibromoacetic acid are regulated with this group but have no MCLGs.

§§§MCLGs were not established before the 1986 Amendments to the Safe Drinking Water Act. Therefore, there is no MCLG for this contaminant.

N/A—Not applicable.

Table 9–3   National Secondary Drinking Water Regulations, 1998

Contaminant	Secondary Standard
Aluminum	0.05 to 0.2 mg/L
Chloride	250 mg/L
Color	15 (color units)
Copper	1.0 mg/L
Corrosivity	noncorrosive
Fluoride	2.0 mg/L
Foaming agents	0.5 mg/L
Iron	0.3 mg/L
Manganese	0.05 mg/L
Odor	3 threshold odor number
pH	6.5–8.5
Silver	0.10 mg/L
Sulfate	250 mg/L
Total dissolved solids	500 mg/L
Zinc	5 mg/L

REFERENCES

American Water Works Association. 1996. SDWA Special Report, 1996 Amendments Emphasize Partnership for Feds, States, Utilities. Washington Report. *Mainstream*. Sept. 1996. Denver, Colo.: AWWA.

Dougherty, C.C. Oct. 1996. Letter. US Environmental Protection Agency, Office of Water Director, Office of Ground Water and Drinking Water.

Federal Register, January 14, 2002, Vol. 67, Number 9, 40 CFR Parts 9, 141 and 142, National Primary Drinking Water Regulations: Long Term 1 Enhanced Surface Water Treatment Rule.

Federal Register, November 2, 1999, Vol. 64, Number 211, 40 CFR Parts 141 and 142, National Primary Drinking Water Regulations; Radon-222; Proposed Rule.

Federal Register, January 22, 2001, Vol. 66, Number 14, 40 CFR Parts 9, 141 and 142, National Primary Drinking Water Regulations; Arsenic and Clarifications to Compliance and New Source Contaminants Monitoring; Final Rule.

Federal Register, June 3, 2002, Vol. 67, Number 106, 40 CFR Part 141, Announcement of Preliminary Regulatory Determinations for Priority Contaminants on the Drinking Water Contaminant Candidate List.

Kramer, M.K. et al. 1996. Waterborne disease: 1993 and 1994. *Jour. AWWA*, 88(3):66–80

Letterman, R.D. 1991. *Filtration Strategies to Meet the Surface Water Treatment Rule*. American Water Works Association. Denver, Colo.: AWWA.

Pontius, F.W. 1997. Future directions in water quality regulations, *Jour. AWWA*, 89(3):40–54

Pontius, F.W. 1998. New horizons in federal regulation. *Jour. AWWA*, 90(3):38–50

US Environmental Protection Agency. Oct. 1990. Guidance Manual for Compliance With the Filtration and Disinfection Requirements for Public Water Systems Using Surface Water Sources. Washington, D.C.: USEPA.

US Environmental Protection Agency. 2000. Clean Water Act: A brief history. http://www.epa.gov/region5/water/cwa.htm.

US Environmental Protection Agency, July 2002, National Primary Drinking Water Regulations Web site, http:/www.epa.gov.

This page intentionally blank

Chapter 10

Environmental Impact Analysis

ENVIRONMENTAL IMPACT PLANNING

Analyses of environmental issues are critical to water resources planning. The issues considered in environmental impact documents include biological, human, and physical resources. Biological resources include fish, wildlife, and vegetation. They may be in aquatic, riparian or wetland zones, or in upland areas that could range from the plains to above the tree line in the mountains. Human resources include considerations for economics, public services, housing, public health, noise, visual, aesthetics, recreation, and cultural resources as well as quality of life considerations. Physical resources consider soils, site geology, air quality, surface waters, and groundwater. All these issues must be considered when developing water resource projects.

Purpose and Need of Environmental Impact Planning

During the 1960s, as the nation's population grew quickly and pollution increased, Congress considered measures to protect the environment, especially from activities related to new construction and the deteriorating condition of surface and ground waters. In 1969, Congress adopted the National Environmental Policy Act (NEPA) in Public Law 91-190 to establish policies and goals to protect the environment. The Act states that Congress recognized the impact of population growth, urbanization, industrial expansion, and expanding technology on the environment and the need to restore and maintain environmental quality. The law further states that it was the continuing policy of the federal government, in cooperation with state, local, and special interest groups, to

> "use all practicable means and measures, including financial and technical assistance, in a manner calculated to foster and promote the general welfare, to create and maintain conditions under which man and nature

can exist in productive harmony, and fulfill the social, economic, and other requirements of present and future generations of Americans."

The law also authorized USEPA to develop rules and regulations to implement NEPA.

Since 1969, NEPA has been interpreted and defined through additional legislation such as the Environmental Quality Improvement Act of 1970 and the Clean Air Act, and specific regulations. The requirements of NEPA and associated regulations have been further defined through state environmental impact planning laws and regulations.

These requirements were developed to provide information to public officials, stakeholders, and citizens before decisions are finalized. The information must provide an understanding of the consequences on the environment of the proposed actions and all reasonable alternatives that would meet the objectives of the proposed actions. Through these documents, participants in the process can make informed decisions to shape the future of their communities.

Projects That Require Environmental Documentation

Environmental documentation should be developed for all projects and discretionary actions that may directly or indirectly change environmental resources or land use patterns. These could include constructing or modifying structures; operating facilities that affect biological, human, or physical resources; or adopting plans (general or master) that will affect future land uses.

Projects that do not require environmental documentation are generally related to continued administrative or maintenance activities such as purchasing supplies or raising fees or taxes to maintain services, submitting proposals for voters or holding an election, implementing a study, adopting some types of legislation such as antidiscrimination laws, or ministerial projects such as issuing licenses. Issuing individual permits by an agency after a Lead Agency (described later) has approved the entire program generally would not require additional environmental analysis; however, a completed environmental impact document may need to be included by reference. Emergency projects to protect or restore property generally do not require environmental planning activities.

NEPA and state legislation are statutory; therefore, the enacting legislative body may provide for exemption of the legislation. All other projects require some type of environmental impact documentation.

Selecting a Lead Agency to document environmental impact. NEPA and similar state legislation were adopted to provide for public agencies to serve as Lead Agencies because the purpose of any public agency is to serve their constituents rather than special interest groups. In addition, the public can influence the public process by participating in public meetings and selecting representatives of public agencies.

The Lead Agency typically is responsible primarily for implementing the project. At the same time, the Lead Agency frequently prepares technical documents. Several agencies may co-lead the environmental impact plan if they have equal responsibility for implementing the project. NEPA and many state programs have provisions for *responsible agencies* that will issue permits or participate in the approval process. These agencies usually comment on issues that are within their area of expertise or responsibility. NEPA and many state programs also have provisions for *cooperating agencies* that have jurisdiction or special knowledge over specific resources but are not involved in implementing or authorizing the project.

Selecting a Lead Agency and responsible agencies is extremely important and frequently very difficult because of the overlapping responsibilities. In sensitive cases, the Lead Agency may request that the responsible agencies adopt the environmental impact document before the Lead Agency does. As a result, the Lead Agency would have an opportunity to review any conditions or mitigation measures adopted by the responsible agencies before the project is adopted. This process also allows informed stakeholders to address agencies with specific expertise on project issues. This type of multiple approval process occurs frequently where multiple land use and resource agencies have overlapping responsibilities.

Initiating the Environmental Planning Process

The environmental planning process must be implemented concurrently with the technical evaluation. Concurrent development of the technical and environmental documents allows the decision-making processes to be integrated. If the technical process precedes the environmental process and identifies final alternatives that may have significant impacts, the cost to redefine and reevaluate new alternatives may be high. In addition, the community may be able to identify the most acceptable alternative. The environmental planning process includes significant public involvement to identify issues that are sensitive to the community, special interest stakeholders, and resource agencies. Public meetings could be held as part of preparing the technical document. However, many stakeholders do not attend the technical meetings because they think they may not understand the information. Therefore, implementing the environmental planning process with the concept development portion of the technical process and presenting information to the public in an understandable and timely manner are important.

The environmental planning process is most successful when the following steps are implemented:

1. Define the scope. This is the first step and is clearly defined in NEPA. A critical aspect of scoping is public participation, a step often left until the end of the process when, in reality, it should be part of the scoping mechanism at the beginning of the process. Public participation identifies potentially affected populations and offers knowledge from the public. Rather than just a public meeting, public participation is an analytical process that can involve interviews, workshops, focus groups, facilitated working sessions, etc. If federally recognized Native American Tribes are part of the public, they should be consulted in a formal government-to-government manner. (See Chapter 2 for guidance on effective public participation and consultation.)

2. Assess environmental compliance needs. Identify the agencies that will provide approvals and permits for the final proposed action. Through direct contacts with these agencies, collect their permit applications and submittal requirements, including mandatory requirements for environmental impact documentation. Discuss their approval processes and schedules for approvals. If possible, ask to view examples of successful submittals.

3. Complete a preliminary analysis of potential issues or constraints. Review information collected from the agencies with the engineering or economic teams on the project. Complete preliminary site visits, if applicable, to identify any specific issues related to special habitats, restraints caused by

adjacent land uses or utilities, or sensitive noise or visual receptors in the area.

4. Develop a strategy to approach the environmental planning process. Prepare a list of relevant regulations and requirements, including key schedule milestones. For each milestone, identify required submittals and the information that will be needed to complete the submittals. Coordinate with the engineering or economic teams to develop a critical path for completing the environmental planning process.

5. Continue to coordinate with all agencies and interest groups. The most frequent complaints about the environmental planning process are related to delays in receiving approvals or permits and applying mitigation measures or requirements on a project at the end of the project. Both issues usually lead to costly delays and redesign of the proposed alternative. Therefore, frequently coordinating with the agencies and interest groups involved and making them part of the alternative development and evaluation program are important steps. They will likely better understand the reasons for the final decisions.

PREPARING ENVIRONMENTAL IMPACT DOCUMENTATION _____

Preparing an environmental impact document includes three critical steps:

1. Determine the type of document.

2. Determine several critical issues.

3. Complete specific analyses and present them in an understandable manner that will meet several uses.

Types of Environmental Impact Documents

There are three basic types of environmental impact documents: exclusions or exemptions, environmental assessments, and environmental impact statements or reports.

Exclusions. Exclusions are used for projects that occur routinely with anticipated outcomes that do not result in significant adverse impacts. Examples include restoring or rehabilitating facilities to a level that does not increase the original design capacity; adding health or safety devices; performing maintenance activities (which may have short-term construction impacts); changing ownership of facilities (though the transfer may result in higher costs that may lead to change in lifestyle of users); or converting small structures (though the conversion may result in a change in use). Most of these issues are not considered when preparing water resource plans. Exclusions cannot be used if the proposed action would have precedent for future actions with potential adverse impacts. Exclusions also cannot be used if the action would have potential adverse impacts on listed species, historic or cultural resources, floodplains, wetlands, water quality, or air quality.

The Lead Agency summarizes the reasons for using an exclusion document and adopts the findings. That agency must notify the public of the decision and allow public comment before implementing the proposed action.

Environmental assessments. Environmental assessments or preliminary studies are frequently used in water resources planning. Through this process a preliminary report is prepared to describe the affected environment, or current conditions, with respect to the biological, human, and physical resources. The level of detail presented is minimal and focused on the elements that may be affected by the proposed action. Generally, the environmental assessment describes only the potential impacts and benefits of the proposed action. If the proposed action could have an adverse impact, it is changed through either the project description or mitigation measures described in the document. Alternatives to the proposed action are described, and the reasons for not pursuing the alternatives are summarized. The environmental assessment is frequently distributed for public comment before the proposed action is adopted and mitigation measures are included in the final document. If the Lead Agency determines that there would be no significant adverse impacts from implementing the proposed action, including mitigation measures, the environmental assessment is adopted and recorded in a public forum. The public must be notified that the final environmental assessment has been adopted and allowed to comment on the decision before the proposed action is implemented.

If the environmental assessment shows that significant impacts could occur or if the public review requires that several alternatives be evaluated in equal detail, the information in the environmental assessment is used to prepare an environmental impact statement or report. Sometimes an environmental assessment is completed to focus the analysis in an environmental impact document. The important issues are defined by distributing the environmental assessment to the public and agencies. This can limit the level of effort for the actual environmental impact report to the sensitive issues.

Environmental impact statements. Environmental impact statements or reports are used when several alternatives need to be evaluated at an equal level of detail. This type of environmental document includes a detailed description of the affected environment and potential impacts and benefits of alternatives. Frequently, a definition of *significant impact* is defined for each element considered in the report. The adverse impacts are measured against impacts that would occur without the project and defined as *significant* or *not significant*. The level of analysis of the impact assessment is more detailed than under an environmental assessment and frequently includes results of numerical models, field investigations, and discussions with community representatives or experts. The environmental impact documentation also includes an evaluation of cumulative impacts of implementing the alternatives with other planned programs that are not specifically part of the alternatives. Mitigation measures are proposed for the alternatives to reduce adverse impacts to a level of less significance. The environmental impact document usually defines an *environmentally preferred alternative* and the *preferred alternative*. Frequently, these alternatives are identical. However, they may be different, and the document must describe the reasons to select the preferred alternative with fewer benefits to the environment.

The environmental impact document generally has more stringent public notification requirements during and following report preparation. For example, NEPA requires scoping meetings during the preparation of the environmental impact document as well as public hearings after the draft environmental impact statement is distributed. In contrast, NEPA requires receiving written public comments on an environmental assessment only after the final environmental assessment has been adopted. Additional public involvement allows concerned stakeholders to participate in the process to identify and evaluate alternatives.

For some complex environmental documents, especially for watershed planning, the draft environmental impact document frequently does not include a preferred alternative or final mitigation measures. This process allows the public to help define the preferred alternative and final mitigation measures. In some cases, this approach has allowed stakeholders to define an acceptable approach to sensitive issues.

Selecting the type of environmental document. Several questions must be answered to decide which type of environmental document to use for each project. The decision may be determined by rules adopted by Lead Agencies or responsible agencies. If not, the Lead Agency should address the following questions:

- Is there only one feasible alternative to meet the proposed purpose and need of the project?

- If no, prepare an environmental impact document. If yes, go to the next question.

- Can the project, including mitigation measures, be defined in a manner that would not result in any significant adverse impact to biological, human, or physical resources?

- If no, prepare an environmental impact document. If yes, go to the next question.

- Is the project part of a larger program that has already been evaluated and adopted under a programmatic environmental impact document?

- If no, go to the next question. If yes, prepare an environmental assessment.

- Is the project part of a larger program that has not been evaluated for potential environmental impacts and could result in cumulative impacts?

- If no, prepare an environmental assessment. If yes, prepare an environmental impact document.

Critical Steps in Preparing the Environmental Document

In many complex projects, including watershed planning, identifying the alternatives is one of the most critical and sensitive steps. With respect to preparing the associated environmental documents, several critical steps, including selecting the study area, study period, baseline conditions, and level of analytical detail, can determine whether the document will be accepted or legally challenged.

Selecting the study area. In many programs, the study area boundaries are evident because of geographical limitations. However, for watershed programs, the study area boundary (for example, evaluating how a proposed dam would affect the inundation area and the area along the stream below the dam) could be extremely broad. In a small watershed, the affected area may extend beyond the basin divide because of animal migration. If the stored water or potential hydropower is to be used outside the watershed, the study area may need to be expanded to identify direct economic benefits or impacts of operating the dam. If the dam would block anadromous fish migration and this would impact regional fish populations, the study area may need to be expanded to include the geographical boundaries of the fish migration patterns. If the fish form the basis of a commercial or sport fishing industry, the study area may need to be expanded to include the geographical locations of this economic sector.

Expanding the study area will allow stakeholders to participate who do not live adjacent to the proposed project. This will help participants better understand the regional limitations, costs, and benefits and may avoid costly litigation or voter challenges. Expanding the study area will increase the cost and time needed to prepare the environmental plan. However, if potential impacts are not disclosed in the environmental document, affected parties may successfully litigate.

Selecting the study period and the baseline conditions. Determining the length of the study period and the baseline conditions frequently depends on the type of project being considered in the document. For many construction projects, the study period may be identified as the current conditions. For utilities that provide public services, the study period extends to the projected future when the capacity of the system will be fully used. For watershed projects, especially those with environmental restoration components, the study period may extend 50 years or more into the future. The extent of the study period becomes a critical issue because it defines the baseline conditions on which the impacts of implementing the alternatives are compared.

If the study period for a program is shorter than 5 or 10 years, the current conditions or affected environment description can serve as the *No Action* or *No Project Alternative* baseline. For programs that will extend for more than 5 or 10 years, the environmental document must define the baseline conditions for the No Action or No Project Alternative as the future conditions without the potential alternatives. This becomes difficult when ongoing programs, including changing legislation, weather conditions, and economics dynamically affect the environment. Under NEPA, the environmental analyses need to compare only impacts of the alternatives with the future No Action Alternative condition. However, many state regulations require that the alternatives to the current and future No Action Alternative conditions be compared.

Utilities also should consider the time for critical species populations to react when selecting the study period for environmental restoration projects. For example, if the life cycle of an animal that would benefit from environmental restoration is 5 years, waiting three life cycles, or 15 years, to determine whether the restoration activities result in sustainable population improvements may be necessary.

Determining the level of detail in the analysis. The level of detail for the impact assessment and presentation of the results is also crucial in determining the usefulness of the environmental impact document. Including all available information about a subject in an environmental document is not desirable. The document should refer to information from readily available publications to avoid duplicating other reports. Detailed analyses that need to be completed may be presented in attachments or appendices to the environmental impact document and summarized in the main document. Presentation of the data in the main document should be at a level that is easily understandable by the public. However, information that would usually be reviewed or prepared by a specialist may be presented in the attachments or appendices. When the information is summarized, the results should not be presented on such a broad basis that the benefits and impacts on specific communities or habitats cannot be identified.

As technical reports have become more reliant on computer models, the level of analysis has become more complicated and intricate. Therefore, the level of detail must be determined before the analyses are completed. Identifying the level of analysis may be constrained by the available analytical tools or input data. For example, if hydrologic data are limited to a main stream in the watershed, constructing a model to simulate operations of all tributary streams would be more difficult than if data are available for all subbasins.

Before initiating the development of a new analytical tool or use of a tool, the Lead Agency must determine the level of detail required by considering the following questions:

- Is the level of detail appropriate to discern the differences between alternatives?

- Is the level of detail appropriate to disclose potential impacts to an individual portion of the study area or community?

The level of detail needed to discern the differences between alternatives depends on the facilities or policies considered. For example, if regional watershed management alternatives range from construction of a new dam to stringent conservation of water, providing a surface water analysis that extends to every tributary in the watershed may not be necessary. However, if the alternatives might affect one part of the watershed to a higher degree than other areas because of changes in groundwater use, a groundwater model for the watershed may be needed.

INFORMATION IN ENVIRONMENTAL IMPACT DOCUMENTS ___

As previously mentioned, the document must address biological, human, and physical resources. Specific issues associated with each are discussed in the following sections.

Human Resources

Issues that could affect the human environment are land use, employment, housing, educational opportunities, transportation, local economics, regional economics, recreation, historic resources, cultural resources, public services, noise, visual, aesthetics, and social factors. Identifying direct impacts of watershed programs on human resources can be determined by reviewing general land use plans and recreational use data, comparing population and economic demographic data and projections, reviewing the site, and reviewing previously identified historical and cultural resources. The results of the review process are compared with the proposed impacts of the alternatives.

The difficulty in evaluating impacts to human resources results from the interrelated nature of the issues. For example, a new dam may increase flat water recreational opportunities but reduce whitewater rafting or upper watershed fishing opportunities. The changes in recreational opportunities would cause a direct change in recreational-related employment. These changes may affect regional income, which in turn may lead to changes in affordable housing. In addition, the quality of recreational activities could affect lifestyles and the responses to these changes, such as the need to travel further to participate in specific recreational activities.

One of the most difficult steps in environmental planning is to determine the significance of the impacts. The overall change in any one issue area may not be quantitatively high. However, the impact to specific community sectors may be very significant. Therefore, presenting the information in a manner that will reflect the significance of the impact is important. For example, the loss of 200 jobs may not be significant in a county with more than 1,000,000 people. However, if the jobs are located in a town with a population of fewer than 5,000, the economic and social impacts would be very high. This type of information must be presented to the Lead Agency in a fair and appropriate manner, and in a way that allows the affected community members to participate in the planning process. An interactive planning process also will allow the utility to define acceptable mitigation measures to reduce the impacts of potential alternatives.

Biological Resources

Biological resources include fish, wildlife, and vegetation. The descriptions of the current conditions and the potential impacts are usually segregated into these three broad categories. Further categorization occurs based on the potential impacts of permitting or approval agencies' proposed actions and requirements.

Surveys are usually completed as part of the environmental planning process. The level of effort in the survey ranges from a review of literature, including information compiled by resource agencies, to detailed delineation surveys. The US Fish and Wildlife Service (USFWS) and similar state agencies have compiled a significant amount of data concerning habitat types and the presence of habitats that may support special status species, including listed or candidate species that may be threatened or endangered. Results from the literature review may be used to screen preliminary alternatives and focus future survey efforts.

Information evaluated in the environmental planning process should be sufficient to identify adverse impacts or benefits on all life stages of fish, wildlife, and vegetation. Therefore, the analysis must consider resident and migrating fish and wildlife species. For special status species, conducting field studies to determine the presence of specie or their habitats may be necessary. If the species migrate or can be viewed only during a specific time period, scheduling the field work becomes part of the critical path. This may occur for migrating species or for species with long hibernation or estivation cycles. For example, some beetles can be viewed for only a four-to-six-week period during the flowering of specific plants because they hibernate the rest of the time.

The analysis of biological resources must also consider the interrelationship of fish, wildlife, and vegetation. If vegetation is restored along a stream, it could reduce water temperatures and provide more food that would increase fish populations. However, the increased vegetation would also provide more cover for foraging wildlife species that may change the balance of predation for fish and wildlife species. This type of change is appropriate in a balanced ecosystem. However, if the ecosystem does not include adequate species diversity, the increased predation could lead to an increased number of species that may be pests for adjacent land uses.

If the habitat is conducive to special status species, the biologists should initiate a consultation immediately with the USFWS for federal projects or projects with federal permits, or with the state resource agency. These types of surveys must provide information in accordance with Section 7 of the Endangered Species Act or similar state laws. For actions subject to Section 7 of the ESA, the USFWS must complete a consultation to assess potential affects on the species. If there are potential impacts, mitigation plans will be required to avoid any activity that could lead to the death of an individual or entire species. If the impacts cannot be fully mitigated, the USFWS completes a biological assessment to determine whether the actions could jeopardize the species or seriously alter its habitat. If a *Jeopardy Opinion* is made, a *Biological Opinion* is developed to identify reasonable and prudent alternatives to avoid jeopardy.

Historically, options considered to avoid jeopardy have been site-specific and frequently would allow only the No Action or No Project Alternative. However, recently, programs of preservation and enhancement of selected areas of considerable size or quality have been implemented in several locations throughout the country under a *Habitat Conservation Plan*. These programs are generally located adjacent to the site of the proposed project, but the areas may be in a more appropriate portion of the watershed. Through this program, special habitat banking can occur to provide for a large area that will support a healthy ecosystem. This has been more successful in restoring populations than in maintaining small areas of undisturbed land within urban or agricultural environments.

Physical Resources

Issues that could affect the physical environment range from surface water, groundwater, air quality, soils including hazardous materials from native materials or waste products, geological risk caused by seismic or land stability, and energy resources. Information concerning these resources can be obtained from field investigations, numerical modeling, literature review, or qualitative analyses. If the information is obtained from numerical modeling, the models can also be used to evaluate the alternatives.

The evaluation of physical resources is interrelated with biological and human resources. For example, surface water affects fishery and wildlife, groundwater, local sector economics, recreation, and other resources. Therefore, surface water resources may need to be evaluated for changes in flow quantity and quality before initiating other resource analyses.

PERMITS AND APPROVALS IN THE ENVIRONMENTAL PROCESS

Environmental planning documents are used for two reasons. First, as previously discussed, decision makers and the public use planning documents to understand potential impacts of the alternatives. Second, the documents are used to obtain permits and approvals for constructing and operating facilities. The remaining sections of this chapter discuss some federal permits and approvals that must be considered for projects with federal interests. State and local agencies grant similar permits and approvals. Sometimes state or local agencies will accept the documentation provided to federal agencies. However, they often require utilities to submit separate documentation.

Many federal laws, regulations, and policies must be considered in approving projects that have a federal interest. Issues that may be related to planning projects are briefly discussed in the following sections.

Lead Agencies also must consider the consistency of a proposed action with approved state and local plans and laws. This requirement is frequently part of approvals for federal and state permits.

National Environmental Policy Act[*]

NEPA provides a commitment that federal agencies will consider the environmental effects of their actions. It also requires that an environmental impact document be included in every recommendation or report on proposals for legislation and other major federal actions that significantly affect the quality of the human environment. The environmental impact document must provide detailed information regarding the No Action Alternative and No Project Alternative, the environmental impacts of the alternatives, potential mitigation measures, and unavoidable adverse environmental impacts. The legislation and associated guidelines also specify public involvement and review requirements.

Endangered Species Act and Critical Habitat

The ESA, most recently amended in 1988 (16 USC 1536), establishes a national program for conserving threatened and endangered species of fish, wildlife, and plants and preserving the ecosystems on which they depend. Section 7(a) of the ESA

---

*www.gsa.gov/Portal/gsa/ep/channelView.do?pageTypeId=81958& channelPage=%2Fep%2channel%2FgsaOverview.jps&channelId=-13909

requires federal agencies to consult with the US Fish and Wildlife Service and/or the National Marine Fisheries Service on activities that may affect any species listed as threatened or endangered. Environmental impact documents must analyze the effects of various alternatives on listed species. These potential effects require utilities to initiate the Section 7 consultation process.

Fish and Wildlife Coordination Act

The Fish and Wildlife Coordination Act (FWCA) requires that parties consult with the USFWS when any water body is impounded, diverted, controlled, or modified for any purpose. The USFWS and state agencies charged with administering wildlife resources conduct surveys and investigations to determine the potential damage to wildlife and to develop mitigation measures. The USFWS incorporates the concerns and findings of the state agencies and other federal agencies into a report that addresses fish and wildlife concerns and recommends ways to mitigate impacts caused by federal projects. Compliance with FWCA is coordinated with consultation for ESA.

National Wildlife Refuge System Administration Act

The National Wildlife Refuge System Administration Act consolidates various categories of wildlife ranges and refuges for management under one program. The act protects wildlife and refuge lands from destruction and injury. It also authorizes the regulation of hunting and fishing within refuge boundaries. If a watershed includes refuges, the environmental planning document should consider the effects of changing adjacent land uses on the refuges.

Migratory Waterfowl Act

The Migratory Waterfowl Act (16 USC 715 *et seq.*) requires that lands, waters, or interests acquired or reserved for purposes established under the act be administered under regulations promulgated by the Secretary of the Interior. These regulations must conserve and protect migratory birds in accordance with treaties between the United States and Mexico, Canada, Japan, and the former Union of Soviet Socialist Republics. Furthermore, these regulations must protect other wildlife, including threatened or endangered species, and must restore or develop adequate wildlife habitats. The migratory birds protected under this act are specified in the respective treaties. In regulating these areas, the Secretary of the Interior is authorized to manage timber, range, agricultural crops, and animal species, and to enter into agreements with public and private entities. If the watershed is located on a major waterfowl flyway in the United States, the environmental planning document should identify and describe impacts to the life stages of the waterfowl that use the watershed.

Clean Water Act

The Clean Water Act (CWA) (33 USC 1344 *et seq.*) was adopted to restore and maintain biological, chemical, and physical qualities of the nation's water. CWA established the National Pollutant Discharge Elimination System to reduce pollutant loads into the nation's water from all point and nonpoint discharges, including stormwater runoff. It provides for development of basin management plans to identify sources of pollution and options to reduce the mass loads. It also requires states or primary agencies to prepare plans to protect wetlands.

Watershed programs must consider several CWA provisions. Most must consider the impacts of nonpoint source runoff, including contributions from undeveloped land such as the forests that may contribute sediment loading. Implementing new programs in a watershed may require the mass loading from the entire watershed to be evaluated to reduce future pollutant concentrations. Recently, watershed programs have been implemented to identify total maximum daily load contributions for critical constituents. Under these programs, one or more contributors of pollutants may coordinate with other dischargers to reduce the pollutant load in the most cost-effective manner. For example, in a watershed with urban and agricultural users, if an urban user plans to increase organics loading for growth, the most cost-effective alternative may be to fund a sediment removal system for the agricultural area rather than providing a high level of treatment in the urban area.

New water resource facilities may require construction methods that include dredging or filling of waters or wetlands. In these cases, CWA provides regulatory authority to the US Army Corps of Engineers (Corps) to regulate these activities through a Section 404 permit program. This program integrates with the Section 401 of CWA, which requires that all such permits comply with the overall water quality plan for each watershed. Section 404 permits require alternatives to be implemented that do not require dredging or filling if any practicable alternative does not have more adverse impacts than a proposed action. The Section 404 permit process should be initiated early in the planning process and modified if the planning process is changed.

Rivers and Harbors Act

The Rivers and Harbors Act of 1899 (33 USC 403) prohibits the unauthorized obstruction or alteration of navigable waters without approval of the Corps. This permit process is usually combined with the Section 404 of the CWA process.

National Historic Preservation Act[*]

Section 106 of the National Historic Preservation Act requires that federal agencies evaluate the effects of federal undertakings on historical, archaeological, and cultural resources and afford the Advisory Council on Historic Preservation opportunities to comment on the proposed undertakings. The first step is to identify cultural resources included (or eligible for inclusion) on the National Register of Historic Places that are located in or near the project area. The second step is to identify the possible effects of proposed actions. The Lead Agency must examine whether feasible alternatives would avoid such effects. If an effect cannot reasonably be avoided, measures must be taken to minimize or mitigate potential adverse effects. Compliance with Section 106 is important, but it is also important to keep it in context with the following:

- It does not require preservation of all historic properties.

- It does not require accurate restoration of historic structures, as accurate restoration may not be possible, economically feasible, or desirable.

- It does not prevent new construction in historic areas.

American Indian Religious Freedom Act (AIRFA)[†]

This regulation comes from a joint resolution from Congress that declares that the US government will protect Native American inherent rights to the free exercise of their traditional religions. This has a broad scope and requires consultation with

---

[*]www.achp.gov/nhpa.html
[†]http://www.cr.nps.gov/local-law/FHPL_IndianRelFreAct.pdf

federally recognized tribes when project actions could affect the practice of traditional religions.

Archaeological Resources Protection Act

The Archaeological Resources Protection Act protects archaeological sites on public and Indian lands, establishes permit requirements for excavating or removing cultural properties from public or Indian lands, and establishes civil and criminal penalties for the unauthorized appropriation, alteration, exchange, or other handling of cultural properties. As part of the cultural resources analysis in an environmental planning document, the potential for archaeological sites must be evaluated. However, disclosure of specific sites or specific information about sites may not be allowed because of the need to preserve the sites from scavengers and tourists. Therefore, the environmental planning document frequently includes a separately bound appendix with specific archaeological information that may be summarized for the Lead Agency.

Indian Trust Assets

The US government's trust responsibility for Indian resources requires federal agencies to protect and maintain trust resources. These responsibilities include taking reasonable actions to preserve and restore tribal resources. Indian Trust Assets (ITAs) are legal interests in property and rights held in trust by the United States for Indian tribes or individuals. Indian reservations, *rancherias*, and allotments are common ITAs. All federal environmental planning documents must consider the presence and potential impacts of alternatives on ITAs in the study area.

Indian Sacred Sites on Federal Land

Executive Order 13007 provides that in managing federal lands, each federal agency with statutory or administrative responsibility for managing federal lands will, to the extent practicable and as permitted by law, accommodate access to and ceremonial use of Indian sacred sites by Indian religious practitioners, and avoid adversely affecting the physical integrity of such sites.

Environmental Justice[*]

Environmental Justice Executive Order 12898 (EJ) pursues equal justice and equal protection for all people under environmental statutes and regulations. EJ helps assure that no one socio/economic group is asked to bear more than its share of adverse environmental impacts. In the past, low-income, minority and/or Native American communities may have borne more than their share of such impacts.

Under NEPA, the NHPA, Endangered Species Act and others, it is important to identify and address EJ concerns. The Executive Order requires federal agencies to analyze environmental and health effects, and the economic and social effects of federal actions. It also requires mitigation measures to be identified. The importance of public participation is emphasized so that affected communities can provide input to the regulatory agencies. (See Chapter 2 on public participation.)

Managing Floodplains

If a federal agency program will affect a floodplain, the agency must consider alternatives to avoid adverse effects in the floodplain or to minimize potential harm.

---

*http://www.epa.gov/compliance/environmentaljustice/index.html

Executive Order 11988 requires federal agencies to evaluate the potential effects of any actions they might take in a floodplain and to ensure that planning, programs, and budget requests reflect consideration of flood hazards and floodplain management.

Protecting Wetlands

Executive Order 11990 authorizes federal agencies to take actions to minimize the destruction, loss, or degradation of wetlands, and to preserve and enhance the natural and beneficial values of wetlands when undertaking federal activities and programs. Any agency considering a proposal that might affect wetlands must evaluate factors affecting wetland quality and survival. These factors should include the proposal's effects on the public health, safety, and welfare caused by modifications in water supply and water quality; maintenance of natural ecosystems and conservation of flora and fauna; and other recreational, scientific, and cultural uses.

Wild and Scenic Rivers Act

The Wild and Scenic Rivers Act designates qualifying free-flowing river segments as wild, scenic, or recreational. The act establishes requirements applicable to water resource projects affecting wild, scenic, or recreational rivers within the National Wild and Scenic Rivers System, as well as rivers designated on the National Rivers Inventory. Under the act, a federal agency may not help construct water resources projects that would have direct and adverse effects on the free-flowing, scenic, and natural values of a wild or scenic river. If the projects would affect the free-flowing characteristics of a designated river or unreasonably diminish the scenic, recreational, and fish and wildlife values in the area, such activities should be developed in consultation with the National Park Service and in a manner that minimizes adverse impacts.

Federal Water Project Recreation Act

In planning any federal navigation, flood control, reclamation, or water resource project, the Federal Water Project Recreation Act requires parties to fully consider opportunities that the project affords for outdoor recreation and to enhance fish and wildlife. The act requires planning with respect to the developing recreation potential. Projects must be constructed, maintained, and operated to provide recreational opportunities, consistent with the purpose of the project.

Chapter **11**

Watershed Management and Groundwater Protection

Watershed protection generally strives to prevent the creation of new contaminant sources or threats to the source waters, whereas watershed management has the connotation of reducing or eliminating contamination sources or threats.

In water supply terms, watershed management is a *source protection* approach. Protecting source water quality is the first line of defense or a protection barrier to the potential transmission of contaminants to the finished water supply. The water treatment facility has historically been viewed as the first and ultimate barrier. Source protection and treatment should be viewed as complementary, not mutually exclusive, actions to optimize the reliable delivery of safe drinking water.

Despite lingering concern about the escalating costs of source protection, recent studies have shown that the benefits of protection are largely positive. There is a direct and cost-effective relationship between source water protection and water quality treatment costs. For example, source water protection programs can result in an estimated savings of about $1.5 billion in avoided costs for compliance with the Disinfectants/Disinfection Byproducts Stages I and II regulations (USEPA, 1993). Another study (USEPA, 1995) found that preventing groundwater contamination is less expensive than cleaning it; remediating groundwater can be 40 times more expensive than taking steps to protect the source. For small community sources, this ratio can be as high as 200:1.

The Safe Drinking Water Act (SDWA) Amendments recognize the direct connection between watershed protection and safe drinking water, and include provisions and financial support for the required source water protection efforts. State regulatory agencies are required to develop Source Water Assessment Plans and work with water supply utilities to delineate watershed boundaries and identify sources of regulated and high-risk unregulated drinking water contaminants. States have the option of using part of the Drinking Water State Revolving Fund (DWSRF), funded at $1 billion per year, to support these efforts. The 1996 amendments offer a great incentive for watershed groups and water utilities to form partnerships and explore common ground.

This chapter is broken down into two main sections. The first presents the major issues and regulations related to surface water source protection. The second section addresses groundwater source protection. Two appendixes included at the end of the book are referred to here: Source Water Protection (a white paper from the American Water Works Association, approved April 11, 1997) and a state government wellhead and source protection contact list.

SURFACE WATER SOURCE PROTECTION

The potential uses of the resources, water and otherwise, in a watershed that contributes to a surface source need to be considered in a source protection program. They might include the following:

- Drinking water supply

- Recreation

- Logging

- Wildlife habitat

- Development

- Agriculture

- Transportation

- Stormwater transport and treatment

- Wastewater treatment and disposal

Often these uses are conflicting. Therefore, the watershed protection plan (WPP) includes several plans, policies, ordinances, and bylaws that must be integrated to best meet the needs of several interest groups or users of the watershed. Forming a watershed planning team that represents the interest of the various users of the watershed can be difficult but is critical to a successful watershed management plan. Community education and outreach are also critical factors in ensuring the acceptance and success of any source protection plan.

Protecting the water source and meeting the needs of multiple users involves a wide variety of management approaches, including some of the following:

- Regulations, bylaws, ordinances

- Enforcement actions

- Land acquisitions

- Monitoring

- Emergency response plans

- Wastewater discharge permits

- Herbicide–pesticide application restrictions

- Stormwater management

- Road-salting restrictions

- Overlay protection zoning

- Public education

- Recreation access restrictions

- Dedicated funding

Many watershed management organizations are involved in implementing any WPP, and a partnership must be formed for any plan to succeed. From a hydrologic or scientific point of view, the watershed (defined by its topographical delineation) is the logical unit of management. However, the water utility, the municipal government, and most regulatory and public agencies are not necessarily delineated by the watershed boundary. Watershed and jurisdictional boundaries that do not coincide present a significant obstacle to the watershed management approach. Many compromises and trade-offs are needed to obtain the cooperative involvement of local, regional, state, and federal players, both public and private, with drinking water source protection as a priority goal. Overcoming these obstacles becomes paramount for a successful protection plan, especially in home rule states where land use controls often reside with the local communities (although this may not always be true).

Watershed management is shown schematically in Figure 11-1.

Delineate and Characterize the Watershed
↓
Identify Players and Form a Planning Team
↓
Develop and Implement an Educational Outreach Program
↓
Identify Regulatory and Community Goals
↓
Classify and Rank Goals
↓
Develop Criteria to Measure Achievement of Goals
↓
Identify Activities Posing a Threat to Goals
↓
Quantify Activities and Impacts on Goals
↓
Rank Threats
↓
Identify Control Measures to Reduce or Eliminate Threats
↓
Quantify the Efficiency and Effectiveness of Control Measures
↓
Identify Administrators of Control Measures
↓
Rank Control Measures
↓
Develop a Watershed/Reservoir Protection Plan
↓
Revise/Modify
↓
Implement the Plan
↓
Monitor/Analyze

Figure 11–1   Watershed protection plan development and implementation flowchart

Delineate and Characterize the Watershed

Many methods are available to delineate watershed catchments. The methodologies range in complexity and cost of implementation. Therefore, the water supplier and the appropriate regulatory agencies must choose a method based on regulatory requirements, available resources, local hydrologic conditions, and specific goals.

Some states have delineated all their major watersheds within the state and may have basin maps in digital format on a geographical information system (GIS). Topographic quad maps from the US Geological Survey (USGS), usually at a 1:24,000 scale, often provide adequate information to delineate the watershed. A base map often is made by adding town boundaries and major roads to the topographic map. Several maps may overlay the base map to help develop the WPP.

A typical scenario of maps might include the following:

- Watershed base map

- Sub-watersheds

- Development

- Major aquifers and public water supply withdrawal points

- Soils susceptible to erosion (Natural Resource Conservation Service)

- Permitted wastewater discharge points, landfills, and hazardous waste facilities

- Underground storage tanks

- Local zoning and overlay districts

- Current land use

- Other hazardous or contaminated sites

- Water quality monitoring stations

- Open space (e.g., parks)

Many of these databases are available in a digital format that allows data to be integrated to produce various maps. GIS also allows text to be attached to the spatial data, resulting in a "smart" map.

Identify Players and Form a Planning Team

The success of any WPP depends on including all relevant watershed organizations on the planning team. Some players will have much more interest in the planning process, but all must be represented. Once the team has been formed, subgroups, responsible for specific tasks, will probably need to be formed. These groups should be formed based on interest and expertise, as well as on authority. Potential planning team members might include the following:

- Municipal officials—representatives from the health department, fire department, historic commission, conservation commission, zoning and planning commission, board of selectmen or city councils, water utility staff, code enforcement officer, and town engineer.

- Public organizations—watershed advisory groups, lake associations, League of Women Voters, community service groups.

- Environmental and planning organizations—Natural Resource Conservation Service, Cooperative Extension Service, USGS, regional planning agencies, state environmental agencies.

- Local citizens—farmers, developers, residents, business and industry representatives, teachers.

All parties with an interest in the watershed must be included on the team. Those who are not part of the utility service district but who reside or own businesses or property in the watershed must also be included. The plan should include benefits to these parties and to the utility's customers. Continual communication about the process is critical for success.

Develop and Implement an Educational Outreach Program

An ongoing outreach program is one of the first steps in developing a watershed management program. The initial objective of the program is to inform people that a watershed management program is being developed, identify its initial goals, assess how it might affect people in the watershed, and invite interested parties to join the team and contribute their ideas. By educating the public about the potential impacts that activities can have on water quality, people become partners in implementing the plan. Many homeowners, for instance, do not understand the link between fertilizing their lawns and the eutrophication of surrounding water bodies. Providing this education is only part of the outreach program; teaching the public about available control measures or *best management practices* is another part. The user must be able to implement the control measures, which must be cost-effective and specific to the threat.

Effective outreach programs keep the public informed of the status of the ongoing protection plan and the benefits or *payback*.

Identify Regulatory and Community Goals

SDWA and its 1986 and 1996 amendments establish the regulatory requirements most critical to the drinking water industry. For the first time, SDWA (i.e., the 1996 Amendments) addresses source water protection requiring states to implement USEPA-approved programs to assess threats. It also provides for voluntary local partnerships to prevent pollution.

The water utility's goal may be to maintain, or even enhance, source water quality. The community may have other goals such as preserving open space, controlling recreation around reservoirs, restricting zoning, expanding the tax base, and limiting lot sizes or impermeable areas. Agreeing on and establishing these goals will dictate the strategy for developing and implementing the source protection plan.

Classify and Rank Goals

Once the primary and secondary goals have been determined, they must be ranked. The goals may be classified as primary (i.e., to maintain or enhance the source drinking water quality), and secondary (e.g., developing a nonresidential tax base in the community, developing public recreation areas, or minimizing restrictions on land use choices in the watershed). Because many goals may conflict, the planning team needs to set priorities. Later in the development of the plan, the identified control measures and their impacts on achieving the identified goals will need to be ranked.

Develop Criteria to Measure Achievement of Goals

The criteria chosen to measure achievement of the goals established in the WPP are extremely important and will serve as the benchmark for the plan. These criteria will also dictate the monitoring program to be followed (i.e., the parameters to be measured, sampling locations, required precision, frequency and duration, program cost). Although knowing the goals of the program is important to establish a sampling program, the utility may need to know the water quality before establishing those goals. In other words, sampling may precede goal setting if those data will help establish goals.

If the primary goal is to maintain the quality of the drinking water source, the criteria may be the current drinking water regulatory constituents sampled in tributaries to the water supply source, at inlet locations to the reservoir, lake, or stream, and at various locations in the distribution system. The list of constituents sampled will vary from sampling point to point (see chapters 5 and 7) but might include the following:

- Secchi depth

- Dissolved oxygen

- Temperature

- pH

- Total coliform

- Fecal coliform

- Conductivity

- Alkalinity

- Turbidity

- Color

- Algae (identification and count)

- Nutrient series

- Chlorides

- Hardness

- Metals

- Organic series

- Silica

- Microbiology

If the goal is not merely to maintain the source water quality but to enhance it (e.g., possibly anticipating more stringent regulations), the sampling program may be expanded to include such factors as *Cryptosporidium*, *Giardia lamblia*, viruses, standard plate counts, and analysis for trihalomethanes and haloacetic acids. Of course, the cost of the monitoring program will increase.

Other possible secondary goals for which monitoring criteria would be needed include

- Sustaining multiple uses of the watershed (e.g., recreation, timbering, wildlife protection and enhancement)

- Minimizing social, financial, and environmental impacts associated with implementing the plan

- Establishing partnerships of watershed users, each able to participate in decision making

The criteria may be categorized as general (directly related to the primary or secondary goals), or specific (related to reducing or eliminating a threat, such as putting septic system users on a centralized sewerage system).

Identify Activities Posing a Threat to Goals

Activities that pose threats to the source water quality in a watershed can be identified, later quantified, and finally ranked by considering several characteristics of the threats

1. Current status of the threat (e.g., immediate or potential)

2. Type of contaminants associated with the activity (e.g., microbial contaminants from a failing septic system or sediment from a construction site—two very different types of contaminants)

3. Location of the activity (e.g., proximity of the activity to the water supply source or distribution system intake—locations of high risk)

4. Magnitude of the contaminant source (e.g., volume of discharge)

5. Frequency of the activity (e.g., continuous or sporadic)

6. Duration of the activity

Threats can also be categorized as either naturally occurring or human-induced and as point or nonpoint sources.

The procedure for identifying threats should include

1. Review current literature on the nature of various threats to water quality.

2. Review watershed data and available mapping.

3. Interview watershed residents and local, regional, state, and federal regulatory personnel.

4. Review historical water quality data for the watershed.

5. Conduct field reconnaissance of the watershed (sanitary surveys).

6. Review databases for regulated activities (e.g., National Pollution Discharge Elimination System discharges, confined feeding operations, land application of sludge).

A list of typical threats in various categories is shown in Table 11-1.

Quantify Activities and Impacts on Goals

To rank threats to the water supply, the threats must first be quantified. The method should be selected based on the relative impact of the threat on the source water supply. One such method was developed to evaluate the Wachusett Reservoir Watershed in Massachusetts. The method evaluates each threat by watershed protection zone and region as well as whether the specific threat is immediate or potential. The watershed is delineated into three zones, as follows:

1. Zone A: areas located within 400 ft of the 100-year floodplain elevation as delineated on the Federal Emergency Management Agency maps.

Table 11-1   Categories of water quality threats

Human-Induced Nonpoint and Point Sources	Natural Sources
Nonpoint	
On-site septic systems	Erosion
Recreational activities	Animal populations
Stormwater runoff	
Logging	
Herbicides, pesticides, fertilizers	
Animal grazing	
Construction	
Gravel mining	
Road salting	
Future development	
Point	
Uncontrolled releases—transportation	
Uncontrolled releases—fixed sites	
Barnyards/feedlots	
Gasoline/petroleum storage	
Permitted activities—wastewater treatment plant discharges	
Permitted activities—solid waste landfills	
Permitted activities—groundwater discharges	
Oil wells not properly abandoned	
Other unauthorized activities	

2. Zone B: areas located one-half mile up-gradient from Zone A or to the watershed boundary, whichever is less.

3. Zone C: areas encompassing the remaining watershed not designated Zone A or B.

Additionally, two regions overlay the watershed:

1. Region 1: the reservoir pool area and Zone A adjacent to the reservoir as well as areas of potentially high risk as a result of intense development, poor soils, steep terrain, bordering wetlands, and tributary streams.

2. Region 2: areas encompassing the remaining watershed not designated as Region 1.

The basis of the criteria is the travel time of the pollutant to the reservoir and, consequently, the time available for the pollutant to be trapped, adsorbed, diluted, or degraded.

In general, immediate threats will dictate remedial action or more aggressive control measures; potential threats will require protective and preventive types of controls. Each threat is rated as high, moderate, or low with general consideration of the following factors related to potential pollutants:

Attenuation/assimilation: the ability of the pollutants to be attenuated through assimilation in the land or water regimes (dilution) is considered. For example, sediment from erosion may be removed from raw water before water is withdrawn or treated. Sediment may be removed by using long detention times allowing sedimentation within a reservoir; oil and grease from parking lot runoff tends to accumulate without attenuation.

Human health impacts: the pollutant's relative threat to human health is considered. For example, nutrients from fertilizer use may promote eutrophication (e.g., algal growth, oxygen depletion) that may in turn affect the aesthetic quality of the water; carcinogenic organic solvents from a large spill may pose severe health risks.

Frequency of occurrence: the relative frequency of releases of a pollutant is considered. For example, failing septic tanks produce virtually continuous releases of pollutants; urban runoff is frequent but associated with specific periodic events. In contrast, accidental spills on a roadway are very infrequent events.

Potential quantity of pollutant: the relative quantity of pollutant typically released by an occurrence of the threat is considered. For example, quantities of oil and grease released in parking lots at recreational facilities would generally be small, whereas quantities of gasoline leaking from underground storage tanks could be considerably greater.

An example of how the method is applied for the Wachusett Reservoir Watershed in Massachusetts is shown in Table 11-2.

Rank Threats

It is important to rank threats to the source water quality so those threats with the highest ratings can be controlled first. The WPP should include a schedule of implementing control measures based on the threats with the highest rating and available resources. Immediate threats should always be ranked higher than potential threats (i.e., Zone A higher than Zone B or C, and Region 1 higher than Region 2).

Identify Control Measures to Reduce or Eliminate Threats

The WPP should include measures designated to control specific threats and broader control measures that provide comprehensive protection measures for a number of threats. Control measures are activities used in the watershed to remediate immediate threats and prevent potential threats. Activities with high threats (i.e., high risk) as identified in the ranking step will require controls that can be implemented easily and reliably.

Structural and nonstructural control measures should be considered in the WPP. Nonstructural controls are behavioral modifications and legislation, regulations, and policies. Legislation, regulations, policies, and practices should be analyzed to evaluate their adequacy in protecting the source water supply. Do these measures provide adequate controls for the specific threats identified earlier? What new nonstructural control measures should be considered for each unique watershed? Important considerations about nonstructural control measures include

1. Who is responsible for administering and enforcing the control measures?

2. Does the administrating agency have enforcement powers?

3. Is the proposed control measure effective for the target pollutants?

The structural control measures are physical controls that, once put in place, do not depend on behavioral compliance to be effective. Examples of structural control measures might include

- detention or retention basins,

- filtration basins and trenches,

Table 11–2   Threat assessment

Threat	Zone A Region 1	Zone A Region 2	Zone B Region 1	Zone B Region 2
Human-Induced				
On-site septic systems (NPS)	*H*	*H*	*H*	M
Recreational activities (NPS)	M	M	L	L
Stormwater runoff (NPS)	*H*	L	*H*	L
Logging on MDC land (NPS)	L	L	L	L
Logging on private land (NPS)	M	M	L	L
Herbicides, pesticides, and fertilizers (NPS)	M	M	M	M
Animal grazing (NPS)	M	L	M	L
Construction activities (NPS)	H	M	M	L
Gravel mining (NPS)	L	M	M	L
Road salting (NPS)	M	L	M	L
Future developments (NPS)	H	H	H	H
Uncontrolled releases from transportation activities (PS)	H	H	H	L
Uncontrolled releases from fixed sites (PS)	H	L	M	L
Barnyards and feedlots (PS)	M	L	M	L
Gasoline/petroleum storage (PS)	*H*	H	*H*	M
Permitted activities (PS)	H	L	H	L
Unauthorized activities (PS/NPS)	L	L	M	L
Natural				
Erosion (NPS)	M	M	L	L
Wildlife (NPS)	*H*	M	L	L

Legend:

H = high existing   H = high potential
M = moderate existing M = moderate potential
L = low existing   L = low potential
NPS = nonpoint source PS = point source

- grass swales,

- filter buffer strips,

- porous pavement,

- oil/grit separators,

- containment systems,

- on-site treatment/disposal systems,

- sediment and erosion control measures,

- animal controls, such as barriers.

These controls are physical in nature and are targeted for defined areas in the watershed and specific threats or types of contaminants. Most are associated with stormwater runoff and function to preclude direct entry of the runoff into the source waters or to mitigate its impact.

Quantify the Efficiency and Effectiveness of Control Measures

A matrix approach can be used to match available control measures to specific threats or contaminants. The cells of the matrix might be classified as low, medium, or high with respect to the efficiency of controlling the specific contaminant. *Efficiency* measures the relative removal capacity of the control measure. For example, a detention basin may be highly efficient in removing incoming suspended sediment but only moderately efficient in removing colloidal organic compounds. Effectiveness measures the ability of the control measure to remove or mitigate the target contaminants. In this example, the detention pond would be inefficient and ineffective if the target contaminant was dissolved organic compounds.

Identify Administrators of Control Measures

The effectiveness of various control measures depends largely on the responsible administrative agency. Many control measures are best administered at the local level but many local agencies are stressed for resources and cannot always provide the needed maintenance and enforcement resources. Also, a watershed may cross several jurisdictions, and resources must be coordinated. Therefore, adequate funding for proper administration or coordination is necessary for a successful WPP. Funding may be available from the Drinking Water State Revolving Fund, USEPA Clean Water Act Section 319, USDA Environmental Quality Incentive Program, River Network Grants, and Emergency Conservation Program. Water utilities should meet with regional USEPA and state agencies to determine the availability of funding in their regions.

Rank Control Measures

To rank the various control measures, utilities first must identify and rank the target pollutants or threats. Next, they must determine the removal or mitigation capability of the control measures for the various target pollutants along with the task and cost of implementation. These criteria result in a general protection philosophy and ranked set of protection measures. The protection philosophy exemplifies the distinctive protection approach that can most effectively achieve the objectives of the WPP. For example, the philosophy adopted for the Wachusett Watershed Protection Plan (Watershed Protection Plan, Wachusett Reservoir Watershed, January 1991) resulted in the following ranked actions:

1. Land acquisition is the best and most desirable method for watershed protection.

2. Current regulatory frameworks are used to the maximum extent possible.

3. Enforcement of regulations is emphasized.

4. Environmental management activities that traditionally have been local responsibilities (i.e., local by-laws and enforcement) are supported as highest priority.

5. Local cooperation and support of public education, financial assistance, and technical support is promoted.

This philosophy resulted in identifying and ranking control measures for specific threats shown in Table 11-1.

Develop a Watershed/Reservoir Protection Plan

Although a partnership must be formed to effectively develop and implement the WPP, usually a Lead Agency (or lead person of the WPP) can be identified. This agency will have primary responsibility for watershed management, usually including land management and protection, water quality monitoring, enforcement of rules and regulations, recreation, sanitary surveys, and policy making and planning. Other agencies and parties play important roles in developing a WPP. State agencies, for example, are responsible for various environmental regulatory and permitting programs to control land use activities; local agencies have an array of local land use regulations that affect water quality. Also, several federal regulations promulgated by USEPA may apply to the WPP. The WPP involves

1. Identifying the geographic and political boundaries.

2. Identifying the goals and objectives.

3. Identifying the threats to degradation of the source water quality and their ranking.

4. Identifying effective measures to control or mitigate threats and their ranking.

5. Identifying available funding for support of the program.

6. Developing a monitoring program to measure the results of implementing the plan and continually provide feedback for modifying and improving the program.

Implement the Plan

The WPP is implemented based on the ranking of the protection or control measures. Generally, protection measures developed for high-priority threats are implemented immediately because they are most critical for protecting the watershed. Protection measures for moderate priority threats are next implemented, possibly over a period of years. Finally, the low-priority measures are scheduled for implementation when financial resources are available.

Although the WPP is developed and implemented to a schedule, the plan is dynamic and must be continually updated and modified based on the ongoing monitoring results. Activities in the watershed will change with growth and land use development; new control technologies will evolve. The partnership needed to make the WPP succeed is a life-long relationship.

GROUNDWATER SOURCE PROTECTION

The guiding steps found in the WPP development and implementation flowchart (Figure 11-1) apply to both groundwater source protection and surface water protection. This section addresses the specific protection issues for groundwater sources.

Local governments and the water supply industry have traditionally been responsible for developing, managing, and protecting groundwater supply in the United States. For most of the country, groundwater is considered the most reliable and safest source of drinking water supply. Many water systems and local governments continue to derive their sources from aquifers with water that requires little or no treatment. Most groundwater treatment removes iron and manganese and controls corrosion (naturally occurring elements); it does not treat groundwater contaminated by land use activities.

Groundwater contamination and water quality threats from land use activities do, however, present a challenge for systems using groundwater. Groundwater has been an economical source to develop because wells could be drilled near the areas to be supplied, reducing transmission costs and lowering infrastructure needs such as transmission piping, pumps, and energy needed to deliver the water. Water quality threats from encroachment of land use activities (such as agriculture, residential development, and industrial and commercial development) introduce organic contaminants, metals, nutrients, and biological pathogens to the land surface or directly into the groundwater. Groundwater contamination rarely can be seen and is often discovered only after a considerable portion of the groundwater resource has become contaminated. Removing chemical contaminants is expensive, and the past practice of abandoning and replacing wells is no longer a viable option in areas with limited resources and growing populations.

Groundwater protection is key to maintaining safe and reliable groundwater supplies. This section describes the groundwater supply characteristics in the United States, presents the regulatory framework for groundwater protection, and proposes a five-step process for groundwater source protection.

Groundwater and Public Water Supply in the United States

There are more than 180,000 water systems in the United States, serving more than 250 million people. Table 11-3 shows the number of community water systems; transient, noncommunity water systems; and nontransient, noncommunity water systems in the United States.

Water systems are classified according to the number of people they serve, the sources of their water, and whether they serve the same customers year-round or only occasionally. Public water systems provide piped water for human consumption to at least 15 service connections or serve at least 25 people for at least 60 days a year. Public water systems are further categorized into the following three major types depending on the type of population they serve:

1. Community water systems serve the same residents year-round. Some examples of community water systems are cities and towns, mobile home parks, and subdivisions.

2. Nontransient, noncommunity water systems do not serve the same people year-round, but do serve the same people for at least 180 days of the year. Examples of nontransient, noncommunity water systems are schools, day-care centers, and many places of business such as factories and offices.

3. Transient, noncommunity water systems are open at least 60 days during the year but generally do not serve the same people every day (that is, they serve a transient population). Some examples of transient, noncommunity water systems are rest stops, some restaurants, and gas stations.

The majority of the US population is served by community water systems (Table 11-4). Fifty-three percent of the US population obtains its drinking water from groundwater sources.

Groundwater is the predominant source of supply for community water systems. About 80 percent of the community water systems rely on groundwater as their primary source (Table 11-5), and most of these systems (85 percent) are small, serving fewer than 3,300 persons each.

Table 11–3   Number of public water systems in the United States

System Type	Number	Percent of Total
Community water systems	50,289	28
Nontransient, noncommunity water systems	23,639	13
Transient, noncommunity water systems	106,436	59
Total systems	180,364	100

Table 11–4   Population served by public water system type in the United States

System Type	Population (*Millions*)	Percent of Total
Community water systems	243.0	93
Nontransient, noncommunity water systems	6.0	2
Transient, noncommunity water systems	13.6	5
Total population	262.6	100

Table 11–5   Community water systems by source in the United States

Source Type	Number	Percent of Total
Primarily groundwater	40,123	79.8
Primarily surface water	4,832	9.6
Primarily purchased	5,334	10.6
Total	50,289	100.0

State and Federal Regulatory Efforts in Groundwater Protection

Water utilities, local governments, state governments, and the federal government share the responsibility for developing measures and programs to protect groundwater quality. SDWA guides drinking water suppliers in the United States in their efforts to protect groundwater sources. SDWA requires USEPA to set standards for maximum contaminant levels (the maximum permissible level of contaminant in water delivered to any user of a public water supply system) in public drinking water supplies, regulate underground injection of wastes into groundwaters, and establish public water supply protection programs.

In 1986, amendments to SDWA increased the authority and responsibility for drinking water protection. The amendments created the Sole Source Aquifer Demonstration Program and the Wellhead Protection Program. Subsequent amendments in 1996 further strengthened drinking water protection by establishing the Source Water Protection Program. The following section describes the components, operation, and current status of the WPP, a summary of Comprehensive State Ground Water Protection Programs (CSGWPP), and the latest update on Source Water Protection.

Wellhead Protection—The 1986 Amendments

Section 1428 of the 1986 Amendments to the SDWA established the Wellhead Protection Program. This program emphasizes prevention rather than treatment of drinking water contamination and remedial actions once groundwater is contaminated.

Each state has developed a program tailored to the specific physical, cultural, and administrative conditions of the area. Variability in hydrology, geology, land use, and management approaches have resulted in a wide range of programs to protect public water supply wells. For a state to have an approved WPP, it must meet the following requirements:

1. Specify the roles and duties of state agencies, local government offices, and public water suppliers regarding development and implementation of the program. Many states have worked cooperatively with public water suppliers and local governments to form local teams to plan and implement wellhead protection efforts. A comprehensive approach, including all stakeholders and the public, is recommended to achieve maximum results. A typical planning team would consist of representatives from local public interest groups (including environmental groups, community service organizations, and public representatives), regulatory organizations (such as health, planning, and public works), public service organizations (water utility, fire department, and extension service), and private organizations (including businesses, farmers, and developers).

2. Delineate a wellhead protection area for each wellhead based on hydrogeologic and other relevant information to define the boundaries of the most critical land areas that provide recharge to the well. The techniques used to delineate wellhead protection areas depend on the well type, hydrogeology, and management approach. Areas that receive recharge that contributes water to a pumping well are referred to as *zones of contribution*. These zones are affected by recharge rates, pumping rates, and hydrogeologic boundaries.

   The methods used to delineate wellhead protection recharge areas include arbitrary fixed radius, calculated fixed radius, simplified variable shapes, analytical methods, hydrogeologic mapping, and computer modeling. If stringent land use controls are to be developed and enforced in the wellhead protection area, the more detailed and scientifically correct methods should be used to delineate the wellhead protection area. If the management approach is only to educate the public and landowners of the connection between their land use activities and water quality in the well, the more simple arbitrary fixed radius or analytical methods are sufficient. Details and examples of delineation methods can be found in several USEPA publications (USEPA, 1987, 1988, 1997a, 1997b). Advantages and disadvantages of various delineation methods are shown in Table 11-6.

3. Identify sources of contamination in each wellhead protection area. The delineated wellhead protection area becomes the boundary within which a land use inventory can be conducted to identify and map potential contamination sources. Not only should current land uses be mapped and assessed for their potential threat to water quality, but also areas of future intended uses on the land. Distance from the well, contaminant type, and contaminant severity are important considerations when assessing water quality threats. For example, a few septic systems in a wellhead protection

Table 11–6   Advantages and disadvantages of WRP delineation methods

Arbitrary fixed radius	Few data necessary Quick and easy to draw Very low cost Not very accurate Not suitable for confined aquifers
Calculated fixed radius	Need limited hydrogeologic data Relatively quick and easy Inexpensive Not highly accurate Not suitable for confined aquifers
Variable shapes	Based on relatively few field data Still fairly quick and easy If data are available, low cost In complex settings, not very precise
WHPA code (Semianalytic model)	Based on substantial field data May require technical assistance Automatic delineation of capture zones Calculates the effects of well interference Danger of hidden errors because the program is simple Most solutions assume homogeneous isotropic aquifers Moderate costs
Analytic models	Based on substantial field data Probably require professional help Moderate costs, if data are available Widely used, fairly accurate Suitable for rock wells (if data are available)
Numerical models	Based on extensive field data Requires computer/technical expertise Can be highly accurate Can be quite expensive

Source: Adapted From Paley and Steppacher.

area may present very little threat to water quality. However, hundreds of on-site systems will definitely create a threat that will most likely result in a lowering of water quality. Many governmental sources are available to provide data on land use threats. States and USEPA regional offices have extensive databases providing information on large permitted facilities such as wastewater treatment plants, landfills, waste sites, and drainage wells. Most quality threats can be identified only by conducting field surveys and inventories. Commercial operations that handle hazardous materials, septic systems, roadway drainage, underground petroleum storage tanks, and other potential contaminants are all land uses that pose a water quality threat but will not be found in any centralized database. Examples of contamination threats and inventory approaches can be found in USEPA (1989, 1993a), and New England Interstate Water Pollution Control Commission (1996).

4. Develop management approaches. Management approaches to protect the water quality of public water supply wells are either nonregulatory or regulatory controls. Nonregulatory approaches include voluntary changes

in behavior through public education, land acquisition, purchase of conservation easements, spill response contingency planning, and increased monitoring. Regulatory controls are used to restrict current and future land uses through the use of zoning, subdivision regulations, local ordinance, and health authorities. Many public water suppliers have worked cooperatively with local governments to help enact overlay-zoning ordinances to implement controls in the delineated wellhead protection area. Most of these regulations are enacted to prohibit the siting of extremely hazardous activities in the wellhead protection area, or to place conditions on uses that will reduce their potential threats. For example, industrial activities using hazardous materials may be allowed in a particular wellhead protection area, but the operator of the facility must include design features to contain, control, and monitor for any potential accidental releases. The stringency of the control measures is a local issue requiring the involvement of the public water supplier and all stakeholders.

5. Prepare contingency plans for alternative sources of drinking water supply in the event of emergencies. Alternative water supply planning ensures that drinking water service can continue uninterrupted if contaminants are released into the wellhead protection area. In addition, detailed contingency plans will identify who should respond and the appropriate level of control to minimize and mitigate water quality threats.

6. Identify sites for new wells that will provide protection from contamination. Water supply planning is an important element of wellhead protection because it requires the local water supplier and the community to look ahead and ensure that sites to develop new wells are protected from potentially contaminating activities. One particularly important tool used in this analysis is a *build-out analysis* to project maximum growth and water demand and to identify land use conflicts.

7. Ensure public participation. Public education is an important element in wellhead protection. Public support, assistance, and involvement will ensure that wellhead protection efforts are successful. Involving and informing the public of wellhead protection activities will help the public understand the need for wellhead protection and provide support to develop and implement the program. If regulatory controls are proposed as a management tool, conducting an effective public education effort is extremely important.

The WPP provides an opportunity for water suppliers, local governments, and state governments to work cooperatively to delineate wellhead protection areas, identify and assess current and potential contaminant sources, and develop management approaches to provide protection from contamination. Thousands of public water supply systems across the United States have active wellhead protection programs working cooperatively with local governments to ensure recharge areas to public water supply wells are protected from sources of potential contamination.

Comprehensive State Groundwater Protection Programs

Although this initiative has largely fallen by the wayside, a brief description follows. In 1992, the USEPA published guidance for comprehensive state groundwater protection programs. The goal of this approach is to achieve a more efficient, coherent, and comprehensive approach to protecting the nation's groundwater resources by coordinating operations of all relevant federal, state, and local groundwater programs in a state.

Under CSGWPP, USEPA asks states to coordinate their groundwater protection actions through six strategic activities:

1. Establish a groundwater protection goal.

2. Establish priorities to guide program efforts.

3. Define authorities, roles, responsibilities, resources, and coordinating mechanisms.

4. Implement efforts to accomplish groundwater protection goals.

5. Coordinate information collection and management.

6. Improve public education and participation in all aspects of groundwater protection.

As of September 1998, nine states (Nev., Okla., Ala., Ga., Wis., Ill. Mass., N.H., Conn.) had USEPA-approved CSGWPPs. CSGWPPs are designed to focus source control programs on preventing contamination of higher priority groundwater, facilitate coordination among the many intrastate programs that protect groundwater, and build a comprehensive approach to protect groundwater that includes all stakeholders. In addition, CSGWPPs strengthen state watershed approaches by providing an essential link between the state's groundwater and surface water protection programs.

Source Water Protection—The 1996 Amendments

The 1996 Amendments to the SDWA require that all 180,000 public water supplies (surface and groundwater systems) be covered under a source water protection program (SWPP). The basic assumption for implementing SWPPs is that multiple-barrier protection of public water supplies will provide for high-quality water supplies and protect public health. Multiple barriers, including source water protection, treatment, distribution system maintenance, and monitoring are proposed to protect the quality and safety of drinking water supplies. Source water assessment and protection represent the first steps in protecting public water supplies.

Source water assessments form the centerpiece of SDWA's focus on prevention. Source water assessments identify the potential threats to the source of a community's drinking water. States can use the assessments to issue water suppliers monitoring waivers for many chemicals regulated under the SDWA. States were directed to develop source water assessments for all public water supplies that included the following (all states have now complied):

1. Delineate the groundwater area or surface watershed contributing water to the water supply intake.

2. Inventory the contaminant sources in the delineated water supply area.

3. Determine the susceptibility of the water system to contamination.

Delineation

Section 1453(2)(A) of SDWA requires that the states delineate the boundaries of the source water protection areas (SWPAs) from which one or more public water systems receives its drinking water supply. The delineations are to account for all reasonably available hydrogeologic information, such as water flow, recharge, and discharge, and any other reliable information the state deems necessary to delineate such areas. The USEPA's Source Water Protection Final Guidance Document (USEPA, 1997c) specifies the following delineation approaches:

For surface water systems, the SWPA should include the entire watershed area upstream of the public water system's (PWS's) intake, up to the state border. The states can segment large watersheds into sub-basins or buffer zones to provide for more cost-effective contaminant source inventories and susceptibility analyses (USEPA, 1997c). Figure 11-2 illustrates a watershed area.

For groundwater systems, delineations should be conducted using one or more of the following methods: (1) arbitrary radii, (2) calculated fixed radii, (3) simplified variable shapes, (4) analytical methods, (5) hydrogeologic mapping, and (6) numerical flow or transport models (USEPA, 1987, 1997d). In addition, conjunctive delineations may need to be completed for PWSs that withdraw water from aquifers with strong hydraulic connections to surface water systems. These delineations should account for the zone of groundwater contribution and the area of surface water contributing to the drinking water intake. For example, high-yield wells in alluvial or sand and gravel aquifers often draw water from the groundwater system and from overlying or adjacent rivers or lakes. As a result, the SWPA should include the groundwater system and upgradient surface waters through which contaminants could reach the drinking water intake.

Identifying Contaminant Sources

States are required to identify the sources of contaminants regulated under SDWA for which monitoring is required (or any unregulated contaminants selected by the state that may present a threat to public health). These contaminants include those regulated under the SDWA (contaminants with a maximum contaminant level [MCL], contaminants regulated under the Surface Water Treatment Rule, and the microorganism *Cryptosporidium*). A variety of regulated and unregulated contaminant sources are found in (SWPSs), including aboveground and underground storage

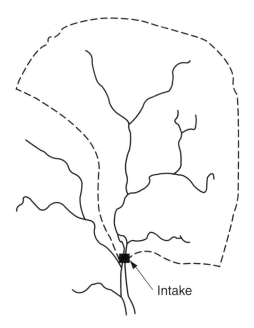

Figure 11–2   Watershed area (USEPA, 1997b)

tanks; animal feedlots; agricultural chemicals; underground injection wells; chemical processing facilities; transportation and road maintenance facilities; septic systems; pipelines; and waste transport, storage, and disposal facilities. The range of potential contaminants and contaminant sources is described in several USEPA publications (USEPA, 1990, 1991a, 1991b).

Because of the wide variety of potential contaminant sources that may be found in SWPAs, a hierarchical approach to source identification is appropriate and most cost-effective. The information sources available to support this approach are summarized here. Figure 11-3 illustrates a segmented watershed area.

Step 1: Search federal and state relational databases to identify regulated sources. The USEPA Warehouse allows for online retrieval of environmental information from seven USEPA databases on Superfund sites (Comprehensive Environmental Response, Compensation, & Liability Information System [CERCLIS]), drinking water (Safe Drinking Water Information System [SDWIS]), toxic and air releases (Toxic Release Inventory [TRI]), hazardous waste (Resource Conservation and Recovery Information System [RCRIS]), and water discharge permits (Permit Compliance System [PCS]), and grants information. As a result, an Envirofacts search allows utilities to rapidly identify extant and abandoned waste management facilities in the SWPA and other ongoing hazardous substance releases to the air, land, or water. In addition, certain states may maintain additional searchable data on underground injection wells, underground storage tanks, oil and gas wells, coal mines, and other potential hazards. The USEPA is currently working to improve and enhance many of its environmental databases. During 1998 and 1999,

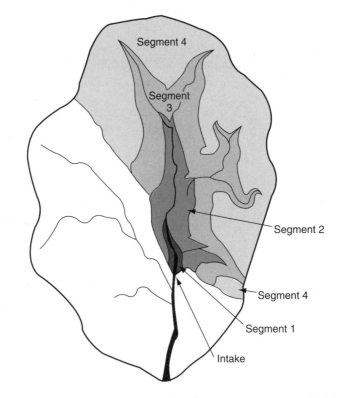

Figure 11–3   Watershed area—segmented for assessments (USEPA, 1997b)

many significant changes in these systems resulted in easier access for the public and better location information.

Step 2: Collect information from local land records, sanitary surveys, or public health records. Information can be collected from local government records, including operating, discharge and disposal, construction, and other permitting information; zoning records; real estate titles and transactions; and health department records (e.g., septic system permits). Maps, aerial photographs, telephone directories, and historic records can be used to locate particular land uses that have been or are continuing to threaten SWPA.

Step 3: Collect new information on past land use practices or contaminant sources that have not been identified. Because many sources, such as product storage facilities, failing septic systems, or abandoned underground storage tanks, may not be tracked at the local level, additional information often must be collected to adequately characterize threats to the PWS. Such information can be collected by door-to-door canvassing within SWPA, windshield surveys, mail surveys, or general public education and outreach to request and gather new information. A number of communities have successfully used local volunteers to collect such information.

Step 4: Target significant sources for further investigation. USEPA (1991b) provides worksheets to help target more significant contaminant sources based on the type and volume of materials managed at the sources and the proximity and vulnerability of the drinking water intake. For sources deemed most significant, the accuracy and reliability of the gathered information should be verified through field checks.

Assessing Vulnerability and Determining Susceptibility

Susceptibility assessments are the least understood (and most important) aspects of source water protection. Assessments are intended to identify the contaminant sources that pose the greatest threat to the drinking water supply so they can be targeted for management. Assessment methodologies include simple, analytical techniques such as hydrogeologic and hydrologic mapping to identify the relative vulnerability of groundwater and surface water supplies, as well as complex contaminant transport models linked to risk assessment matrices. Surface water assessments have relied on predictive models such as USEPA's Qual2E and Stormwater Management Model. Packaged assessment products such as Better Assessment Science Integrating Point and Nonpoint Sources developed by the USEPA Office of Science and Technology present a new method to incorporate point source and nonpoint source pollution into source water assessments. When the source water's susceptibility is assessed, a vulnerability determination must be produced and made available to the public.

Managing the Sources of Contamination

The SDWA Amendments of 1996 do not require management controls; however, many water suppliers and local governments are actively controlling contamination sources and preventing new contamination sources from threatening drinking water quality through various management controls. These controls were discussed previously in the section, *Identify Control Measures to Reduce or Eliminate Threats.*

Public Involvement/Consumer Confidence

These initiatives will also foster a greater need for outreach, education, and other nonregulatory tools. Public outreach and education designed to influence behavior has been effective in preventing pollution, conserving water, and developing supplies. Such approaches have been developed effectively as part of wellhead protection programs for groundwater-based systems and for large surface water-based utilities with limited, vulnerable supplies.

Public involvement and participation are needed for all utilities attempting to implement source water protection and management measures. As the water supply and public utility industries adopt integrated resource planning and watershed and source water management practices to ensure sustainable, long-term drinking water supplies, the need to build public support for and understanding of critical management issues becomes increasingly important. Through trial and error, utilities are developing new approaches for communicating with the variety of stakeholders and stakeholder groups that have an interest in water supply development, treatment, distribution, and demand management issues. Furthermore, other utilities and environmental programs are learning how to work with interested stakeholders in meaningful ways. By adopting these approaches, drinking water utilities can build stakeholder alliances that will foster better communication with the public and inform utility decision making. The emerging challenges of new water supply development, source water quality management, and the consumer awareness and public outreach provisions of SDWA make the need for such stakeholder involvement and alliance building especially critical.

Water utilities have historically interacted with a variety of stakeholder groups. At the local level, utilities regularly deal with individual customer service and rate issues. Such local stakeholders may also be represented by developers, subdivision managers, or other bulk purchasers of residential water supply. High-demand users, such as industry or large public or private institutions, may also band together to represent the interest of such users. Finally, public utility commissions or citizens' utility boards are often charged to represent local residential water users in determining the adequacy of water supply rate structures and public utility spending plans.

On a regional level, water supply development and management initiatives intersect with the activities of municipal, township, and county governments; planning authorities; homeowners' associations; and agricultural and industrial trade groups. These stakeholder groups may become critically involved in the developing and managing water supply watersheds or regional aquifers that encompass multiple political boundaries. Effectively communicating with such a diverse range of interests can drain the time and resources of even large utilities.

Finally, new monitoring and reporting requirements mandated under SDWA will change the relationship of individual utilities with state and federal regulators and will require new approaches for communicating with the public. In addition, a growing number of utilities are choosing to work with national programs, such as Groundwater Guardian, which focus on community-based water supply protection.

The growing need for interaction with these stakeholders has led utilities to conclude that public awareness of utility concerns is key to obtaining support for management initiatives and is critical when responding to the need for new resources and system improvements. Customers and other stakeholders are always more likely to *buy in* to management decisions when they are consulted early in the decision-making process.

REFERENCES

New England Interstate Water Pollution Control Commission. 1996. *Source Protection. A Guidance Manual for Small Surface Water Supplies in New England*. New England Interstate Water Pollution Control Commission.

US Environmental Protection Agency. 1985. *Protection of Public Water Supplies from Ground-Water Contamination, Seminar Publication*. EPA 625-4-85-016. Washington, D.C.: Center for Environmental Research Information, USEPA.

US Environmental Protection Agency. 1987. *Guidelines for Delineation of Wellhead Protection Areas*. EPA 44016-87-010. Washington, D.C.: Office of Ground-Water Protection, USEPA.

US Environmental Protection Agency. 1988. *Developing a State Wellhead Protection Program: A User's Guide to Assist State Agencies Under the Safe Drinking Water Act*. EPA 440/6-88-003. Washington, D.C.: Office of Ground-Water Protection, USEPA.

US Environmental Protection Agency. 1989. *Wellhead Protection Programs: Tools for Local Governments*. EPA 440-6-89-002. Washington, D.C.: Office of Water, USEPA.

US Environmental Protection Agency. 1991. *Managing Ground Water Contamination Sources in Wellhead Protection Areas: A Priority Setting Approach*. EPA 570/9-91-023. Washington, D.C.: Office of Ground Water and Drinking Water, USEPA.

US Environmental Protection Agency. 1992. *Final Comprehensive State Ground Water Protection Program Guidance*. EPA 100-R-93-001. Washington, D.C.: USEPA.

US Environmental Protection Agency. 1993a. *Wellhead Protection: A Guide for Small Communities*, Seminar Publication. EPA 625/R-93/002. Washington, D.C.: Office of Research and Development and Office of Water, USEPA.

US Environmental Protection Agency. 1993b. *Guidance Specifying Management Measures for Sources of Nonpoint Pollution in Coastal Waters*. Washington, D.C.: Office of Water, USEPA.

US Environmental Protection Agency. 1997a. *The 1995 Community Water Supply Survey*. EPA 815-R-97-001. Washington, D.C.: Office of Water, USEPA.

US Environmental Protection Agency. 1997b. *State Source Water Assessment and Protection Programs—Final Guidance*. EPA 816-R-97-009. Washington, D.C.: Office of Water, USEPA.

US Environmental Protection Agency. 1997c. *Catalog of Federal Funding Sources for Watershed Protection*. EPA 841-B-97-008. Washington, D.C.: Office of Water, USEPA.

US Environmental Protection Agency. 1997d. *Guidelines for Wellhead and Springhead Protection Area Delineation in Carbonate Rocks*. EPA 904-B-97-003. Region 4, Groundwater Protection Branch, USEPA.

US Environmental Protection Agency. 1997e. *Delineation of Source Water Protection Areas, A Discussion for Managers; Part 1: A Conjunctive Approach for Ground Water and Surface Water*. EPA 816-R-97-012. Washington, D.C.: Office of Water, USEPA.

US Environmental Protection Agency. 1997f. *Water on Tap: A Consumer's Guide to the Nation's Drinking Water*. EPA 815-K-97-002. Washington, D.C.: Office of Water, USEPA.

This page intentionally blank

Chapter **12**

Economic Feasibility

MULTIOBJECTIVE DECISIONS: ECONOMICS AS ONE OF SEVERAL OBJECTIVES

The choice of one or more water resource alternatives for further study or implementation depends on a process in which multiple objectives and a number of factors must be considered. Although certain objectives or factors may play dominant roles in early screening of alternatives, all must be considered when selecting water resource alternatives. These factors, many of which have been discussed in previous chapters, include

- technical feasibility (Can an alternative be implemented given the knowledge, available technology, equipment, and labor force and skills available?);

- policy issues (Are specific constraints imposed on projects as the result of policy determinations in the water resources arena or in other areas of policy?);

- political issues (Must specific political influences, issues, constraints, special interests, or constituencies be considered?); and

- economic factors (Does the alternative represent an efficient, effective use of the resources available?).

This final factor—the determination of whether a project represents an efficient or effective use of available resources—is discussed in this chapter.

ECONOMIC FACTORS

Limited Resources

In general, a production process requires at least one of three basic inputs: effort (labor), equipment (capital), and raw materials. The ways in which these inputs are combined to produce a product is determined by their relative availability in the environment and the level of technology. If an abundance of a resource is always available, whether its application is being used in the most efficient or effective manner does not need to be considered. There will always be enough to satisfy all needs. However, most resources are not sufficient to satisfy all needs, and their best uses must be determined.

Historically, the US economy had an abundance of raw materials, but faced limited labor resources. Other economies, such as China, have historically had an abundance of labor resources and raw materials, but relatively scarce capital resources. Other economies, such as in Japan, may have adequate capital and labor resources, but limited supplies of raw materials. Over time, resources typically become scarcer as growing populations pressure the availability of raw materials and capital.

Economic analysis of resources evolved because resources are generally limited in some way. Water resources planning faces this problem of scarce resources, as do all other segments of the economy. Identifying new sources of water supply (scarcity of raw materials) and developing the assets (scarcity of capital—both physical and financial) necessary to deliver a product (safe, reliable water) to customers is becoming increasingly costly. Water resource planners must compete for resources with other economic and social needs. The planners must also help determine how available resources are to be allocated between different projects or different objectives.

Allocating Scarce Resources

The goal of economic analysis is to provide a process by which decisions can be made on how to allocate the available but scarce resources to the most efficient or effective uses. This goal is applicable whether viewed from the standpoint of allocating resources throughout the economy to determine how much is available for water resources planning and development or viewed from the point of allocating resources that have already been made available for water resources between competing projects.

In economic analysis, the allocation process is typically discussed in terms of the *net benefits* to be derived from projects so they can be ranked according to a quantitative, objective measurement. Net benefits, in economic analysis, are defined as being the difference between the benefits created by the projects and the costs of completing and operating the projects. For quantitative analysis, these costs and benefits are almost always expressed in monetary units.

Net Benefits = Total Benefits – Total Costs

ECONOMIC VARIABLES: COSTS AND BENEFITS _____

The primary elements in an economic analysis are the benefits derived as a result of the project and the costs of implementing the project. For most projects, the costs of implementation are easier to define and quantify than are the benefits. For instance, although the costs of providing drinking water that is free of *Cryptosporidium* or *Giardia* may be estimated based on known supply and treatment practices, the benefits of *Cryptosporidium* and *Giardia*-free water are much more difficult to assess. Estimating the number of avoided cases of these waterborne inflictions is possible; however, evaluating the cases avoided is not a straightforward task.

Often complicating the economic analyses of any project, and particularly of water resource projects, is the determining of the proper perspective from which to view the costs and benefits that accrue to the project. As discussed in the following section, a project may be viewed from the utility perspective, the ratepayer perspective, or the society perspective. Determining the benefits and costs for projects will vary according to the perspective from which the analysis takes place.

Perspectives

The differing perspectives of costs and benefits follow definitions developed by the California Public Utilities Commission and California Energy Commission (*Standard Practice Manual: Economic Analysis of Demand-Side Management Programs*, December 1987). The discussion in this standard practice manual was aimed primarily at evaluating energy conservation programs, but the premises and analytical techniques apply directly to the analysis of water resources projects. The perspective that is appropriate for evaluation must be determined for each project; no one perspective is appropriate for all cases.

Utility. Benefits and costs from the utility perspective reflect the direct impacts on the utility, without regard to any others. As such, only costs imposed directly on the utility would be included in cost determinations. Costs include payments the utility makes for land, equipment, supplies, fees, consultants, engineers, contractors, other agencies, operators, financing costs, and utility staff that apply to the project. If the project under evaluation contributes toward increased costs for other utility operations, those costs should also be included. On the other hand, to the extent that private parties or governmental agencies provide subsidies or contributions, the costs the utility must directly pay are reduced and should be excluded from costs in this perspective. The utility programs that provide rebates or subsidies to customers, such as water conservation, represent a cost to the utility that should be included as costs related to the project. Costs borne by others outside of the utility, including the environment, would not be included in this perspective.

Similarly, only benefits that directly affect the utility should be included in this perspective. A water utility benefits from a new water supply project if it can sell more water and increase its overall revenues. Other benefits include

- reduced overall utility operating costs as a result of a project,

- new water supply cost lower than the best alternative previously available to the utility, and

- reduced water usage as the result of a conservation program, thereby reducing utility operating costs.

Costs and benefits that are not included in the perspective—because they are imposed on or provide benefit to an entity external to the utility implementing the project—are referred to as externalities. For example, if, as a result of the project, a neighboring community benefits from reduced flooding, those benefits would not be included (unless the community provided a payment to the utility in return for the benefit).

Ratepayer. The ratepayer perspective incorporates most of the costs and benefits that apply to the utility perspective. This perspective also includes all costs and benefits carried by those who pay the rates for the utility. Higher rates, which translate into less income the ratepayer has to spend on other products (including savings), represent an additional cost borne by the ratepayers. A new water supply that is perceived to be lower in quality than the current one may induce ratepayers to purchase bottled water for drinking purposes, thus imposing an additional cost that would be recognized from the ratepayer perspective.

On the other hand, a new water supply with greatly reduced mineral content may allow ratepayers to reduce or eliminate expenditures for water softeners, thus providing them with a benefit that would not be included in the utility perspective. A supplemental water supply project that provides the additional water necessary to support construction and inhabitation of new homes that could not otherwise have been built provides benefits to at least some ratepayers. Any negative impacts on other ratepayers would cause the additional costs to be counted against the additional benefits.

Society. The costs and benefits included in the utility and ratepayers perspectives are generally also included in the society perspective. The society perspective, however, also includes all costs and benefits that would be considered externalities from the other perspectives. In other words, since all of society (including the environment) is included in the analysis, those external costs and benefits become internal to the analysis. The society perspective represents a more comprehensive perspective that attempts to incorporate all impacts.

For the society perspective, payments from one entity to another are considered to be simply transfers of funds for which the costs to the granting entity are negated by the benefits to the receiving entity. For example, a conservation rebate that would have been considered a cost for the utility under the utility perspective and a benefit to the ratepayer under the ratepayer perspective, effectively cancel each other out when examined from the society perspective. Similarly, a grant program in which the federal government provides a substantial portion of the costs of construction for a project would provide a benefit under the utility perspective, but under the society perspective nationwide, would represent a transfer because one segment of society is receiving benefit at the expense of another. Because transfers can affect the distribution of income, wealth, and well-being, they are often subject to additional policy (such as equity or fairness of the distribution) and political considerations.

Perspective choice. The choice of the perspective to analyze a project determines which costs and benefits are appropriate. The society perspective provides the broadest coverage of costs, including those related to the environment, but the utility perspective should also always be examined to make sure the program is affordable to the utility and its ratepayers. Projects should be evaluated from each perspective to assure the decision makers that significant, relevant impacts have not been overlooked.

Costs

In the following discussion, costs are classified as internal or external to the utility. Internal costs are borne by the entity (utility) that benefits from the project. Internal costs would be included in analyses performed from the utility perspective. Costs borne by any another entity that does not receive a benefit from the project are external costs. Those costs classified as external would not be included in the utility perspective, but would be considered in the society perspective (along with most internal costs).

Costs for project alternatives are also likely to be distributed differently over time. Some projects require large initial capital expenditures, with relatively small ongoing operating expenditures. Other projects may require modest initial capital expenditures but have several increments phased in over time and high operating expenditures. Because alternative projects will differ in the combination of initial and incremental capital spending and ongoing operations and maintenance (O&M) expenditures, the analysis must be based on the full life cycle of the projects. Consequently, the pattern and timing of project costs is an important factor in determining whether a project will be economical.

Internal costs.   The internal costs of a water resources project typically fall within two main categories:

- Capital

- Operations and Maintenance (O & M)

Capital costs.   Capital costs consist of all expenditures necessary to create a productive asset. They are relatively large expenditures that must be made in a short time. Capital costs are sometimes referred to as "lumpy" expenditures because they must occur during short time frames and cannot easily be incrementally changed. The expenditures tend to be all-or-nothing expenditures and must be made before any production can occur.

Financing.   Developing a new water resource generally requires substantial resources, usually over a short time, and must be made before benefits (receipt of revenues) are realized. In most cases, the amounts required are well beyond the ability of the utility to fund through internally generated revenue sources. Consequently, the projects are often financed through external sources, particularly by issuing debt instruments such as bonds.

Debt financing is the interest and associated costs that must be added to the overall lifetime project cost. Even though the additional interest costs add to project cost, because they are distributed over time, their economic impact will be less. As discussed in a later section on the value of time, an expenditure in the future is economically less than an equivalent expenditure today.

Because costs to the utility are spread over the term of the debt (often 20 to 30 years) rather than entirely up front, a revenue stream can be developed that pays for the debt service (principle and interest). Debt financing may be more equitable or fair because it allows a matching of costs with benefits over time: the benefits of a large project are distributed over an extended time frame; debt financing allows the costs to be distributed over a corresponding time frame. Although debt is spread over many years, it is seldom for the entire life cycle of the project.

Subsidies and grants.   Because of the large capital expenditures required for many water resource projects, cost offsets may be available that reduce the internal costs to the utility. Grants or subsidies from other entities, particularly other governmental entities, may be available. To the extent that these can be used, the internal cost to the utility is reduced. If the analysis is performed from the utility perspective, the project cost is reduced by the amount of the grant or subsidy and the project becomes more feasible. If, however, the analysis is performed from the society perspective, the grant or subsidy is a transfer and has no impact on project costs; costs decrease for the utility but increase equivalently to the granting entity.

Operations and maintenance costs.   O&M costs represent the ongoing expenditures necessary for the utility to operate the project over time, including keeping facilities in good repair. Unlike capital costs, O&M costs are continuous over the lifetime of the project, depending to some degree on the level of production from the project.

External costs.   Capital and O&M costs are internal to the firm or utility that creates the project. These are paid by the utility, directly or indirectly, to achieve a result. They are factored into the decision by the utility depending on how it allocates its resources. Many projects, on the other hand, also have the potential to affect parties not directly related to the project. When decisions are made by a utility, these external costs may be overlooked because they must be paid by another entity. Indeed, from the utility perspective, they are not relevant. For overall economic efficiency, all costs should be accounted for, as under the society perspective. This requires that the external costs be included to the fullest extent possible.

Imposed costs.   Most production processes, whether they occur in a factory, office building, or water treatment plant, have the potential to impose costs on someone else. Air pollution from a chemical factory imposes additional costs on those who must breathe the polluted air. Other businesses may have to spend more funds to filter or clean the air to make conditions palatable for their employees or customers. A farmer whose pesticides run off into a river used for drinking water imposes costs on the water utility to remove any residue from the pesticide. These all represent costs imposed by a production process on another entity that has neither consented to the imposition of the cost nor directly benefits from the production process. Imposed costs may be estimated based on the cost of efforts by the other entities to undo their impacts.

Where external costs are not factored into the decision-making process, the product tends to be underpriced and overproduced. Because prices are determined, at least in part, by the costs to produce a product, they will be lower than otherwise. Because prices are lower than they otherwise should be, customers will desire more of the product and overproduction occurs. On the other hand, for production processes that have had costs imposed on them, production costs (to remove pesticides from drinking water, for example) and prices charged tend to be higher than they would otherwise be, leading to a tendency to underproduce. For the most efficient allocation of resources, costs should be internalized to the extent possible.

Environmental costs.   Some external costs are imposed not on a specific entity but rather on the environment. Where imposed costs can be estimated and quantified based on the additional costs other producers must pay to offset the imposed costs, environmental costs are not as easily determined or valued. Valuation of the loss of habitat or of an endangered species is nearly impossible.

Because valuation of environmental costs is very difficult, the costs are often not included in economic analyses, even though they may be recognized in other ways. Integrated resource planning efforts commonly screen alternatives for environmental effects before performing the economic analysis. Although the economic analysis does not explicitly include environmental costs, only projects already determined to have acceptable environmental impacts are typically considered. Some regulatory agencies include an environmental cost to recognize additional impacts that are not in the cost analysis. For example, a project deemed likely to have greater environmental impacts than others might have a 10 percent cost applied to account for at least some of the real costs.

Benefits

Identifying and quantifying the benefits of water-related projects can be difficult. Some benefits such as additional revenues generated by sales, are fairly straightforward, but most are more troublesome. Many economic analyses for water projects concentrate on the cost side only, assuming the benefits are adequate to make all projects economically feasible and the main task is to identify the lowest cost option to achieve the positive benefits.

Internal benefits.

Value of production.   The most direct measurement of benefits for water resource projects is the value of additional water sales generated as a result. Because both the price and the quantity of additional water can be projected, valuation of the benefits, at least from the utility perspective, is straightforward. Other sources of benefits from water projects could include power generation and sales, recreation use fees, additional impact fees from growth supported by a new water supply, and additional tax revenues from growth in the service area. All are related directly to increased production and are relatively easy to quantify.

Avoided costs.   Many benefits of a project may be indirect, coming about as a result of not having to use resources in some other way. For example, a surface water supply project that replaces a groundwater supply that is seriously overdrafted and is creating saltwater intrusion provides benefits that cannot be measured in additional water sales. Rather, the benefits come from avoiding the costs associated with the saltwater intrusion. If adding 500 acre-ft (615×10^3 m^3) of surface water supply can avoid the need to build a desalination facility costing $5 million, the benefit of the surface supply is equivalent to the avoided $5 million in costs. As discussed later, this amount should be adjusted to reflect the time value of money. These avoided cost-benefits can come about as the result of avoiding capital and O&M expenditures.

External benefits.   External impacts are negative or cost impacts imposed on outside entities, including the environment. Water resource projects, however, may also provide positive external benefits that should be included in determining total benefits, just as the external costs should be included in total costs. For example, creating a lake for water supply purposes may also provide recreation benefits, habitat for wildlife, or flood control benefits. As with external costs, the allocation of resources can be distorted by failure to include these benefits in the economic analysis.

TIME AND DISCOUNT RATE

Because many water resource projects require large initial investments, comparing the costs and benefits of alternative water resource projects critically depends on the value of time and the discount rate used in economic analyses.

Value of Time

For most water resource projects, initial expenditures may be quite large, followed by ongoing O&M costs extending over the life of the project. Substantial up-front capital expenditures may be required for a project, but the benefits are realized over an extended period of time. Consequently, any analysis must be based on the times over which the spending and benefits occur, particularly when comparing two projects with cost and benefit streams that differ in timing and quantity. The different timing patterns can make determining which of several options is financially preferable very difficult.

Policy makers must carefully consider how these differences in timing and quantity or size will affect the decision process. A typical question a policy maker should ask with regard to timing of a specific project spending is "Am I better off spending $100,000 today on this project or is it better to wait a year when the project would cost $110,000?" or "Are savings (benefits) of $1,000 from a conservation measure in the first year of greater value than a $1,200 savings achieved in year three?" To provide a common basis for comparisons, economists and financial analysts use the concept of "present value," which adjusts future amounts of costs or savings to equivalent values today. To answer the questions, a planner needs to know the earnings that are possible for investing available funds. If the best earnings rate on investments available amounts to 5 percent per year, that becomes the basis for answering the questions. The interest rate used is referred to as the "discount rate." The discount rate is the highest rate of return (interest rate) that could be earned by investing available funds with the same level of risk. For a utility, the discount rate may be determined by the utility's long-run cost of capital, which is the interest rate it must pay to borrow in the long-term bond market.

To understand the value of time, a good analogy is investing funds in a savings account. With $100,000 available today invested at 5 percent interest the total value would be $105,000 ($100,000 × [1 + 0.05]) at the end of the year. Receiving $110,000 in one year would be better than $100,000 today. If the interest rate on investment happened to be 10 percent per year, $100,000 would be $110,000 in one year ($100,000 × [1 + 0.10]). Both decisions would have the same result. On the other hand, if the interest rate were 20 percent, the $100,000 would be $120,000 in one year ($100,000 × [1 + 0.20]). Because more could be earned by investing the funds ($100,000) than the amount being offered for one year ($110,000), receiving the $100,000 up front would provide greater value.

The concept of present value is essentially a reversal of the process just described. When the value in the future is known, what is its worth today? With a 5 percent interest rate, what is the value of $110,000 spent or received one year from today? The calculation for this simple situation is to divide the $110,000 by the interest-earning factor (1 + 0.05), such that the present value is calculated as ($110,000 / [1 + 0.05]) = $104,762. In other words, $104,762 today would earn, at 5 percent interest, $5,238 in one year, so the full amount available in a year's time would equal $110,000. Because the present value of $110,000 is $104,762, it would be economically better to accept $110,000 in one year than $100,000 today.

For periods of comparison longer than one year, as in the second example, the calculation must also take into account that funds invested today would have the additional years of earnings potential, assuming the annual earnings are reinvested and compounded. So an initial investment of $1,000 at 5 percent interest would be worth $1,050 ($1,000 × [1 + 0.05]) at the end of one year. For the second year, $1,050 would be earning 5 percent interest and be worth $1,102.50 ($1,050 × [1 + 0.05]) at the end of the second year. The $1,102.50 would earn 5 percent and be worth $1,157.62 ($1,102.50 × [1 + 0.05]) at the end of the third year. This chain of calculations could be expressed more concisely as $1,000 × (1 + 0.05)^3. Reversing the process, as was done above, implies that the present value of $1,157.62 would be $1,000 ($1,157.62 / [1 + 0.05]^3).

For the second example, because both the savings from conservation are out in time, the present value of each program must be determined and compared. The present value of $1,000 in conservation savings achieved in one year, with a 5 percent discount rate, is $952.38 ($1,000 / [1 + 0.05]). The present value of $1,200 in conservation savings achieved in 3 years, again with a 5 percent discount rate, is $1,036.60 ($1,200 / [1 + 0.05]^3). Comparing the two options, the second is preferred, with a present value that is higher by $84.22. So even though an additional 2 years must pass before the savings from the conservation program are achieved, the values of those savings will be greater than for the program that generates savings at the end of just one year.

In general, when the timing of money flows differs between alternative projects, their time value must be considered to determine which will provide the best or most economical use of available resources. As projects are deferred, eliminated, or reduced in size as a result of reduced levels of demand, the present value of the spending flows determines the real amount of savings.

The present value of money represents the value of a future payment if its equivalent was received today.

$$PV = FV/(1 + r)^n \qquad \text{(Eq 12-1)}$$

Where:

PV	=	present value
FV	=	future value
r	=	discount rate
n	=	number of periods

Spending on water resource projects often consists of multiple-year capital programs, with O&M costs spread out over time, and yield benefits that may be even further spread out over time; therefore, using present value calculations to determine program effectiveness or to compare alternative programs is essential.

Discount Rate

The discount rate is highly influential in determining the present value and the choice of the discount rate can significantly influence the overall results. A high discount rate will cause future values to quickly diminish in importance, thus placing greater influence on near-term values. With a low discount rate, on the other hand, future values will not diminish as rapidly and will therefore carry greater influence in the present value calculation. The discount rate must be chosen with care.

As discussed in the previous section, the discount rate should reflect either the best alternative use of the funds available or the cost of capital (which for most public agencies is equivalent to the interest rate on long-term debt). For federal government projects, the Office of Management and Budget provides guidelines (*Circular A-94,* Appendix C), for choosing the discount rates, based on interest rates for Treasury notes and bonds, with maturates that can be matched to project lives. The guidelines are updated annually. For 1998, the 30-year discount rate was established at 6.1 percent, based on 30-year Treasury bonds. For public agencies that can raise funds through issuance of long-term, tax-exempt municipal bonds, interest rates could be a percentage point lower, depending on ratings of bonds and conditions. A discount rate in the range of 5.0 percent to 5.5 percent would, therefore, be appropriate.

As implied here, the discount rate depends on the entity for whom the analysis is being performed. It will vary depending on the perspective used in the analysis. From a utility perspective, the discount rate would likely be based on long-term, tax-exempt bonds of the utility. However, from the society perspective, the rate based on Treasury bonds would reflect a broader social valuation. From a ratepayer perspective, the discount rate should be equivalent to the expected rate of return on investments. An appropriate measure would be the average rate of return on the Standard & Poors' 500 Index. For individuals, the discount rate would depend on the best investment alternative. For some, the best alternative might be a bank savings account. For a person unwilling to accept risk, the return might be based on 90-day Treasury notes, which are both liquid and secure; for a person willing to accept average risk, the return might be based on the average returns on a stock market index or money market fund.

An additional consideration in choosing a discount rate is whether it should be the nominal or real discount rate. The nominal discount rate reflects current market conditions, taking into account expected inflationary impacts of money. Market rates are nominal rates. The real discount rate is the nominal rate less expected inflation, which erodes the purchasing power of money over time. Because the real discount rate is an inflationary adjusted value, it is sometimes referred to as a constant-dollar rate. *Circular A-94* specifies 3.8 percent for the 30-year real discount rate. The difference of 2.3 percent between that amount and the 6.1 percent nominal rate reflects the expected rate of inflation.

The choice of real or nominal discount rates depends on whether costs and benefits are evaluated based on a real (constant-dollar) or nominal basis. If costs and benefits are expressed in terms of today's dollars, without adjustment for inflationary impacts, the real discount rate should be used in the evaluation. However, if costs and benefits have been adjusted to reflect costs expected in the future, including any projected inflation, the nominal discount rate should be used.

COMPARISON METHODOLOGIES

The goal of economic analysis is to allocate resources in the most efficient and effective manner, given insufficient resources to satisfy all needs. The methodologies discussed provide alternative methods for arriving at resource allocations, given that alternative uses have been defined. Another way of expressing the goal of economic efficiency or effectiveness is maximizing the net benefits, where net benefits represent the difference between total benefits and total costs. Projects can be ranked, then accepted or rejected, based on whether they contribute to increasing net benefits.

Evaluating alternative projects is often difficult because of the varied mix of resources used in the projects (combinations of capital and O&M expenditures) and the timing of the expenditures and benefits received as a result of the project. The same end results (benefits) can often be achieved through various combinations (high capital, low O&M; low capital, high O&M). The goal is to determine which combinations will contribute the most to net benefits.

In several of the methodologies presented, projects are typically ranked on costs alone. The basic assumption underlying this type of approach is that each project alternative achieves the same goals, and therefore has identical benefits. The cost-only approach also assumes that the projects are beneficial, that is, they increase net benefits.

Annualized Costs

The goal of the annualized costs method is to rank projects based on the costs that are imposed annually on the utility by alternative projects that achieve the same end result (the benefits are assumed to be equal for each alternative and, therefore, need not enter into consideration). O&M expenditures occur regularly throughout the project life and can be estimated annually with little difficulty. Capital costs, however, are expenditures that occur in large amounts early in the project, but contribute toward production throughout the life of the project. This method converts capital costs into annual equivalents that can then be added to O&M to get total annual costs to be attributed to the project. Projects can then be ranked according to their annualized costs.

The calculation of the annual cost of capital takes into account the useful life of the capital facility and the utility's cost of capital. In essence, this calculator determines the amount that would have to be charged annually over the life of the facility to recover the capital investment. This calculation is technically equivalent to determining a mortgage payment spread evenly over the expected life of the facility. This recovery factor can be calculated by the following formula:

$1/[1 - (1/r)^n]/r$, which can be simplified to $r(1 + r)^n/(1 + r)^n - 1$ (Eq 12-2)

Where:

r = utility's cost of capital
n = useful life of the facility

The capital recovery factor is multiplied by the capital cost to determine the annualized capital cost:

annualized capital cost = capital cost capital recovery factor   (Eq 12-3)

The annualized capital cost is added to annual O&M expenditures to determine the annualized costs for the project. After this calculation is performed for each alternative project, the projects are ranked according to annualized costs. The least cost alternative would be chosen, assuming equivalent benefits.

Example:
Assumptions: capital cost = $5,000,000; interest rate = 6.0%; project life = 40 years;

Annual O&M costs	= $250,000
Annualized capital cost	= $5,000,000 × [(0.06)(1 + 0.06)^{40} / (1 + 0.06)^{40} - 1]
	= $5,000,000 × 0.0664615 = $332,308
Total annualized costs	= $332,308 + $250,000 = $582,308

Projects with annualized costs of less than $582,308 would be preferred over the example project; the example project would be preferred over projects with higher annualized costs. This method becomes much less useful when capital costs occur in phases or if O&M costs are not constant. The stream of benefits is also assumed to be equal for each alternative. This is a simple, inexpensive method for ranking similar projects.

Present Value

Present value analysis explicitly considers the value of time in analyzing costs and benefits. Using present value allows for comparing alternative spending and benefit patterns over time, converting each to its equivalent value today. Key to present value analysis is the discount rate, which adjusts values to reflect present day equivalents. Economic efficiency is based on maximizing the present value of the net benefit stream. Both the internal rate of return and benefit–cost ratio methodologies, which are commonly used as indicators of economic efficiency, are based on present value calculations.

Like the annualized cost method, the present value approach can be carried out based on costs alone, assuming again that benefits occur equally over time among the projects. The present value approach is more robust, accommodating unequal spending patterns over time. Unlike annualized costs, O&M costs need not be assumed equal every year. Capital spending in phases can be readily handled. Alternative funding sources can be incorporated into the analysis so either revenue funding or debt funding alternatives can be explored. As with annualized costs, the present value method allows projects to be ranked based on least cost.

The present value method also has the advantage of being able to become a full economic analysis, with costs and benefits evaluated. The assumption of equally distributed benefits over time is not necessary because the benefits can be evaluated directly. The term "net present value (NPV)" is generally used to distinguish use of the present value technique based on benefits and costs from the technique based on costs only. The process of calculating the present worth is the same. To calculate NPV, costs are subtracted from the benefits for each period, then the present worth of the net benefit for the year is discounted back to its present value.

Present value (whether net or cost only) for a series of values can be calculated based on the formula

$$PV = \sum t = 1^t = [FV_t/(1+r)^t] \qquad \text{(Eq 12-4)}$$

Where:

FV_t = the future value in year t

r = discount rate

t = periods ranging from year 1 to year t

Project alternatives are ranked according to their present values; the lowest present value is preferred over higher present values when comparing costs. When ranking projects based on NPV (benefits in excess of costs), the alternative with the highest NPV is ranked highest as it contributes the greatest amount to net benefits. Projects with lower, but positive NPV, contribute to net benefits and are therefore economically viable. However, given budget and resource constraints, these lower ranked projects may not be possible.

The following Example 1 illustrates the calculation of the NPV at an 8 percent discount rate for a project with initial capital costs of $500,000, increasing O&M costs, and benefits that are constant after the project goes into service. The total costs just equal total benefits over the project life ($900,000 total project benefits versus $900,000 total project costs); the NPV is negative. This is due to the pattern of costs (large up-front capital costs) compared to later benefit receipts, which are discounted in value compared to the earlier capital costs. This project would not be economical, as shown by the negative NPV. A lower discount rate would decrease the negative NPV. Only at a discount rate of 0 percent would the project not have a negative NPV.

In Example 2, the initial capital costs are lower, but annual O&M costs are higher. The slightly positive NPV indicates that this project configuration would contribute to net benefits and be economically effective. Given the low NPV, this configuration would, however, rank low on a list of alternatives. If the projects shown in the two examples were the only alternatives available, the project in the second example would be chosen as the preferred project because of its positive NPV.

In addition to selecting a preferred project from several alternatives, NPV rankings can be used to allocate limited resources (budget) among unrelated projects. In Example 3, seven projects are given hypothetical rankings based on NPV. Projects A through E all have positive NPVs and would therefore be worthwhile. Project F, with a zero NPV and Project G, with a negative NPV, should not be undertaken even if funding is available since they do not contribute to net benefits. Of course, budget limitations may make it impossible to undertake all beneficial projects. Those providing the highest value should be implemented first, until the budget is exhausted. In Example 3, the cost of each project is also provided. Given a budget of $5,000,000, Projects A, B, and C would be chosen for implementation because they

Example 1
Discount Rate: 8.0%

Year $t =$	Capital Cost ($)	O&M Cost ($)	Total Cost ($)	Benefits ($)	Net Benefit ($)	Net Present Value ($)
1	500,000	10,000	510,000	0	(510,000)	(510,000)
2		20,000	20,000	100,000	80,000	74,074
3		30,000	30,000	100,000	70,000	60,014
4		40,000	40,000	100,000	60,000	47,630
5		50,000	50,000	100,000	50,000	36,751
6		50,000	50,000	100,000	50,000	34,029
7		50,000	50,000	100,000	50,000	31,508
8		50,000	50,000	100,000	50,000	29,175
9		50,000	50,000	100,000	50,000	27,013
10		50,000	50,000	100,000	50,000	25,012
Totals	500,000	400,000	900,000	900,000	—	(144,793)

Example 2
Discount Rate: 8.0%

Year $t =$	Capital Cost ($)	O&M Cost ($)	Total Cost ($)	Benefits ($)	Net Benefit ($)	Net Present Value ($)
1	200,000	20,000	220,000	0	(220,000)	(220,000)
2		30,000	30,000	100,000	70,000	64,815
3		40,000	40,000	100,000	60,000	51,440
4		50,000	50,000	100,000	50,000	39,692
5		60,000	60,000	100,000	40,000	29,401
6		70,000	70,000	100,000	30,000	20,417
7		80,000	80,000	100,000	20,000	12,603
8		90,000	90,000	100,000	10,000	5,835
9		100,000	100,000	100,000	—	—
10		100,000	100,000	100,000	—	—
Totals	200,000	640,000	840,000	900,000	60,000	4,204

provide the highest contribution to net benefit and their costs fit within the budget. With a budget of $6,000,000, Project D could be added.

Benefit–Cost Ratio

An alternative method for determining whether a project is economically feasible is based on the benefit–cost ratio. In this method, the ratio of the present value of benefits to the present value of costs is calculated.

B/C = present value of benefits / present value of costs

Example 3

	NPV ($)	Total Cost ($)	Cumulative Cost ($)
Project A	245,000	3,000,000	3,000,000
Project B	200,000	1,500,000	4,500,000
Project C	125,000	500,000	5,000,000
Project D	50,000	200,000	5,200,000
Project E	10,000	1,000,000	6,200,000
Project F	—	100,000	6,300,000
Project G	(20,000)	50,000	6,350,000

Where the present value of benefits is higher than the present value of costs, the ratio will be greater than 1.0 and the project would be economically feasible. Where the present value of benefits is less than the present value of costs, the ratio will be less than 1.0, indicating that the project is not economically feasible. The B/C ratio reflects the same information that comes from the calculation of NPV discussed earlier. Whenever the NPV is positive, the B/C ratio will be greater than 1.0. When the NPV is negative, the B/C ratio will be less than 1.0. Therefore, economic feasibility can be determined with either method.

Unlike NPV, the B/C ratio is not useful for allocating resources among projects. A higher B/C ratio does not mean a greater contribution to overall net benefits, as does a higher NPV. The table in Example 4 assumes the same projects as shown in Example 3. Assuming that total costs and total benefits are stated in present values, the B/C ratio is calculated for each project. Note that Project A, with the highest NPV, has a lower B/C ratio than any of Projects B, C, or D. The B/C ratio provides information about the economic feasibility of the project but should not be used to develop a ranking of those feasible projects.

Example 4

	NPV ($)	Total Cost ($)	Total Benefits ($)	B/C Ratio ($)
Project A	245,000	3,000,000	3,245,000	1.082
Project B	200,000	1,500,000	1,700,000	1.133
Project C	125,000	500,000	625,000	1.250
Project D	50,000	200,000	250,000	1.250
Project E	10,000	1,000,000	1,010,000	1.010
Project F	—	100,000	100,000	1.000
Project G	(20,000)	50,000	30,000	0.600

Internal Rate of Return

A project's economical viability can be determined by calculating the internal rate of return (IRR), the interest rate that would make the NPV zero. In other words, at what discount rate would the present value of benefits just equal the present value of costs over the life of the project?

Previously the formula for calculating the present value was given:

$$PV = \sum t = 1^t[FV_t/(1+r)^t] \qquad \text{(Eq 12-5)}$$

Where:

FVt = the future value in year t

r = discount rate

t = periods, ranging from year 1 to year t

The IRR is based on the same fundamental equation, but solving for the value of r, the discount rate, with PV set to zero. This rate of return on the investment can then be compared to rates of return on other types of investments to determine whether the project will help to maximize overall benefits. Typically, a target rate of return is determined based on some alternative investment opportunity. If the target return level is 10 percent, all projects with an IRR greater than 10 percent would be considered feasible. Projects with an IRR less than 10 percent would not be considered.

Like the B/C ratio, the IRR method provides a means for screening projects for economic feasibility but should not be used to rank projects for implementation. For public projects, it can be difficult to determine the target return level.

SUMMARY

Projects are determined to be economically feasible if they contribute more to benefits than to costs. To recognize that the timing of costs and benefits is important, all benefits and costs should be calculated in terms of today's dollars, or more specifically, in terms of present values. The net present value, B/C ratio, and IRR methods all provide means by which economic feasibility can be determined. However, the NPV method also provides a means to rank projects and allocate limited budget dollars.

This page intentionally blank

Chapter **13**

Integrated Resource Planning

Integrated resource planning (IRP) is a method of addressing the myriad issues raised in this manual. IRP is an overall process for guiding and developing a water resource plan. This chapter explains how this process works, showing the difference between IRP and traditional planning. The chapter highlights methods and criteria used to compare alternatives and select a plan.

Defining Integrated Resource Planning

Although the individual elements of IRP have been used for many years, IRP is a relatively new concept for most water utilities. No definition for IRP is broadly accepted, so the definition used in this manual is contained in AWWA's White Paper on IRP.

> IRP is a comprehensive form of planning that encompasses least-cost analyses of demand-side and supply-side management options as well as an open and participatory decision-making process, the development of water resource alternatives that incorporates consideration of a community's quality of life and environmental issues that may be impacted by the ultimate decision, and recognition of the multiple institutions concerned with water resources and the competing policy goals among them. IRP attempts to consider all direct and indirect costs and benefits of demand management, supply management, and supply augmentation by using alternative planning scenarios, analyses across disciplines, community involvement in the planning, decision making, and implementation process, and consideration of other societal and environmental benefits.

> IRP includes planning methods to identify the most efficient means of achieving the goals while considering the costs of project impacts on other community objectives and environmental management goals. These planning

315

methods specifically require evaluation of all benefits and costs, including avoided costs and life-cycle costs.

Another, slightly different definition is contained in a report on IRP conducted for the AWWA Research Foundation (AwwaRF).

> IRP is a continuous process that results in the development of a comprehensive water resource management plan. It identifies and gives balanced consideration to supply and demand management planning alternatives. It includes analyses of engineering, economic, societal, and environmental costs and considerations while balancing the needs of competing users and multiple objectives of the use of the resource. It is an open and participatory process involving all stakeholders and striving for consensus, while encompassing least-cost analyses of short- and long-term planning options, and satisfying utility and regulatory policy goals. Finally, IRP explicitly seeks to identify and manage risk and uncertainty and provides for coordination of planning between water and wastewater utilities in a specific region.

The AwwaRF definition is more practical as it meets the primary mandate of most water utilities: "Providing a safe, adequate, and reliable supply of water at a reasonable cost to its customers." When appropriately applied, IRP is an effective process for preparing a water resource plan.

AWWA sponsored a research project on IRP that contained case studies and published a guidebook on the topic called, *Integrated Resource Planning: A Balanced Approach to Water Resources Decision Making.* This guidebook is a good primer on IRP.

Agencies Typically Involved in IRP

Most IRPs have been prepared by wholesale or retail water agencies who control their water supply. Most wholesale water agencies, while taking the lead in resource planning, have involved their retail customers in a meaningful way. The AWWA White Paper encourages water and wastewater agencies to work together. The availability of a significant amount of reclaimable wastewater can make working together mutually beneficial. Water resource schemes that generate or conserve significant energy, or where the power company is a major competing user of water, may indicate that a joint IRP with the energy utility would also be beneficial.

Utility Experience

A number of water utilities started and completed IRPs in the early 1990s. Many more are expected to complete them. A sampling of IRPs is contained in Table 13-1. Most of these are being updated in 2006-07. Some common elements are a conservation program, wastewater reclamation where it is cost-effective, and in some cases, development of a new surface water supply. Note the long-range planning horizon of about 25 to 50 years.

OVERVIEW OF THE IRP PROCESS

The AWWA and AwwaRF definitions clearly show that many factors must be considered in preparing an IRP. Essentially, the first ten chapters of this book present the elements of the IRP process, and the information generated must be dealt with logically. Every IRP will have unique features that make the process somewhat

Table 13–1   Utility experience with IRP

Utility	Year Completed and Time Horizon	Alternatives Considered	Plan Selected
East Bay Municipal Utility District, California	1995–2020	Imported water Groundwater storage Reclamation Conservation	Groundwater storage Conservation Reclamation
Denver Water, Colorado	1997–2045	Small and large storage Potable, nonpotable reuse Conservation	Conservation Nonpotable reuse Long-term consideration Additional storage Potable reuse
Southern Nevada Water Authority (Las Vegas)	1995–2050	Seasonal groundwater Additional imported Colorado River water Virgin River water Conservation, reuse	Colorado River Shallow aquifer Artificial recharge Reuse Conservation
Metropolitan Water District of Southern California	1996–2020	Additional imported State project water Water transfers Groundwater recovery Water recycling Desalination Conservation	Additional imported water Water transfers Water recycling Conservation
Portland, Oregon	1996–2050	New sources (Clackamas, Willamette, Columbia rivers) New dam on Bull Run Aquifer storage and recovery Water recycling Conservation	Aquifer storage and recovery, Clackamas River intake, Conservation New source after 2025
Columbus, Ohio	1992–2020	Onstream reservoirs Offstream storage Groundwater Conjunctive use Conservation	Conservation Groundwater—new wellfield Offstream storage
Alameda County Water District, California	1995–2030	Agricultural water purchase Additional reservoirs Reclamation Desalination Conservation	Additional storage Reclamation Water transfers Conservation
Colorado Springs, Colorado	1995–2040	Pipeline from Arkansas River Local groundwater System improvements Water recycling Conservation	System improvements Develop groundwater System improvements Conservation Plan pipeline from Arkansas River

different from a *model process*. This section presents a model process and shows some variations. Finally, the components of an IRP are described.

Model IRP Process

Figure 13-1 illustrates a model process that contains all the elements as chapters in this book.

- Demographic trends, historic water use, economic indicators, and climate data are needed to prepare a **water demand forecast**.

- The current and planned **conservation programs**, such as plumbing codes, landscape ordinances, and rebate programs should be accounted for in the forecasts.

- **Forecasts** are needed for normal, dry-year, and critical dry-year conditions, wet years in future years.

- **Supply-side planning** starts with the safe yield of supplies and, if inadequate for future needs, locates alternative groundwater or surface water supplies to meet all or some future demands.

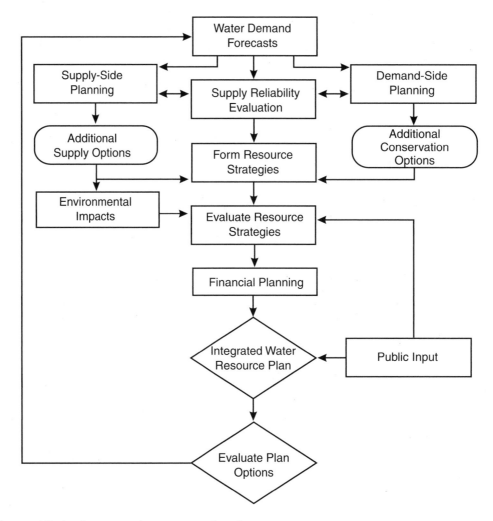

Figure 13–1   Integrated resource planning

- **Demand-side planning** identifies additional conservation methods and wastewater reclamation projects to reduce demand and quantifies their costs and savings. In addition, short-term demand reduction possibilities in critical dry years are quantified.

- The **supply reliability evaluation** ties together the probability of a supply shortage with the short-term demand reductions that could be used to balance supply and demand during droughts. The result is a tabulation of the magnitude and frequency of imposing mandatory short-term demand reduction programs.

- **Resource strategies** are the alternatives that combine new supply development and demand reduction alternatives into a manageable number of combinations.

- **Evaluate resource strategies** involves traditional economics analysis plus consideration of **water quality** and other **environmental impacts**.

- The utility **goals and policies** enter into the evaluation of supply reliability and the resource strategies.

- **Financial planning** is needed at the end to ensure the IRP projects can be funded. The **water rate design** may be radical enough to cause a reduction in water demand that needs to be factored in.

- **Public input** is shown at a couple of key points but needs to be recognized as continuous throughout the process.

- **Evaluation of the results** is a feedback loop to keep the plan updated.

What are the benefits from IRP? Figure 13-2a shows some of the benefits which relate to better utility management.

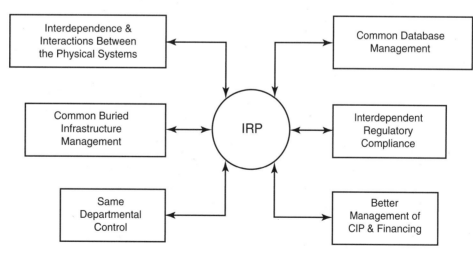

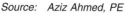

Source: *Aziz Ahmed, PE*

Figure 13–2a   Integrated resource planning–why?

Two Example IRP Process Diagrams

Two variations on the model diagram demonstrate how local situations involve tailoring the model process to fit local conditions. Shown in Figure 13-2b is Denver Water's IRP process. Separate options for Denver and other agencies were accounted for as well as preparation of separate demand forecasts. Demand management was also investigated before being used to form resource strategies.

A different process was used by Alameda County Water District (ACWD) (Figure 13-3). The impact of water supply deficiencies on customers and the groundwater supply was evaluated before considering new supply-side alternatives. If the groundwater is allowed to be drawn down too low, salt water begins to intrude into the aquifer. This intrusion can be avoided by considering shortages (at an acceptable magnitude and frequency) and purchasing new imported water supplies. The goal of an acceptable reliability (shortage management) drives the solution of the alternatives for this IRP.

These two examples demonstrate that the IRP process can be, adapted to local conditions and appropriate aspects emphasized.

Key Components of IRP

The process flow diagrams show how all the information flows together. Certain key components must be included if the process is to be considered an IRP:

- Clear goals and policy objectives adopted by the utility management

- A planning horizon or future design year

- An interdisciplinary process, considering not just engineering details but also a range of key policy objectives

- Equal treatment of supply-side and demand-side options (a level playing field)

- Consideration of supply reliability

- Explicit consideration of uncertainty

- An open process with a heavy dose of public participation

Comparison of Traditional Supply Planning and IRP

IRP evolved from traditional or limited water supply planning that focuses on finding the least-cost solution. Although economic analysis is also important in IRP, environmental impact analysis and reliability analysis are considered. Table 13-2 compares some key criteria that helps explain the enhancements that IRP offers over traditional or *least cost* planning.

Table 13-2 shows that IRP cannot be labeled as "the same old thing." IRP includes extensive analysis of demand management so these options can compete equally with supply options. IRP explicitly considers uncertainty and turns constraints into decision variables. Public participation is used to seek consensus. IRP is inclusive and proactive, as opposed to sporadic public meetings normally associated with traditional supply planning. IRP seeks to identify and analyze trade-offs rather than treat external factors as constraints or *givens*.

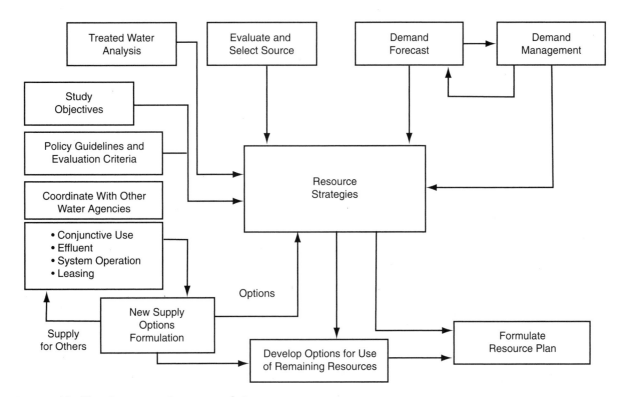

Figure 13–2b   Integrated resource plan

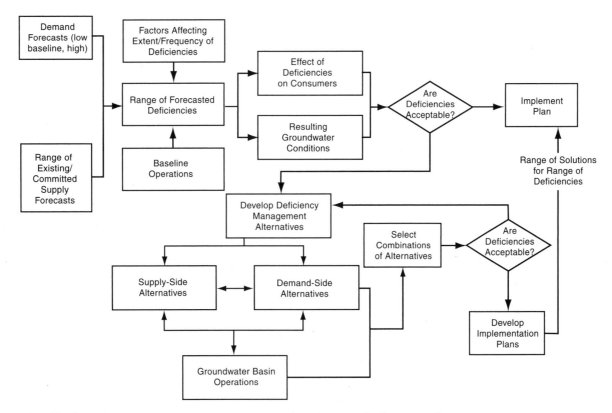

Figure 13–3   Water resources management planning study framework

Table 13–2 Comparison of traditional supply planning and IRP

Criteria	Traditional Planning	Integrated Resource Planning
Resource options	Supply options (demand taken as given)	Demand and supply options (demand can be manipulated)
Resource ownership and control	Utility-owned and centralized	Some resources owned by other utilities, other producers, customers
Plan selection criteria	Minimize costs and maintain system reliability	Diverse criteria, including risk reduction, environmental quality, economic development
Focus of economic cost analysis	Cost to utility	Multiple perspectives (society, program participants, ratepayers, individuals, etc.)
Conduct of planning	Internal to the utility, mainly system planning and financial planning	Several utility departments as well as outside experts commissions staff, public
Role of public groups	Intervenors	Participants
Objectives	Single	Multiple
Supply reliability	Constraint and high priority	Decision variable
Environmental quality	Constraint, comply with regulations	Planning objective
Risk	Should be avoided	Should be managed

Adapted from Beecher, J., *Jour. AWWA,* June 1995.

PLAN OUTLINE

The remainder of the chapter focuses on what needs to be done to gain project approval. Following is a suggested inclusive outline for an integrated water resource plan. Some of these considerations may not be appropriate for all settings.

    I. Executive Summary
        A. Background
        B. Need for a Plan
            1. Increasing Demands
            2. Yield of Sources
            3. Environmental Regulations
        C. Recommended Plan
            1. Process Used to Select Plan
            2. Plan Features
                a. Demand Management
                b. Supply Development
            3. Benefits of Plan
            4. Cost
        D. Implementation Considerations
            1. Institutional

2. Financing
3. Next Steps

II. Introduction
    A. Purpose
        1. Statutory and Regulatory
        2. Management Tool
    B. Objectives and Scope
        1. Level of Service
        2. Costs and Rates
        3. Environmental Impact
        4. Risk of Shortage
    C. Basis of Planning
        1. Planning Horizon
        2. Demographic Projections
        3. Information Sources
        4. Level of Detail
    D. Organization of Report
    E. Acknowledgments

III. Description of Study Area
    A. Map of Study Area
        1. Municipalities, Districts
    B. Watershed Areas
        1. Source of Water Supply Boundaries
        2. Location of Major Streams and Rivers, Groundwater Zones
    C. Demographics
        1. Historical and Future Population
    D. Employment
        1. Historical and Future Projections
    E. Land Use
        1. Tabular Summary by Category for Study Area
        2. Map of Vicinity of Current and Future Water Supply Sources
    F. Wastewater Facilities
        1. Location
        2. Flows
        3. Ongoing Reclamation/Reuse Projects

IV. Water Resource System
    A. Map of Water Supply System
        1. Location of Reservoirs and Well Fields
        2. Location of Major Transmission Facilities
    B. Water Treatment Facilities
        1. Location on Map
        2. Capacity and Type of Treatment
        3. Age and Physical Condition
    C. Finished Water Storage
        1. Capacity by Pressure Zone
    D. List of Known Deficiencies

V. Water Supply Quantity and Quality
    A. Historical Yields of Current Sources
        1. Surface Water Sources
        2. Groundwater Sources

      3. Drought History
   B. Expected Impacts on Current Yields
      1. Land Use
      2. Other Water Right Holders
      3. Environmental
   C. Quality of Sources
      1. Current and Potential Contamination Issues
      2. Compliance With Safe Drinking Water Act

VI. Current and Projected Water Demands
   A. Historical Water Use by Customer Class
      1. Analysis of Monthly Consumption Data
      2. Explanation of Any Trends
   B. Basis of Future Water Demands
      1. Population, Employment, Land Use Projections
      2. Future Service Area

         a. Possible Expansions
         b. Need for Water
   C. Future Demand Projections
      1. Breakdown by Customer Class
      2. Annual Demands at Five-Year Increments
      3. Typical Monthly Fluctuation
      4. Peak Month and Peak Day
   D. Description of Demand Management Program
      1. Codes and Standards
      2. Quantifiable Programs
      3. Replacement of Potable Demands With Recycled Water
         a. Current and Planned Projects
   E. Impact of Current and Planned Conservation
      1. Demand Reduction Caused by US Energy Policy Act
      2. Other Measures Being Implemented
      3. Impact on Peak Month and Peak Day
   F. Future Water Supply Deficits
      1. Future Yields of Current Sources Less Projected Demands
         a. Normal Year/Dry Year/Wet Year
      2. Expected Frequency and Magnitude of Shortages
      3. Water Supply Needs
      4. Water Treatment, Infrastructure Needs

VII. Identification and Preliminary Screening of Demand-Side Management Options
   A. Long-Term Conservation Measures
      1. List of All Feasible Options
      2. Preliminary Screening
         a. Qualitative Criteria
         b. Unit Cost
      3. Description of Most Viable Options
         a. Unit Water Savings
         b. Market Penetration
         c. Unit Costs
      4. Conservation Alternatives
         a. Basis of Alternative—Level of Savings

        b. Projected Water Savings Over Planning Period

        c. Initial and Annual Costs

  B. Short-Term Conservation Measures

    1. Drought Management History in Service Area

        a. Savings Achieved

        b. Costs and Impacts

    2. Drought Contingency Alternatives

        a. Description of Programs for 5 to 35 percent demand cutbacks

        b. Voluntary and Mandatory Programs

        c. Screening

VIII. Identification and Screening of Water Supply Options

  A. New Surface Water Supplies

    1. Water Purchased From Wholesalers

        a. Availability

        b. Cost

        c. Contract Provisions

    2. Source Developed by Utility

        a. Technical Issues

        b. Water Rights Issues

        c. Quantity and Quality Available

        d. Facilities Required and Costs

        e. Expected Approval Process and Time Frame

    3. Preliminary Screening

        a. Technical Feasibility

        b. Reliability

        c. Cost of Water Produced

        d. Probable Environmental Impacts

  B. New Groundwater Development

    1. Location, Yield, and Costs of New Well Fields

    2. Water Quality Issues

        a. Mineral Quality

        b. Status of Any Hazardous Waste Remediation

    3. Infrastructure Required

        a. Location and Capacity

        b. Recharge Opportunities

        c. Costs

    4. Preliminary Screening

        a. Water Quality

        b. Cost of Water Purchased

  C. Conjunctive Use Alternatives

    1. Integrated Surface Water/Groundwater Operation

        a. Recharge Ability During Wet Years

        b. Withdrawal Rates During Dry Years

    2. Aquifer Storage and Recovery Projects

    3. Preliminary Screening

  D. Wastewater Reclamation and Reuse Alternatives

    1. Potential Markets

    2. Relevant Regulations

    3. Potential Projects

        a. Potable Water Replaced

        b. Cost and Time Frame

    4. Preliminary Evaluation
      a. Technological Factors
      b. Cost of Water Produced
      c. Environmental Impact
      d. Description of Viable Projects

IX. Forming Resource Scenarios
  A. Matrix of Possible Combinations of New Supply- and Demand-Side Management (DSM) Possibilities
    1. Scaling Project Size to Meet Future Demands
    2. Timing of Project Development
      a. Use of DSM to Defer New Supply Development
  B. Preliminary Screening
    1. Identify Manageable Number of Options
    2. Describe Features in Detail

X. Evaluation of Resource Options
  A. Economic Evaluation
    1. Selection of Criteria/Methods
      a. See Chapter 12
    2. Present Worth of Options
      a. Rank Order
      b. Cost of Water Produced/Saved
  B. Regulatory Considerations
    1. Water Rights
      a. See Chapter 4
    2. Permitting Issues
    3. Compliance Issues
  C. Risk and Reliability
    1. Probability of Shortage Versus Magnitude of Storage
    2. Frequency of Using Coping Mechanisms
  D. Environmental Impact
    1. Evaluation
      a. See Chapter 10
    2. Qualitative Ranking
  E. Implementation Considerations
    1. Institutional Arrangements
    2. Ease/Difficulty of Financing
  F. Overall Ranking
    1. Matrix Comparison
    2. Ranking According to Incremental Costs
    3. Benefits of Each Option
    4. Results of Public Input
  G. Selection of Recommended Plan
    1. Criteria for Selection
    2. Reasons for Selection

XI. Impact Analysis of Recommended Plan
  A. Economic Impacts
    1. Capital/Debt Financing
    2. Affordability
    3. Impacts on Rates and Charges
      a. Alternative Rate Structures

        b. Guidelines for Rate Study
- B. Environmental Impact Analysis
  1. Regulatory Requirements
  2. Environmental Impact Report (as required)
     a. See Chapter 10
  3. Guidelines for Obtaining Necessary Permits
- C. Drought Contingency and Emergency Management Plan
  1. Sources of Emergency Water
     a. Local Sources
     b. Agreements With Other Utilities
  2. Phased Plan
     a. Expected Shortage Frequency/Magnitude
     b. Actions to Reduce Consumption, as needed
- D. Public Participation
  1. Summary of Public Involvement
  2. Summary of Comments on Draft Integrated Resource Plan
- E. Regional Impacts
  1. Relationship to Nearby Water Utilities
  2. Regional Economic, Environmental, and Social Impacts
  3. Consisting of State and Federal Plans and Policies

XII. Implementation
- A. Utility Organization
  1. Organizations Charts
  2. Roles of Utility Departments
- B. Approval Process
  1. Local (Utility)
  2. Regulatory Agencies
- C. Project Schedule
  1. Tasks Needed to Implement Projects
  2. Key Decisions Points
  3. Milestones
- D. Coordination With Other Agency Planning
  1. Demographic and Land Use
  2. Regional Water Supply
- E. Financing
  1. Financial Plan
  2. Cost Allocation
- F. Ongoing Monitoring and Evaluation
  1. Plan Performance Measurement Criteria
  2. Evaluation Methods

FORMING RESOURCE COMBINATIONS

The water planner usually has many options available to meet future demands. For example, water demands can be reduced through water conservation, certain potable uses may be replaced with recycled (reclaimed) wastewater, new wells drilled, new reservoirs constructed, or new water purchased from regional water suppliers (wholesalers). Evaluating all the options can be tedious and time-consuming. Therefore, a manageable number of alternatives or combinations of resources should be developed that meet certain objectives and criteria and will generally meet future demands in some fashion. This section describes how to compile the options discussed in earlier chapters into resource combinations.

Demand-Side Management

As discussed in chapter 6, resources available to reduce demands during normal years include long-term water conservation and wastewater recycling. During droughts, short-term water conservation programs could help balance available water supply and demand.

Long-term conservation. Conservation measures should be consolidated into three to four programs that can be combined with supply options to meet future demands. Each program could consist of several and as many as 10 or 15 measures. Suggested grouping is listed below.

- **Current codes and regulations.** These programs, including the US Energy Policy Act and landscaping regulations, should be accounted for separately because the decision has already been made to implement these programs. Because these changes are likely to be recent, they are not yet reflected in historical water use patterns. Ordinarily, they will not be accounted for in the base water demand. These programs can be used to produce what can be called a *net demand* projection as described in chapter 3. Net demand means base demand less the effects of implemented conservation programs.

- **Minimum program.** A minimum program contains water conservation measures currently being planned for the next 10 years.

- **Moderate program.** A moderate program contains cost-effective water conservation programs that save more water than the minimum program.

- **Maximum program.** A maximum program consists of a very aggressive conservation program that goes beyond the moderate program and is made of measures that save the most water.

These programs will each have a time stream of costs and water savings that can be integrated with various supply options.

Short-term conservation. The utility's drought history should be examined to gauge the effectiveness of prior short-term programs. Different levels of voluntary to mandatory programs should be formulated to deal with possible water supply shortages. Shortages can also be treated as a resource as managed shortages are a way to meet demand. Shown in Table 13-3 is a typical array of shortage management programs. These programs have been used to achieve 5 to 35 percent cutbacks for months or years, depending on drought severity, location, and system usage patterns.

Table 13–3   Model drought demand management plan

Drought Phase	Water Storage	Actions	Expected Range of Use Reduction (%)
I	Moderate	Voluntary/Public education	5–10
II	Severe	Restricted uses	10–20
III	Critical	Allocation/Rationing	20–35

Source: Urban Drought Guidebook, *Brown and Caldwell (1989).*

Supply-Side Resources

Resource alternatives for water supply include the options covered in chapter 5. These range from groundwater to surface water to conjunctive use.

Increased surface water storage. Reservoirs can be built for carryover storage to increase surface water yield or emergency storage for a drought reserve. New reservoirs are typically difficult to permit because of environmental concerns. Sometimes raising a dam or constructing an off-stream reservoir that is filled by a pipeline from a nearby surface water supply is easier than constructing a new reservoir. In some cases, the reservoir might be constructed by a regional water supplier or another retail water agency that is willing to share the yield.

Groundwater. New well fields can be constructed in the agency service area or in a nearby valley and imported. Wells can be deepened or renovated to increase yield. In some cases, the supply may be from a previously contaminated subsurface reservoir that has been cleaned up. In many coastal areas groundwater development is restricted or discouraged because of saltwater intrusion concerns related to overdrafting. Groundwater modeling, described in chapter 8, can be used to assess the possible increase in water supply.

Conjunctive use. Combining surface water and groundwater resources is conjunctive use. Surface water can be used as the major supply when available and groundwater can be stored for use during dry periods. Excess surface water can also be used to recharge the groundwater basin, to be pumped out later when needed. Conjunctive use is like having two water supplies, one that is highly weather dependent (surface water) and one that is less so (groundwater).

Supplemental supply. Many retail water agencies have the option of purchasing water from a regional supplier. Some have long-standing contracts with their supplier with the possibility to purchase additional water. Local water sources should not be ignored. Although often small, they can increase yield sufficiently to carry the water agency for a number of years.

Water transfers and exchanges. In areas with regional water transmission networks, the possibility to transfer supplies from an agency with a surplus to one with a deficit can be investigated. Sometimes agricultural water agencies are willing to discuss selling the rights to a water supply during dry years, while continuing to use their supply during normal years. The transfer requires a physical way to move water from one agency to another. Sometimes the cooperation of a regional water supplier, who owns the transmission network, is required. These exchanges usually require considerable legal work but a minimal amount of construction.

Additional treatment capacity. Sometimes all that is required to make more water available is to increase treatment capacity. The additional water supply may come from added water purchase, more water from the same source, or a new source requiring treatment. Treatment capacity is optimally expanded incrementally, ahead of the need.

Wastewater Reclamation

As discussed in chapter 6, recycled wastewater, appropriately treated, can be used as a source of water to offset certain current or future potable water demands. For example, golf courses can be irrigated with recycled water, removing them from the potable supply and freeing up water to support growth. Incorporating dual water systems in new developments is considerably less expensive than retrofitting an already developed area. Successful reuse projects usually have the following characteristics:

- Source of treated wastewater discharge reasonably close to high-demand areas.

- High irrigation or industrial demands that can accommodate the recycled water quality (possibly high total dissolved solids and other minerals and organics).

- Ease of constructing pipelines.

- Ability to comply with state regulations at a cost of water produced that is the same as or lower than the marginal cost of new supplies.

Recycled water projects should be characterized by potable use displaced in million gallons per day (mgd), construction cost, annual operating cost, and cost of water produced ($/acre-ft). In some cases, recycled water projects should be interfaced with conservation projects targeted at the same end user. For example, a golf course reuse project may overlap with a turf water audit at the same site. These interactions can be handled as resource options are formulated.

Preliminary Screening

Screening at this stage is based primarily on technical feasibility and institutional factors. Criteria could include the following:

- Technical reliability. Does the technology exist? Has the alternative been proven elsewhere with operational and performance data available?

- Environmental impact. Would some impacts be difficult or impossible to mitigate?

- Institutional feasibility. Does the agency have the water rights to carry out the project or is the cooperation of other agencies required (and unlikely to be achieved)?

- Are extensive institutional or administrative changes required to implement the alternative?

The objective is to eliminate alternatives that have fatal flaws. As many alternatives as possible should be eliminated because the next detailed evaluation phase can be expensive, such as preparing an environmental impact report on a new reservoir. The next section describes the detailed evaluation process for the alternatives that pass the preliminary screening.

EVALUATING RESOURCE COMBINATIONS

Resource combinations are water supply and demand reduction scenarios or alternatives that improve water supply reliability at some cost and may have environmental and other impacts. The evaluation process helps decision makers understand the trade-offs between meeting future demands and improving supply reliability and associated costs. The evaluation process must be rigorous, fair, and address all reasonable issues raised by the public, technical advisory committee members, and other stakeholders. The process begins with selecting objectives or evaluation criteria and then analyzing the alternatives with respect to the objectives and criteria. Finally, the results of the evaluation must be presented in a clear and unbiased manner because they will be subjected to intense public scrutiny and public input is likely to change how alternatives are rated.

Select Objectives or Evaluation Criteria

The first step is to identify appropriate measures of effectiveness. Evaluation does not mean that costs should be minimized or effectiveness maximized. Rather, a balance should be struck. This balance should be developed in the public arena, through negotiation among the stakeholders. Evaluation criteria should include various measures of performance or effectiveness as well as environmental impacts and public acceptability. Listed here are a few suggested criteria that can be tailored to specific projects. In some cases, the evaluation is enhanced if objectives are written that quantify or at least qualify what is meant by the criteria. For example, a criterion might be cost but the objective could be stated to *minimize agency costs* or *minimize water rate impacts*, both of which are more specific and easier for comparative ratings of alternative scenarios. Suggested criteria include

- costs

- risk and reliability

- environmental impact

- public acceptability

Some general guidelines for applying each suggested criterion are provided here.

Economic Analysis

As discussed in chapter 12, the economic analysis should be based on present worth, which is a way of equalizing alternatives that have different time streams of costs and benefits. Cost categories include capital (including project design, construction, and mitigation) and operations and maintenance expenditures. Key issues in present worth analysis include the length of the time period and the discount rate. Typically, 20 to 50 years are used in the analysis of water resource projects, because they have very long useful lives. Discount rates are usually selected to reflect the true cost of money, which is defined as the cost of borrowing money (by a public utility) minus the inflation rate. Historically, the true cost of money has been 3 to 4 percent.

In some cases, a benefit–cost (B/C) analysis is a desirable way to compare alternatives. If the benefits can be quantified, the present worth of their time stream can be calculated. Many of the reservoirs currently operating in the United States were justified with a B/C analysis. This necessitates putting a value on such benefits as flood protection, recreational opportunities, and water supply, as well as negative benefits such as environmental impacts. Most IRPs have not used B/C analysis, instead relying on displaying costs, project features, and impacts in qualitative or numeric terms that allow the public to establish relative worth and make value judgments related to project attributes and impacts, such as improved reliability. If a B/C analysis is to be conducted, selecting the discount rate and evaluation period is critical. Longer periods favor staged alternatives, those with deferred costs, or those with benefits that increase over time. Shorter periods favor alternatives with high initial benefits.

Supply Reliability

A goal of an IRP is to improve water supply reliability for the water agency's customers. Reliability refers to the degree to which customers receive their water within acceptable quality and service standards. Future water demands may instigate supply shortages reduced to acceptable levels. Specifically, water supply reliability can be defined in three ways:

- Reliability to meet short-term local emergencies. These emergencies involve sudden catastrophes, such as a main break or major fire. Typically, goals are to have one to 10 days of locally stored water.

- Reliability to meet medium-duration delivery system emergencies. Some agencies may want to maintain local storage to meet demand over a more extended period, such as might result from a seismic event, a major spill, or an imported water supply disruption. For example, goals might be to have two to seven months of storage, based on an assumed reduction in demand, of 25 percent.

- Reliability to meet long-term demands. In this case, goals should be set to balance supply and demand during below-normal water supply years. Quantified goals may include a maximum 15 to 25 percent shortage in dry periods and a maximum 25 to 30 percent shortage in a worst-case drought.

If the alternative being evaluated includes sufficient local storage, the first goal can be met. Meeting the second goal requires an analysis of the likely system failures and the length of the outages at current and future demands. Alternative sources or mandatory restrictions may be sufficient to meet the third goal; otherwise, the alternative must be downrated. Meeting the third goal can be evaluated with hydrologic simulation modeling. Such a model would simulate the historical record of water supply on a monthly (or shorter interval) basis and compare water availability with future monthly water demands. Water supply deficits during dry periods would be recorded and the probability of a shortage of a certain magnitude and duration computed. Alternatives would be scored on their ability to meet goals, and would be down-rated depending on the frequency and magnitude of shortages that are greater than planned.

An example of how to display the results of an alternative's ability to avoid long-term shortages is shown in Figure 13-4. This analysis can be performed assuming average demand or dry year demands (in which cases the shortages would be greater). For example, 2020 demands could be superimposed on the hydrologic record and years with a shortage determined. The frequency distribution of the shortages would be constructed as shown in Figure 13-4. From an analysis of this type, the planner will be able to state the percent of the years that a given or higher level shortage will occur. As shown in Figure 13-4, a 10 percent shortage will occur 40 percent of the time. This alternative would probably be down-rated on reliability.

Another simpler approach is to evaluate system performance during a *design drought*, selected from the historical record or possibly from a modified record. In California, many reservoirs built from 1950 to 1970 were designed to meet demands during the worst drought on record, which was the 1928 to 1934 dry year sequence. As always seems to be the case, a worse drought has since occurred. The drought period from 1987 to 1992 caused the available yield from many reservoirs to be downgraded, because there were serious shortages. One way to evaluate delivery capacity from extant and new reservoirs in such cases is to assume a design drought consisting of the 1987 to 1992 period, extended, for example, by two years (with the recent droughts in many areas from 2002 on, design drought for each area needs to be evaluated and more recent information used, if applicable). Comparing the yield during the design drought with future demands may produce a shortage that would establish the reliability of the system under the worst-case scenario. Comparing how alternatives perform during a design drought is another way to quantify and compare reliability.

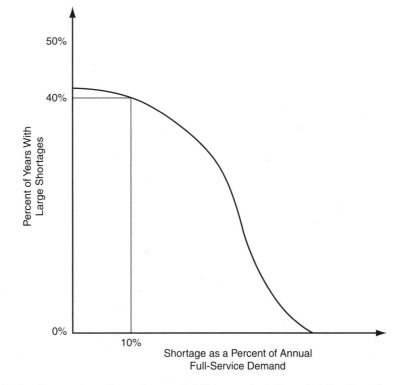

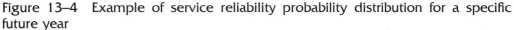

Figure 13–4   Example of service reliability probability distribution for a specific future year

Environmental Impacts

Environmental impacts may be positive or negative, and sometimes can be dealt with as environmental externalities. For water agencies, externalities are defined as costs (or benefits) that relate to providing water service but are external to the agency and are not included in the agency's cost of service, such as the use of a resource for which it does not pay, like a river. Someone or something (e.g., fish or wildlife) is paying the cost. Many external costs and benefits, including effects on the quality of an estuary or river, effects on the source of supply, aesthetics, air quality, recreation, wildlife, jobs, and energy use or savings, can be identified. Jordan (1995) described methods for evaluating externalities. Chapter 10 describes the procedure for preparing an environmental impact report, including factors that can be used to rate an alternative. If the impacts cannot be quantified and dealt with as externalities, they should at least be rated in a matrix, with scores assigned based on qualitative information.

Public Acceptability

Later in this chapter, guidelines are provided for running an effective public education program. It is difficult for a water resource planner to gauge public acceptability of an alternative without asking customers. Advisory committees and public meetings can provide feedback on alternatives. This feedback can be translated into screening criteria that will eliminate alternatives that have severe institutional problems or unacceptable public impacts.

Ranking the Scenarios

The performance of a scenario can be rated against a criterion or objective and then compared in a matrix format. There are different ways to rate alternatives, and two examples will be given from actual IRPs. Table 13-4 shows the evaluation matrix used by the ACWD. The ACWD calls its resource combinations *sequences*. The ACWD rated its nonquantifiable criteria on an ordinal scale of 1 to 3. Lower numbers were preferred. Numerical values for each scenario were calculated by adding the values of individual resource options in proportion to the amount of new supply provided. In this case, no clear winners emerged, only trade-offs that are appropriate for decision makers to discuss and evaluate. In the end, sequence 3 was determined to best meet the ACWD's policy objectives.

Another example is provided in Figure 13-5. In this example, the Santa Clara Valley Water District staff evaluated four hybrid (resource) strategies against six primary objectives. Other objectives are shown but not evaluated because stakeholders asked the staff to focus on these six objectives. The strategies are rated against each objective using high, medium, and low performance and with pluses and minuses within each level. Stakeholder comments are reflected in the rankings. By displaying alternatives in this manner, a preferred strategy may become obvious, taking the best features of each alternative to maximize the ranking.

In some cases, the costs can be plotted versus the rankings. In this case, the criteria should be weighted and the weighted summations of all the scores plotted versus cost. Spending more and more money at some point nets very little in terms of improved rankings or scores. Beyond a certain point, the additional costs do not add measurable value, so the planner can compare alternatives that deliver approximately the same performance for similar costs and select from a subset of the initial scenarios.

A plan is usually selected by developing a preferred strategy from the alternative scenarios considered. The selection may seem to be the end of the IRP process, but it is actually the beginning of the implementation phase. The IRP is designed to be a dynamic document that must respond to changing times and be periodically updated.

SELECTING AND IMPLEMENTING A PLAN

Considering Cost-Effectiveness

In least-cost planning, selecting the preferred plan is relatively simple. The minimum cost plan that meets a reliability goal and other constraints is selected (often displayed graphically as in Figure 13-6). The total cost is the sum of the cost of new resources and the customer costs or willingness to pay. The latter is the inverse of customer costs for not having sufficient reliability. As reliability declines, customers must pay to mitigate the shortages or they will incur losses. Data on customers' willingness to pay can be obtained through public input or contingent valuation surveys. In one study, residential customers in California were willing to pay \$12 to \$17 more per month to avoid water shortages similar to those during the 1970s, 1980s, and 1990s. The amount of money that should be invested is represented by the least amount of cost needed to meet the reliability goal. In the real world, least-cost planning is not sophisticated enough to identify the preferred option. Environmental impacts and mitigation costs can complicate the selection process. Environmental mitigation costs add to the resource costs and shift the optimum point as shown on

Table 13-4 Evaluation of resource sequences

Evaluation Criteria	Sequence 1	Sequence 2	Sequence 3	Sequence 3A	Sequence 4	Sequence 5	Sequence 6	Sequence 6A	Sequence 7
Cost ($ millions)*	$25	$104	$62	$61	$41	$54	$51	$34	$49
Reliability (expected unserved demand in drought years)†	24%	10%	10%	10%	10%	10%	10%	10%	10%
Maximum monthly hardness (mg/L)	238†	150	150	150–175‡	150–175‡	150–175‡	150	175–238§	150
Environmental impact	1.3	1.8	1.3	1.4	1.3	1.2	1.2	1.0	1.4
ACWD control	1.3	1.5	1.3	1.3	2.1	1.9	1.9	1.9	1.8
Water availability risk	1.2	1.5	1.1	1.1	2.0	1.8	1.8	1.8	1.5
Financial risk	1.5	1.9	1.7	1.7	1.5	1.8	1.7	1.5	1.6
Water quality risk	2.4	2.1	2.2	2.1	2.6	2.3	2.5	2.5	2.4

NOTE: Lower numbers are preferable.

*Net present value of capital and variable operating costs of new resources.
†1 in 30 years probability of occurrence. Expected *annual* unserved demand expressed as a percentage of full-service *annual* demand.
‡Seasonal increases in hardness.
§175 mg/L annually, up to 238 mg/L during drought years.

Alameda County Water District, 1995

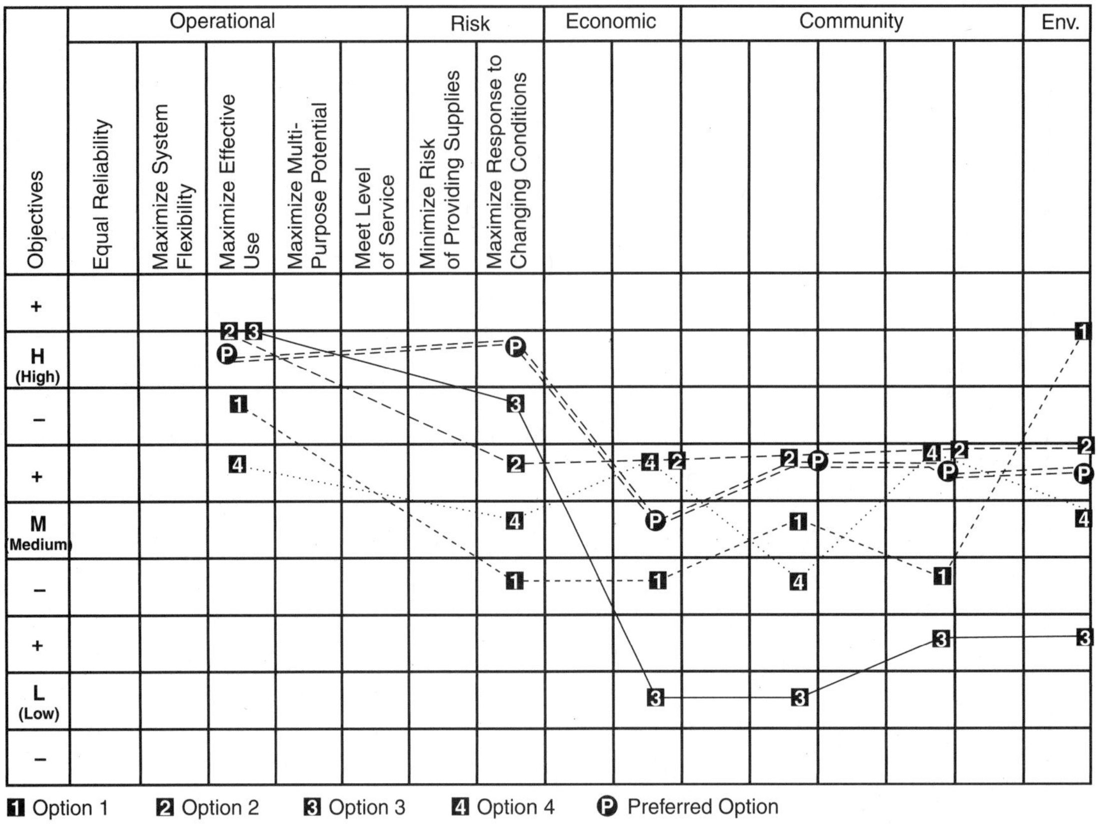

Objectives	Operational					Risk		Economic	Community					Env.
	Equal Reliability	Maximize System Flexibility	Maximize Effective Use	Maximize Multi-Purpose Potential	Meet Level of Service	Minimize Risk of Providing Supplies	Maximize Response to Changing Conditions							
+			**2 3** **P**				**P**							**1**
H (High)														
–			**1**				**3**							
+			**4**			**2**		**4 2**	**2 P**		**4 2** **P**			**2 P**
M (Medium)						**4**		**P**		**1**				**4**
–						**1**		**1**		**4**		**1**		
+												**3**		**3**
L (Low)								**3**		**3**				
–														

1 Option 1   **2** Option 2   **3** Option 3   **4** Option 4   **P** Preferred Option

Figure 13–5 Consideration and ranking of many alternatives is a feature of integrated resource planning

Figure 13-7. A higher cost is the likely result, with the possibility of a new reliability goal.

Identifying Near-Term Actions

For the preferred option to remain focused on a long-term vision, the plan should be updated every three to five years as conditions change. What is important in the present is what should be done in the near-term. Actions could include

- carry out activities to ensure that baseline assumptions continue to be valid,

- establish a budget and schedule for implementing individual preferred strategy components,

- develop contingency plans as conditions change,

- begin environmental documentation to implement the preferred strategy,

- monitor water demands,

- monitor the availability and quality of selected new supplies, and

- continue public outreach and participation for subsequent approvals required.

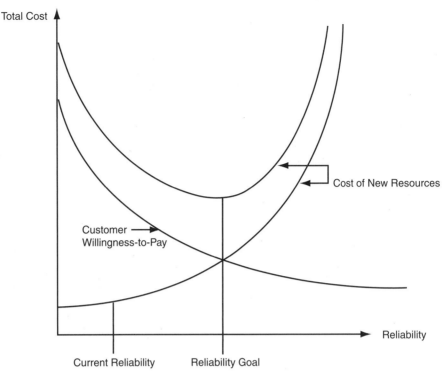

Source: Courtesy of Gary Fiske, Fiske & Associates

Figure 13–6   Determining the optimum (least-cost) level of water supply reliability

Identifying Contingency Actions

To keep the preferred plan flexible and to respond to changing conditions, utilities should develop contingency plans of action. Contingency actions would be activated by *trigger* events that may significantly affect assumed baseline conditions or the agency's ability to implement the preferred strategy. These events would require the utility to either reevaluate the IRP or adjust the preferred strategy. Potential triggers could include

- resolution or change in regional or statewide water controversies
- failure of a component to perform as expected
- unexpected changes in water demands (increasing or decreasing faster than expected)
- source water quality degradation
- performance of a component that exceeds expectations
- partnerships with other agencies
- failure to obtain a key permit
- emerging technologies

NEPA and Environmental Permitting Issues

Very often, one or more resources that comprise the preferred option will require that an Environmental Impact Statement (EIS) be prepared under the National

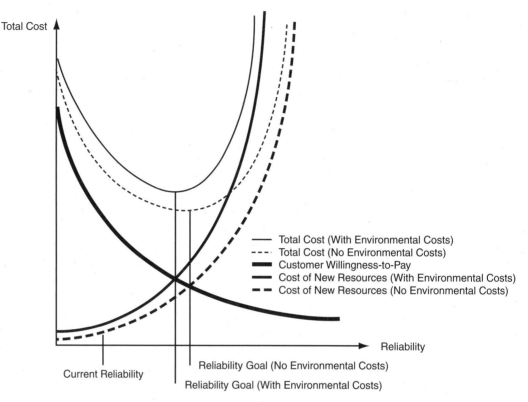

Source: Courtesy of Gary Fiske, Fiske & Associates

Figure 13–7   Effect of environmental costs on water supply reliability

Environmental Policy Act (NEPA). As described in chapters 9 and 10, the EIS and permit applications can have very detailed and onerous requirements. In some cases, the IRP may be completed as a part of the EIS process. The EIS process requires consideration of alternatives and doing an EIS after the IRP may require redoing some steps in the evaluation process. On the other hand, the EIS should not be started until it is clear that the likely preferred option will require an EIS. An agency must decide at what point a formal NEPA review should be initiated. That decision will affect the scope, schedule, and budget of the planning effort, particularly concerning the range of alternatives and level of detail that must be considered.

Financing the IRP

The IRP should include a financial element. Financing options to pay for the IRP elements fall into several categories:

- Bond financing, normally used for large capital projects

- Borrowing, often used for smaller capital projects

- Connection and other new account fees, often used to create a capital reserve fund to pay for incremental expansions of the water system

- Water rates, normally used to pay for ongoing administrative, operation, maintenance, and debt financing costs

The AWWA manual M1, *Principles of Water Rates, Fees, and Charges*, should be consulted as the financing plan is created.

REFERENCES

Alameda County Water District. 1995. Integrated Resources Planning Study. Alameda, Calif.

American Water Works Association. December 1993. White Paper on Integrated Resource Planning in the Water Industry.

Barakat and Chamberlin. 1992. Water Supply Reliability in California: How Much Do We Have? How Much Do We Need? Phase 1, prepared for the California Urban Water Agencies. Sacramento, Calif.

Barakat and Chamberlin. August 1994. The Value of Water Supply Reliability: Results of a Contingent Valuation Survey of Residential Customers, Prepared for the California Urban Water Agencies. Sacramento, Calif.

Barakat and Chamberlin. 1994. Integrated Resource Planning: A Balanced Approach to Water Resources Decision-Making, prepared for American Water Works Association Research Foundation. Denver, Colo.

Beecher, J. 1995. Integrated Resource Planning Fundamentals. *Jour. AWWA*, 87(6).

California Department of Water Resources. 1989. *Urban Drought Guidebook*, Brown and Caldwell. Walnut Creek, Calif.

Integrated Resource Plan. 1997. Denver Water Board. Denver, Colo.

Jordan, J. 1995. Incorporating externalities in conservation programs, *Jour. AWWA*, 87(6).

Santa Clara Valley Water District. 1997. Integrated Water Resources Plan Executive Summary. Santa Clara, Calif.: Santa Clara Valley Water District.

Vista Consulting Group. 1997. Guidelines for Implementing an Effective Integrated Resource Planning Process, prepared for American Water Works Association Research Foundation. Denver, Colo.

This page intentionally blank

Chapter **14**

Case Studies

To illustrate the planning principles discussed in the preceding chapters, this final chapter will briefly discuss several water resources planning case studies. There is no claim that these case studies are representative of the resource planning activities being undertaken in the industry. Rather, they are designed to amplify and make more concrete the material presented to this point.

In each case, the salient features of each planning process are described, as are the outcomes of that process, to this point. No normative judgments are made. Particular plans are not labeled as *successes* or *failures* for several reasons:

- Identifiable *bad* outcomes (e.g., a permit application being rejected) may be caused by a variety of factors other than the manner in which a plan was carried out. A *good* plan could well lead to a bad outcome.

- A particular outcome may be viewed as a success by some and a failure by others.

- The fairly recent completion of many of these plans makes it difficult to forecast some of the ultimate outcomes.

- The shock of a bad outcome can have some benefits, such as redirecting the water resource thinking of an agency or a region. A near-term failure can lead to long-term successes.

Case studies were prepared by staff at the named utilities. While there are no specific references for each, the material is a summary of events and outcomes that occurred over a number of years. For additional details on the case study, the reader is advised to contact the utility named directly.

CASE STUDY #1: CITY OF NEWPORT NEWS, VA AND THE KING WILLIAM RESERVOIR PROJECT

Background

Since 1987, the cities and counties of the lower Virginia Peninsula in southeastern Virginia have engaged in finding and completing water resource projects to meet future water needs through 2050. These communities, populated by close to 400,000 people, include the cities of Newport News, Hampton, Poquoson, and Williamsburg, and the Counties of James City and York. They also include eight military/federal installations that will receive water from this project as well as two water supply host communities west of the Peninsula. This work complements and builds on an earlier effort by James City County to build a reservoir, an effort vetoed by the US Environmental Protection Agency (USEPA).

After extensive evaluation of thirty-five possible alternatives, the Peninsula communities selected a three-part program that included more intensive water conservation, desalting of brackish groundwater and construction of an off-stream storage reservoir in King William County. The first two parts of the solution (more intensive water conservation and desalting brackish groundwater) have been implemented. A federal permit for the reservoir is still in process.

The proposed King William Reservoir (KWR) is to be located in the upper reaches of Cohoke Creek, a small tributary of the Pamunkey River in King William County, Virginia, approximately 3.5 miles upstream of the existing Cohoke Millpond dam. It will have an 8.9 square mile drainage area, a 1,526 acre surface area, and a total storage volume of 12.2 billion gallons at a normal pool elevation of 96' MSL. The reservoir will occupy 27 percent of the watershed, but the primary water source will be the nearby Mattaponi River. Water will be withdrawn from the river in times of high to moderate natural flows. There will be no withdrawals during low flows, when salinity and other aquatic factors may be a concern. Water will be pumped from the new KWR to Newport News Waterworks' existing Diascund Reservoir, in New Kent County.

Issues

From the beginning, the regional Peninsula partners worked closely with state and federal agencies as a team to address environmental and cultural issues. Until the late 1990s, this seemed to be an effective strategy. Agencies and localities worked together to address several issues, and they successfully produced complex mitigation plans.

Environmental

The primary environmental issues relate to the impacts to 403 acres of wetlands and 34 acres of open waters in the Cohoke Creek project area. Other issues have to do with actual or potential wetland impacts downstream of the new dam, in the new pipeline easements, and at the Diascund Reservoir outfall on Beaverdam Creek; potential changes to water quality (principally salinity concentrations) and fish populations in the Mattaponi River; and potential impacts to species protected under the Endangered Species Act.

The proposed wetland mitigation plan includes restoration and creation of 822 acres of wetlands, more than double the 403 acres in the footprint of the Reservoir, and a 110-acre contingency site. Most of the mitigation project sites are adjacent to surface watercourses and extensive tracts of existing wetlands and uplands that will be protected and preserved. There are 822 acres of primary mitigation sites and 80 percent of these, or 655 acres, would be restoration of previously degraded wetlands.

After four years of detailed cooperative investigations by an interagency mitigation team, which included the US Army Corps of Engineers (Corps), the US Fish and Wildlife Service (USFWS), the USEPA, the Virginia Department of Environmental Quality (VDEQ), and others, a wetland mitigation plan was drafted. The interagency team accepted all of the sites in the proposed mitigation plan as suitable wetland mitigation sites for the KWR project. There are also plans to preserve 400 acres of existing wetlands adjacent to mitigation project sites, and approximately 322 acres of shoreline wetlands and shallow water habitat are expected to develop around the reservoir itself.

Mitigation plans for two threatened plants—the small whorled pogonia and sensitive joint-vetch—were completed. However, since the plants were first discovered, the small whorled pogonia has disappeared as a result of beaver activity and private logging in the area. A series of studies indicated that impact to the small joint-vetch population by the project is unlikely.

Cultural Resources

There are three Native American Indian tribes, with cultural/historic ties to the area, in the county where the reservoir is to be built. Two tribes are on reservations, and the third tribe maintains property in the county. The Corps' (Norfolk District) 1997 Final Environmental Impact Statement (EIS) concluded that the project would not result in any disproportionately high and adverse human health or environmental effects on minority populations and low income populations, and it documented several objective, persuasive reasons for its conclusion. The project will not encroach on any tribal lands, and the proposed water intake structure is 5.5 river miles upstream of the closest reservation.

The Peninsula communities established contacts with the three tribes beginning in 1990. By 1997, a team of state and federal agencies, Native American tribal representatives, and Newport News as the applicant (representing the Peninsula communities) began two years of work to draft a Memorandum of Agreement (MOA) that addressed potential effects and mitigation of effects on historic resources and cultural properties. The draft MOA was undergoing final negotiations by June 1999.

Outcomes to Date

In the mid-1990s, opposition to the project, led primarily by the Sierra Club, began growing. The group linked the project to their national campaign to "stop sprawl." Despite the applicant's ongoing consultation with Native American tribes in King William County, one Native American tribe filed a lawsuit against the state regarding its permit for the project.

The Virginia Water Protection Permit was issued for the project in late 1997, but at the federal level, one delay after another was occurring. The Corps required a new needs assessment, despite the fact that one had been part of the EIS that they published in 1997. The Corps contracted with Planning and Management Consultants, Ltd. (PMCL) to review the Peninsula's water use forecast, and this was followed by a needs assessment by the Corps' Institute of Water Resources, IWR, completed in 2000. IWR validated the need for additional water but did not agree on the exact amount that was needed for the planning period.

In June 1999, the Norfolk District Engineer issued a letter stating a preliminary position to deny a federal permit. His letter effectively terminated consultations with interested Native American tribes and suspended the Corps' review of the applicant's proposed wetland mitigation plan. Several other essential activities also came to a halt. That same month, Virginia's Governor Gilmore requested the Corps to reconsider its position. This activated a Corps regulation that refers decisions by a district that are in conflict with a sitting governor to be referred to the division level, in this case the North Atlantic Division in New York.

During 1999 and 2000, the Peninsula communities produced additional reports on the primary issues of contention and contracted for an updated and extensive needs assessment. Despite these efforts, the Norfolk District Engineer's final recommendation, submitted to the North Atlantic Division in July 2001, was to deny the 404 permit.

The Peninsula communities waited for more than a year while the Corps' North Atlantic Division conducted a thorough review of the project's record. In October 2002, the Peninsula communities received stunning and welcome news. The Corps' North Atlantic Division commander issued a decision to continue the permit process. General M. Stephen Rhoades said, "The project's purpose and need as submitted by the City of Newport News were valid." He also found that the King William Reservoir is the least environmentally damaging practicable alternative to meet that need based on current information. However, General Rhoades required the satisfactory completion of three steps before a permit decision could be issued:

1. Coordination must be completed under the National Historic Preservation Act of 1966, including resolution of Native American issues.

2. The applicant must submit an updated wetland mitigation plan for review and approval by the Corps.

3. The Commonwealth of Virginia must determine whether the project is in compliance with its *Coastal Zone Management Act* (CZMA) program.

At this writing, the Peninsula communities are still awaiting guidance from the Corps on the first two issues and are working with the state on the CZMA permit. Two lawsuits against the state regarding its Water Protection Permit (Virginia's CWA 401 certification) for the reservoir are in process, one from an alliance of opponents and one from a Native American tribe. These cases continued through 2003 and on.

The earliest that this project can be built, filled, and functioning is 2012. Meanwhile, the region, along with most of the state of Virginia and much of the country, suffered a serious drought in 2002. Water utilities on the Peninsula had called for mandatory water restrictions, and some had gone so far as to consider at what point water rationing would be necessary. The drought, while significant, was not historic, and it underscored the need for the project for the near term as well as for the long term.

The communities backing this project have often asked themselves why this project took the turn that it did with the Corps' District office and with at least one Native American tribe. Efforts were made since the beginning of the project to avoid such roadblocks. Region 3 of the USEPA lauded this project as a model project because of the level of consensus process that had been established. The Peninsula communities will be evaluating the project's history to see what corrective actions might have made a difference.

CASE STUDY #2: CASE STUDY FOR REGIONAL WATER PLANNING IN TEXAS

Background

Texas is a large state with widely varying hydrological conditions, particularly from west to east. The Texas Water Development Board (TWDB) has been charged with developing a state water plan through a consensus process with other state agencies, river authorities, municipalities, agricultural interests, and others since the drought of record in the late 1950s. While these plans all had significant local and regional involvement, they were all top-down initiates, i.e., proposed by TWDB.

The 1997 Texas Legislative session saw the passage of what was then known as Senate Bill 1, the Brown-Lewis Bill. This bill authorized TWDB to pursue the development of a statewide water plan by first establishing regional planning areas within Texas. Sixteen regional planning areas, primarily based on river basin associations, were created and each regional planning area submitted a list of names for potential appointment to a regional water-planning group (RWPG). Each RWPG was composed of representatives from eleven interest groups, including municipalities, counties, water districts, water utilities, industries, small businesses, agriculture, electric power generation, environmental groups, river authorities, and the general public.

The Planning Process

Each RWPG was funded through appropriations from the Texas Legislature and administered through the TWDB. Each group selected a consultant to perform the necessary tasks to develop a consensus plan for each area. Each group was required to develop a public involvement plan and to hold public meetings to discuss various milestones in the plan with the general public. Records of comments received at all public meetings were kept and comments were responded to throughout the planning process and in the final report from each RWPG to the TWDB.

TWDB provided baseline population and water demand data through their own demographers and outlined the strategy that must be followed for those regions that desired to adjust the TWDB numbers. Each region then used existing data to identify the groundwater and surface water availabilities for their region, with particular emphasis paid to waters that were shared by one or more regions to ensure that the water was correctly allocated by region. Use of groundwater in Texas is generally under the right of capture unless the right of capture is modified through rules of a properly constituted groundwater conservation district. Use of surface water was traced through rights, contracts, and other means of allocating firm yield water from all sources.

Available supplies were compared with projected demands through a 50-year planning horizon. Shortages were identified through this comparison, and management strategies were developed to provide the additional water necessary to meet these shortages. Conservation was generally the first strategy, even to the extent that TWDB water demands had conservation built into their projections and often to the level of advanced conservation. Greater utilization of existing supplies through contract renewals and expansions were generally the next strategy, followed by increased use of groundwater where available, and then by development of new surface water supply sources, including both new reservoirs and desalination of both brackish groundwater and seawater.

Each of the management strategies developed had to be evaluated based on the following criteria:

- Estimated costs for development of the water, including transmission and treatment costs at the point of introduction to the distribution system;

- Environmental flows impacts;

- Impacts on wildlife and wildlife habitat;

- Impacts on cultural resources;

- Impacts on other water resources;

- Ground/surface water interrelationships; and,

- Socioeconomic impacts.

The regional plans from each of the RWPGs were developed between June of 1998, and December of 2000, with the completed plans submitted to TWDB in January 2001. The TWDB then used these regional plans to develop a unified statewide plan by meeting with the RWPGs to resolve any conflicts and differences between the plans. A final series of hearings on the state draft plan were held in 2001, and the adopted state plan was finalized in January 2002.

The 2002 State Water Plan identified approximately $17 billion of improvements that are needed over the next 50 years to provide the necessary water for the populations and water uses anticipated during that time period. The regional RWPG process saw significant progress made in interregional cooperation as win/win strategies were identified through intergroup meetings and an understanding that if the needs were not met through cooperative strategies, everyone lost the ability to control their own resources and control would default to TWDB. One significant example of this cooperation is the interregional strategy that was proposed to provide water supplies to one region from another region for municipal use; and in exchange, the recipient region paid to develop additional agricultural water supplies in the other region. Without this compromise, those agricultural needs could not be met.

Plan Outcomes

Many of the large 2002 State Water Plan projects are associated with a major water provider who has shown the commitment and capability to follow through with large projects. TWDB is providing limited planning grants to entities interested in developing regional facilities plans for implementing the State Water Plan on a local basis. TWDB has also gone forward with a request for Statements of Interest for a Desalination Demonstration Project in Texas.

In addition, the State Water Plan is set on a 5-year cycle for updating and incorporating new information into the plans. The first cycle is almost complete, with the aim of identifying those strategies that are less likely to be implemented and developing more feasible strategies to replace them. The 2007 State Water Plan was adopted by the TWDB on November 14, 2006.

CASE STUDY #3: PORTLAND, OREGON, REGIONAL WATER SUPPLY PLAN

Background

The tri-county Portland metropolitan region is a water-rich but rapidly growing area. Much of the region is currently served from the city of Portland's Bull Run system. The Bull Run is a protected watershed on federal land, the water rights of which are held by the city of Portland. The Portland Water Bureau operates two seasonal storage reservoirs on Bull Run. Parts of the region are served by other primarily surface water sources.

In 1992, 27 water providers in the region banded together to develop Phase 2 of the Regional Water Supply Plan (RWSP). Partway through the process, Metro, the regional land use planning agency, officially became a plan participant. The Phase 1 work, which had already been completed, had narrowed the field of feasible supply options to six possibilities, all of which, along with conservation and transmission options, were to be examined in Phase 2. The Phase 2 planning horizon was through the year 2050.

The Planning Process

The RWSP Project was funded and managed through an intergovernmental agreement that set up a participants' committee, consisting of all participating agencies, and a smaller steering committee. The participants' committee met monthly, and the 6-member steering committee met at least every two weeks, over a period of three years. The project also included an extensive public involvement program.

The planning process included development of a detailed econometric regional and subregional demand forecasting model. The model estimated average annual, seasonal, and peak-day demand, and reflected the impacts of naturally occurring conservation through a vintaging algorithm.

An early task that involved participating agencies and stakeholders was to develop a set of policy objectives and associated measurable evaluation criteria. Strategies were ultimately evaluated against these criteria, and information was developed for each resource option to facilitate this evaluation. Objectives were developed to cover such areas as

- costs and rates

- water supply reliability

- environmental impacts

- system efficiency

- raw and treated water quality

- vulnerability to catastrophic events

The RWSP included an extensive assessment of potential conservation measures and the development of a set of conservation programs. It also included an analysis of transmission alternatives to move water around the region.

As part of the planning effort, a simulation model was developed as the major tool to analyze and compare resource strategy alternatives in terms of their performance against the evaluation criteria. This modeling tool enabled the development and evaluation of many strategy alternatives.

A preliminary RWSP was issued in August 1995, after approximately 27 months of work. It was circulated for review and comments by all governmental decision-making bodies involved in the plan, as well as by citizens and stakeholders. Comments were solicited through a newsletter, workshops, and public meetings. After a five-month review period, all participant entities responded to the plan. During the early months of 1996, a package of plan changes to respond to the received comments was prepared and issued in March 1996. These proposed changes underwent further review over the summer and by October 1996, the final plan was prepared.

The final RWSP contains recommended near-term and long-term strategies for meeting future water needs through 2050. In all cases, these strategies indicate that water needs for the Portland Metropolitan region through 2025 can be met through conservation efforts, by constructing transmission interties, and by developing or improving regional water sources currently on line (including the Columbia South Shore well field), already under construction or programmed for development before 2005. Many regional water providers are active participants in the Columbia/Willamette Conservation Coalition to coordinate and develop effective conservation programs. Major new development of sources such as the Clackamas River, aquifer storage and recovery, or a currently unidentified source increment would likely not be required before 2023.

Plan Outcomes

As of September 1998, most plan implementation actions focused on conservation. A number of the region's providers, through the Columbia/Willamette Conservation Coalition, began to implement the more extensive conservation programs recommended in the plan. A critical outcome of the RWSP process was the formation of the Regional Water Providers Consortium. Almost all participants in the RWSP signed a new intergovernmental agreement to join and fund this consortium. Members pay dues based on their current size and forecasted growth. A portion of the dues funds a part-time staff. The consortium will be responsible for implementing and updating the RWSP and will function as a coordinating body for other issues affecting the provision of municipal water services.

Since September 1998, the consortium has continued to function and has addressed many regional water supply and infrastructure concerns. Among other things, the consortium funded a large study of regional transmission alternatives. In addition, the functions of the Columbia/Willamette Conservation Coalition were incorporated into the consortium to ensure better coordination of supply-side and demand-side planning for the region. In mid-2002, the consortium began the first five-year update of the RWSP, which was completed in December 2004.

CASE STUDY #4: CITY OF COLORADO SPRINGS, COLORADO, INTEGRATED RESOURCE PLAN

Background

Colorado Springs Utilities (CSU) supplies 70 mgd ($0.26 \ m^3/d$) of surface water from the Rocky Mountains to approximately 380,000 people. The first diversion project, the local Pikes Peak system, began in the 1870s. Several other systems have been developed since that time, bringing water from as far as 200 miles (321 km) away. The delivery systems for these remote supplies are adequate until 2010, but by 2040 another 55 mgd (0.21 m³/d) of delivery capacity will be needed to accommodate a projected growth of 561,000 more people.

Planning Process

Planning for new delivery capacity began in the late 1980s. New options focused on delivering supplies from the Arkansas River basin. A new raw water delivery pipeline from the federally owned Pueblo Reservoir to a terminal storage reservoir in Colorado Springs and an associated water treatment plant were selected from among the alternatives studied. The project involves pumping water up 1,700 feet (518.2 m) over about 50 miles (80 km) and providing major facilities, at a cost of $300 to $450 million. Because of the high cost and long lead time, participants recognized that local supply and demand management options should be researched and compared and an integrated resource plan (IRP) developed. Local resource options studied included conserving water, developing local groundwater, expanding wastewater reuse, and improving systems. The costs for these options ranged from $12 million to $108 million and produced 2 to 13 mgd (0.01–0.05 m³/d). By themselves, they would not meet demands to 2040 but could defer the need for the Arkansas River delivery system and would buy time to prepare the project.

Public Participation Process

CSU formed a citizens review committee to participate in the studies and reports. Resource options were presented to the committee, which played an important part in building consensus in the local community and acceptance in other potentially affected communities. In addition, six public meetings were held over a three-month period to explain the development of the draft plan. Another citizens advisory group worked with the department to select and implement appropriate and acceptable conservation measures for the community. The department continued to communicate with other Arkansas River interest groups and successfully reached agreement with these groups on several key issues.

Plan Outcomes

The city council formally adopted the final plan, which includes a combination of conservation, irrigation of parks, campus areas, cemeteries, and golf courses with local groundwater and reclaimed wastewater, improving the water delivery system, and starting on the Arkansas River delivery project. Negotiations for regulating storage space in the Arkansas River basin and permitting activities are under way. Land has been acquired for some facilities. Appropriate recreational use of the terminal storage reservoir and adjacent property is being studied in partnership with the city's Parks and Recreation Department.

CASE STUDY #5: DENVER, COLORADO, METROPOLITAN AREA _

5A. Two Forks Reservoir Planning Process

The Two Forks Reservoir was proposed during the early 1980s to meet rapidly growing demands in the Denver Metropolitan Area. The reservoir, on the South Platte River, was to impound 1.1 million acre-ft (1.3 million m³) behind a 555-ft (169-m) dam. The pool surface area was to be 7,300 acres (2,954 hectares), inundating 29 river miles (46.4 km). The project was cosponsored by 43 water providers in the region, including the Denver Water Board, which, in addition to providing retail service to the city of Denver, provides wholesale service to many suburbs. An environmental impact statement (EIS) was completed in March 1988.

In 1989, after project sponsors spent $40 million on permitting and an environmental impact assessment, USEPA vetoed the issuance by the Corps of a Clean Water Act (CWA) Section 404 permit for the project. The rejection was based on Section 404(b)(1) of the act, which precludes approval of a project "if there is a practicable alternative to the proposed discharge, which would have less adverse impact on the aquatic ecosystem, so long as the alternative does not have other significant environmental consequences."

USEPA held that the planning process did not adequately consider a broad enough set of alternatives to the Two Forks process, including conservation; rather, the process focused on analyzing the impacts of the Two Forks project and potential mitigation efforts. Opportunities for stakeholder involvement in the planning process were limited, and environmental advocates played an important role in the ultimate outcome.

The planning process did not explicitly address contingencies, such as regulatory failure of Two Forks; thus, when Two Forks was rejected, the region had no viable alternatives.

The Two Forks rejection was a rude shock to the water providers of the Denver region. It resulted in some fundamental rethinking of the direction of water resources planning in the area and the relationship between Denver Water and many suburban water agencies. It also led directly to the development of an IRP by Denver Water.

5B. Integrated Resource Planning Process

The July 1997 report issued by the Denver Water Board begins as follows:

> From the perspective of 1997, it seems almost inevitable that EPA in the late 1980s would veto the proposed Two Forks dam and reservoir project. The mammoth project—1.1 million acre-feet in storage—would have inundated dozens of relatively pristine miles of trout stream in a pastoral valley setting, at a cost of about half a billion dollars. No matter that the dam site, a natural for a reservoir, had been on Denver's drawing board for almost a century, or that 44 Metro Denver communities and four counties cooperated to design this locally funded project, or even that all state and federal agencies, including the regional EPA office, had agreed to the project. Despite all this, Two Forks was vetoed, and its veto helped signal that the values of a nation and region had changed, that water was viewed by many as more valuable in the stream than stored or moved to other locations, and that the high tide of massive on-stream storage projects had receded, leaving other alternatives as the people's choice.[*]

This passage clearly illustrates the evolution of the thinking of Denver Water in the wake of the Two Forks rejection. Two years after that, the Denver Water Board issued a policy statement, which reads

> . . . Denver's Water Board may no longer serve a central planning role for water supply under current institutional and political constraints. Having assessed Denver assets and obligations in light of current events,

---

[*]Denver Board of Water Commissioners. *Water for Tomorrow: The History, Results, and Projections of the Integrated Resource Plan*. July 1997.

the Water Board is preparing for a different role in metropolitan water supply and development.

In 1994, Denver Water officially began a three-year IRP process to develop a long-term resource strategy. Consistent with the "different role" set forth in the policy statement, the process focused on meeting the needs of Denver's "Combined Service Area," which includes the city and county of Denver and 75 contractual suburban distributors. The IRP scope of work included the following 10 tasks:

Task 1: Study Objectives
Task 2: Resource Decision Guidelines/Evaluation Criteria
Task 3: Treated Water System Analysis
Task 4: Evaluation and Selection of Supply Options
Task 5: Water Demand Forecast
Task 6: Evaluation and Selection of Demand Management Options
Task 7: Resource Strategy Formulation and Evaluation
Task 8: Development of Options for Remaining Resources
Task 9: Report Preparation and Review
Task 10: Public Information and Involvement

This work scope and the work that was done by staff and consultants are, in many ways, diametrically opposed to the previous focus on a single project. The work began with a careful description of the current raw and treated water system. Current Denver water supplies come from a combination of east slope (South Platte) and imported Western Slope sources. The Western Slope water is delivered to the Eastern Slope via a series of tunnels under the Continental Divide. Reliable annual supplies are estimated at 345,000 acre-ft (424 million m^3). This compares to current demand of 265,000 acre-ft (326 million m^3), and projected needs of 445,000 acre-ft (547 million m^3) by 2045.

The treated water system includes three treatment plants and an extensive system of pump stations, reservoirs, and distribution lines divided into more than 140 pressure zones. The combined delivery capacity of the treatment plants is currently 645 mgd (2.4 m^3/d), expandable to some 900 mgd (3.4 m^3/d).

The IRP was characterized by extensive analysis of supply-side and demand-side options. About 200 supply options were identified, including structural and nonstructural alternatives. These options were then screened for fatal flaws, and the remaining 154 were divided into five functional categories:

• Effluent reuse

• South system storage

• North system storage

• New stream diversions

• System refinements

Representative options from each category were then analyzed in detail. A detailed analysis was also performed of the treated water system, including needs for additional treatment plant and transmission system capacity.

Denver's IRP also included an extensive conservation component, which looked in detail at a variety of innovative conservation programs to supplement Denver's programs. These programs were segmented into three levels of aggressiveness. They were screened and reviewed both internally by Denver Water staff and externally by a citizens advisory committee and a group of outside water conservation experts. This process resulted in a set of programs that are estimated to save about 29,000 acre-ft (3.6×10^7 m^3) annually by 2045.

These supply and conservation options were then considered in an iterative process of strategy development that heavily involved Denver Water's board members. The adopted strategy focused on actions over the next 30 years and emphasized system refinements, nonpotable reuse, and conservation. Participants recognized that, toward the end of the period, new supply will likely be needed and that cooperative actions with other suppliers were also to be carefully considered. The plan also included a 10-year *prove-up* period to monitor and verify conservation savings and adjustment of other strategy components if conservation savings vary from projections.

The Denver Water IRP process included extensive public involvement from the beginning. This effort included workshops, media briefings, paid advertising, a telephone survey, and focus groups. In addition, meetings were held with a variety of stakeholder groups, and presentation materials were developed for use at these meetings. Staff also compiled a list of 2,000 people who had interest in Eastern Slope and Western Slope water issues. This list received a quarterly newsletter that reported on the IRP process.

Outcomes

In October 1996, the Board issued its *Resource Statement*, which, among other things, directed staff to aggressively pursue additional conservation programs, a nonpotable reuse project, and small system refinements. Staff began that process, and projects have been reflected in Denver Water's 10-year capital improvement program.

Denver Water has retained consultant services to predesign the nonpotable reuse project. Final design and regulatory permitting occurred in 1999. The goal was to have Phase 1 (about 7,000 acre-ft [8.6×10^6 m^3]) online in 2001. Phase 2 (about 5,000 acre-ft [6.2×10^6 m^3]) is scheduled to be online in 2008 with Phase 3 (about 4,000 acre-ft [4.9×10^6 m^3]) online in 2011.

Denver Water is also aggressively pursuing the purchase of gravel pits below Metro Wastewater to maximize the yield from the nonpotable reuse project and to maximize the reuse of transmountain effluent in an exchange for additional South Platte water at Denver's intake structures. The goal is to purchase 12,000 acre-ft (14.8×10^6 m^3) of gravel pit storage: 8,000 acre-ft (9.8×10^6 m^3) to maximize South Platte River exchanges and 4,000 acre-ft (4.9×10^6 m^3) to maximize the yield from the nonpotable reuse project. To date, Denver Water has purchased about 8,000 acre-ft (9.8×10^6 m^3) of gravel pit storage at a cost of $15.6 million. The expectation is that the remaining 4,000 acre-ft (4.9×10^6 m^3) will be tied up within a few months. The greatest impediments to these efforts are court challenges to Denver Water's exchange decree and potential problems with environmental site assessment for depletions to the Platte River.

Also in late 1996, the Board issued a *Guidance Document for Cooperative Actions with Metropolitan Water Suppliers Outside the Board's Service Area* (Guidance Document). The Guidance Document clarified the Board's interest in pursuing cooperative actions with other providers with the following statement:

> The Board intends to fulfill its primary responsibility to the CSA by implementing the near-term strategy outlined in the Resource Statement. Therefore, the effort to identify potential cooperative actions with others is a secondary priority.

One of the potential cooperative actions, conjunctive use, has raised some interest and concerns on the Western Slope. Some on the Western Slope are concerned that Denver Water and others will blindly pursue a conjunctive use option without first exploring ways to maximize the use of the groundwater resources in the Denver Basin. However, Denver Water will require the proponents of any conjunctive use proposal to analyze all groundwater management options to ensure the most efficient and practicable use of that nonrenewable resource.

In part, based on this very concern, the Board determined that any proposal would have to

> Demonstrate an effort by the proposing entity to gain acceptance of the proposal from those outside the Denver Metro Area who might be impacted by the proposal. This would include efforts to mitigate those impacts. (Guidance Document)

Hence, Denver Water has been working with Douglas County water users and Western Slope interests to design an IRP process for meeting Douglas County's water needs. The Douglas County IRP process began in early 1999.

CASE STUDY #6: KENTUCKY–AMERICAN WATER COMPANY'S INTEGRATED RESOURCE PLAN

Background

As of January 1998, Kentucky–American Water Company (KAWC) served water to more than 90,000 customers in Fayette (City of Lexington), Woodford, Scott, Harrison, Bourbon, Jessamine, and Clark counties. The system is growing, with more than 2,000 new customers added annually in recent years. System demand has averaged 40 mgd (0.15 m^3/d), and the maximum day demand has exceeded 64 mgd (0.24 m^3/d). Water supply is obtained from the Kentucky River and one reservoir. The Kentucky River comprises a series of 14 locks and dams; therefore, the yield of the river is a function of both river flow and pool storage. Water is treated at two filtration plants, the 40-mgd (0.15-m^3/d) Kentucky River Station and the 25-mgd (0.09-m^3/d) Richmond Road Station. The KAWC distribution system consists of 1,250 miles (2,000 km) of main and ten storage tanks with a combined capacity of 16 MG (7,273.6 m^3).

Description of Integrated Resource Planning Study

The planning study for KAWC, published in July 1992, included a detailed analysis of projected customer demands, including a weather normalization to account for projected demands during a hot, dry summer. A demand management study was undertaken in which the projected savings from more than 40 potential demand management measures were estimated. Cost-effective, demand-side management measures are being implemented by KAWC. These include residential fixture retrofits, a public education program on outside water use, and audit programs. A specialized study was conducted as part of the planning study to determine the impact of low river flow on aquatic life in the river. This study was coordinated with the Kentucky Division of Water and Kentucky Department of Fish and Wildlife and helped determine the optimum passing flow, which provides maximum yield of the supply while maintaining appropriate protection of aquatic life and minimum impact on downstream users.

From these studies, KAWC determined there will be a significant supply deficit if and when a severe drought occurs. KAWC also determined that there is production capacity deficit also compared to maximum day demands.

Public participation occurred during and after the preparation of the planning study. State regulatory agencies, including the Kentucky Public Service Commission and the Kentucky Division of Water, KAWC's Consumer Advisory Council, environmental groups, and the public have all been involved.

Outcomes

The Kentucky Public Service Commission (PSC), which oversees the water rates that KAWC can charge to its customers, initiated hearings into the question of whether KAWC has a source-of-supply deficit, and if so, how large it is. PSC concurred with KAWC's earlier finding that there was a supply deficit of approximately 20 mgd (0.08 m^3/d), and that KAWC needed to undertake a supply development program.

Many alternatives for additional supply to the Lexington region had been studied, with two primary alternatives given detailed consideration. These alternatives are

- Install valves and increase the size of the dams on the Kentucky River.

- Construct 55 miles (88 km) of pipeline to obtain finished water supply from the Ohio River, purchased from the Louisville Water Company.

The Kentucky River Authority (KRA), a public agency with oversight of the Kentucky River, proposed construction on the dams. However, the regulatory approval, public acceptance, and funding of such dams made their implementation uncertain. In its planning study, KAWC used a decision tree approach, whereby KAWC began to undertake steps in its own control to provide additional supply for its customers, while concurrently monitoring and supporting KRA's planned activities.

KRA finished rehabilitating valves in the dams, which allows some water to be transferred to downstream pools where it is needed when natural river flow is low. This helped reduce the deficit but did not fully resolve KAWC's need for additional supply.

KAWC's chosen option is the construction of a 36-in.-diameter (91 cm) finished water pipeline to purchase and deliver treated water from Louisville to Lexington. KAWC will enter an agreement with the Louisville Water Company for the purchase of treated water. During normal times, only 1 to 2 mgd (0.004–0.008 m^3/d) will be delivered continuously through the pipeline. However, during a drought, or during peak demand periods, as much as 25 mgd (0.09 m^3/d) or more can be delivered through the pipeline. There are several unique advantages to the pipeline project. It gives KAWC access to water from the Ohio River, which is virtually an unlimited source of supply. Also, it makes use of available treatment capacity at Louisville and resolves both the source of supply and production capacity deficits for KAWC. KAWC does not need to build new treatment facilities.

The pipeline interconnecting Louisville and Lexington is currently under design. The project also includes two booster stations. It was put in service in 2001. Total estimated project cost is $44 million.

CASE STUDY #7: WICHITA, KANSAS, INTEGRATED RESOURCE PLAN

Background

Since the 1980s, Wichita, Kansas, has recognized that its current water resources would not adequately meet the city's water needs beyond the first decade of the next century. One of the first water supply options the city explored was using a water reservoir located more than 100 miles (160 km) away. Because of high, front-end economic impacts and significant social, environmental, and political opposition, the city decided to reevaluate using locally available water resources. That evaluation led the city to develop a more holistic approach to water resources in a manner that is environmentally, socially, and economically acceptable to the community.

The primary elements of the IRP include water conservation, optimization of the six available local supplies when available to enhance productivity and protect water quality, conjunctive water use permitting, and communication with regulatory agencies, other water users and the public. The key to the IRP is the recharge of the City's Equus Beds Well Field area from excess flows in the Little Arkansas River. This area has experienced extensive groundwater drawdown since the 1950s as a result of pumping by irrigators, municipalities, and industries and can hold as much as 100 billion gallons (454 million m^3) of water.

The city has worked closely with the Kansas State Board of Agriculture, Kansas Department of Health and Environment, Kansas Water Office, Groundwater Management District No. 2, and other state and federal agencies throughout the development of the IRP. For the IRP to be feasible, a conjunctive use water permit must be issued by the Kansas State Board of Agriculture. This will represent a significant policy change by the state in that water rights are currently issued for water sources individually, without considering the integrated or conjunctive use of multiple water sources.

The city currently has individual water rights on file with the state for average day and maximum day water use rates for these three supply sources. A conjunctive use permit will allow the city to use its excess river and bank storage water, groundwater, and reservoir water to maximize water supply during wet and dry hydrologic cycles. This will result in the greatest beneficial use of the area's water resources for water supply, as well as greater operating flexibility. The city's total water rights may be used for very little or almost all of river water pumpage, groundwater pumpage, or reservoir pumpage. Other activities include perfecting water rights, purchasing water rights, performing extensive water quality evaluations, and working within the state's minimum desired stream flow requirements.

Outcomes

As a result of recommendations made in the IRP, the city of Wichita has optimized the use of its two major water supplies, the Equus Beds Well field and Cheney Reservoir. Using more surface water from Cheney Reservoir during wet years, the city conserved more than 2 billion gallons (9 million m^3) of water as of mid-year 1998 by reducing pumping from the Equus Beds Aquifer.

In addition, a $7 million demonstration project, referred to as the Equus Beds Recharge Demonstration Project, began operating in 1997 to explore the feasibility of aquifer recharge from the Little Arkansas River basin near the communities of Halstead and Sedgwick. As of July 1998, more than 330 million gallons (1.5 million m^3) were recharged to the aquifer. The purpose of the demonstration project was to develop design and operation information and to obtain approvals from local, state, and federal agencies for the full-scale project, which includes $110 million in recharge, storage, and recovery facilities. Implementation of the full-scale plan should meet the needs of the city and surrounding communities through 2050.

Finally, the city's Groundwater Management District No. 2 is working with the state to develop groundwater recharge regulations and a groundwater recharge accounting process. The city and the state are also working to establish procedures for approving conjunctive use concepts for future evaluations of water rights for new surface water and groundwater supplies.

CASE STUDY #8: WARE CREEK RESERVOIR, VIRGINIA _____

Background

James City County is the second fastest growing county in Virginia and has many summer visitors. In 1981, the county had approximately 24,000 residents. By 1987, the county's population had grown to about 31,000 residents. Projections indicate that by 2030, the county's population will exceed 50,000. James City County water demand was about 9.3 mgd (0.04 m^3/d) in 1996. Projected water demands for 2030 are about 18.2 mgd (0.07 m^3/d).

The Ware Creek Reservoir project was proposed in the early 1980s. The project was estimated to yield about 9.4 mgd (0.04 m^3/d) of water. In 1984, James City County applied to the Corps for a Clean Water Act Section 404 permit to place fill for the dam. The Corps, US Fish and Wildlife Service, National Marine Fisheries Service, and USEPA jointly completed an EIS in 1987. The Corps subsequently issued a notice of intent to issue the permit in 1988. After further review and public hearings, the USEPA regional administrator recommended (in early 1989) that USEPA veto the Corps' decision.

Initially, the veto was based on the potential availability of practical water supply alternatives that would have fewer adverse environmental effects than the proposed project. However, the basis for the veto evolved to focus solely on the significance of potential environmental impacts given that the courts found the water supply alternatives to be impractical. Subsequent litigation between James City County and USEPA spanned an additional 4½ years, resulting in a decision by the US Fourth Circuit Court of Appeals to uphold USEPA's veto of the project based on anticipated "unacceptable adverse environmental impacts" alone (pursuant to CWA Section 404 (c)).

USEPA found that the project would result in the loss of 381 acres (1,660 hectares) of vegetated wetlands and 44 acres (192 hectares) of palustrine, estuarine, and lacustrine open water systems. USEPA also asserted that the project would severely and adversely alter the natural nutrient regime for the York River and Chesapeake Bay ecosystem. USEPA noted that the project would represent a *profound cumulative loss* of functional wetlands that contribute to the *environmental well being* of the river and the bay.

James City County had proposed to mitigate wetlands impacts caused by the Ware Creek project by purchasing and reconnecting about 500 acres (2,178 hectares) of wetlands to their natural hydrologic systems. USEPA reviewed and rejected the county's mitigation plan on the grounds that it would not adequately offset the adverse impacts resulting from the project. According to James City County staff, the presence of the threatened and endangered plant species was not the major issue associated with USEPA's action on the project. According to written opinions of the US Court of Appeals, USEPA recognized that the proposed reservoir and mitigation proposal would increase the freshwater habitat, but the agency found that the dam would harm fish species currently living in the Ware Creek watershed because it would convert the free-flowing stream into a lake. The project would also have potentially destroyed a productive Great Blue Heron Rookery, eliminate water fowl foraging areas, and adversely affect several threatened or endangered plant species. USEPA also had concerns about the county's proposal to mitigate wetland impacts because the mitigation site was not in the same drainage basin as the proposed project.

In the Ware Creek case, USEPA expressed concern about the apparent lack of regional cooperation among water providers. USEPA noted that the Ware Creek project would supply only *local* (versus regional) needs, and cited obstacles to a regional system posed by the lack of cooperation among localities. James City County staff confirm that there was resistance among certain localities to the option of a jointly owned project.

As in the Two Forks case, the involvement of several environmental organizations strongly influenced the outcome of the project. Groups including the National Wildlife Federation, Sierra Club, and the Southern Environmental Law Center participated in the decision-making process at the administrative and judicial levels.

Litigation regarding the Ware Creek project ended in October 1994 when the US Supreme Court elected not to hear an appeal filed by the county. This action was the culmination of 15 years of project activity. After the veto, the city of Newport News proposed to develop a regional water storage project that would yield about 24 mgd (0.09 m^3/d) and could provide some supply to neighboring localities including James City County.

According to county staff, this project proposal essentially *sealed the fate* of the original Ware Creek project. Currently, James City County anticipates about 4 mgd (0.02 m^3/d) from the regional storage project. However, the Virginia Department of Environmental Quality has placed downstream release conditions on the CWA 401 certification. These conditions would effectively reduce the available storage to about 15 mgd (0.06 m^3/d) and would preclude James City County from obtaining stored water. The ultimate outcome of the situation is pending appeal.

In addition, James City County is pursuing water conservation measures that focus on long-term per capita demand reductions associated with installation of low-flow plumbing fixtures (including incentives) and aggressive tiered rates.

CASE STUDY #9: SOUTHERN NEVADA WATER AUTHORITY INTEGRATED RESOURCE PLAN

Background

The Las Vegas region currently has a population of about 1.2 million people and receives less than 4 in. (10 cm) per year of rainfall; 85 percent of its water supply comes from the Colorado River, the rest from groundwater. Until the mid-1980s, supplies were expected to last well into the 21st century. Since the tremendous growth that began in 1987, however, water usage increased by as much as 13 percent annually. If trends continued, Las Vegas would be out of water in less than 10 years.

This awareness spurred an intense water supply and demand projection process in 1990 among all the local water and wastewater agencies, complete with computer models and consultants. The bad news was confirmed in early 1991: Supply shortfall by 2007 with conservation, by 1998 without. The good news was the creation in 1991 of the Southern Nevada Water Authority (Authority), a regional water and wastewater agency with members from all seven local water and wastewater agencies and municipalities. The Authority would manage current supplies, find new supplies, and promote conservation. Conservation was instituted in various forms in the member agencies, including increases in water rates, and the Authority acquired more water. Even so, the latest demand projections showed that demand would exceed current supplies before 2010.

An even more immediate problem of facility shortages loomed. Las Vegas receives most of its water from the Colorado River through a single "straw" called the Southern Nevada Water System (SNWS)—a 400-mgd (1.5-m^3/d) treatment and transmission facility system. The water is piped from Lake Mead through the River Mountains tunnel and into the valley to the utilities. Some utilities were facing the inability to meet peak summer demands as soon as 1996 because of lack of facility capacity. Although 6 percent conservation had been achieved by the end of 1993, none was occurring during the summer, when it was needed most.

To buy the community a few more years, plans to expand SNWS as quickly as possible began immediately. However, additional capacity was still needed soon after 2000. In 1993 the Authority began plans for a second "straw," the Authority's Treatment and Transmission Facility (TTF). Projects of this magnitude normally take as long as twenty years to plan and build; TTF staff had seven years.

Phase 1 IRP

At the same time, the IRP concept in water planning was beginning to surface, and in early 1994, the Authority began its own IRP effort. Authority consensus was that it did not have many options to meet its resource and facility needs. Colorado River water was the best resource option to pursue, conservation was imperative, and new facilities were sorely overdue. Since IRP was supposed to look at the *big picture* of resources, facilities, and conservation, however, the Authority wanted to make sure it was going down the right path before it went much further.

The Authority hired a consultant to do a Phase I IRP in six months. With plans, studies, and a technical work group, the consultant was asked to create strategies that would meet future water demands and then rate them against various objectives determined by the work group.

The Colorado River dominates the SNWS supply picture. Nevada is one of three lower-basin states (along with California and Arizona) that have an allocation of Colorado River water under the Colorado River Compact. Nevada's annual demand is approaching that state's allocation. The ability of Nevada and its neighboring states to bank or market their annual allocations is very uncertain, and is currently a subject of ongoing negotiation among the states and the US Bureau of Reclamation. Thus, the availability of additional Colorado River water is very uncertain.

In addition to the Colorado, a variety of other resource and facility alternatives were examined. The two major possibilities include

- the Virgin River, either through a new pipeline or by wheeling that water through Lake Mead, and

- the Cooperative Water Project, which involves importing groundwater via pipeline from four southeast Nevada counties north of Las Vegas.

In June 1994, the Authority Board created the SNWA Integrated Resource Plan advisory committee (IRPAC), consisting of 21 citizens—and 24, later—from the local community. As a part of the IRP process, IRPAC reviewed and discussed the technical work provided throughout the process by Authority staff and finalized a number of recommendations.

At the end of Phase 1 in June 1995, the Authority Board adopted the 19 recommendations made by IRPAC. These recommendations focused on the overall planning issues—what resources to pursue, what facilities to build (if any), and what levels of conservation to achieve.

Summary of primary IRPAC recommendations.

- Colorado River water is the top priority resource option, rather than the Cooperative Water Project or the Virgin River pipeline.

- Build phased Colorado River treatment and transmission facilities as soon as possible.

- Achieve a 10 to 15 percent reduction in maximum day water demand by summer 2000.

- Study conservation to determine whether higher savings levels are feasible.

- Include the use of short-term, temporary supplies in an annual *Resource Plan*.

- Study *elasticity* (rate impact on demand) and ways to finance facilities.

Phase 1 Challenges

Citizen involvement.   Three months into the IRP, Authority staff realized that it should involve citizens as soon as possible, because important decisions might be made with the Phase 1 IRP findings. A 21-member IRPAC was created from a cross-section of the community to provide input on which strategies the Authority should pursue. The problem was keeping ahead of IRPAC. People wanted to act immediately, before analysis was complete.

Multijurisdictional.   The IRP was under control of the Authority, but other water and wastewater planning efforts in various stages were not. In such a rapidly growing community, different agencies' efforts could not be put on hold while the IRP churned through a two- or three-year process. With constant communication, the IRP and other efforts would begin to influence one another in later stages.

Time.   The biggest timing issue was the TTF schedule. TTF staff could not put the TTF on hold until results of a lengthy, detailed IRP process would conclude that the Authority needed a TTF. So TTF planning continued on a parallel path with the IRP, with no commitment to build, while the IRP process determined whether to build a TTF.

Data.   Initially, staff thought they had all the data the IRP could possibly need, but soon found they did not. Much had been collected but not as part of a whole picture. People were constantly reminded that this was a first phase of a process and that data would always be changing. In the first phase IRP, there were enough data to see the relative merits of different strategies, even if not the precise merit, and enough on which to make some general decisions.

Uncertainties.   The Authority had uncertainties in its future demands and supplies. The major future supplies would all have to be negotiated. Although projections generally showed the community continuing to grow, in a volatile economic climate such as Las Vegas', it was extremely difficult to forecast the rate of that growth. *Low* and *high* demands were analyzed throughout the IRP process, with fingers crossed that the high was high enough. Fortunately, the uncertainties were included in the analysis, because real-world decisions must consider uncertainties. However, the uncertainties made the strategies that the Authority might follow more complicated. The Authority had to make short-term facility decisions now, before knowing what resources might become available, yet try to avoid eliminating future supply possibilities resulting from current facility decisions. Thus, possible strategies were more like decision trees, rather than specific courses of action. Although "trees" best represented reality, they were more difficult to understand and explain.

Phase 2.1

In October 1995, the Authority began Phase 2 of its IRP to develop recommendations to the Board on regional water facilities charges (water rates and connection charges). In December 1995 the committee made eight recommendations, which the Board adopted.

Summary of primary recommendations.

- Phase-in a regional connection charge to avoid disrupting businesses.

- Phase-in water rates to avoid rate shock.

- Study and implement alternative revenue sources as quickly as possible.

- Provide conservation incentives immediately.

Phase 2.2

In February 1996, the Authority continued Phase 2. This time IRPAC focused on potential alternative revenue sources to help fund the regional water facilities and the level of water treatment to be included. In November 1996 the Board adopted all of IRPAC's recommendations.

Summary of primary recommendations.

- Sales tax and water excise tax are the most promising alternative revenue sources.

- Connection charges should still provide at least 50 percent of the total revenue.

- Part of the sales tax increase should be used for regional wastewater facilities.

- Pricing water for conservation should be pursued but left to local purveyors.

- Ozonation should be added to direct filtration at the regional water treatment facilities.

- Highly advanced water treatment should be studied but postponed until cost-effective.

Conclusion

As is often the case, this IRP effort had to balance the potential for lengthy analyses and *scope creep* with the need for rapid action. In a rapidly growing community such as Las Vegas, where the window of opportunity for action is very small, it is imperative to stick to the agreed-on project scope and determine and act on the essential data. Detailed analysis may not be needed for certain decisions.

The SNWS IRP was not just an event, it was, and continues to be, a process. The primary goal was to show to the public and the decision makers, in explicit and consistent language, the trade-offs among different solutions to the Las Vegas region's problem. Perhaps, though, an equally important thing to come out of this IRP might be the process: people with different backgrounds learning to look at possible solutions that transcend their own personal issues.

CASE STUDY #10: EUGENE, OREGON, WATER AND ELECTRIC BOARD WATER SUPPLY PLAN

Background

Eugene is the second largest city in Oregon, with a 1995 population of about 120,000. It is located in the Willamette River valley about 100 miles (160 km) south of Portland, just south of the confluence of the Willamette and McKenzie rivers. The Eugene Water & Electric Board (EWEB) is the combined water and electric utility serving the City of Eugene and surrounding areas. The 1995 EWEB water service area population was about 152,000.

Currently, EWEB relies on the McKenzie River as its sole supply source. McKenzie River water is treated at the Hayden Bridge Filtration Plant, which has a capacity of 72 mgd (2.7×10^5 m^3/d). The 1998 system peak-day demand was 70 mgd (2.65×10^5 m^3/d). The capacity of the treatment plant is augmented by some 73 million gallons (2.8×10^5 m^3/d) of in-town treated water storage. These storage tanks must also smooth diurnal variations in demand and meet emergency storage requirements.

The need for the IRP is largely determined by the diurnal variations in EWEB system demand. For purposes of the IRP, summer days were divided into four subperiods, which corresponded to the typical bimodal pattern of demand seen by many municipal suppliers. On hot summer days, there is generally a morning and late afternoon peak in demand, with reduced demand during the midday and nighttime periods. For EWEB, the average hourly demand in the 4-hour late-afternoon/early evening period was more than 30 percent higher than the average demand over the 24 hours of a hot summer day. Focusing on the demands during this period therefore more accurately summarizes system constraints.

EWEB Supply Options

The EWEB Water Supply Plan (IRP) considered a variety of options to augment EWEB supply:

- Hayden Bridge expansion. Expansion of the Hayden Bridge intake and filtration plant on the McKenzie River.

- Fish Hatchery. A new intake and treatment plant at the fish hatchery directly across the river from the Hayden Bridge site.

- Jordan Pit. A new intake and treatment plant on the McKenzie just above the confluence with the Willamette.

- Willamette downstream. A new intake and treatment plant on the Willamette just downstream of the confluence.

- Willamette upstream. A new intake and treatment plant on the Middle Fork of the Willamette southeast of the city.

- Deep aquifer. Deep wells in the Willamette–McKenzie confluence area.

- Shallow aquifer. Shallow wells in the Willamette–McKenzie confluence area.

The IRP also evaluated potential additional storage and transmission infrastructure.

EWEB Conservation Options

The IRP also carefully considered conservation program options. An underlying premise of the IRP is that conservation is a resource option to be combined with supply options to form complete resource strategies that must be evaluated and compared. Thus, a major element of the IRP focused on these demand-side resources.

EWEB currently has a rather extensive set of conservation programs. The IRP considered a variety of additional conservation measures. The following measures were felt to have sufficient potential and were therefore considered for inclusion in EWEB resource strategies:

- Single-family residential water audits
- Single-family new construction standards
- Multifamily residential audits
- Government audits
- Commercial audits
- Residential/commercial informational brochures
- Industrial auditor training
- Low-cost financing of conservation measures
- Various conservation rate designs
- Landscape ordinance

The Working Group

At the outset of the process, EWEB convened a group of citizens, senior staff, and elected EWEB Board members to form a working group that would play a central role over the entire course of the IRP. The composition of the group is somewhat unique and was designed as a more effective way of reflecting community needs into the planning process. This group was heavily involved in all stages of the planning process and was a key liaison with the community at large.

EWEB Policy Objectives and Evaluation Criteria

EWEB staff and consultants worked closely with the working group over several iterations to develop a set of policy objectives that would guide the evaluation of resource strategies. The wording of each objective was critical to ensure that the intent was correctly established. Policy objectives were developed in the following areas:

- Minimize cost
- Maximize reliability
- Minimize environmental impacts
- Maximize conservation
- Minimize vulnerability to catastrophic events
- Maximize flexibility
- Maximize public acceptability

Strategy Development and Evaluation

Strategies were developed and evaluated using *Confluence*, a sophisticated but easy-to-use IRP model that uses Monte Carlo simulation techniques. The strategy that was ultimately recommended and adopted by the elected EWEB board included the following key features:

- Enhanced conservation programs, focusing primarily on outdoor end uses

- Infrastructure investments to *optimize* the system, including transmission and storage facilities

- Expansion of the Hayden Bridge Filtration Plant

- Investigation and development of wells to tap the deep aquifer. Initially, these wells would be used only for emergency backup, rather than as a production source

- An as-yet-unspecified long-term supply to maintain system reliability for the remainder of the planning period, which was through 2040

Plan Outcomes

The plan was completed and presented to the EWEB Board in the fall of 1998. The Board formally adopted the plan in December 1998. Much of the initial work tasks that are included in the recommended strategy, including system optimization investments, wellfield reconnaissance, and expanded conservation efforts, are reflected in the proposed water division fiscal 1999 budget. These tasks are expected to move forward expeditiously. Work is also anticipated on a water supply shortage contingency plan, which was also recommended in the IRP.

This page intentionally blank

Appendix **A**

Preliminary Cost Guide
for Water Supply Dams

For reconnaissance level evaluations, the following guidance provides relative cost estimates when comparing dam alternatives. Guidance is presented for selecting earth fill and concrete gravity dams, including developing opinions of cost to provide a reasonable framework for initial site screening assessments. For simplicity, this approach is limited in scope; it does not replace the counsel and input of an experienced dam design professional.

Most new concrete gravity dams are constructed using roller compacted concrete (RCC), because RCC is significantly less expensive than conventionally placed concrete for most applications. Therefore, the cost guidelines for gravity dams presented later in this section were developed assuming the use of RCC.

SELECTING THE APPROPRIATE DAM TYPE

A far more extensive set of site conditions, opportunities, and constraints than those presented in this section could be developed. However, the issues and considerations presented are generally sufficient to initially identify and assess a dam type that is conducive to most sites. Table A-1 presents key site characteristics and their importance in selecting an appropriate dam type.

If a key factor for one dam type is identified to have an overriding detrimental impact on technical viability or cost (e.g., bedrock at substantial depth precluding an RCC dam), the other dam type should be selected by default. It is also not uncommon to encounter dam sites that lack clear merits for either dam type. In such cases, the utility needs to assess both types.

The preliminary cost-estimating techniques used do not consider pumping stations or pipelines, water supply intake and outlet works, property acquisitions, reservoir clearing, structure relocations, and bridges; or any other considerations not directly related to the impounding structure. The utility will need to consider the magnitude of these and other costs separately.

Table A–1   Considerations for selecting dam type

Assessment Factor	Earth Fill Dam	RCC Gravity Dam
Foundation Conditions		
Overburden	Significant concerns if highly permeable to depth or if excessive settlement likely; overburden cutoff trench typically used.	Typically built on rock foundation, with overburden excavated to competent rock.
Bedrock quality	Of concern if shallow overburden with open bedrock fractures. Generally not a significant concern unless soil cover is either minimal or relatively pervious.	Rock surface needs to be relatively uniform (no overhangs or ledges) and surface fractures treated. Rock grouting typically is used to treat dam foundation.
Construction Materials and Access		
Borrow availability	Need large quantities of suitable earth borrow relatively close to the proposed fill placement site.	Either a local quarry site (rock crushing) or minable sands and gravels are needed for larger projects. Commercial aggregates common for RCC volumes smaller than 30,000 yd^3.
Access, stockpiling, and staging areas	Typically require access for hauling, spreading, compaction equipment, and concrete transit mix trucks, plus nominal staging areas.	Access as for earth dam, plus staging for RCC mix plant, aggregate stockpiles, drilling and grouting equipment, conveyors, rock crushers, etc.[*]
Spillway Requirements		
Spillway design flood (SDF) magnitude	Normally need to locate major spillways away from the dam. Requirement for large spillway can significantly affect layout, design treatments, and project costs.	Spillway facilities can normally be accommodated as part of the impounding structure and normally do not significantly affect project costs.
Site topographic setting	If necessary, a large remote spillway can be accommodated more readily in valleys with a mildly sloping abutment or a reservoir perimeter saddle area.	Because the spillway is readily incorporated into the dam, an RCC dam benefits from a deeply incised valley, but can be used for a variety of site settings.

*A much smaller footprint is needed for an RCC dam.

ESTABLISHING DAM PROFILE LAYOUT

The topography along the dam axis (from US Geological Survey [USGS]) 7.5 minute quadrangles or other available mapping) should be used to plot a profile of the valley as much as 20 ft (6.1 m) above the proposed reservoir pool elevation, with the top of dam set 10 ft (3 m) above the proposed operating pool elevation as shown in Figure A-1.

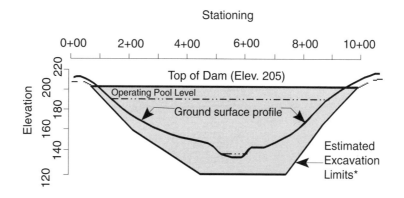

Figure A–1   Dam profile layout

PROFILE LAYOUT AND BASIS FOR ESTIMATING QUANTITY ___

An approximate quantity take-off is developed from the profile layout presented in Figure A-1. The utility should estimate the abutment and foundation excavation lines required to found the dam on firm bedrock for a RCC dam and on competent overburden for an earth dam (a minimum of 5 ft [1.5 m]). The base length and top length of the dam (L_b and L_t) and the abutment contact slopes should be set to best fit the dam profile geometry as shown in Figure A-2.

County soil surveys will generally include the approximate thickness of soil strata and depths to bedrock for use in this assessment. Additionally, USGS geologic maps and bedrock outcropping noted during field reconnaissance can provide added guidance in this regard.

RCC Gravity Dam Assessment—Preliminary Layout and Opinion of Cost

For concrete gravity impounding structures, single-stage overflow spillways are typically incorporated into the dam. The cost of a spillway for a gravity dam generally is not an overriding factor affecting feasibility, because a large spillway can readily be incorporated into a gravity dam. In general, by applying only the larger cross-sectional area of the nonoverflow portions of the dam (see Figure A-3), the added volume of RCC will reasonably counterbalance the cost of treatments needed for safe flood passage over the spillway (a nominal spillway cost factor is added).

Developing RCC Dam Layout and Quantity

Once an outline profile of the dam is established, its volume can be estimated based on the characteristic dimensions illustrated in Figure A-3. Volume estimating procedures assume the width of the top of the dam is 20 percent of the maximum dam height, the top of the dam elevation is 10 ft (3 m) above the operating pool, the slope of the downstream face of the dam is 0.8(h):1.0(v), and the slope intersects the top of the dam elevation at the upstream face (see Figure A-1). Should the top of the dam need to support a roadway, the additional costs for a wider top of the dam and a spillway bridge would need to be separately considered.

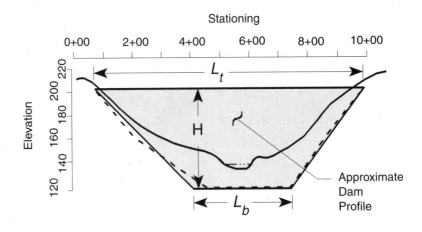

Figure A–2 Profile layout for estimating quantity

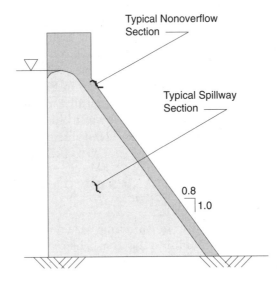

Figure A–3 Typical RCC dam geometry

The required volume of RCC is approximated using the following equation:

$$V_{RCC} = 0.008 \times H^2 \times (2L_b L_t) \qquad \text{(Eq A-1)}$$

Where:

V_{RCC} = total estimated volume of RCC in cubic yards
H = maximum height of dam in feet (see Figure A-3)
L_b = total length of the base of the dam in feet (see Figure A-3)
L_t = total length of the top of the dam in feet (see Figure A-3)

RCC Dam—Opinion of Cost

Figure A-4 provides a graphical presentation of estimated RCC unit cost versus placement volume. High, low, and median cost curves are provided to reflect factors such as construction costs for the region in question, RCC aggregate availability, and access and staging areas for materials and equipment. Aggregate availability and processing costs can significantly influence the selected unit price for RCC. Additional cost factors are included for spillways and general mobilization. The estimated cost for an RCC gravity dam is computed as:

$$\text{Cost (\$)} = V_{\text{RCC}} \times UC_{\text{RCC}} \times (1 + CF_s + CF_{gm}) \qquad \text{(Eq A-2)}$$

Where:

V_{RCC} = the RCC volume

UC_{RCC} = the RCC unit cost

CF_s = the spillway size cost factor

CF_{gm} = the cost factor for general mobilization that includes mobilization, site work, control of water, foundation treatment, and other incidental items

Utilities should apply considerable judgment when selecting cost factors.

CFs should be selected in the range from 0.2 to 0.5, depending on the magnitude of the spillway design flood. In general, the smaller value would apply to

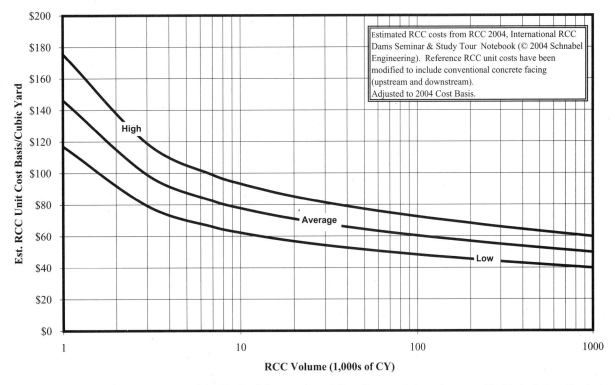

NOTE: Estimated RCC costs courtesy of the Portland Cement Association. Base costs have been modified to include estimated dam facing costs.

Figure A–4   RCC unit cost

nonmountainous drainage areas of 10 mi^2 (25.6 km^2) or less, with the high end value for mountainous drainage areas of about 40 mi^2 (102.4 km^2).

For dams with moderate foundation excavation and treatment, or diversion and dewatering considerations, use a CF_{gm} of 0.4. Where a project will require extensive foundation excavation and treatment, and significant construction diversion and dewatering facilities, a CF_{gm} of 1.0 is recommended. Values should be selected to reflect likely project requirements.

This estimating technique does not include costs for stilling basins, pumping stations, and pipelines, water supply intake and outlet works, property acquisition, reservoir clearing, structure relocations, and bridges; or any other facilities not directly related to the impounding structure. The magnitude of these and other costs will need to be considered on a site-specific basis.

EARTH FILL DAM ASSESSMENT—PRELIMINARY LAYOUT AND OPINION OF COST

Developing reliable cost opinions for earth fill dams is generally more complex and difficult than for RCC dams, because of the significant influence spillway facilities can have on project layout and cost. Four basic earth fill dam options are presented to accommodate a range of site settings and spillway requirements.

When developing concepts and layouts for an earth dam, the first consideration is the magnitude of spillway discharge required. Where a large spillway design flood (SDF) needs to be handled, spillway siting and layout often dictates the efficient use of site opportunities and approaches to treating other site conditions. If feasible, an RCC dam should be selected in these cases.

For most earth dams, constructing a major spillway within the dam footprint is also more costly and difficult than for an RCC dam. Where the SDF magnitude is more nominal (such as for a pumped-storage reservoir site on a small tributary watershed), or where the local topography and geology provide ample opportunity for locating an abutment or reservoir perimeter spillway, the layout of project facilities is more straightforward.

Selecting an Earth Dam Alternative

Four alternative dam concepts are presented for consideration. Based on the information presented in Table A-2, the embankment and spillway option considered

Table A–2   Embankment dam alternative layout selection factors

Layouts for Earth Embankment Dams	SDF Normally Accommodated	Impact of Steep Abutments	Impact of Difficult Foundations	Local Borrow Material Availability	Range of Economical Dam Heights
Principal/emergency spillway	Small to intermediate	Significant	Intermediate	Intermediate to significant	<100 ft
Central overflow spillway	Small to large	Nominal	Significant	Reduces need for borrow	<50 ft
Remote service spillway	Intermediate to large	Intermediate	Significant	Intermediate	>50 ft
Closed conduit spillway	Nominal	Nominal	Low	Negligible	Any

most conducive to the site setting and SDF magnitude should be selected. Where two alternatives appear to be equally suited to the site conditions, the first listed alternative from Table A-2 should be selected.

Developing Earth Dam Layout and Quantity

Volume estimating procedures assume the width of the top of the dam is 40 percent of the maximum dam height, the upstream and downstream slopes are 3 horizontal to 1 vertical, and a foundation cut-off trench is provided. The required volume of earth fill is approximated using the following equation:

$$V_{earth} = 0.05 \times H^2 \times (2L_b + L_t)$$ (Eq A-3)

Where:

V_{earth} = the total estimated volume of earth fill in cubic yards
H = the maximum height of dam in feet (see Figure A-3)
L_b = the total length of the base of the dam in feet (see Figure A-3)
L_t = the total length of the top of the dam in feet (see Figure A-3)

Because the reduction in earth fill for a central overflow spillway is generally offset by the need for a more costly structural spillway, the utility should not reduce earth fill volumes for this option. Figure A-5 provides a graphical presentation of estimated earth fill unit cost versus placement volume. High, low, and median cost curves are provided to reflect factors such as construction costs for the region, earth

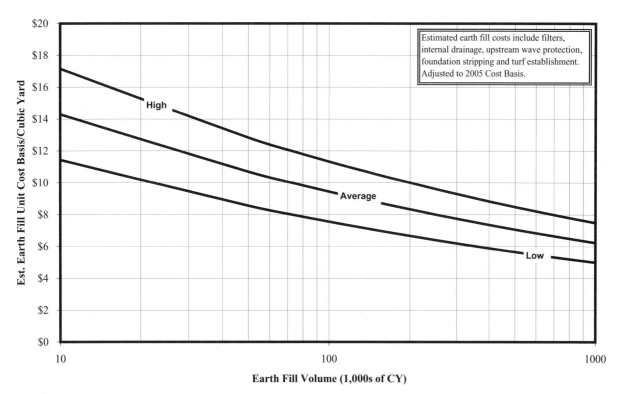

NOTE: Considerable judgment needs to be applied in selecting cost factors.

Figure A–5   Earth fill unit cost

borrow availability, and access and staging areas for materials and equipment. Additional cost factors are included for spillways and general mobilization.

EARTH DAM—OPINION OF COST

The estimated cost for an earth dam is computed as:

$$\text{Cost (\$)} = V_{earth} \times UC_{earth} \times (1 + CF_s + CF_{gm}) \qquad \text{(Eq A-4)}$$

Where:

$$
\begin{aligned}
V_{earth} &= \text{the earth fill volume} \\
UC_{earth} &= \text{the earth fill unit cost} \\
CF_s &= \text{the spillway size cost factor} \\
CF_{gm} &= \text{the cost factor for general mobilization that includes mobilization,} \\
&\quad \text{site work, control of water, foundation treatment, and other} \\
&\quad \text{incidental items}
\end{aligned}
$$

CFs should be selected in the range from 0.5 (small) to 1.0 (intermediate) to 1.5 (large), depending on the magnitude of the spillway design flood. In general, the smaller value would apply to nonmountainous drainage areas of 10 mi^2 or less, with the high-end value for mountainous drainage areas of about 40 mi^2 (101.6 km^2). For pumped-storage projects on tributary streams less than 5 mi^2 (12.8 km^2), CFs can be reduced to 0.3 (nominal).

For dams with moderate foundation excavation and treatment, and diversion and dewatering considerations, use a CF_{gm} of 0.4. Where a project requires extensive foundation excavation and treatment, and significant construction diversion and dewatering facilities, a CF_{gm} of 1.2 is recommended. Values should be selected to reflect likely project requirements.

Appendix **B**

A White Paper From the American Water Works Association Source Water Protection (approved April 11, 1997)

STATEMENT OF PRINCIPLES

The American Water Works Association (AWWA) is dedicated to providing the public with an adequate supply of clean, safe drinking water. AWWA is committed to ensuring that water resources are managed in a manner consistent with the protection and enhancement of source waters for current and future supplies of drinking water. Source water protection (SWP) is a program of actions, policies, and practices to be undertaken by water suppliers, government agencies, institutions, and individuals to advance these goals.

AWWA promotes a multiple-barrier approach to providing safe drinking water that includes SWP, treatment as appropriate, distribution system maintenance, and monitoring. SWP may reduce health risks and treatment costs and improve finished water quality. SWP programs may also provide ancillary benefits of enhancing water quality for other users and improving the natural and aesthetic environments of communities. Accordingly, SWP should be pursued diligently for every water supply source.

SWP programs must be implemented in a context of supporting and competing public needs. They also must be flexible enough to address threats to source water quality and opportunities for improvement that vary from site to site and evolve over time. Regulatory programs and subsidies at all levels of government that are related to water resource protection should focus on current or potential sources of drinking water. In these programs, SWP goals should be added or elevated in importance.

Water suppliers, regulators, landowners, and municipalities share responsibility for protecting source water. Property owners must bear responsibility for preventing and abating pollution emanating from their holdings. AWWA supports the interests of water suppliers and of consumers whose health and welfare could be affected by unrestricted exercise of property rights upstream. However, AWWA recognizes the need to be sensitive to property rights and to avoid imposing undue burdens on parties who may be affected by source water protection measures.

THE ROAD TO A SOURCE WATER PROTECTION PROGRAM

A basic premise for implementing source water protection programs is the multiple-barrier approach to protecting water supplies and public health. By establishing multiple barriers that include source water protection, treatment as appropriate, distribution system maintenance, and monitoring, water suppliers are able to ensure the quality and safety of drinking water for their consumers. SWP represents a first and most important step in safeguarding public water supplies.

Some common elements for successful SWP programs are: they account for local conditions, incorporate diverse interests, require commitment to the SWP process by all involved parties, and are sustainable over the long term. SWP requires a sustained commitment of policy, as well as financial and technical resources over a time span of decades, not just years. Some important water quality benefits of source water protection may not be measurable in the short run. In addition, a long-term commitment is necessary to ensure the protection of high-quality water sources so they remain available for future generations.

One of the most difficult issues in an SWP plan is the establishment of equity in sharing the responsibility and expense of these programs. SWP efforts often are hampered by issues of who benefits and who pays. The following guidelines have been used to resolve these issues:

- Sources of pollution bear the responsibility for remediation; in other words, the polluter pays.

- Open and active communication, flexibility, and participation in the SWP process by involved parties can overcome actual and perceived imbalances of equity.

- Federal, state, and local resources can be applied to help address the equity issue.

- Consideration should be given to the value that SWP programs can provide to a community through environmental benefits—such as wildlife habitat and open space—as well as improved quality and quantity of available resources.

- Compensation for lost or diminished use of property because of SWP restrictions may be considered in some cases.

These guidelines can help balance the rights of property owners and others affected by SWP measures with the rights of consumers whose health and welfare depend on the quality of source waters that could be degraded by the exercise of unrestricted property rights.

DEVELOPING RESOURCES FOR SOURCE WATER PROTECTION

A challenge incumbent on successful, sustainable SWP programs is developing adequate structural and financial resources to support them. Some specific options include

- State and federal governments tailoring legislative and regulatory agendas, resources, and programs to support SWP.

- State governments refocusing and allocating a portion of resources and funding to SWP. The states should secure adequate legislative and regulatory authority, e.g., planning and regulatory enforcement, for SWP programs. This could also include levies on polluters or pollutants (pesticides, herbicides, fertilizers, etc.), with the proceeds supporting cleanup efforts.

- Local governments supporting SWP with appropriate land use management and regulatory enforcement and by encouraging support from local grass-roots efforts, environmental groups, and community groups.

- Water suppliers taking an active role in protecting their source waters by providing organizational, technical, monitoring, and financial resources and by harnessing resources available from federal, state, and local programs and institutions and from volunteers.

- Private organizations initiating SWP programs and participating in cost-sharing arrangements.

RECOMMENDATIONS

1. Water suppliers, regulators, and local landowners and municipalities share responsibility for SWP. Federal and state programs need to be tailored to support a local and regional approach to developing and implementing SWP programs and activities.

2. Recognizing that drinking water sources are becoming significantly polluted now, federal and state legislative and regulatory programs should be directed to stress the protection of water resources for current or potential drinking water supplies on a priority basis. SWP goals should be included in programs and, where already included, elevated in importance.

   Where necessary and appropriate, new or expanded regulatory SWP programs should be implemented for specific river basins, watersheds, or aquifers via state or regional initiatives. This implies an integrated look at all the activities within an aquifer or watershed to assess priorities and place priority on certain pollution protection programs that offer the best net economic and environmental benefits.

3. Water suppliers should develop written source water management plans to prevent or reverse water quality degradation. The SWP plans should delineate and characterize specific source water areas (watershed, well-head, or recharge areas), identify threats to water quality, and provide a strategy for ongoing management of conditions and activities within these

areas that may affect source water quality. The plans should also specify resource requirements for communications, implementation, and program assessment.

Appendix **C**

State Wellhead and Source Water Protection Contact List

For a current updated list of the State Wellhead and Source Water Protection Contacts, please go to http://www.epa.gov/safewater/.

For inquiries on national drinking water source protection programs, call the SDWA Hotline, 1-800-426-4791.

This page intentionally blank

Index

NOTE: *f.* indicates a figure; *t.* indicates table.

AWWA Manuals

M1, *Principles of Water Rates, Fees, and Charges*, Fifth Edition, 2000, #30001PA

M2, *Instrumentation and Control*, Third Edition, 2001, #30002PA

M3, *Safety Practices for Water Utilities*, Sixth Edition, 2002, #30003PA

M4, *Water Fluoridation Principles and Practices*, Fifth Edition, 2004, #30004PA

M5, *Water Utility Management Practices*, Second Edition, 2006, #30005PA

M6, *Water Meters—Selection, Installation, Testing, and Maintenance*, Second Edition, 1999, #30006PA

M7, *Problem Organisms in Water: Identification and Treatment*, Third Edition, 2004, #30007PA

M9, *Concrete Pressure Pipe*, Second Edition, 1995, #30009PA

M11, *Steel Pipe—A Guide for Design and Installation*, Fifth Edition, 2004, #30011PA

M12, *Simplified Procedures for Water Examination*, Fifth Edition, 2002, #30012PA

M14, *Recommended Practice for Backflow Prevention and Cross-Connection Control*, Third Edition, 2003, #30014PA

M17, *Installation, Field Testing, and Maintenance of Fire Hydrants*, Fourth Edition, 2006, #30017PA

M19, *Emergency Planning for Water Utility Management*, Fourth Edition, 2001, #30019PA

M20, *Water Chlorination/Chloramination Practices and Principles*, Second Edition, 2006, #30020PA

M21, *Groundwater*, Third Edition, 2003, #30021PA

M22, *Sizing Water Service Lines and Meters*, Second Edition, 2004, #30022PA

M23, *PVC Pipe—Design and Installation*, Second Edition, 2003, #30023PA

M24, *Dual Water Systems*, Second Edition, 1994, #30024PA

M25, *Flexible-Membrane Covers and Linings for Potable-Water Reservoirs*, Third Edition, 2000, #30025PA

M27, *External Corrosion—Introduction to Chemistry and Control*, Second Edition, 2004, #30027PA

M28, *Rehabilitation of Water Mains*, Second Edition, 2001, #30028PA

M29, *Water Utility Capital Financing*, Second Edition, 1998, #30029PA

M30, *Precoat Filtration*, Second Edition, 1995, #30030PA

M31, *Distribution System Requirements for Fire Protection*, Third Edition, 1998, #30031PA

M32, *Distribution Network Analysis for Water Utilities*, Second Edition, 2005, #30032PA

M33, *Flowmeters in Water Supply*, Second Edition, 2006, #30033PA

M36, *Water Audits and Leak Detection*, Second Edition, 1999, #30036PA

M37, *Operational Control of Coagulation and Filtration Processes*, Second Edition, 2000, #30037PA

M38, *Electrodialysis and Electrodialysis Reversal*, First Edition, 1995, #30038PA

M41, *Ductile-Iron Pipe and Fittings*, Second Edition, 2003, #30041PA

M42, *Steel Water-Storage Tanks*, First Edition, 1998, #30042PA

M44, *Distribution Valves: Selection, Installation, Field Testing, and Maintenance*, Second Edition, 2006, #30044PA

M45, *Fiberglass Pipe Design*, Second Edition, 2005, #30045PA

M46, *Reverse Osmosis and Nanofiltration*, Second Edition, 2007, #30046PA

To order any of these manuals or other AWWA publications, call the Bookstore toll-free at 1-(800)-926-7337.

M47, *Construction Contract Administration,* First Edition, 1996, #30047PA

M48, *Waterborne Pathogens,* Second Edition, 2006, #30048PA

M49, *Butterfly Valves: Torque, Head Loss, and Cavitation Analysis,* First Edition, 2001, #30049PA

M50, *Water Resources Planning,* Second Edition, 2007, #30050PA

M51, *Air-Release, Air/Vacuum, and Combination Air Valves,* First Edition, 2001, #30051PA

M52, *Water Conservation Programs—A Planning Manual,* First Edition, 2006, #30052PA

M53, *Microfiltration and Ultrafiltration Membranes for Drinking Water,* First Edition, 2005, #30053PA

M54, *Developing Rates for Small Systems,* First Edition, 2004, #30054PA

M55, *PE Pipe—Design and Installation,* First Edition, 2006, #30055PA

M56, *Fundamentals and Control of Nitrification in Chloraminated Drinking Water Distribution Systems,* First Edition, 2006, #30056PA

To order any of these manuals or other AWWA publications, call the Bookstore toll-free at 1-(800)-926-7337.